Changing Urban Bureaucracies

Changing Urban Bureaucracies

How New Practices Become Routinized

Robert K. Yin

With the assistance of
Suzanne K. Quick
Peter M. Bateman
Ellen L. Marks

Lexington Books
D.C. Heath and Company
Lexington, Massachusetts
Toronto

Library of Congress Cataloging in Publication Data

Yin, Robert K
   Changing urban bureaucracies.

   Bibliography: p.
   Includes index.
   1. Municipal services—United States—Technological innovations—Case studies. 2. Bureaucracy—Case studies. 3. Organizational change—Case studies. I. Title.
HD4605.Y55 1979   301.18'32'0973   78-20378
ISBN 0-669-02749-9

Published simultaneously in Canada.

Printed in the United States of America.

International Standard Book Number: 0-669-02749-9

Library of Congress Catalog Card Number: 78-20378

Contents

List of Figures
and Tables

Preface

For much of 1976, the book *Passages: Predictable Crises of Adult Life* by Gail Sheehy was a nationwide bestseller. Sheehy's book influenced this one beyond the loosely analogous use of life histories, passages, and cycles. Her volume was, by traditional standards of social science, a courageous attempt to describe a set of developmental stages in American adulthood. What made the rendition courageous was the book's grand scope, despite its limited information base. The author, who is not an academician, could explore an exciting new frontier without the typically distracting, hedged statements found in social science efforts.

Sheehy's book did not affect a friend, Robert Weiss, in quite the same way. Weiss, a capable social scientist noted for both his methodological contributions and his research on family and adult crises (see his study *Marital Separation*, 1975), like many others, was critical about what Sheehy had done. She had collected a biased set of evidence, mainly from acquaintances in New York City; her conclusions were overly dogmatic and often went beyond the evidence; and her insights were crowded by glib superficialities. Nevertheless, social scientists are constantly understating their own work and allowing others to make those simple but penetrating insights about human behavior. What Sheehy had done on the topic of adult development was to remind us that adults continue to develop in significant ways (for which most of us are unprepared), and that male and female developmental patterns are different and are occasionally in conflict. Although one could quarrel endlessly with Sheehy's specific principles and stages of development, the book's message seemed clearer and more thought-provoking than most social science versions of the same topic. What was most disturbing was that we social scientists had a tendency to be afraid of looking at the larger picture and were constantly hiding behind our data.

In a Rand manuscript on technological innovation in local services, *Tinkering with the System,* coauthored with Karen Heald and Mary Vogel (1977), we, too, had allowed our thoughts to be led by the data; and the reader will find that manuscript dominated by chi-square, multiple regression, and even step-wise regression analysis. In retrospect, it was the sort of effort a competent group of Rand analysts might undertake, but it lacked the challenge of creation and imaginative thinking. The appearance of Sheehy's volume was therefore a propitious one, making us wonder why social scientists write less bravely than journalists. In fact, social scientists should be able to do better, not merely by using their heads, but also by applying those methods for collecting and analyzing evidence that only they are trained to use.

Of course, this was an approach only suitable to certain types of topics, and organizational change was undoubtedly one of them. Where there is an analytic concern about the dynamics of change over time in studying behavioral processes, most of the standard statistical techniques only serve as weak tools of inquiry. This is not a new insight; in fact, it has been shared most recently by George Downs in his *Bureaucracy, Innovation, and Public Policy* (1976), and by our colleagues at Rand, Paul Berman and Milbrey McLaughlin. Each of us has had to confront the limitations of statistical and linear models that were mainly designed for cross-sectional study and mechanistic systems. Thus, in writing this book, our standards have been provided by those works that appear all too infrequently but that have produced important insights into organizational processes. Among these are such works as Herbert Kaufman's *Are Government Organizations Immortal?* (1976), Graham Allison and Peter Szanton's *Remaking Foreign Policy: The Organizational Connection* (1976), Jeffrey Pressman and Aaron Wildavsky's *Implementation* (1973), and such standbys as Anthony Downs' *Inside Bureaucracy* (1967) and Graham Allison's *Essence of Decision: Explaining the Cuban Missile Crisis* (1971).

A common denominator of all these works, as well as of the present one, is the reliance on case studies as a source of evidence. High-quality case study research appears to have suffered in the gradual shift of the social sciences toward quantitative models and techniques. The apparent simplicity of whatever quantitative evidence is produced by a case study has come to be mistaken for a lack of rigor, and the method has been widely criticized. Nevertheless, case study research cannot be replaced by other methods. The goal of this study is thus to improve the methodology by creating a rigorous and replicable *chain of evidence*. In particular, our case study materials were designed with aggregate analysis in mind—that is, the conduct of each case study follows a similar protocol or set of questions—and the case materials are presented in two forms: the standard narratives (see appendix D) and a "table of events" (see chapter 4). The latter represents a methodological innovation which attempts to capture the key characteristics of each case study in explicit form. Accordingly, this study is based on the "data" presented in the table of events, and the reader is encouraged to follow the entire chain of evidence from (1) field protocol to (2) narrative case study to (3) table of events to (4) findings and conclusions. This chain, fully presented to the reader, has not been made explicit in previous uses of the case study method. This is a new procedure, and perhaps it will set an example for further research on organizational processes.

It is difficult to relate to the readers the sense of discovery that this approach has produced. Some of the most complex topics in organizational theory—routinization or institutionalization among them—can now be addressed, and we can begin to build "normal" theory. Again, drawing from Sheehy's example and the organizational studies just cited, the insights that appear most useful are the ones that tell us how organizations or people normally behave. This development of normal theory is a necessary precursor for designing any strategies for intervention, much as most clinical psychology (an intervention of sorts) is based on theories of normal behavior. Yet, policy research has until now been dominated by the development of interventionist strategies that have treated normal behavior as a black box. As politicians and policymakers have found in the last two decades, such interventions have been rooted in completely artificial worlds; take as examples the imposition program budgeting (PPBS) or other service interventions that did not even inquire about an organization's routine processes. Such interventions have produced a dismal record of failure. Some of us have had the luxury of viewing these failures from an external vantage point and at a time in our careers when our own thinking has not yet solidified. We remain optimistic that better theories of normal behavior, and hence better interventions, will emerge in the years to come.

Acknowledgments

This book represents the conclusion of a study that was initiated in August, 1976 and supported by the National Science Foundation. Many persons have contributed in one way or another to the effort. Our major debt, of course, is to the officials in the local agencies that we visited or telephoned, without whose assistance the study could not have been conducted. Similarly, The Rand Corporation's office in Washington, D.C., provided a supportive and stimulating environment for conducting research.

Throughout the course of the study, many colleagues were also kind enough to comment on the work or to review preliminary drafts of the book. These occasions included two conferences held in Washington, D.C., on October 20 and 22, 1976. The purpose of these conferences was to suggest ideas about routinization by engaging (1) a group of local officials who had themselves had direct contact with service innovations, and (2) a group of research investigators who had recently conducted empirical studies of service innovations. Within each group, an attempt was made to invite participants acquainted with different local services. The participants were: Rae Archibald, former deputy fire commissioner, New York City Fire Department; Philip Cook, former Budget Bureau administrator, City of Buffalo, New York; Todd Endo, former assistant to the superintendent of public schools, Arlington, Virginia; James Morgan, Jr., former director of public safety, St. Petersburg, Florida; John Teipel, director, Street and Sanitation Services, Dallas, Texas; Richard Bingham, Department of Political Science, University of Wisconsin at Milwaukee; Ernest House, School of Education, University of Illinois; Henry Lambright, Syracuse University Research Corporation; David Tansik, Management Department, University of Arizona; and Bruce Vladeck, School of Public Health, Columbia University.

The final manuscript was immeasurably improved by suggestions made on an earlier version by three persons: Rae Archibald (The Rand Corporation), Senta Raizen (former director, Dissemination and Resources Group, National Institute of Education), and Lloyd Rowe (chairman, Department of Political Science, Indiana University, Northwest). J. David Roessner, who was with the Division of Policy Research and Analysis (National Science Foundation) also reviewed the earlier version, but his contributions to this work go beyond these specific comments; Dave has continually provoked new insights into organizational innovation during our numerous conversations.

None of the aforementioned persons, of course, is to be held responsible for the accuracy of the final manuscript; nor should Karen Brown (a most unusual editor) and Donna Betancourt, both of whom tried to make the words more precise and the sentences shorter, be held culpable. Appreciation is due to all these persons for their efforts, but any shortcomings can only be attributed to the author's own lack of imagination and occasional stubbornness.

1 Life Histories of Innovations

It was not so long ago that most people took urban services for granted. As with daily mail delivery, every neighborhood was assumed to have a school, police and fire protection, and garbage pickups and other street services. Most residents were only aware of these services through direct contacts with teachers, police officers, and sanitation and other service workers; but such contacts were few and far between. By and large, the services seemed to take care of themselves. Like the letters that appeared in one's mailbox everyday, the services were just there.

The 1960s changed this. We learned that many urban services were suddenly inadequate. Massive migratory shifts and rising expectations had resulted in new demands that urban schools, police, and other services could not fulfill. The number of problem neighborhoods rose, and people began to talk about "block-busting," "tipping," and "white flight." Although technological advances had helped the space program and created continued improvements in consumer products, urban bureaucracies remained labor intensive, noninnovative, and inflexible. Whatever the urban riots indicated about the human condition in cities, for instance, they did show that the police still had a lot to learn about peace-keeping tactics.

We also learned that urban services could be costly. And that they could stop. The New York subway workers' strike in 1965 and the citywide teachers' strike of 1968 (which followed community control initiatives in Ocean Hill-Brownsville and other neighborhoods) were just the beginning of strikes and strike threats across the country that continue to this day. Work stoppages, "sickouts," and collective bargaining became part of the concerned citizen's vocabulary. With the fiscal dilemmas faced by cities and suburban areas over the past several years, urban services have by now been frequently at the center of public controversy. Residents know only too painfully that, if they want services to continue at previous levels, tax rates may have to continually increase or cities may have to find other sources of revenue.

The shift in awareness about urban services also drew Congressional and Presidential attention. Massive federal education aid programs, large-scale assistance to law enforcement agencies, and widespread community development programs were all initiated during the 1960s. Such programs, however, did not evolve from any master plan for improving urban areas or urban services. Thus, each federal program developed its own policies for delivering federal aid. In some cases, as in education aid programs, grants were made to existing state

1

and local agencies; in other cases, as in community development programs, new, locally-based nonprofit organizations supported the efforts. For urban residents, the negative effects of federal aid were often more obvious than the positive ones. Local political conflicts—over issues such as the use of federal resources, housing scandals, court-ordered desegregation, and law enforcement assistance that was used for new police gadgets but did not necessarily result in greater public safety—all gave the appearance of further disrupting urban services rather than improving them.

Nevertheless, the message was clear. Something had to be done to change urban services so that they would be more responsive to contemporary demands. Gradually, citizens felt that such changes had to affect the structure of urban agencies. Somehow, changes had to be made in the way that urban services were organized, and such changes required more than the adoption of a few new practices. In different cities across the country, at least three types of structural changes were attempted. In some cities, "super" agencies were created, with the hope that power would shift upward to a level closer to the municipal executive. At that higher level, it was hoped that residents' priorities could be more easily incorporated into the actions of elected officials, and that the inertia of individual agencies could be overcome through better coordination and closer supervision from the executive level. In other cities, decentralization and neighborhood governments were considered, with an equally compelling but opposing rationale: If service agencies had to relate more closely to residents at a district level, the agencies would more responsively serve residents' needs. In yet other places, new nonprofit organizations were initiated to augment the services already provided by existing agencies. Such organizations as Model Cities agencies or community development corporations were usually highly dependent upon federal funds. Once again, however, these various strategies for structural change were developed in an uncoordinated fashion. Most cities, for instance, attempted all three types of reform simultaneously without understanding that conflicting pressures were often created.

In retrospect, these attempts at structural reform have had little lasting impact. Super agencies were easy to create, but also easy to dismantle; effective neighborhood governments were difficult to implement in urban areas because of the time and effort required to amend city charters and were never fully developed; newly-developed nonprofit organizations had difficulty surviving their original federal auspices, and many failed to become "institutionalized." Moreover, as political priorities shifted at both the local and federal levels, many of the earlier initiatives were reversed. From the vantage point of the late 1970s, in other words, the remarkable accomplishment of the past decade has been the persistence of schools, police and fire departments, sanitation services, and other urban agencies to maintain their basic organizational structures.

This is not to imply, however, that new service practices have not evolved. Parents have learned to tolerate classroom procedures, different from those of their childhoods, that have created a new educational environment for their children. Residents have also become aware of changes in police operations. Some changes, such as the increase in motorized patrol, the common use of walkie-talkies (which did not begin until the 1960s), and the expanded community relations role of the police officer, have become part of the usual police activity currently depicted in television dramas; yet the activities are far different from those romanticized in earlier versions of the old-fashioned "cop on the beat." To take another example, many of the earlier complaints about noisy garbage collection have been eliminated because noise has been reduced through the use of plastic trash bags. There are even some new services, such as the installation of emergency medical teams in many urban and suburban communities. The teams provide paramedic aid that is totally different (and far better) than that traditionally available at the scene of an accident.

The point is that, underlying the political rhetoric, and despite the failure of large-scale attempts to change the organization of urban bureaucracies, urban services have survived and have continued to adopt new practices. Whereas we may have been largely ignorant of how such services were organized before the 1960s, the new perspective of the late 1970s has suggested another blind spot: We do not know much about the normal evolution of new service practices. In many respects, the excitement of the 1960s created an unfortunate diversion. People expected rapid change, and policymakers took what they believed to be radical initiatives. Attention was incorrectly focused on understanding and even evaluating organizational initiatives. However, whether they were ever properly conceived or not, we ignored the obvious—that service practices are constantly changing (albeit not in the ways that we would always like), and that there is a continuing process of change that must be understood before lasting reforms can be expected.

The research in this book attempts to uncover the processes by which new service practices become routinized. Knowledge about these processes is important for two reasons. First, as already indicated, to the extent that policymakers and residents would like to instigate bureaucratic reforms in the future, such knowledge will help to assure that reasonable initiatives are made, and that the results are productive and longlasting. Second, we believe that the normal change processes have been neglected far too long. If the evolution of urban bureaucracies can be considered analogous to the development of a biological organism, then we have failed until now to appreciate the natural ways in which bureaucratic practices grow and become modified. Like child or personality development, urban bureaucracies may well follow certain predictable patterns, but these can only be determined if a more naturalistic and less interventionist perspective is used to identify the appropriate patterns.

The naturalistic perspective requires service practices to be analyzed in their own terms—that is, to accommodate the budgetary, personnel, and organizational reality of every agency. It requires an appreciation for the common features that make school districts operate in a similar manner in different jurisdictions, or that make different police departments appear to operate consistently from site to site. The naturalistic perspective also asks that one accept the incremental nature of urban bureaucratic change. Thus, although a specific innovation may appear to be only "tinkering with the system," the aggregate effect over the long-term may be substantial.[1]

Only one previous research study, Anthony Downs' *Inside Bureaucracy* (1967), has strikingly captured this naturalistic perspective in the past. However, Downs was mainly concerned with the birth and death of federal bureaus. He also conducted his study at an earlier time when case study analysis for policy purposes was not a refined activity, and he thereby had less access to specific experiences as evidence for his conclusions. Nevertheless, Downs provided many insights into the nature of the federal bureaucracy, and we hope that our research as reported here, based on nineteen case studies and a telephone survey of ninety other sites, will equally enlighten the reader.

The Life History Approach

Focus on Innovations

To analyze changes in service practices, this study takes advantage of the numerous specific innovations, or new practices, that different agencies have implemented in the past. The major objective has been to trace the "life history" of different innovations, a term first used by Tansik and Radnor (1971), from the point at which they were first adopted to a point where the innovations have more or less disappeared as "innovations" and are regarded as an integral part of standard practice. The focus on specific innovations does injustice to the richness and complexity with which urban bureaucracies are constantly changing. Nevertheless, without such a focus, the study of organizational change would be too slippery; like the chronicler but not the historian, one would not know what changes were significant nor could one produce a meaningful picture.

Innovation life histories provide such a focus. In fact, any innovation appears to undergo a complex sequence of changes before it can be said to have become a part of the agency's routine functions. An innovation that has been integrated into standard practice has generally passed through three phases of change:

1. Initiation and adoption. A specific series of events occurred, during which the innovation was considered for adoption; some pilot testing may have occurred on a small-scale basis, and the results of that testing resulted in a decision to adopt the innovation.

2. Implementation. A subsequent series of events occurred, during which broader support for the innovation was developed; plans were made for instructing and training relevant practitioners throughout the service; the innovation was introduced as widely as resources would permit; and implementation results were monitored.
3. Routinization. Another series of events occurred, as a result of which the innovation no longer appeared as an innovation but became part of the common services routinely provided. (One characteristic of this stage is when a local agency can no longer return to a previous way of doing business, although some new innovation may occur to supplant the routinized one.)

These phases are not easily defined, nor do they necessarily bear simple relationships to each other. The labels may be considered akin to such other life-stage labels as infancy, childhood, adolescence, and adulthood. For instance, by certain criteria, adolescence may begin much earlier and end much later than by other criteria. Similarly, some aspects of childhood may be found in adulthood, even though the stages are separated by adolescence.

The general notion, however, is that the phases in the bureaucratic change process have distinct characteristics, and that the phases occur sequentially over time. Unfortunately, the vast majority of research on innovations has been concerned with the earlier phases of the innovative process, either adoption or implementation.[2] In contrast, the available research on the *routinization* process —also referred to as *incorporation* or *institutionalization*—is sparse. Thus, little is known about the factors that facilitate or discourage routinization. In short, previous research on urban services has failed to focus on how new practices ultimately become institutionalized in a bureaucratic setting.

Without understanding routinization, researchers cannot appreciate the nature of bureaucratic change, and policymakers cannot intervene if routinization fails to occur where desired (or vice versa). This lack of understanding can have serious consequences. For instance, failure at the routinization phase can be more costly than failure at either of the two phases, because an innovation is likely to have incurred full-scale costs and shown some merit, unlike innovations that may have failed at the implementation stage. Second, failure to routinize can be a disruptive process for the specific persons who have been associated with an innovation; they may have invested significant portions of their careers in developing skills associated with an innovation, often at the expense of foregoing other opportunities. For these reasons, it is important to understand the routinization process and to develop guidelines for federal and local officials concerned with innovations. There may even be strategies that these officials can undertake at the outset of an innovation's life history to assure subsequent routinization.

Illustrative Life Histories

The value of using specific innovations as an opportunity to study bureaucratic change may be illustrated by reviewing a few life histories. The following are derived from the nineteen case studies conducted as part of this study, and subsequent chapters refer to various aspects of these studies. The four examples presented here are typical of many of the life histories and include one where routinization has been completed, one where the innovation has been operating at an incompletely routinized stage for several years, one where the nature of the innovation changed, and one where the innovation is no longer in use.

In Life History A, the innovation consisted of a mobile intensive care unit (MICU) program that began early in 1973 with the purchase of a single emergency vehicle and the training of seventeen firefighters to serve as paramedics. A one-year federal grant helped to support the operation, but the community had been anxious to initiate such a service for several years. This was in part because of two accidents, a furnace explosion that killed nine people and another accident that killed two young high school coaches; many felt that more lives would had been saved if on-site medical attention had been available.

After the first year, local fire department funds were used to support the innovation, which has subsequently undergone substantial expansion. The MICU service currently consists of six vehicles, and seventy-six firefighters (about 15 percent of the entire department) have received paramedic certification. Nearly half of the fire alarms in the city now call for an MICU vehicle, and the program has attracted considerable public interest. Recently, the mayor made city funds available for fire officers to begin a large-scale citizen training program in cardiopulmonary resuscitation. The head of the MICU committee that oversees the service also serves as chairman of the state and national MICU committees.

Changes have occurred within the fire department as well. MICU equipment and supplies are now purchased with the same procedures as other fire equipment, but the procedure has been facilitated by the fact that the purchasing agent has taken a paramedic course, is an MICU enthusiast, and understands in detail the variety of necessary equipment. The paramedic position has been given civil service status; more important, however, the MICU program has been structured so that the paramedic assignment will not be a dead-end job. One paramedic and one lieutenant typically comprise an MICU unit. When the lieutenant is promoted to captain, he leaves the unit and thus creates a position to which others can be promoted. This also means that, in time, officers who have been part of the MICU service will move to higher-level positions in the department. Other changes in the department have included the establishment of standard operating procedures for the service, the initiation of a regular training program, the formalization of paramedic certification and recertification procedures as part of state licensing requirements, and the development of solid working relationships between fire and health practitioners. For instance, emergency room nurses have worked with the emergency medical teams in answering calls to become familiar with the MICU operation, and the paramedics have demonstrated their skills to various hospital staffs.

Two other events are particularly noteworthy. In the last year or two, the MICU service has enabled the fire department to maintain its established level of staffing due to the increased workload imposed by the MICU service, while other city agencies have experienced budgetary cutbacks. In addition, the title of the fire department has been expanded to include the words "rescue service." In sum, the MICU innovation, in an interval of only a few years, has become an integral part of the services provided by the fire department.

In Life History B, the innovation was a computer-assisted instructional (CAI) program for a school district. Although the school district had used its own computer for administrative purposes since 1961, it was not until 1972 that teletype terminals were acquired for instructional applications. In such applications, a student does his or her own programming on a terminal, or simply solves mathematics problems on an individual basis. The innovation was initiated by a mathematics teacher who had become the mathematics supervisor for the district; complementary technical support in maintaining the equipment has been provided by the district's data processing unit.

Financial support for the CAI innovation has consistently come from the district's own funds. As a result of the innovation, computer programming and advanced computer mathematics courses are now offered by the district. Over the years, however, the number of CAI terminals has only increased from nine to ten terminals, one each for all but one of the high schools. In part, the small number has been due to the limited amount of core computer time, which is mainly dedicated to adminstrative and other school-related functions but not to instructional use. In part, however, the limited size of the innovation is related to a lack of strong demand by students or teachers for CAI applications. Many teachers are enthusiastic about CAI but only one round of in-service training was formally offered, and most teachers, including those in subjects other than mathematics, are largely unaware of the ways in which CAI can be integrated into their classroom activities.

The innovation in life history B has thus survived an initial period of adoption and implementation, but has remained at a stable level since its initiation. Other than the creation of special computer mathematics courses, CAI has not become an integral part of the school curriculum. Most students and teachers in the district have no contact with CAI; there is no formal training program for teachers; practitioner certification to teach in the school district does not include any requirement to have a computer background or CAI training; and there have been few changes in formal operating procedures, and no adoption of CAI-oriented textbooks. Nevertheless, CAI may continue in this fashion for an indefinite period of time. Individual schools have purchased their own minicomputers and additional terminals as part of the capital expenditures for a new wing of a school building, and the mathematics supervisor remains enthusiastic about CAI. In sum, the CAI innovation in this district is still active, but it has not yet become an integral part of the educational services provided by the district.

In Life History C, a closed-circuit television system (CCTV) was installed in a school district, and the first television programs were transmitted in 1969. Each week, two fifteen-minute programs for grades three, four, and five were produced in social studies, science, and art. The programs were designed to correspond with the topics that students would study in their classes, and students in nine elementary schools viewed the programs as part of their classroom work. The main goal of the CCTV operation was to improve the education of students from low-income families, and much of the initial funding came from a three-year state and federal award.

Although this innovation operated successfully for a year, with appropriate in-service training available to teachers, and although the district had made viewing such programs a mandatory part of the curriculum at these nine schools, the innovation had dramatically changed two years later. This was because the entire district implemented a formal decentralization plan in 1970, in which the original district was divided into three administrative subdistricts. Each of these subdistricts had full control over the development and administration of its own instructional program, with its own superintendent and citizen advisory committee. Moreover, the nine original elementary schools were equally divided among the new subdistricts. The decentralization made it impossible to continue the program of mandatory viewing of the CCTV programs, and the whole CCTV operation stagnated for about a year and a half.

Eventually, a new television coordinator was appointed as part of a central service, the educational media department. Since 1974, this new coordinator has helped the subdistricts to develop a considerably revised innovation, focused around instructional television (ITV) but not CCTV. The new coordinator has rejected the "down the line" transmission arrangement in which a single program is sent to many classrooms simultaneously; instead, he has fostered a grass roots approach in which teachers are encouraged to adapt television to their individual classroom needs. Thus, when the five-year lease with the telephone company for cable services expired shortly after the new coordinator's arrival, he decided not to renew that contract and instead applied the funds to the purchase of video equipment such as videotape recorders, monitors, and portable cameras to be shared by schools throughout the district.

The new system is itself now being slowly integrated into the district's organization. The district is able to maintain and repair the television equipment; new civil service classifications have been established for the technical staff positions associated with the operation; a variety of local funding sources is used to support the system; and a television production studio has emerged as a mandated part of the curriculum of one of the high schools. However, the innovation as presently implemented is not a CCIV system in which programs are actually transmitted from one classroom to another or from one school to another. Thus, in this life history, the original innovation has ceased, but it has been replaced by a related innovation that appears more suitable to the needs of a decentralized school district.

Life History D also involves a CCTV system. In this case, state funds were initially used to help purchase and install a microwave-cable system in which three channels were made available to transmit programs to about 1,200 television sets located in classrooms throughout the district. Because it was an ambitious project, most of the period of the state grant (1963-68) was used to implement the system. Various technical difficulties were encountered. The wiring process progressed slowly, but, by 1967, fifty-two schools were wired and receiving programs. In addition, the district had a fully equipped television studio, two full-time technicians to service the system, new civil service classifications for the staff related to the CCTV system (who were located in a separate television department in the district), and a sufficient number of self-produced or purchased television programs to utilize all three channels fully during the school day. In addition, when state funding finally ended (the grant had involved a declining share of state funds for the five-year period), the system was then entirely supported by local funds. The system had also received consistently strong support from the district superintendent.

Budget cutbacks during 1969 and 1970, however, increased pressure on the district to reduce and eliminate the CCTV system. The original superintendent departed; teacher resistance to the innovation increased in the form of formal union opposition; and, by 1971, the entire television department had been disbanded and much of the television equipment sold to another district and to the local public television station. Today, there is only sporadic use of the original CCTV system, even though the microwave and cable connections are still functional. Individual schools may use television in the classroom, and at least one high school has its own production studio. However, there is little or no central coordination, and the sporadic use has not been sufficient to warrant the judgment that the CCTV system as a whole has survived. In fact, the earlier budget cuts quite clearly eliminated the system, along with other specialized educational programs such as driver education.

Changes in Service Practices—The Key Questions

The four life histories offer a glimpse of the variety of experiences that different innovations can undergo within local service agencies. Yet, their experiences can also tell us a lot about the nature of change within urban bureaucracies.

A fundamental question has to do with the routinization process itself: *What operational characteristics reflect the life history of a new service practice as it becomes routinized?* Few previous investigations have defined the concrete organizational changes that occur, and such concepts as routinization until now have remained abstract and only loosely amenable to empirical study. In contrast, the major contribution of this study will be to define the routinization process in an operational and rigorous form.

A second question has to do with explanations for routinization outcomes: *Why do some innovations survive over a long period of time and eventually become routinized, and why do others fail to do so?* The common initial responses to this question are not satisfactory. For instance, it has generally been thought that the new practices that survive are those that demonstrate a clear service improvement. Indeed, much of the work in evaluation research for public programs is based on this premise. However, in the four cases just described, the service payoffs for the first innovation were not any more evident than those for the last three, and this is thus an insufficient explanation for the eventual outcomes. In fact, in none of these four cases, and in few of the other case studies among the remainder, was there any formal evaluation of service payoffs or a clear understanding of the possible payoffs. A second common notion has been that the decision to fund an innovation with local monies is the major distinction between those that survive and those that do not. Again, all four cases described, and nearly all the remaining cases, had become fully supported by local funds, and yet this did not guarantee long-term survival. A third common observation is that innovations that fail to become implemented properly are those that fail to survive. Yet, in Life History D, the innovation was fully operational and covered most of the schools within the school district. Thus, success during the implementation stage does not assure that an innovation will survive. A fourth common hypothesis is that the passage of chronological time itself is a major factor in routinization. Yet, of the four illustrative cases, the one that had been most routinized, Life History A, was also the case with the shortest history.

Other apparent explanations are actually somewhat circular. An observer close to Life History D, for instance, noted that the budget cutbacks that had led to the end of the CCTV system also affected other special education programs, such as driver education. Thus, one common explanation has been that innovations that only result in "special" activities or programs are not likely to survive. But this explanation begs the question, for it is the very distinction between a "special" and a "routine" activity that we would like to understand. In short, we need to know what makes an innovation remain special, and, conversely, which factors lead to an innovation becoming a routine activity of a bureaucracy.

Any deeper probe, of course, fully reveals the weak nature of our knowledge base. None of the previous explanations offered, for instance, can even begin to distinguish the two situations in Life History A and Life History B: In both cases, the innovation had clearly survived for a period of time beyond any "pilot" or "demonstration" period, but the first innovation continued to grow and became a part of much of the basic organizational routine of the agency, while the second innovation remained in a stagnant state.

In summary, the task of this study is to describe the process of change in urban bureaucracies and thereby to begin to explain these different outcomes. Only with such information will we be able to understand how new practices typically evolve in urban bureaucracies. And only an understanding of the typical will enable us to think about designing successful interventions.

Evidence Used in This Study

The subsequent chapters of this book provide more detail on the procedures used in this study. However, the general features are worth summarizing here.

Case Studies and Telephone Interviews

The actual life histories of six types of innovations in different cities were based on nineteen on-site case studies augmented by telephone interviews covering ninety additional cities. The six types of innovations, which are fully described in the next chapter, were:

Type of Innovation	Urban Service
Computer-assisted instruction (CAI)	Education
Police computer systems	Police
Mobile intensive care units (MICU)	Fire
Closed-circuit television systems (CCTV)	Education
Breath testing for driver safety	Police
Jet-Axe (an explosive device)	Fire

The data were all collected during the winter of 1976-77 and spring of 1977.

The two methods of data collection were used because of their complementary nature. (Appendix A describes their differences and some recent research that has applied them to the study of bureaucratic innovation.) On-site case studies involved a series of personal interviews at the same site. The case study also enables an investigator to observe an innovation in practice and other characteristics of the local service organization. The case study approach was used because the state of knowledge about organizational change processes is still primitive, and the approach thus provided the flexibility needed to trace life histories and to develop notions about a bureaucratic change process that has only been poorly understood in the past. Such case studies, however, were limited in number because of the time and effort required to conduct each case study. For this reason, other sites were more superficially covered through the use of structured telephone interviews, in which a single respondent was queried about the situation at a whole site.[3] The larger number of sites thus permitted generalization to a wider array of cities than was possible with the case studies alone.

Aside from these inherent differences between on-site case studies and telephone interviews, the two methods of data collection were treated similarly in other procedural respects. These included: (1) the selection of cites to be studied, (2) pilot-testing and the development of specific instruments, and (3) preparation of the data for analysis.

City Selection

The innovations pertinent to this study were those that had been adopted some time ago by a local agency. Therefore, six lists of cities were developed, one for each type of innovation. Each list was based on previous studies that had specified that an adoption had occurred.[4] For the case studies, a sample of cities from each list was pre-screened via a brief telephone call to determine whether the innovation had survived or not over the years.[5] The sites for the case studies were chosen to ensure three types of variations with regard to this outcome: over five years and still used, between two to five years and still used, and once used but subsequently undergoing some cutback or curtailment. However, it was not always possible to find such sites with the brief pre-screening procedure, and travel and scheduling constraints did not always allow the precise implementation of this plan. Nevertheless, the nineteen case studies represented a stratified sample, covering a variety of routinization experiences for each type of innovation. The cities that were subsequently visited are listed, according to type of innovation, in table 1-1.

For the telephone interviews, all cities in the original six lists corresponding to the six types of innovation were used, excluding those that had been selected for site visits. The initial telephone interview occasionally revealed, however, that the city did not really qualify for study, usually for one of the following reasons:

1. The initial adoption had actually not occurred.
2. The innovation had been incorrectly defined at the outset and was not one of the six types.
3. The adopting agency was incorrectly defined at the outset and was not a school district, police department, or fire department.

Table 1-1
Nineteen Case-Study Sites, by Innovation

Innovation/City	1970 Population (thousands)
Computer-assisted instruction	
Dallas, Tex.	844
Oakland, Calif.	362
San Diego, Calif.	697
Tampa, Fla.	278
Police computer	
Boston, Mass.	641
Indianapolis, Ind.	746
Miami, Fla.	335
Nashville, Tenn.	448
Mobile intensive care units	
Birmingham, Ala.	301
Dallas, Tex.	844
Denver, Colo.	516
Closed-circuit television	
Omaha, Nebr.	347
Portland, Oreg.	380
Rochester, N.Y.	296
Breath testing	
Akron, Ohio	275
Cincinnati, Ohio	451
Memphis, Tenn.	624
Jet-Axe	
Omaha, Nebr.	347
Rochester, N.Y.	296

These disqualifications limited certain innovations such as police computers and CCTV to about sixteen cities each; it was thus decided to randomly select from the lists of the four other types of innovations until sixteen cities for each had been identified. Thus, except for police computers and CCTV, where the entire universe was included, the telephone interviews represented a random sample of previously identified adoption sites. Table 1-2 shows the full list of cities in which telephone interviews were conducted.[6] (Some cities appear more than once because the list for each type of innovation was separately developed, and the same city may have adopted more than one innovation.)

In general, the cities that were studied, both by on-site case study and by telephone interview, ranged from 250,000 to 1 million in population. (A few cities under 250,000 had to be included for some of the innovations in order to fill the necessary sample size; the five major cities over 1 million in population

Table 1-2
Ninety Telephone Interview Sites, by Innovation

Innovation/City	1970 Population (thousands)	Innovation/City	1970 Population (thousands)	Innovation/City	1970 Population (thousands)
Computer-assisted instruction		Mobile intensive care units		Breath testing	
Atlanta, Ga.	497	Baltimore, Md.	906	Atlanta, Ga.	497
Baltimore, Md.	906	Cincinnati, Ohio	451	Austin, Tex.	252
Birmingham, Ala.	301	Gary, Ind.	175	Baltimore, Md.	906
Denver, Colo.	516	Jacksonville, Fla.	529	Dallas, Tex.	844
Fort Worth, Tex.	393	Kansas City, Kans.	507	Indianapolis, Ind.	746
Honolulu, Hawaii	325	Madison, Wis.	172	Jacksonville, Fla.	529
Kansas City, Mo.	507	Memphis, Tenn.	624	Jersey City, N.J.	260
Louisville, Ky.	362	Phoenix, Ariz.	582	Kansas City, Mo.	507
Newark, N.J.	382	Portland, Oreg.	380	Minneapolis, Minn.	434
New Orleans, La.	593	St. Paul, Minn.	310	New Orleans, La.	593
Phoenix, Ariz.	582	Salt Lake City, Utah	176	Oklahoma City, Okla.	368
Rochester, N.Y.	296	Seattle, Wash.	531	St. Louis, Mo.	622
St. Louis, Mo.	622	Toledo, Ohio	383	San Diego, Calif.	697
Toledo, Ohio	383	Tucson, Ariz.	263	Seattle, Wash.	531
Tucson, Ariz.	263	Warren, Mich.	179	Tampa, Fla.	278
Wichita, Kans.	277			Tucson, Ariz.	263
		Closed-circuit television		Jet-Axe	
Police computer		Anaheim, Calif.	166	Charlotte, N.C.	241
Baltimore, Md.	906	Atlanta, Ga.	497	Cincinnati, Ohio	451
Birmingham, Ala.	301	Fresno, Calif.	166	El Paso, Tex.	322
Buffalo, N.Y.	463	Honolulu, Hawaii	325	Honolulu, Hawaii	325
Denver, Colo.	516	Indianapolis, Ind.	746	Jacksonville, Fla.	529
Kansas City, Mo.	507	Milwaukee, Wis.	717	Kansas City, Mo.	507
Long Beach, Calif.	359	Phoenix, Ariz.	582	Louisville, Ky.	362
Louisville, Ky.	362	St. Louis, Mo.	622	Minneapolis, Minn.	434
Oakland, Calif.	359	Salt Lake City, Utah	176	St. Paul, Minn.	310
St. Louis, Mo.	622	San Jose, Calif.	447	St. Petersburg, Fla.	216
San Diego, Calif.	697	Santa Ana, Calif.	156	Salt Lake City, Utah	176
Seattle, Wash.	531	Seattle, Wash.	531	San Francisco, Cal.	716
Tucson, Ariz.	263	Springfield, Mass.	164	Santa Ana, Calif.	156
Washington, D.C.	757	Tucson, Ariz.	263	Tucson, Ariz.	263

were categorically excluded from study because of their size.) It is important to note, however, that the relevant organizational unit was not a city per se, but one of three service agencies: a school district (for CAI and CCTV), a police department (for police computers and breath testing), or a fire department (for MICU and Jet-Axe). Thus, if it was found that a city had adopted one of the six innovations but that the adoption had not been by one of these three agencies, the city was not considered eligible for study. This exclusion criterion mainly affected police computers, where a large number of police departments are now users of a city computer system; the eligible cities only included those where the department owned (or leased) and operated a core computer itself.

Pilot-testing and Instruments

Two different types of instruments were used for data collection. For the on-site case studies, an interviewer's guide was prepared (see appendix B). For the telephone interviews, six different questionnaires were designed, one for each type of innovation (also see appendix B).

These instruments and other field procedures, such as the problems of identifying the main respondent to be interviewed (usually the official who coordinated the use of the innovation), were developed in an explicit pilot-testing phase of the study that preceded the formal data collection effort.[7] The pilot phase was aimed at developing hypotheses about routinization, clarifying certain substantive issues, and identifying potential methodological problems. For instance, it was found during this phase that no single instrument was sufficient to conduct telephone interviews for six different types of innovations. The pilot testing was conducted during the period from August to December of 1976; final instruments were designed in January 1977, and the final case studies and telephone interviews were conducted from February to July of 1977.

Preparation for Data Analysis

For case studies, a problem that is often overlooked by investigators conducting a series of case studies is the aggregation problem. This problem has to do with the manner in which general lessons are drawn from the array of case studies that has been conducted. Few investigators understand that the problem is aggravated by certain types of data collection, and that the problem must therefore be anticipated in the design of the initial fieldwork. For instance, if information is collected in an inconsistent manner at different sites, later aggregation is nearly impossible. As another example, the individual case studies may contain too much information and thereby create an enormous problem of data reduction.

Because each case study followed the same interviewer's guide, each was written in a narrative form that was organized around the same subtopics. Eight representative case studies have been fully edited, reviewed by the relevant local agency, and reproduced in appendix C. (The other eleven are available from the author on request.)[8] After the narratives were completed, a summary table of events was prepared (see chapter 4), dividing the life histories of each innovation into three chronological stages. This summary table serves as the main evidence from which the general observations and conclusions from the case studies have been drawn. In short, the chain of evidence from data collection instrument to narrative case-study to master table-of-events to general findings has been traced as explicit steps, and the entire procedure is, in principle, susceptible to replication.

For the telephone interviews, the responses to each of the six original instruments were separately tabulated. Identical and comparable questions were then combined across instruments so that the responses for all ninety sites could be tabulated together. The results of these tabulations, in simple descriptive form, are contained in appendix D. These data were then used for all the telephone interview analyses described in chapter 7.

For both the case studies and the telephone interviews, the emphasis throughout the data collection was on the occurrence of organizational events. For this reason, the measurements used mainly consisted of items scaled along nominal or ordinal dimensions. Such items were analyzed individually in relation to routinization outcomes, but no multivariate analysis was attempted. Because the objective of the study was to describe life histories of innovations and to provide a new framework for assessing routinization, the study did not attempt to develop the refined set of interval-scaled items that would have allowed multivariate analysis. Such refinements have been suggested as appropriate tasks for further research (see chapter 8).

Limitations

Because any single study must be limited to some set of specific innovations and body of evidence, the generalizability of the conclusions can always be questioned. Thus, although the conclusions presented in this study should demonstrate internal validity by drawing logically from a research design and data collection methods that are internally consistent and unbiased, it is important to discuss the extent to which the study is either generalizable or limited regarding external validity, or the degree to which the conclusions are applicable to situations other than those directly studied.

The study appears to be generalizable beyond the immediate innovative situations in the following manner. First, the case-study visits and telephone interviews covered a variety of geographic areas and appear to fully reflect a national sample of cities of 250,000 to 1 million in population. (The five largest cities—New York, Chicago, Los Angeles, Philadelphia, and Detroit—were omitted from the study because of the distinctive complexity of their local public agencies.) Second, the study covered a sample of innovations that has been divided according to a meaningful conceptual distinction—task-specific and task-diverse innovations (see chapter 2)—and the results may, therefore, be extended to other types of innovations to the extent that they can be classified into this scheme. Third, the study included three of the most common types of urban services, and the results should be generally applicable to the entire array of urban service-agencies found in medium-sized local jurisdictions. Whether the organizational principles that emerged from the study may also be applicable to bureaucracies in general, and not just local public agencies, can of course be further tested. Informal observations of other public and private bureaucracies suggest that the routinization process described here may not be different from that found in other types of organizations.

In contrast, the study appears to be limited in the following manner. First, the study focused on innovation life histories that occurred in the last fifteen years. Although some of the innovations had begun earlier, the bulk of the results are constrained by the political and bureaucratic environment of the last fifteen years. Such a period of time covers more than a single cohort of innovations because, among other things, local and federal conditions have changed so rapidly even within this period of time; nevertheless, it may be true that future innovations will be taking place in a very different environment, and, to this extent, the generalizability of the study's conclusions will be limited. Second, although the study focused on six different types of innovations, all were embodied in some hardware or physical apparatus. The life histories of "hardware" innovations were the target of study because their artifacts and functions could be more easily traced over time. Innovations that do not have such a physical embodiment may result in different experiences in local organizations; however, it is also possible that "software" innovations involve the same routinization process but are more difficult to trace. Overall, the distinction between hardware and software innovations has been inadequately studied, so the study's conclusions must tentatively be considered limited to hardware innovations.

On balance, the results and guidelines from the study do not suffer from the idiosyncrasies that would have occurred had the study been limited to: one type of innovation (many adoption and diffusion studies are of this nature); one type of service agency (many policy studies are of this nature); or one or two specific jurisdictional sites (many academic case studies are of this nature). On the contrary, the conclusions regarding routinization may be applicable to most of the innovative situations encountered by a contemporary local service agency in medium-sized cities.

Summary of Study

New service practices continually emerge in urban bureaucracies. However, little is known about how such practices become routinized, or part of "standard practice." Ironically, many changes in service practice have continued to occur at a time when federal policymakers have become convinced of the intransigent and rigid nature of urban bureaucracies. The goal of the present book is, therefore, to describe the routinization process. The lessons drawn are an attempt to develop insights into how service practices normally change. This development of "normal" theory is a necessary precursor for designing any intervention strategies, and it has been a void in previous policy research.

The routinization process was studied by examining the life histories of six types of innovations, described in chapter 2 at nineteen case-study sites and ninety telephone-interview sites. The life histories were analyzed in terms of the achievement of ten specific organizational events, which have been conceptualized as either *passages* (transitions from one organizational state to another) or *cycles* (survival over periodic organizational events). These concepts, as well as several factors hypothesized to facilitate the achievement of passages and cycles, are fully elaborated in chapter 3.

According to the findings, routinization occurs in a series of stages: the *improvisation stage* (chapter 4), the *expansion stage* (chapter 5), and the *disappearance stage* (chapter 6). During the latter two stages, the achievement of the ten passages and cycles serves as the operational criteria for routinization. These include: the passage from external to internal funding, the establishment of personnel classifications or certification, changes in organizational governance (in one case, the name of the agency was actually changed to accommodate the new practice), and the appropriate turnover of personnel. Several strategies were found to be effective in promoting routinization:

1. At the outset, it was important to get the new practice operating on a daily basis, even if this was done by limiting its scope.
2. The new practice had to have concrete benefits for service practitioners: convenience, reduced physical effort, greater potential for promotions, additional sense of safety on the job. These types of benefits were not necessarily the same as those covered by external evaluators.
3. If the new practice displaced an old one, specific steps needed to be taken to eliminate the old way of doing business, such as eliminating the forms and procedures associated with the old way.
4. The new practice had to be ultimately expanded to its fullest logical extent, or else it continued to be regarded as a "special project," which precluded it from becoming a standard practice.
5. The time lags for achieving the various passages and cycles were different, so that it was important to get an early start on certain activities—

establishing the personnel classifications for any new job skills that may be required by the new practice, for example, to insure later routinization.

The findings were also analyzed in relation to the specific factors hypothesized to facilitate routinization (chapter 7). The development of support for the innovation by an active innovator, by service practitioners, and by administrators, as well as the establishment of a core application and minimal competition among applications, appear to be important to routinization; in contrast, external assistance—whether in the form of federal or state funds or of technical assistance—was found unrelated to routinization. Lastly, the implications of the study for further public policy research are discussed in chapter 8.

Notes

1. The author has previously written about the usefulness of the naturalistic perspective and the degree to which change in urban bureaucracies takes an incrementalist form. See Yin, Heald, and Vogel (1977), especially pp. 4-7 and 126-130.

2. In fact, so many individual studies have been done that entirely separate volumes (e.g., Zaltman et al., 1973; Rothman, 1974; and Public Affairs Counseling, 1976) have summarized the numerous findings on the initial importance of performance gaps, slack resources, chief executive support, practitioner training and preparation, and impetus for innovation from *within* the adopting agency.

3. The selection of a single respondent represented a tradeoff between an attempt to gain a diverse set of responses about a single innovation and an attempt to cover numerous innovations. The latter was chosen, with the single respondent identified as a person knowledgeable about the innovation (usually the coordinator). To minimize biases, the telephone interview emphasized "facts" about the innovation (e.g., the initiation date, the services provided, the existence of an in-service training program or of federal funds, etc.) rather than interpretations concerning its use. Nevertheless, for such a complex topic as organizational innovation, telephone interviews of additional respondents for the same innovation would be desirable in the future.

4. The studies were as follows: for CAI, Bukoski and Korotkin (1975); for police computers, Colton, (1972a), Kraemer et al. (1976), and Bingham (1976); for CCTV, Wigren et al. (1967); for MICU, National Emergency Medical Services Information Clearinghouse (n.d.); for breath testing, no specific study but sites randomly selected from cities between 250,000 and 1 million in population; for Jet-Axe, Feller, Menzel, and Kozak (1976).

5. The six prescreening instruments (one for each type of innovation) are contained in appendix B.

6. The telephone interviews ultimately covered only ninety of the ninety-six sites selected because of call back difficulties at six of the sites.

7. The pilot phase is fully described in an unpublished paper, R.K. Yin et al., "Routinization III: Research Methods for Phase II," The Rand Corporation, January, 1977.

8. Each case study was sent in draft form to the local agency for corrections and editing. In addition, the agencies were asked whether their jurisdictions could be named or whether they wished to be cited anonymously in the final case study. Eight jurisdictions indicated their willingness to be named, and these are the case studies reported in appendix C. The remaining jurisdictions asked to be anonymous.

2 The Innovations

General Characteristics of Innovations

Studying Life Histories of Innovations

There are two ways of recording life histories of specific innovations. One way is to select relevant innovations now being adopted by local agencies, with life histories based on the subsequent events that occur for each innovation. The study would then follow a true longitudinal research design, tracing the changes that occur at each site over the next several years (Kimberly, 1976a). Such a longitudinal design, however, entails heavy costs and great risks:

1. A large number of innovations would have to be monitored at the outset because the dropout rate would be unknown, and too small an initial sample could result in few innovations with extensive life histories.
2. The study would have to be conducted over a long period of time because the routinization process, unlike adoption or implementation, is by definition a process that occurs over the course of many organizational events.
3. The innovations to be studied would be somewhat peculiar because all would have begun during the same calendar period, and the universe would actually form a special cohort from which the results of the study might not be easily generalized.

These problems create sufficiently major barriers that a true longitudinal design appears unfeasible.

An alternative approach is to select innovations that have been adopted and implemented by local agencies some time in the past. A study would thus begin by identifying similar innovations that had been implemented at different sites on a periodic basis over a span of years. A quick spot-check could identify those innovations that had survived as well as those that had not. Appropriate life histories could then be reconstructed for a sample of these innovations. This approach would avoid wastefully commiting resources to an unnecessarily large number of innovations, would capture some variation in outcomes, would produce results generalizable to more than one cohort, and would be less costly because old innovations could still be included, but not on a real-time basis. The research design would, however, not be a true longitudinal design but a post-hoc longitudinal design, in which data collection occurs at a single point in time. In other words, changes that had occurred since the initial adoption would have to be traced by artifacts, documents, and the recall of human respondents (Kimberly, 1976a).

This alternative approach appears to be the most suitable for topics that of necessity cover events over a long period of time. A extensive study of the invention and development of notable technological innovations, for instance, followed this design (IIT, 1968).[1] The study selected several major new technologies such as magnetic ferrites, the video tape recorder, and oral contraceptives, and established for each innovation a series of key developmental events that had occurred. In some cases, the TRACES—as the study methodology became known—covered a period of 100 years or more. The research design differed from that proposed here, however, in that the study only focused on famous technologies that had been successfully developed and marketed; no histories were collected of technologies that had failed (by whatever criterion).

For the present study of routinization, the use of this post-hoc longitudinal design required a listing of innovations previously adopted by local agencies. To create some pragmatic and realistic boundaries for such a list, it was decided to develop the list from previous studies of innovation adoptions; the studies were limited to those on technological innovations,[2] those published since 1962, and those that covered any of three local services—public education, police protection, and fire protection. In other words, although there have been numerous innovations in local agencies, our universe was defined by what previous studies had already documented, rather than by a new survey addressed directly to local agencies. This choice was made because it was well known that previous studies had already identified large numbers of innovations adopted by local agencies.[3]

The Shifting Nature of Innovations

Because this study of routinization was based on life histories of specific innovations, there were several issues to be resolved concerning the final selection of innovations. Until recently, research was dominated by the seemingly straightforward assumption that "an innovation" existed in some clearly recognizable form that corresponded to the theoretical conception adhered to by the researcher.[4] Inherent in this assumption was the implication that the innovation as employed by one adopter was essentially the same as that used by all other adopters.

The assumption appeared to be a justifiable one, especially in cases where new practices had been adopted by individual, as opposed to organizational, users. It was reasonable to assume that a farmer would recognize a particular farm practice by name and that he could cite the year he first adopted it. The same could be expected when one tried either to trace the rate of adoption of a certain birth control method or to identify schools that were among the first to teach particular subjects that had not been part of the traditional curriculum. In either case it was expected that upon hearing the name attached to the innovation (birth control pills or the new math), the adopter could easily say whether the practice was in use and, if in use, when it had begun.

In recent years, however, as studies of innovations have broadened, there have been sharp challenges to the notion that "the innovation" is a clearly identifiable entity that varies little across adopting individuals and organizations (see Warner, 1974).[5] The assaults on the conception of the innovation as a static entity have been especially prevalent in research concerned with innovations in organizational settings. As researchers have examined the implementation of innovations in organizational settings, they have found that the innovation as implemented can be quite different from the one originally planned for study. Moreover, it has become increasingly apparent that what was supposedly identified as the same innovation may vary substantially from site to site.

The work of Berman and McLaughlin (1974) readily demonstrates this phenomenon (see also McLaughlin, 1975). In their study, they found that the introduction of an educational innovation was often followed by a period of *mutual adaptation.* This was a period in which both the organization and the innovation underwent change: the organization adjusted to the presence of the innovation, and the innovation was simultaneously modified to suit its organizational environment. Thus, an observer returning to an organization several years after the introduction of an innovation could find that many aspects of the innovation were different from the innovation as first adopted. These findings were similar to those reported by Charters and Pellegrin (1973), who set out to observe the course of events for an educational innovation known as "differentiated staffing." Instead of finding that there was a consistent formulation of the innovation, they found that "there was no 'it' to select, implement, [or] evaluate. In fact, the very task of the so-called 'initiation period' was to define what the innovation—the blueprint—was to be." It is encouraging, therefore, to find that recent work in the innovation field has been careful to emphasize that innovations do, in fact, vary widely across sites and over time.

Such research also indicates the necessity of carefully considering the nature of the innovations to be selected for any study of routinization. Routinization is an organizational process that occurs over a long period of time in different organizations. During such a process, a wide range of changes is likely to occur in an innovation, making empirical study more difficult. As a result, the selection of innovations for study was based on two sets of criteria: (1) some common features for all the innovations included in the study, and (2) some variable features along which the innovations selected for study were deliberately varied.

Common Features of the Innovations Studied

All the innovations included in the study had four attributes: technological, historical, service, and behavioral emphases.

Technological Emphasis. For the purpose of study, technological innovations have been defined as innovations whose day-to-day operation relies on machines, equipment, computer hardware, or other apparatus. These are the technological artifacts of the innovation. This definition of a technological innovation excluded certain analytic techniques and processes, such as operations research models or specific software for computer simulation models, that are often considered technological in nature.[6]

The decision to limit this inquiry to innovations with a material component reflected a basic assumption that, when first inquiring into a complex organizational process such as routinization, it is necessary to begin with as concrete an innovation as possible. Thus, a definite advantage of limiting innovations to those with material artifacts is to assure that there will be something tangible to focus on when trying to trace the agency's experience with an innovation. A disadvantage, however, is that it is not possible to generalize the findings to those innovations that are without material components. This, of course, does not mean that the findings cannot be informative with respect to such innovations, but any statements about the routinization of innovations other than those having material artifacts will necessarily be tentative.

Historical Emphasis. To be included in this study, the material artifacts necessary for the operation of the innovation must have been adopted by a local agency after 1960. This restricted the study to those innovations that had generally come into use in the last fifteen years. It eliminated from consideration such older innovations as the overhead projector or the police car, or even gasoline-driven fire trucks, whose initial adoption occurred in an era when local service agencies were organizationally and politically very different from those of the present time. Moreover, because the study covers the more contemporary period of the last fifteen years, it includes many innovations whose development or initial use by local agencies was prompted by the availability of federal funds or other federal resources such as information dissemination efforts. This historical context thus forms an appropriate policy context for the study.

Service Emphasis. All the innovations in the study were service-oriented in function. That is, they currently are, or in the past have been, used by practitioners in a local agency to assist in the delivery of agency-specific services. Thus, schools have the explicit mandate to instruct students in a variety of subjects. Similarly, police are responsible for maintaining law and order. These service functions may be contrasted to administrative functions such as budgeting, payroll, billing, and similar functions that only indirectly relate to an agency's mission. Some innovations may be used for both service and administrative functions, and these innovations were, therefore, eligible to become subjects of study. However, innovations dealing solely with the administrative operations of an agency were excluded from consideration.

Behavioral Emphasis. All the innovations had some behavioral component. That is, their day-to-day operation relied on frequent and continuing direct or indirect interaction between practitioners in the service agency and the technology. Direct interaction refers to physical manipulation of the material artifacts. Indirect interaction refers to: (1) providing verbal instructions to an individual on how to manipulate the technology, or (2) processing output produced by or communications received through the material artifacts.

This attribute excluded those innovations in which the adopting unit may have been a local agency, but in which there was little behavioral involvement, such as windowless schools, a new boiler system for heating firehouses, or new solid-state circuitry for communications equipment. Restricting the selection of innovations in this way assured that the innovations to be studied were those most likely to involve some of the most difficult problems in routinizing an innovation.

Variations in the Innovations Studied

At the same time, the innovations studied varied along certain dimensions. This allowed the study to test certain propositions about the possible effect of innovation characteristics on the routinization process. What became apparent during the pilot study phase of this study was that the life history of an innovation was largely influenced by the breadth and nature of its functional applications.[7] In other words, innovations can be placed into one of three classes, depending on the nature of the functional flexibility made possible by the technology. Once the innovations are so divided, the routinization fate of the innovations in one class appears to be explained by a different set of factors than those factors influencing the extent of routinization in the other two classes.[8] Furthermore, the distinction among the three classes appeared more important than those innovation attributes such as compatibility, communicability, or simplicity (see Rogers, 1962; and Rothman, 1974), typically associated with the initial act of adoption.

The pilot study suggested two criteria for sorting innovations into the three classes reflecting functional flexibility. The first criterion distinguished task-specific from task-diverse innovations. An innovation is task-diverse if it is possible to use the hardware for at least two service applications. In general, the distinction between task-diverse and task-specific is made on the basis of the inherent nature of the innovation, independent of how it is used at any given site. Thus, one would expect task-diverse innovations to be used in a somewhat different manner from site to site, whereas task-specific innovations would vary only a little from site to site.

The second criterion distinguished task-diverse innovations whose applications are distinctly service-limited from task-diverse innovations that have both

Table 2-1
Technological Innovations Classified into Three Groups, According to Functional Flexibility

Service	Task-Specific Innovations	Task-Diverse Innovations	
		Service Only	Service and Administration
Fire protection	Helmet with radio receiver and transmitter capability (In-helmet communications)	Emergency medical vehicles	
	Jet-Axe	Light, versatile vehicles for extinguishing small fires (minipumpers)	
	Automatic device for changing water pressure in fire hose (automated nozzle)		
Police protection	Lightweight, bullet-proof vests (body armor)	Minicomputers	Police computers
	Breath-testing machines	Videotape recorders	
Education	Language laboratories	Educational television/closed circuit television	Computer-assisted instruction
	Hand-held calculators	Videotape recorders	Video systems that provide up-stream and downstream video signals (two-way television)

service and administrative applications. As pointed out earlier, these administrative functions include budgeting, payroll, maintenance of personnel records, and so on. An important hypothesis to be examined was that innovations with both service and administrative functions have unique routinization patterns, setting them apart from those innovations that only have service applications.

Table 2-1 lists a set of innovations according to these three classes. Routinization is hypothesized to occur for different reasons, depending upon which of the three classes an innovation falls within. This is not to say that many factors will not also remain constantly important across all the three classes.

Task-Specific Innovations. For these innovations, several conditions are hypothesized to promote the routinization of the innovation:

1. *Widespread practitioner acceptance* based on the ease of substitution for an older, core practice and on a practitioner's self-interest in innovation benefits.
2. *Service payoffs*, namely cost savings or some other clearly visible and measurable advantage over a previous practice.
3. *Minimal retraining* needed for practitioners.

These conditions stem directly from the nature of task-specific innovations. Such innovations are usually adopted by an agency to perform a narrowly defined task that represents some clear improvement over previous practice. Moreover, there is usually an explicitly defined way of using the innovation— a set of rules that can be followed to achieve a specified objective. The automated fire-nozzle is an example. It is intended to permit firefighters to adjust the intensity of the water stream, thus, in theory, eliminating the need for a man to be stationed at the pumper to adjust the water intensity manually. There is a clearly specified and simple technique for using the nozzle, and, once this technique has been practiced during training sessions at the fire academy, firefighters can proceed to apply the nozzle to fight fires exactly as they had with the traditional system.[9]

Practitioner satisfaction with the innovation appears to be an important determinant of whether or not the innovation will be routinized. In some cases, as with lightweight body armor in police departments, practitioner satisfaction as a result of nonofficial trials can even lead to pressure on management to adopt an innovation. Practitioner opposition is likely if the practitioners do not perceive that the innovation serves their interests or if there are problems in the innovation's initial use, thus making it difficult for practitioners to substitute the innovation for an established practice.

Task-Diverse (Service-Only) Innovations. In contrast, the factors that are hypothesized to enhance the routinization of these innovations are:

1. Support from agency administrators.
2. Many complementary, service-related applications, though not necessarily a clear service payoff.
3. Support from some core group of practitioners, who may even require substantial training in the use of the innovation.

Task-diverse innovations are often brought to an agency either to perform a function that was not previously included in the agency's services or to supplement a previously established function. New jobs are frequently created in connection with the innovation, and practitioners may require extensive in-service training.

Moreover, if the innovation fails to work in the context of the original application that spurred its introduction, the equipment may be used for other applications as long as there is support from those in management who have the ultimate control over budget and personnel decisions. Thus, the flexibility in service applications increases the likelihood of some practitioner support, because different practitioner groups will become involved for different applications. For instance, if educational television (ETV) does not succeed with the English teachers who were the first intended users, it may be possible to build constituency among mathematics teachers that support ETV even though they were not involved when it was first introduced. Of course, the ideal situation for assuring that ETV has continued use in a school would be for its application to extend across many subjects—English, mathematics, science, languages, and so on—and across many activities, such as drama productions, sports events, and special events.

Whereas practitioner support for task-specific innovations is closely tied to the ease with which the innovation can be substituted for an existing practice, practitioner support for task-diverse innovations may well be influenced by two other factors. One of these appears to be the opportunity for practitioners to influence the early decisions on applications and equipment design. For example, in emergency medical vehicles, paramedics may take great pride in the fact that they have had a chance to help design the vehicle's internal layout.

The other factor hypothesized to influence sustained and growing practitioner support for task-diverse applications is the practitioner perception that the quality of service delivery has been enhanced. However, unlike the case with task-specific innovations, in which it is typically possible to point to "objective" or "documentable" evidence of innovation advantages, the evidence in favor of continued use of task-diverse innovations may often tend to be more "subjective" and "anecdotal." Thus, with computer-assisted instruction (CAI), enthusiastic teachers may claim that anyone can see that students with motivational problems improve their behavior when they have the opportunity to use the computer.

Task-Diverse (Service and Administrative) Innovations. Routinization for the innovations is hypothesized to be facilitated by several conditions within an agency—in addition to the conditions facilitating task-diverse (service-only) innovations.

1. A single, active innovator dedicated to maintaining service functions.
2. Continued opportunities for practitioner training in relation to service functions.
3. Minimal competition between administrative and service applications.

Each of these conditions places emphasis on maintaining support for the service function, which may compete strongly with the administrative applications.

It is noteworthy that any savings or improvements that result from administrative applications of new technology may be easier to document objectively than those resulting from service applications. Thus, a school administrator can claim that a new computer system can ". . . now run the payroll in fifty minutes, where it used to take six people working three days to do the same thing. I don't know if we could ever go back to doing it the old way." In a budget-review situation, such claims might be accepted as more persuasive evidence for continuing to use the computer for payroll than the diffuse claim that "the problem kids become more motivated" would be for continuing to use the computer for instruction.

In addition, growth in administrative functions is likely to threaten the service functions if a situation arises where trade-offs must be made between the two. In such situations, the routinization of the service applications is hypothesized to occur more readily if there has been a respected middle-level manager or coordinator who has actively worked to maintain such applications. This person will typically have foreseen potential conflicts between the administrative and service applications, and may have taken several steps, such as making service applications known to the public, to assure that they are not discontinued. Another condition that helps secure the service applications is the availability of ongoing training opportunities for practitioners, which provides a mechanism for generating practitioner support.

Six Innovations

From the array of innovations identified in searching the literature and during the pilot study phase, six innovations were selected for inclusion in the study (see table 2-2). Several factors influenced the selection:

1. The availability of information that identified a sufficient number of sites where the innovation had been adopted.
2. Representation, if possible, of three different service areas (police, fire, and education).
3. A spread of the innovations per service between the task-specific and task-diverse types.

Table 2-2
Six Innovations Selected for This Study

Type of Urban Service	Functional Flexibility Class
Computer-assisted instruction (education)	Task-diverse (service and administrative)
Police computer systems (police)	Task-diverse (service and administrative)
Mobile intensive care units (fire)	Task-diverse (service only)
Closed-circuit television (education)	Task-diverse (service only)
Breath testing (police)	Task-specific
Jet-Axe (fire)	Task-specific

The reason that six innovations were selected as an appropriate minimum number to be studied was to assure that at least two types of innovations would be included within each flexibility class. The following subsections contain brief descriptions of each type of innovation.

Computer-Assisted Instruction

Advances in computer technology have been responsible for the gradual installation of computer educational systems across the country. In general, school districts have adopted computers to perform both administrative as well as instructional functions. The latter have been referred to as computer-assisted instruction (CAI), and CAI applications received their major impetus following the development of computer time-sharing systems. In such systems, many terminals can be served by the same computer, and a student working at a terminal can follow an instructional routine that is individually tailored to his or her needs.

In most schools, CAI consists of several terminals linked to a central computer. The terminals and leased telephone lines may be paid from an individual school's budget, whereas the central facility is usually part of a school district's central administrative offices. The terminals are normally located in a classroom, so that several students, depending upon the number of terminals, may work at the terminals, while other students follow the more traditional teaching methods. The students may rotate so that each is given an equal amount of terminal time, or a few students may be the dominant users. The terminals can be of two varieties: (1) the older teletype terminals, that tend to be noisy and slow but that operate reliably and provide a hardcopy printout, or (2) the newer cathode ray terminals (CRTs), that are quiet and fast but are more expensive and cannot provide hardcopy without a companion printer.

The students may use the terminals for different educational purposes. In some cases, a computer-science course is the subject of study, and the students have enrolled in the elective subject to learn how to do programming and to use a computer. Such a course is not usually a part of the core curriculum, however, and may be cancelled if the school budget is tight. In other cases, students in mathematics classes learn to use a terminal, but not necessarily to program, so that they can solve mathematics problems with the computer's assistance. Finally, there are a number of software packages that allow students to practice solving mathematics problems; to learn materials in science, reading, social studies, language; or even to receive job counseling by following a preprogrammed curriculum. A frequent application is a drill-and-practice routine, in which the student does not do any programming but merely follows the simple directions given by the terminal.

CAI applications have usually been installed or developed as an adjunct to administrative computer applications. According to a recent survey, the majority of school computers (54 percent) are used for administrative purposes only; 38 percent are devoted to instructional and administrative purposes, and only 8 percent are used exclusively for instructional purposes (Bukoski and Korotkin, 1975 and 1976). These proportions have not changed much during the last five years, if such results are compared with those from an earlier survey (Darby et al., 1970). Administrative applications include the business management functions that might be found in any public agency such as payroll, inventory, personnel, and accounts, as well as school-related applications that are nevertheless not CAI, such as student scheduling, maintenance of student records, transportation scheduling, and testing and evaluation.[10] Additional school-related functions cover some of the special functions of schools, such as processing library information or providing vocational guidance. (For a description of counseling services, see Ellis and Tiedeman, 1970.)

Early interest in CAI was facilitated by federal monies from the National Science Foundation. The federally sponsored activities included such demonstration projects as the PLATO system that began operating in 1959[11] at the University of Illinois (House, 1974) and the research on CAI conducted at Stanford University beginning 1963-64 (Suppes and Morningstar, 1970). In recent years, the use of CAI has received support through federal grants under the Elementary and Secondary Education Act of 1965 (Title III), but it should also be pointed out that the vast majority of school computer systems have been totally supported with local funds (Bukoski and Korotkin, 1975).

Early applications of CAI were largely based on the assumption that it could provide individualized instruction at low cost. However, the rhetoric that developed in the early years around the promise of CAI (see Atkinson and Wilson, 1968; and Margolin and Misch, 1970) has had unfortunate effects. First, many of the promises have not been fulfilled, which has added to the skepticism about the potential payoffs from educational innovations. Second, the early rhetoric served to antagonize teachers, who felt that CAI was a long-term threat to their jobs. Today, some form of CAI is used in only about half of the country's public secondary schools. The median number of terminals is two per school (Bukoski and Korotkin, 1975 and 1976). Moreover, there have been no clear payoffs from CAI in terms of student achievement. Although there has been no nationwide evaluation of CAI, individual evaluations of specific systems, such as those made by Oregon Board of Education (1971) and Street (1972), have had mixed results. CAI programs have not necessarily produced gains over non-CAI programs (see also Zinn, 1970; and Hunter et al., 1975). A frequent positive result has been that students from low-income families view CAI as a more equitable form of instruction than traditional classroom instruction; for example, the terminals allow a student to avoid interacting with teachers who might be perceived as discriminatory (Clark, 1973; and Beard, 1976).

A recent development in CAI has involved the installation of minicomputers in individual schools. Such minicomputers have usually been defined, as by Knight (1975), in terms of their small storage capacity (64 K bytes or less), low cost (less than $25,000 for the central processing unit), and compactness (less than fifty pounds for this unit with no special air conditioning required). The minicomputer can serve one or more terminals, and it allows an individual school to avoid the frequent problems of coordinating CAI use with either the central facility or other schools. Competition for terminal time, both within and among schools, appears to be a frequent problem. Bukoski and Korotkin (1975), in fact, noted in their survey that the "lack of terminals appears to be the single most frequently mentioned concern of school staffs currently using a computer to aid their instructional program." The minicomputer is one way of reducing such problems, especially where the central computer is mainly occupied with the administrative functions. At the same time, unless there is coordination among schools, each school then has to go through the same learning process in deciding which minicomputer to purchase and in maintaining and servicing the unit.

In summary, CAI is now used in many school systems. The main subjects involve mathematics and computer science, rather than English, the sciences, or social sciences. The CAI function is usually part of a larger computer operation that also provides administrative services to the school district. In most cases, there is direct competition between CAI and the business applications for computer time, and the CAI applications can be reduced to the point of disappearing as the computer continues to be used for administrative purposes. Most computer systems are supported totally by local funds, and the major apparent savings or increases in service have been associated with the administrative services, although there have been few formal evaluations of the actual nature of administrative improvements. Specific improvements in student achievement from CAI have not been consistently demonstrated, and the use of CAI has most commonly been justified on the grounds that exposure to the computer is a valid goal in itself, independent of any instructional gains, simply because computers are so prevalent in American society that a student who has had such exposure will be better prepared to cope as an adult.

Police Computer Systems

Computer use by urban police departments has also been a major innovation of the last two decades.[12] Although such use was virtually unknown twenty years ago, almost all large departments located in cities of 500,000 population or over now employ some type of computer; for cities of 100,000 to 500,000 population, about 70 percent of the police departments use a computer (Colton, 1974). The increased use has resulted from at least four factors. First, the rising incidence of crimes and broadened police activity have led to enormous increases in record-keeping requirements. Second, the development of national information systems, such as the FBI's National Crime Information Center in 1967, as well as the continued need to make the Uniform Crime Reports every month, have increased the incentives for establishing a computer operation. With such an operation, a police department can, for example, consult the records that the FBI maintains on offenders, thereby increasing the information available at the local level. Third, advances in computer technology, especially in the use of on-line systems, have expanded the potential applications for police use.[13] For instance, an officer on the street can have immediate access to records concerning the existence of a warrant on a suspected offender. This is done by communicating with a dispatcher, who operates an on-line terminal. Fourth, large amounts of federal funds have been made available by the U.S. Law Enforcement Assistance Administration (LEAA), following the Safe Streets Act of 1968, for purchasing and developing hardware systems (Colton, 1972a).

Police departments can use a computer system for a variety of important functions (see Fyke, 1971). These include the everyday administrative applications related to the operation of any public agency, such as payroll, accounts, personnel, and property inventory. They also include an increasing number of applications specifically related to the operation of a police department, such as crime reporting, issuance of traffic citations, maintenance of records of outstanding warrants, stolen property, as well as criminal histories, and patrol allocation and dispatching. Some of these latter applications, such as criminal histories, involve large amounts of data or complex systems, such as computer-assisted dispatch, in which the full implementation of the application may take years.

Although a police department may now have integrated numerous applications into its computer system, only a few applications may have been added at any single time. Typically, the earliest applications tend to involve traffic citations and crime reporting, neither of which require on-line access to the computer; subsequent applications cover the links to regional and national information systems and police management and patrol. Only in later years will the computer system be extended to such complex functions as case reporting and computer-assisted dispatch (Colton, 1972a and 1974). Moreover, the increases in computer applications will also typically follow turnover in computer equipment. For instance, many police departments have gone through the three generations of core computers typified by the IBM 1401, 360, and 370 systems.

The variety and complexity of applications can create a constant competition for computer time. The ensuing scheduling difficulties may be especially aggravated by periods in which the computer is not functioning properly (downtime). Not surprisingly, the need to set priorities and establish the most efficient pattern of computer use has been continually cited as the most important computer problem (Colton, 1974). In most cities, this problem is compounded because the police department may be only one of several users of a municipal data processing operation. In such cases, the police department does not itself own or manage the core computer system. To the extent that the municipal data processing operations have organizational problems, all users, including the police department, will be adversely affected (Bingham, 1976). However, the coordination problems with a municipal data processing operation are not necessarily greater than the problems that arise when a police department manages its own computer system, so that no clear advantage has been found between the arrangements (Colton, 1972a). For instance, having sole ownership may be too costly and may require too many technical skills not available in a department (Whisenand and Tamaru, 1970). One new trend has been for police departments to install their own minicomputers that mainly perform message switching and that are linked with the municipal data processing operation.[14] The advantages of this arrangement have not been fully determined and are not likely to be known for some time.

In contrast to other computer operations such as CAI, the service payoffs from police systems may be readily enumerated. A more efficient traffic citation system, for instance, can have the specific effect of increasing revenues from violations. On-line access to police and court records can result in a higher rate of arrests and an increase in a police officer's workload. Similarly, computer-assisted dispatch systems can be evaluated in terms of changes in the quality of police response and the duration of response time. However, in spite of the specificity and magnitude of these potential payoffs, there have been few attempts to evaluate existing computer systems along these lines. In part, this has been because of the weak tradition of evaluation research within local departments. However, it has also been because the diversity of police applications from site to site has discouraged national evaluations. Unfortunately, greater attention for evaluating computer systems has been given to municipal and regional computer systems than to the experiences of line agencies such as police departments (see Hearle and Mason, 1963; Kraemer et al., 1976; and

Eveland, Rogers, and Klepper, 1976). The diversity of the larger systems has made assessment difficult and has potentially led to incorrect inferences about the lack of service benefits in line agencies.[15] Whatever the other differences and similarities, police computer systems share an important attribute with most other administrative computer systems: There is little awareness or knowledge of the system by the urban residents, who might be considered as the "clients" of police services. In this respect, police computer systems do not have the same level of visibility as, say, CAI in school districts.

For purposes of the present study, police computer systems were considered as a primary innovation regardless of the number or type of applications developed by the system. This definition thus differs from CAI, in which the innovation was defined as having one or more instructional applications, regardless of the business and other uses of the school computer. Furthermore, because our study focused on organizational changes within a line agency such as a police or fire department or a school district, the universe of police innovations was limited to those instances in which the police department owned and operated the computer system whether it was a large system or a minicomputer.[16] Without such a restriction, our study would have been diverted by the variety of organizational arrangements that characterize municipal computer operations, and the relevant institutional forces would not have dominantly involved any single user such as a police department.

Mobile Intensive Care Units

A mobile intensive care unit (MICU) provides emergency care away from a hospital facility. The unit consists of a specially equipped vehicle and a paramedic team that can administer a range of medical care upon instruction from a centrally located physician. The key technological element of this innovation is thus the communication capability of the MICU; the mobile staff can maintain voice contact with a physician, and physiological data about the patient's condition can be sent to the physician via radio telemetry (see Lewis et al., 1972; and Hirschman et al., 1974). As such, the MICU goes much beyond either the traditional ambulance service, which provides transport service only, or the traditional first-aid provided by fire or police officers, which is limited to basic first-aid and is not based on immediate physiological measurements or advice from a physician. The MICU has another distinctive feature—the use of specially trained paramedic personnel. These personnel receive extensive training, which includes several hundred hours of training by medical doctors and nurses, and they may be alternatively referred to as paramedics, advanced emergency medical technicians (advanced EMTs), or firemedics. These paramedics can perform a variety of medically sophisticated tasks: for example, cardiac defibrillation, intravenous therapy, electrocardiographic (ECG) telemetry, drug administration, and endotracheal intubation (Page, 1976). The paramedic personnel should not be confused with less advanced technicians usually referred to as EMT-Ambulance or EMT-A's. The latter are generally ambulance personnel who have received an eighty-one-hour course in basic life-support, and they can perform such tasks as cardiopulmonary resuscitation, spinal injury management, splinting, hemorrhage control, and emergency childbirth. Nor should paramedics and MICUs be confused with mobile coronary-care units, which were under experimentation several years ago and in which physicians and nurses, rather than paramedics, traveled as part of the unit (see Grace and Chadbourn, 1969; and Pyo and Watts, 1970). As one can imagine, the mobile coronary-care units involved much higher personnel costs and were an inefficient use of physician time.[17]

The MICUs have primarily dealt with victims of heart attacks or other coronary disorders. ECG and blood pressure data are the main physiologic symptoms that are transmitted to a centrally located physician. Based on these data as well as the visual symptoms reported by the paramedics, the physician can recommend the appropriate steps to be taken by the paramedic team. The apparent need for such a service has been based on the common observation that the first few minutes and hours of care are the most critical for patients suffering from myocardial infarctions, and that with the traditional ambulance service, many patients died while en route to the hospital (Pantridge and Geddes, 1967). However, in spite of the focus on coronary disorders, the MICU is capable of fulfilling a variety of medical functions. For this reason, MICUs were regarded in our study as a functionally flexible innovation—but one that did not involve the built-in conflicts as between the administrative and instructional uses of school computer systems.

Although the MICU has some basic service features and flexibility, the most distinctive variations result from the fact that MICUs can be operated under a wide variety of organizational arrangements in any given jurisdiction. For instance, the MICU may be part of the fire department (see Smith, 1971, and Page, 1975), police department (see Murphy, 1973), local health department, or even some other emergency service organization. Furthermore, the service may be coordinated at a city level, a county level, or some other regional level. For less populated areas, a common expectation has been that regional arrangements would have greater payoffs (see Renner, 1974), even though regional systems may be difficult to implement because they require new institutional arrangements among existing agencies.[18] Because our study focused on highly urbanized areas, however, all of our observations were made on MICUs operated by city agencies; in particular, our study was limited to those cases in which the municipal fire department had implemented and was operating the MICU service.

Whatever the organizational arrangement, a citizen usually summons the MICU by calling an emergency telephone number—often 911. If the dispatcher feels that it is appropriate, he sends an MICU unit, which may have been housed in a local fire station or in a hospital facility. In most cases, the vehicle is used as an MICU only, and, after the patient is treated, it can also transport him or her to the hospital; in some cases, however, the vehicle may be a specially equipped fire apparatus, and, after treating the patient, the paramedic team will call an ambulance (often operated by a private contractor) to transport the patient to the hospital. Thus, the basic nature of the MICU innovation requires cooperation among two or more city agencies. For instance, an MICU operated by a fire department will almost certainly require technical assistance and training from the local health department, will involve cooperative arrangements with the local hospital's emergency room, and may often depend upon the 911 communications center operated by the police department. Similarly, an MICU operated by a local hospital may have to rely on dispatching messages that come through both the police and fire departments.

In most jurisdictions, MICU services have only been initiated during the last ten years. This growth has probably followed the development of efficient and portable physiological equipment, such as that used to transmit ECG and blood pressure information via radio telemetry.[19] In addition, many policy initiatives have come from the federal government during the last decade. This has included the National Highway Safety Act of 1966, which established state training and licensing requirements, and specified the standards for equipping, organizing, and operating MICU vehicles (see Gibson, 1977, for an excellent review of federal activities in this area). These requirements were to be implemented with only a modest sum of new grant monies; the main financial incentive was the threat to withhold national highway construction funds. This threat has apparently never been fulfilled, even though several states continue to be noncompliant (see Gibson, 1977). Other early federal initiatives included activities by the Department of Health, Education, and Welfare, mainly under the Regional Medical Programs. A specific federal mandate was created in 1973, when Congress passed the Emergency Medical Service Systems Act, which provided grants for regional systems (reauthorized in 1976). Regional systems have also been the focus of a major program financed by the Robert Wood Johnson Foundation (see Chaiken and Gladstone, 1974).

As with both CAI and police computer systems, there have been few specific evaluations of the service payoffs from MICUs. This has been unfortunate, because the obvious impression at any MICU site is that service payoffs have occurred and can easily be determined. The payoffs can include: lives saved (paramedics describe their life-saving experiences in almost religiously fervent terms), amount and type of treatment provided at the scene, and greater satisfaction by clients and practitioner personnel. The absence of evaluations, however, has led to confusion because the organizational payoffs, as in regional systems, have been unclear and are confused with the service payoffs.

The federal initiatives have been responsible for the widespread use of standardized training programs such as the eighty-one-hour course designed by the Department of Transportation for emergency medical technicians—ambulance (EMT-A's). In addition, the initiatives have been responsible for the passage of state legislation with regard to these training programs, training for paramedics (advanced EMTs), and certification and update training procedures (Collins, 1974, and Plaas, 1974). Finally, the federal initiatives have led to the development of certain standards for MICU vehicles and equipment. Nevertheless, there has been considerable variety in the implementation experiences of different local jurisdictions (see Page, 1975; Gunter, 1975; and Comptroller General, 1976). Some jurisdictions have never adopted MICUs or, like New York City (see Sullivan, 1977), are just beginning to do so. Other jurisdictions have indeed initiated such services, only to witness subsequent difficulties and service interruptions due to inter-agency problems. Overall, the active federal role has not led by any means to the uniform provision of MICU services (Gibson, 1977), and the MICU thus serves as a good example for examining the routinization process.

Closed-Circuit Television Systems

A closed-circuit television system (CCTV) is a dedicated system that provides programs for specified television receivers that are placed in specific locations. Unauthorized receivers cannot view any of the programs because the target television receivers are either connected by cable to a central transmitting source or are equipped with special converters to receive and unscramble the over-the-air signals. The central source may be used to transmit live productions, video-tape replays, or retransmissions of over-the-air broadcasts to the target receivers. A CCTV system is thus different from regular, over-the-air broadcasting in that the system is limited to a specific group of receivers (though these receivers may still also tune into regularly broadcast programs). The system has its own production facility (if only a videotape recorder to play videotapes), signal-sending or transmitting capacity, and transmission system (such as cable connections leased from the telephone company or microwave links using dedicated over-the-air frequencies).

CCTV can be used by a variety of public and private organizations, including school districts. For school districts, CCTV potentially offers considerable advantages over the educational use of regular over-the-air television. Schools and classrooms, of course, have increasingly used over-the-air television in the classroom. Programs such as "The Electric Company" are designed for both at-home and in-school viewing (see Yin, 1973, and Liebert, 1973), and a teacher may use a classroom television set to show such a program to the class. The use of over-the-air television, however, has major shortcomings that can only be overcome by CCTV. The advantages of CCTV include the following.

1.   Teachers are not limited to those programs that are being shown by com-

mercial or public broadcasting stations; there can be access to special educational programs designed specifically for the needs of a class.

2. Teachers are not limited to the specific schedules of over-the-air programming; the use of television can thus be tailored to the classroom schedule.

3. CCTV systems can have a much larger number of channels, all dedicated for educational use. The entire school, offering a diverse array of subjects, can potentially generate the need for using these different channels at the same time.

4. Students are not limited to a passive role but can learn about the production process and create their own television programs.

For these reasons, educational and communications policymakers have attempted to make it easier for school districts to develop CCTV systems. In 1963, the Federal Communications Commission (FCC) reserved the use of four channels for such CCTV systems in education. These four were for the construction of an Instructional Television Fixed Service (ITFS), which is a microwave system designed to serve a school district or a set of neighboring districts. In 1972, the FCC again attempted to encourage educational uses by specifying that new cable television systems in the 100 largest television markets had to set aside one channel for educational use (see Booth, 1972; Borko, 1973; Baer, 1974; and Carpenter-Huffman, Kletter, and Yin, 1974). Finally, the Office of Education, through its programs under Title III of the Elementary and Secondary Education Act of 1965, has supported the use of CCTV systems in different school districts.

In theory, CCTV offers a wide variety of service benefits to the classroom teacher. First, existing over-the-air programs can be videotaped or acquired as part of a videotape library. The program can then be shown repeatedly at different hours of the day, so that teachers can use the programs for different classes and at the most suitable times (see WCET-TV, 1973). Second, the videotape library can include films and other software that are specially designed for educational use. A televised segment can therefore be a preprogrammed part of the curriculum for a specific subject. Third, teachers and students can produce their own programs. The production process in recent years has been technologically facilitated by the evolution of the "portapak," which is a small, battery-operated vidicon camera that can be easily carried to produce videotapes of indoor or outdoor activities (see Bretz, 1976).

A CCTV system can also be used under a variety of organizational arrangements. For instance, teachers can use the system in their classrooms; or a school's media center can be the location of television carrels where students can gain individualized instruction. Because CCTV systems can cover a variety of school subjects and organizational arrangements, we have regarded the innovation as a functionally flexible one for the purposes of our study. However, possibly because of the diverse applications, there have been few studies of the actual experiences or payoffs from CCTV. Some reports (Gebolys, 1974) are merely preliminary descriptions of systems that ultimately did not even become operational. Other reports (WCET-TV, 1973, and Smith and Cooper, 1974) give actual evaluative evidence that student achievement improved as a result of a CCTV system, but only cover a short period of time that does not allow the evaluation to rule out the effects of contaminating factors. Finally, there have been a few surveys of CCTV use throughout the country (see Wigren et al., 1967, and Feinberg, 1976), but these surveys have only noted adoption rates and future intentions, and have not probed the nature of individual local experiences.

In general, it can be said that CCTV systems have not spread as rapidly as once might have been hoped, even though there have been continued advances in television technology that have produced several generations of new equipment. The major difficulties appear to be related to high front-end costs (Feinberg, 1976), the difficulties of organizing a sophisticated media program in which production can be carried out without technical flaws (American Association of School Librarians, 1975), the training of teachers to use CCTV in a creative manner, and the limited availability of high-quality films, videotapes, and software programs (Carpenter-Huffman, Kletter, and Yin, 1974). On this last point, it might be noted, for instance, that many of the early CCTV systems predated the development of special educational programs such as "Sesame Street" or "The Electric Company"; attractive television programs were thus especially scarce before the early 1970s.

As a whole, microwave, cable, and other closed-circuit systems have remained more experimental and less integrated into the educational program than the classroom use of over-the-air television (Wigren et al., 1967). In other words, the instructional uses of television have been dominated by individual classroom viewing of available programs rather than coordinated, district systems. CCTV nevertheless serves as a relevant innovation for the purposes of the present study. This is because of the inherent nature of the innovation. It is a complex innovation whose main applications are service-related and not administrative, and it is an innovation that must be adopted by a school district or group of schools and not merely adopted by an individual classroom teacher.

Breath Testing for Driver Safety

Local law enforcement agencies have recently implemented many improvements for testing and analyzing the amount of alcohol found in a person's breath. These improvements have been a response to both technological developments in breath testing, which can be conducted through processes involving gas chromatography, photometric colorimetry, or infrared photometry, as well as to the continued rise in traffic accidents attributable to persons driving while intoxicated (DWI).[20]

The main breath-testing instruments that have been adopted include the Breathalyzer, the Alco-Limiter, the Gas Chrometograph, and the Alcohol Screening Device. The most common breath-analyzing instrument has been the Breathalyzer, a machine that uses photometric colorimetry and that infers the blood alcohol concentration (BAC) of a person from a sample of his or her breath. The innovation, a model of equipment that has only had one generation, consists of a semiautomatic instrument about the size of a small typewriter. The subject, seated next to the Breathalyzer, blows into a tube attached to the instrument, and a sample of 55 ml. of breath is collected in a cylinder. A small piston then forces the sample out of the cylinder and through a 3 ml. solution. If there is any alcohol in the breath sample, this alcohol will react chemically with the solution, producing visible changes in the color of the solution. Such changes are automatically measured by the Breathalyzer, allowing an officer to read the BAC from a calibrated gauge. The BAC is marked on a special piece of graph paper and is submitted as evidence in court. The entire test takes about five minutes.

Before such breath-analyzing instruments became available, law enforcement agencies typically had to collect a sample of a person's blood or urine for blood analysis by a laboratory. In comparison to breath testing, these older procedures were highly complex, costly, and inefficient (Hoffman, 1973). Thus, breath testing offers the following advantages over older procedures:

1. Less discomfort and inconvenience for the person being tested.
2. No need for medical personnel to be present during testing.
3. A shorter period of time away from patrol duty by the arresting officer.
4. No delay of several days between the administration of the test and the reporting of the laboratory results.
5. No need to coordinate law enforcement procedures with those of a central laboratory. (The older procedures had to be careful to establish a direct chain of evidence to assure that none of the samples had been exchanged or had accidentally become contaminated.)

The use of the Breathalyzer or any other instrument for breath analysis to present evidence on BAC is based on two important assumptions. First, the amount of alcohol detected in a person's breath is assumed to be related to his or her BAC. Second, the BAC is assumed to be related to behavioral impairment in driving a car. Research has gradually established the validity of the latter assumptions, with a BAC of less than 0.05 percent now being regarded as evidence of no behavioral impairment, a BAC of 0.10 percent or more as presumptive evidence of impairment, and a BAC of between 0.05 and 0.10 percent as an equivocal range within which impairment may or may not exist. However, research has not yet definitively established the validity of the former assumption—that breath alcohol content is related to BAC. Two experts (Mason and Dubowski, 1974; see also Mason and Dubowski, 1976) who reviewed the major studies on this latter topic concluded:

The reliability of properly performed breath tests for the purpose of determining alcohol in breath is, indeed, adequate. It is the transmutation of a breath quantity to a blood concentration that is less than satisfactory. These considerations lead us to conclude that in actual law-enforcement practice, when a breath sample is analyzed for alcohol, the quantity found cannot be used to calculate the simultaneously existing actual blood alcohol concentration (with acceptable accuracy) without making assumptions having uncertain validities in any given case because they have not been assessed. (The Committee on Alcohol and Drugs of the National Safety Council has since recommended that the Uniform Vehicle Code §11-902.1 (5) be amended to read "(5) Alcohol Concentration shall mean either grams of alcohol per 100 milliliters of blood or grams of alcohol per 210 liters of breath.——) [Parenthetic statements added at request of authors.]

Nevertheless, there have been no findings that actually challenge the link between breath alcohol content and blood alcohol concentration. Thus, the results of breath tests have been successfully used in court in conjunction with observations of an offender's motor behavior at the time of arrest, and in most jurisdictions the combined evidence has led to higher conviction rates for DWI cases.

Federal agencies have played an important role in the implementation of Breathalyzers and other breath testing equipment. The formation of the National Highway Traffic Safety Administration in 1966 led to the issuance of standards and regulations for breath testing. Thus, federal regulations now cover:

1. The standards that should be applied to the operation and monitoring of breath testing equipment ("Standard for Devices To Measure Breath Alcohol," 1973).
2. The certification of specific brands of equipment that meet those standards (*Federal Register*, 1976; see also Flores, 1975).
3. Guidelines for state laws on: agreement to submit to blood alcohol tests (implied consent statutes), automatically-presumed guilt for BAC levels of 0.10 percent and over ("illegal per se" statutes), and submission to roadside screening to make on-site determinations of whether a person's BAC appears high enough to justify the making of an arrest, and the administration of a breath analysis test (pre-arrest screening statutes).[21]

The states have also been required to establish special agencies to deal with alcohol and traffic programs. As a result, most states have passed the appropriate statutes to regulate the use of breath testing equipment, although there are variations among states.[22]

It is important to note that, in spite of these federal and state initiatives, there is still substantial variation in the use of breath testing equipment by local law enforcement agencies. First, the agencies are by no means required to conduct breath tests. The major statutes cover issues concerning BAC (and not breath analysis levels), and the most definitive evidence can still only be derived by direct BAC tests, such as a blood analysis or urinalysis. The traditional methods of testing BAC, in other words, can still play an essential role for which breath testing has not become a total replacement. Second, the specific procedures for using breath testing equipment may vary. Some police departments have mobile units that transport the breath-testing equipment to the scene of an arrest; other departments place such equipment in one or more precinct houses. Third, agencies vary in the degree to which they use videotapes as supplementary evidence. In some cases, an agency may videotape a series of motor tests but not the actual administration of the breath tests; in other cases, an agency may videotape both; in yet other agencies, there may be no videotapes used at all.

Jet-Axe

Jet-Axe is the trade name for a product that is manufactured and distributed across the country by a single company located in Fairfield, California. The device is an explosive unit that can be attached to a wall or door and then detonated from a remote location. The ensuing explosion creates a hole of about three feet in diameter through which firefighters can either gain entry into a building or can ventilate a fire. The device is entirely self-destructing; if another hole is needed for subsequent entry or ventilation, another Jet-Axe must be used and detonated.

The Jet-Axe's development followed advances in space technology, with demonstrations for use by urban fire departments first taking place in 1968-69 (Frohman et al., 1972). The presumed need for the Jet-Axe in urban firefighting was based on estimates that one-third of the some 150,000 annual fires in urban areas required forcible entry, and that in 10 percent of these 50,000 cases, entry through traditional methods such as using crowbars or conventional fire axes, required twenty minutes or longer (Frohman et al., 1972). With the Jet-Axe, entry can be created in a matter of minutes. The fire officer in charge at a fire determines whether a situation requires the use of a Jet-Axe and, if so, where it should be placed. A firefighter then hangs the Axe on a nail or magnetic hook so that it hangs vertically against the wall or door to be cut. A safety device is then removed from the Jet-Axe's container and a 35-foot firing line is laid out. When the line is fully extended and all nearby personnel are behind some protective barrier, the firefighter or fire officer will detonate the Jet-Axe with a spring-loaded firing pin.

There are several models of the Jet-Axe, differing in size and amount of explosive force. However, there has been no updating or new generation of models. A fire department may purchase the Jet-Axes at a cost of about $125 each. Although this amount is small and can usually be paid out of a chief's discretionary budget, the fact that the device is entirely self-consuming precludes massive testing and demonstration at a fire academy for training purposes. Therefore, although many firefighters in a department are likely to receive oral instructions and may even view a film about the Jet-Axe's use, only a few in any given department will actually have had direct training with the device. This lack of exposure is compounded by the fact that only few firefighters will have opportunities to use the Jet-Axe in firefighting. The tendency has been to apply the Jet-Axe only in cases where the conventional methods are likely to fail or are judged to require an inordinate amount of time or effort, such as in cutting through steel doors, heavy-gauge metal screen, or industrial roofing. For any given fire department, the number of such fires is much smaller than those merely requiring forcible entry of any kind. Moreover, the Jet-Axe will not be used even in these situations if some person is still on the other side of the barrier because of the strong possibility of inflicting injury to that person. Thus, few firefighters actually gain direct experience with the Jet-Axe, either through training or firefighting opportunities.

Nevertheless, the Jet-Axe does provide a number of potential service pay-offs: Some barriers that cannot be penetrated with conventional methods can be cleared by the Jet-Axe; the entry is often cleaner and creates minimal damage to surrounding walls or doors than conventional methods; and access and entry time is significantly reduced by using the Jet-Axe. Moreover, the physical effort in using conventional methods can often exhaust firefighters so that they are less capable of combating a fire once they have gained entry through conventional methods, and the use of the Jet-Axe can minimize this problem.

In sum, the Jet-Axe is a reliable explosive device that was designed to penetrate particularly difficult physical barriers in fighting fires. The device comes in several sizes and has been on the market for about seven years. During this period, it has been purchased and used by many fire departments across the country.[23] The firefighting application followed extensive research and development related to space programs, as well as intensive demonstrations before urban fire chiefs, during 1968-69.

Summary

This chapter has described the six types of innovations whose life histories at specific sites were the subject of study: computer-assisted instruction, police computer systems, mobile intensive care units, closed-circuit television systems, breath testing, and the Jet-Axe.

The six represent a conceptual distinction among task-specific, task-diverse (service-only), and task-diverse (service and administrative) classes of innovations. Each class has been hypothesized, on the basis of observations made during a pilot study phase, to become routinized for different reasons. A different set of factors were specified for each class of innovations.

The innovations to be studied were selected according to a post-hoc longitudinal research design. In this design, innovations known to have been adopted during the last fifteen years were identified. For a sample of these innovations, the life histories from the time of adoption to the present will be traced in chapters 4-6. To facilitate the tracking of important organizational events, the six types of innovations were all selected because they had some technological artifact. This attribute made tracking easier because of the added concreteness of the innovation but may limit the conclusions of the study to "hardware" innovations.

Notes

1. A second study (Battelle-Columbus Laboratories, 1973) also used the same method and was based in part on the original TRACES data.

2. See the following subsections for a discussion and definition.

3. For example, the literature consists of studies that have frequently involved national surveys of the adoption patterns for specific innovations.

4. The term "innovation" is commonly used in three different ways (see Zaltman et al., 1973). In one context, it is synonomous with invention. Here, innovation is akin to the act of perceiving or creating something new. In another context, it is ascribed to a particular kind of organizational process as in Mohr's (1969) definition of an innovation as "the successful introduction into an applied situation of means or ends that are new to that situation" (see also Myers and Marquis, 1969). In a third context, which is the one employed in this paper, the innovation is an artifact of some sort that is newly introduced into an organization (see also Yin, Heald, and Vogel, 1977).

5. Everett Rogers, who conducted many of the earlier studies on individual adoption, has given new attention to the instability of innovations by noting that a process of "re-invention" often occurs from site to site.

6. For example, Schon (1967) speaks of technology as "any tool or technique, any product or process, any physical equipment or method of doing or making, by which human capability is extended." Leavitt (1965) offers a similarly broad perspective when he describes technology as "direct problem solving inventions." Leavitt includes sets of activities, methods, or processes and layouts, arrangements, or patterns in his definition, as well as equipment, machines, and tools.

7. For a full description of the pilot work, see an unpublished paper available from the author: R.K. Yin et al., "Routinization III: Research Methods for Phase II," The Rand Corporation, January 1977.

8. This is not the same as saying that one class of innovations will tend to become more routinized than another—which is not hypothesized to be the case.

9. It is again important to point out that the significant characteristics are those inherent in the innovation, and not those that may have emerged during implementation at a particular site. The actual implementation experience may reveal many unforeseen problems.

10. For discussions of the various applications, including CAI, see Holtzman, 1970; and Salisbury, 1971.

11. The PLATO I system did not have any time-sharing capability, and only the subsequent PLATO II, III, and IV systems were able to service more than one terminal at a time (see Bitzer and Skaperdas, 1970; and Watson, 1972).

12. For a brief history, see Whisenand and Tamaru (1970).

13. The first police on-line system was installed in St. Louis in 1964.

14. See the CAI discussion for a definition of minicomputers.

15. This excessive variation in organizational arrangements may have been one reason that Eveland, Rogers, and Klepper (1976) found it difficult to discern any clear pattern of experiences in their study of regional computer systems.

16. With the restriction to police-owned and operated computer systems, there is always the possibility of unrepresentative findings, because the more common national experience has been where police departments have been users of municipal systems. However, existing research has shown that there is no consistent pattern of differences between police-owned and municipally-owned systems, either in terms of the distribution of such systems or of the success of the computer operations for police use (Colton, 1972b). Furthermore, the major concern of our study is with change in organizational settings such as police departments, and not with any assessment of the use of computer technology.

17. See Hartley (1971) for a survey of emergency service practice, broadly defined. This survey covers all kinds of assistance, of which MICUs are but one type. Similarly, see National Highway Traffic Safety Administration (1976) for a bibliography on emergency services, broadly defined.

18. A recent GAO report had as its main target the vulnerable nature of these regional systems (see Comptroller General, 1976). The report doubted that most regional systems would survive the period of federal or other external funding, because the regional systems had failed to develop access to local government revenues or cooperative relationships with local agencies.

19. For instance, the TELECARE II apparatus performs these functions as well as defibrillation, is battery-operated, and weighs 37 pounds.

20. According to one estimate, alcohol was involved in one-half of the 45,000 traffic fatalities in 1976. (See Dozier and Moulden, 1977.)

21. A person must be arrested on DWI charges before a breath test can be conducted. The pre-screening procedure facilitates a preliminary judgment on whether the arrest should be made, but only the results of the subsequent breath test are used as evidence in court. (See Moulden and Voas, 1975.)

22. For instance, all states except Idaho and Utah have a presumptive 0.10 percent BAC law; in Idaho and Utah, the level has been set at 0.08

percent. Only a minority of the states, however, have passed pre-screening laws. (See Dozier and Moulden, 1977.)

23. One preliminary estimate was that 400 Jet-Axes were sold during 1970-72 (Frohman et al., 1972).

3 Passages and Cycles

The major lines of argument for thinking about routinization have thus far taken the following form. First, routinization represents the process by which new service practices become an integral part of urban bureaucracies; the evolution of such practices, it has been argued, has been poorly understood in the past but is an essential component of any future strategy for changing urban bureaucracies. Second, the routinization process can best be revealed if one traces the life histories of specific innovations. These innovations are new service practices and, if successful over time, can become a part of standard bureaucratic practice.

The discussion now turns to the most critical part of the conceptual framework: determining how to identify and assess the specific organizational changes that mark routinization. This chapter contributes an original conceptualization of organizational change that focuses on the notion of passages and cycles. This, however, is discussed in later portions of the chapter. First, the traditional approaches to the study of bureaucratic innovation need to be briefly reviewed.

Traditional Approaches for Studying Bureaucratic Innovation

Four general approaches have dominated traditional ways of thinking about bureaucratic innovation.[1] These approaches are fully reviewed in appendix E, but, in brief, they are marked by the following characteristics:

1. Research, development and diffusion. Emphasizes the macro-institutional environment in conducting R&D and in producing, marketing, and implementing new technologies; gives little attention to events within specific organizations that implement and routinize the new technologies.
2. Social interaction. Emphasizes the communication network and adoption pattern for specific innovations; individuals rather than organizations have been the main adopters studied, and the main focus has been the spread or diffusion among adopters rather than the events following adoption at a given site.
3. Innovative organizations. Correlates a wide range of organizational characteristics with the occurrence of bureaucratic innovation; typical result is a profile of innovative versus noninnovative organizations, but such a profile is cross-sectional in nature and cannot fully capture such processes as

49

implementation or routinization, which take place over time within the same organization.

4. Organizational change. Examines events over time within the same organization; usually specifies a stage theory, such as adoption → implementation → routinization, but few studies have specified a set of critical events or the operational characteristics of the innovation process.

In general, even though many revisions have occurred in these approaches, they still form the foundation for various empirical studies of local services and bureaucratic innovations. For studying routinization, only the organizational change approach provides even rudimentary assistance for analyzing life histories of innovations. Nevertheless, it is useful to show how recent empirical studies of local service innovation still tend to follow one or another approach. Each approach implies a different research design, and this in turn dictates the issues that a study can address.

Research, Development and Diffusion Approach—
Radnor (1975), and Baer et al. (1976)

These first two studies follow the research, development and diffusion approach. The Radnor (1975) study examined the use of new equipment in the law-enforcement field, based on interviews of over 200 organizations, including users, producers, distributors, and related organizations. Thus, the study investigated the institutional relationships at each step in the development of new equipment, including: needs assessment, investment in and funding of the appropriate R&D, production, marketing, sales, and implementation feedback. The study attempted to identify the problems at each step, and thus to specify policies that could be followed by the federal government to alleviate these problems. However, no attempt was made to understand the life histories of innovations within specific organizations.

The Baer et al. (1976) study contained case studies of twenty-four federal demonstration projects, of which about six involved applications in local services, such as a mechanized system for collecting refuse, a computer-assisted electrocardiogram analysis, a dial-a-ride transportation system, and an expressway surveillance and control system. The study defined demonstration projects as representing ". . . the final stage of 'scaling up' from the laboratory to commercial use," and, as a result of the case study analysis, six factors were identified as being associated with successful demonstrations:

1. A technology well in hand
2. Cost and risk sharing with real participants
3. Project initiative from a nonfederal source

4. Existence of a strong industrial system for commercialization
5. Participation during the planning stage of all institutional elements needed for commercialization
6. Absence of tight time constraints

The Baer et al. study dealt with the relationships among various public and private institutions in producing and using a new technology and therefore illustrates the main strengths and weaknesses of the research, development and diffusion approach. The approach is useful for identifying the various institutions involved in producing a new technology. However, at the point of adoption, implementation, or routinization, it provides little guidance for analyzing the key organizational events within a given local agency.

Social Interaction Approach—Feller, Menzel, and Kozak (1976)

This study was based on extensive surveys of agency officials in four services: traffic control, air pollution, firefighting, and solid waste. The officials identified new technologies used in each service and gave their reasons for adopting or not adopting the various technologies. A major finding of this study was that, in all but the solid-waste area, there was an extensive pattern of diffusion, with 60 to 80 percent of the respondents indicating their agency had adopted such innovations as:

1. Induction loop detectors
2. Solid state traffic-control devices
3. Optically programmed traffic signals
4. Lightweight fire hoses
5. Lightweight hose couplings
6. Continuous SO_2 monitoring

Many other innovations had been adopted by a large number of the agencies surveyed. The study thus challenged the traditional stereotypes of public services as noninnovative organizations. Reflecting the social interaction approach, the study further analyzed the pattern of diffusion. For instance, one finding was that there were no "innovative" cities in which the four services all tended to be innovative; another finding was that innovative attempts tended to be located in jurisdictions near the site of the relevant manufacturer. Feller, Menzel, and Kozak also attempted to conduct an analysis of the intra-organizational factors that characterized adoption behavior, but the results were inconclusive, suggesting only that individual adoptions were not to be explained by any model in which the magnitude of the problem (prior need or performance gap) or the availability of extra resources (slack resources) were the main components.

Although the Feller, Menzel, and Kozak study attempted to go beyond the social interaction approach by studying organizational characteristics, the main findings and contribution deal with the diffusion patterns of different technologies in local services. This contribution represents the inherent strengths and weaknesses of the social interaction approach. It is only this approach, for instance, that does an adequate job of analyzing diffusion patterns across agencies and sites over time. None of the other studies cited here contains a diffusion curve. At the same time, such a perspective yields little appreciation for organizational changes within an adopting agency.

Innovative Organizations—Bingham (1976), Nelson and Sieber (1976), and Danziger and Dutton (1976)

These three studies fall within the innovative organizations approach, although the Bingham (1976) study also covers some diffusion and hence social interaction issues. The Bingham study examined the use of eight innovations in four services: public housing, public schools, public libraries, and general municipal government. The diffusion aspect of the study was based on the results of surveys of agencies in cities over 50,000, and it was found that there were no "innovative" cities, that is, cities where there was a high degree of innovativeness in all four services in the same city.

The bulk of the Bingham study, however, dealt with the identification of factors correlated with the adoption of innovations. The main finding was that an agency's environment, including existence of federal or state assistance, slack resources, and overall professionalism in local government, was one of the strong determinants of adoption behavior. Except for organizational size, whose role is statistically difficult to disentangle from that of community size and wealth, the study found no organizational characteristics that were correlated with adoption behavior. Two conceptual contributions by the study were that: (1) innovations in method (process innovations) followed the predicted patterns more than innovations involving physical changes (product innovations); and (2) some agencies could and often did innovate to improve already adequate levels of performance (amenity condition), as well as to upgrade substandard performance (need condition). The latter finding may help to explain the failure to find, as in the Feller, Menzel, and Kozak (1975) study, a performance gap as one of the correlates of innovation.

The Nelson and Sieber (1976) study was based on a survey of school principals in cities over 300,000; the survey asked the respondents to indicate whether any of seventeen innovations were in use or were being tested. Most of the innovations were curriculum changes, and only a minority of them constituted technological innovations, such as televised instruction, teaching machines, and language laboratories. The analysis focused on the characteristics of the innovation as well as of the adopting agency as potential determinants of adoption. Among the findings, it was shown that the potential high cost of an innovation was not necessarily a barrier to its use; cost, however, was not related to the perceived quality of the innovation; and there was only a moderately negative relationship between administrative difficulties during implementation and subsequent use.

The Danziger and Dutton (1976) study followed almost the same research design as that of Nelson and Sieber: a survey of city and county governments for the extent of their use of electronic data-processing (EDP) innovations. Over seven-hundred jurisdictions were surveyed; the responses by each jurisdiction were used to calculate an innovativeness score. Highly innovative jurisdictions were found to be: large in size with a complex governmental organization; in sites where there was professional-managerial control over EDP decisions; where there was not a highly developed industrial activity; and where control over EDP decisions was decentralized.

These three studies in the aggregate give an indication of the problems with the Innovative Organizations approach. Although each study was more than adequately designed and contained sophisticated single and multivariate analyses, the studies each defined a very different set of innovations and examined different organizational attributes. It is this variation that has led Downs and Mohr (1976) to question the ultimate utility of the Innovative Organization approach; the results may always be idiosyncratic to the innovations chosen, characteristics examined, and measures used. Little convergence of findings from different studies can be expected.

Organizational Change Approach—Bale (1976) and Berman and McLaughlin (1977 and 1978)

Both studies examined innovations in schools; Bale (1976) focused on the use of a single innovation—instructional use of the television program "The Electric Company"—and Berman and McLaughlin (1977 and 1978) examined a wide variety of federally instigated innovations, only some of which involved new technology.

The Bale (1976) study actually followed an innovative research design in which the investigator explicitly attempted to combine the innovative organizations and organizational change approaches. This was done by establishing several stages of change, and then examining the organizational characteristics that were important at each stage of change. Figure 3-1 summarizes the research design. It shows the stages of change and the organizational characteristics investigated, and it provides the results of the study. A typical finding was that pupil characteristics were an important correlate in the initial stage in determining whether a school should consider an innovation; at later stages, however,

Figure 3-1. Summary of Bale's Conceptual Framework and Findings

Stages in Kaplan's Model of the Process of Organizational Change	Influencing Factors											
	Attributes of the Innovation	Strategies of Introduction	Characteristics of Organization Members	Structural Properties of Organization	Characteristics of Organizational Environment	Characteristics of Throughput (Pupils)	Results of Stage 1	Results of Stage 2	Results of Stage 3	Results of Stage 4	Results of Stage 5	Results of Stage 6
Stage 1: Essence of a problem condition	///	///	0	+	+	+	///	///	///	///	///	///
Stage 2: Diagnosis	?	?	+	0	+	0	0	///	///	///	///	///
Stage 3: Initiation	?	?	+	+	+	0	+	+	///	///	///	///
Stage 4: Introduction	?	?	+	0	0	0	+	0	+	///	///	///
Stage 5: Transition	?	?	0	+	0	0	0	+	+	0	///	///
Stage 6: Routinization	?	?	?	?	?	?	?	?	?	?	?	///
Stage 7: Stabilization	?	?	?	?	?	?	?	?	?	?	?	?

Source: Richard L. Bale, "Organizational Change and Innovation in American Elementary Schools: The Case of 'The Electric Company,'" Ph.D. diss., Florida State University, 1976. Reprinted with permission.

[a] The hatch marks indicate cells that are illogical or redundant; for filled cells, + indicates factor had impact at that stage, 0 indicates factor had no impact at that stage, and ? indicates factor and/or stage not addressed by study.

pupil characteristics, as one might readily expect, had little to do with successful diagnosis, initiation, introduction, and transition. The figure also indicates the limited scope of the Bale study; there was no attempt to define the later stages of change—routinization or stabilization—or to identify the correlates of these stages.

The Berman and McLaughlin (1977 and 1978) study covered a wide variety of innovations sponsored by the U.S. Office of Education. The key findings were that the innovations often differed unpredictably from site to site, and that this, in part, was the result of a process of mutual adaptation whereby the innovation and the site both modified each other. Another key finding was that the overwhelming majority of the innovations failed to become incorporated—as measured by the transition from federal to local sources of funding. Because of this finding, however, the authors were unable to examine routinization in any detail.

These two studies illustrate the potential of the organizational change approach. Unlike the other three approaches, an explicit attempt is made to examine events over time within specific organizations. In theory, the full life history of an innovation—from adoption to routinization— can be traced. Unfortunately, most studies that follow the organizational change approach (including the Bale and Berman and McLaughlin studies) have failed to trace the full process. Adoption and implementation remain the primary focus because few innovations appear to become routinized. Moreover, most studies have still not provided operational guidelines to determine whether routinization has occurred. As a result, the next section attempts to develop a more comprehensive conceptual and operational framework.

Organizational Passages and Cycles as a Way of Defining Routinization

When an innovation has become a stable and regular part of organizational procedures and behavior, it is defined as having become routinized. In the local service setting, a routinized innovation would be part of the common services normally provided by an agency; the practice would no longer be regarded as a special innovation. For innovations that have replaced older service practices, complete routinization implies that the agency cannot revert to the displaced service practice. However, the innovation may be replaced by some newer innovation at a later date.

The acceptance of this framework still leaves one far short of being able to analyze routinization because so many of the important concepts have not yet been made specific. We need to further define routinization, discuss the implications for routinization strategies, and then review various hypotheses about why routinization occurs. The existing literature on organizational change provides meager assistance for answering certain key questions:

1. What are the characteristics of routinization?
2. Is routinization an absolute condition, or are there different degrees of routinization?
3. How can the state of routinization be assessed through empirical study?

The main contribution of this study is to answer these questions by establishing an initial set of categories and then by describing the events in specific life histories. Previous research has not covered these key questions adequately. For instance, although the stages of organizational change appear to be commonly accepted theoretical notions, even discussions that claim to assist in the design of field studies do not describe how such stages are to be assessed (Barnes, 1971). At another level of analysis, the research that deals with the birth, growth, and death of an organization (Downs, 1967; and Kaufman, 1971, 1975, and 1976) has primarily been concerned with organizational size as the main outcome measure.[2] None of these studies, however, has attempted to determine the changes occurring within an organization as a new practice becomes routinized.

Routinization must be assessed by focusing attention on discrete organizational conditions—documentable occurrences—such as the following:

1. A new set of procedures exists in the police department's orders of the day.
2. An agency is operating on a new fiscal year budget and management plan.
3. A biology teacher has been replaced during the past year.
4. Equipment has been obtained through a new leasing contract.
5. A newer organization plan has been implemented as organizational positions have been redefined.

These conditions are not necessarily simple; they can involve a series of decisions that are difficult to trace. Moreover, the conditions may not be easily defined in terms of the specific dates when the conditions first existed. The budget process, for instance, may take place over a multi-week period and still require modifications throughout the year. The important characteristics of such conditions, however, are: (1) that they are, in principle, sufficiently self-contained to serve as units of analysis; and (2) that they constitute, in the aggregate, a way of assessing the current status of an organization.

Any focus on organizational conditions immediately raises the same problem that nags all organizational change theories: the need to distinguish important conditions or changes from unimportant ones. Clearly, the daily life of an organization can consist of an almost infinite array of conditions:

1. The manager was out because of illness.
2. The paper in the Xerox machine was replaced.
3. There was an office party.
4. The supervisor wrote a reply to some employee suggestions.

How should conditions be defined so that only those that are relevant to routinization are assessed? What is needed is a set of categories of organizational conditions in which each category reflects an important facet of routinization status. To the extent that routinization is considered as the normal occurrence of a specific practice that began as an innovation, these categories should cover the organizational resources or operations that sustain innovations over a period of time.

In a local service agency, an innovation may be sustained by five major resources: budgetary resources, personnel resources, training programs for service personnel, appropriate rules of organizational governance codified in a statute, regulation, or procedural manual, and supply and maintenance operations. In general, the innovation that has received the most sustained support from these resources may be regarded as being the most routinized. To gain support from these resources, an innovation must achieve a series of passages or cycles. These are the two critical concepts that will recur throughout this study.

A "passage" occurs when a formal transition from one organizational state to another has taken place. For instance, new job skills often require the establishment of specific personnel classifications in the civil service system. The actual establishment of such classifications would constitute a passage. Similarly, the establishment of a new component in an in-service training program, the issuance of a new entry in an agency's operating manual, or the change from an external to internal source of funding would also serve as passages. The term "passage," then, is used to define significant changes in organizational procedures or structure that reflect increased organizational support for an innovation. In most cases, such passages occur only once and mean that an innovation has become a more integral part of an organization. The more passages that have been achieved, the more routinized an innovation may be regarded—all other things being equal.

In contrast, a "cycle" is an organizational event that occurs repeatedly during the lifetime of an organization. Each time a cycle occurs, the use of an innovation may be questioned and threatened. However, the more cycles that an innovation survives, the more routinized it may be regarded—again, all other things being equal. The term "cycle" thus applies to repeated events that occur as part of an organization's operations and that may affect an innovation.

The routinization of an innovation may be described in terms of its ability to negotiate several passages as well as its ability to survive a period of organizational cycles. To further elaborate this concept of routinization, the following paragraphs identify the major passages and cycles related to the five types of resources needed to sustain an innovation:

1. Budgetary resources
2. Personnel resources
3. Training programs for service personnel

4. Organizational governance
5. Supply and maintenance operations

Budgetary Resources

The initial budgetary support for an innovation will evolve as a result of budgetary proposals, review, deliberation, and decision making at different organizational levels, not all of which are within the target agency. A routinized innovation, however, is one that has survived numerous budgetary cycles. For most agencies, the cycle occurs annually. The more cycles that occur, the more the innovation would be considered routinized and the less it would be regarded as an innovation.

Within local service agencies, another important budgetary distinction arises because of the pervasive nature of federal funding at the local level. This is the distinction between budgetary items supported by local revenue (hard money) and those supported by externally derived sources, generally federal grants or aid (soft money). Because the soft money is typically time-limited, as in a project grant of three years' duration, an innovation is more routinized if it is supported by hard rather than by soft money. For an innovation that began with soft money, the passage or transition to hard money may thus be regarded as a significant step toward routinization.[3]

Personnel Resources

Personnel resources are present in any innovation, whether they are used for operating, managing, or coordinating the use of the innovation. As with budgetary resources, the important components of the personnel resources in terms of the routinization process also involve passages and cycles. The resources include the jobs themselves as well as the incumbents. In local service agencies, job classifications should reflect job responsibilities and duties. For an innovation that began with a temporary or ad hoc definition of job functions (typically, the functions may have been defined by an outside consultant or equipment manufacturer), the passage or transition of such functions into civil service classifications may be regarded as a significant step toward routinization.[4] Similarly, the passage of the function into job prerequisites or promotional requirements would also be a significant step.

In spite of the fact that job functions are documented in this manner, each incumbent will nevertheless perform a specific job in a slightly idiosyncratic manner. The more routinized innovation is thus one whose personnel requirements have been carried out by more generations, or cycles, of incumbents (Hage and Aiken, 1970). Of course, turnover rates vary according to job and agency, so that it is impossible to relate such cycles of incumbents to any calendar period of time. However, it is generally true that the longer the period of time, the more personnel cycles will have occurred.

Such turnover is often difficult to measure. This is because high turnover rates are not desirable at the outset of an innovation's life history; yet, low turnover rates are not desirable when an innovation has matured, as this will tend to (undesirably) identify the innovation with a specific group of incumbents. Thus, turnover should occur during the later stages in the life history. In addition to bringing new incumbents into contact with the innovation, turnover may also mean the promotion of the original incumbents—presumably supportive of the innovation—to higher positions of authority in the agency. Such promotion will add further support for the innovation and is thus a desirable cycle of events.

Training Programs

Training requirements, particularly for practitioners, vary from innovation to innovation. Some innovations are easy to operate and require little instruction to be used; others require training that can last over many weeks. Thus, training resources, unlike budgetary and personnel resources, may not be required by every innovation. (The discussion only pertains to those that do.) Nevertheless, it will be seen that training again involves a passage and a cycle.

In local service agencies, the practitioners typically belong to a practice-oriented profession like teaching, medicine, law enforcement, and social work. The profession will set standards for practice, which may be incorporated into the curriculum of the professional school—police academies, medical schools, and educational schools—or into the certification requirements for practice, or both (Yin, 1976). When the skills needed to operate an innovation become part of a profession's standards, the professional school curriculum, or the certification requirements, the innovation has thus made a significant passage toward routinization. An example here would be the use of CAI in the classroom. Most state educational agencies do not yet require that mathematics teachers have any formal training in computer science to be certified. Consequently, there are teachers who not only lack that training, but who may also have a negative attitude toward the use of CAI. If such training were required and if all incoming mathematics teachers could only gain certification by having this training, the likelihood of CAI becoming a regular part of the mathematics classroom practice would be increased.

For many local service agencies, there is also continual inservice training. Fire and police officers typically participate in daily or weekly drills. The officers also return two or three times a year to special training facilities, where they learn about new practices and refresh their knowledge about old ones, and

tests are often administered to assure that they have maintained a basic performance standard. Teachers may similarly have formal in-service training
requirements that are linked either to on-the-job performance or to promotions,
and personnel in most services are generally subject to periodic training sessions.
Under such conditions, the more routinized innovation is one with skill requirements that have been conducted in more training cycles.[5] In this manner, the
skills will not only have been taught to more personnel, but they will also have
been taught over a period of time to more generations of personnel.

Organizational Governance

The formal rules by which a local service agency operates are usually specified
quite explicitly.[6] The rules may occur in many different contexts; for example,
in:

1. Statutes that authorize an agency or appropriate funds to it
2. State or local laws (ordinances) that deal with agency revenues or work
   practices
3. Regulations that describe an agency's authority, organizational structure,
   or procedures
4. Agency collective bargaining agreements or other contractual obligations
5. Agency operating manuals or other written procedures for day-to-day
   operations and the maintenance of service standards[7]

Often the formal rules are manifested in the administrative forms used within
an agency, the specific data collected by the agency, or the flow of paperwork
from desk to desk.

For most of these governance rules, the notion of a passage is slightly more
important than that of a cycle because the rule-generating process may not occur
on a cyclic basis. Thus, wherever some aspect of the innovation becomes part of
the organization's formal governance, such a passage may be regarded as a
significant step toward routinization. For instance, an innovation may become
part of a formal reorganization (a change in organizational status), which would
integrate the innovation into the organization. Some innovations may not
necessarily become a formal part of an organization's governance, but may be
closely associated with some condition of governance. A state law, for instance,
may mandate a certain distribution of the agency's work force over different
hourly shifts. To create such a distribution, an agency may use an innovation,
such as a computer-based analytic program, which has thus not been mandated
by the law but which has been very closely associated with its implementation.

Finally, organizational governance can also be affected by normative practices. That is, even in the absence of formal mandates, a practice that becomes

widespread will become an integral part of an agency's responsibilities. Thus, an innovation that has attained widespread use will have made a major step toward routinization. Conversely, an innovation that is continually operated on only a limited basis will tend to be seen as a special project or operation, no matter what the formal mandate. Because widespread use may be gradually achieved on a phased basis, the notion of cycles appears more appropriate than that of passages.

Supply and Maintenance Operations

These are also key resources in providing sustenance to any innovation. A key piece of equipment that is part of the innovation (or the entire hardware component of the innovation), may need to be replaced or upgraded. The innovation may also require a specific set of supply or special maintenance procedures. Again, with each type of operation, there tend to be passages and cycles.

A passage occurs when the agency establishes the necessary supplies as part of its regular inventory, and not as items for special order. Thus, for many innovations, the initial supply and maintenance services may have been provided by the vendor (external to the agency). These services may have been part of a leasing arrangement, may have been contracted separately, or may have been provided by some other agreement. When such innovations are first serviced by an agency itself or are contracted on a long-term basis, however, this may be regarded as a significant step toward routinization. This internal capability means that the necessary supplies are maintained as part of an agency's regular inventory and that the agency's own maintenance shop can make any repairs and perform the periodic servicing of the innovation.

Cycles occur when equipment is upgraded or replaced. The calendar time of these cycles varies and is related to the type of equipment involved. For instance, fire departments generally purchase new fire trucks at a very low rate because the lifetime of a fire truck is often more than twenty years. In contrast, the mobile fleet of a police department will turn over about once every five years. Regardless of the calendar time, one procedure that may be important for successful survival is the development of new purchasing specifications for equipment related to the innovation, to be used for all subsequent purchases.

The Complete Passages and Cycles Framework

The state of routinization of an innovation may be defined in terms of a number of organizational conditions, each of which reflects some essential aspect of organizational operations in maintaining an innovation over time. For every condition, routinization has been defined as a combination of passages and survival over a number of cycles. In general, an innovation shall be considered more routinized the more passages or cycles it has achieved. Table 3-1 summarizes these conditions; all but two became the subject of actual study in the following chapters.[8]

The framework of passages and cycles appears to have certain appealing characteristics in providing operational insights into the routinization process. For a particular agency or locale, certain passages or cycles may be difficult to accomplish. It may be well known that changes have rarely occurred, for instance, in the supply and maintenance operation of an agency, and that any investment of energies to routinize any innovation will be wasted. Before any changes can be made to routinize an innovation, the whole subsystem may have to be revamped. Typically, the head of the supply and maintenance operation may have to be replaced. Under such conditions, advocates for routinizing a specific innovation would be better off if they concentrated their efforts on other passages or cycles. In the long run, of course, the existence of numerous institutionally blocked passages could then become an operational definition of a stagnant, or non-innovative, agency.

Three other issues should be raised that are especially relevant for designing an empirical study. First, because it is difficult to keep track of all the various cycles, an initial empirical achievement would simply be to note whether the first cycle had occurred or not, for any given category. This will be the strategy pursued in the following study. Second, in conducting any analysis of routinization, the various passages and cycles represent separate dependent variables. Currently, there is no rationale for deciding which passages and cycles may be more important, or for believing that the passages and cycles are similar units of measure that can be aggregated even if weighted. Thus, the creation of any aggregate index of routinization should only be undertaken with great caution but may still be a necessary shorthand for analyzing empirical data. Third, although the definition of routinization has attempted to be comprehensive in order to be conceptually complete, there is no reason that a single empirical study should be expected to cover the entire scope of what has been conceptualized. Indeed, our intention has been to define routinization in such rich terms, because it is a complex process which can only be adequately investigated by a large number of empirical studies.

Factors Affecting Routinization

Because the passages and cycles framework just described represents a considerable elaboration of previous thinking on organizational change, the framework will be the main focus of the empirical analysis to follow in chapters 4, 5, and 6. However, some rudimentary thoughts may be presented regarding the factors leading to routinization. Although empirical evidence will be examined in chapter 7, this is a topic in which substantial further research will be needed.

Table 3-1
Organizational Passages and Cycles Related to Routinization

Type of Resource or Operation	Passages	Cycles
Budget	Innovation supports changes from soft to hard money (2)[a]	Survives annual budget cycles
Personnel		
Jobs	Functions become part of job descriptions or prerequisites (5)	–
Incumbent turnover	–	Survives introduction of new personnel (9)
		Survives promotion of key personnel (8)
Training		
Prepractice	Skills become part of professional standards, professional school curriculum (7)	–
Inservice	–	Skills taught during many training cycles
Organizational governance	Establishment of appropriate organizational status (3)	Attainment of widespread use (10)
	Use of innovation becomes part of statute, regulation, manual, etc. (6)	
Supply and maintenance	Supply and maintenance provided by agency or on long-term (contract) basis (4)	Survives equipment turnover (1)

[a]Numbers refer to ten passages and cycles studied in actual life histories (see table 7-1).

During the period that an innovation is being introduced, there can exist any number of factors that may affect the routinization outcome, such as the specific passages or cycles that will be achieved. Each of these factors is a complex set of circumstances which can also change over time, so that the process suggested here goes far beyond the Innovative Organizations approach, in which static factors are correlated with innovative outcomes. For instance, a key factor in achieving routinization may be the continued support of an external constituency, such as clients of the service, potential clients, or the community at large. Such support can rise and decline over time, and there is no single point for measuring support that would necessarily represent the characteristics of support during other points in time. Although this causes immense problems of measurement for any empirical study, the spirit of the following discussion is an attempt to describe the importance of a group of factors, independent of any concern for establishing definitive measures for empirical study.

The factors that may be hypothesized to affect the routinization of an innovation can be classified into five subgroups, those that are related to:

1. Inherent characteristics of the innovation
2. Service applications and outcomes of the innovation as experienced by an agency
3. The external environment of the local agency
4. The internal characteristics of the agency
5. Federal or state support for the innovation

Of these five subgroups, the last four are discussed in the following subsections. The first, which deals with the inherent characteristics of the innovation, was covered in chapter 2.

Service Applications and Outcomes

Three factors are hypothesized to be relevant here: The innovation has involved a core application; competition among applications has been minimized; and the innovation has shown some service-related payoff. An innovation may be used in a number of ways by a local agency, and this application may vary from site to site. Previous research has suggested that innovations are more likely to be routinized if the innovation is applied to a core application rather than to a peripheral function of the agency (see Berman et al., 1975). The core is not easy to define. For instance, each agency can have core administrative functions, such as administering the payroll, as well as core service functions, such as providing medical treatment to a patient. For administrative functions, it might be possible to enumerate core activities such as budget, personnel, and maintenance; for service functions, it might also be possible to enumerate as core functions those that directly reflect service goals or standards. However, there appears to be no completely satisfactory approach for defining what a "core" function is, even though there may be some degree of consensus among service administrators when they set their priorities.

One suggestion from previous research has been to determine whether an innovation has displaced some significant function (Berman et al., 1975). If displacement has occurred, as opposed to a new function that has been merely added on, the argument is that a core function is more likely to have been involved. Such a view, however, precludes the notion that core functions might be increased, as in the case of a paramedic rescue squad that provides on-site medical treatment that was never provided in the past, so displacement can only be part of the story. Nevertheless, for most innovations, displacement can be one criterion for determining whether a core function has been involved. Where no displacement has occurred, there must be some compelling evidence before one can conclude that a new core function has involved.

Competition among applications occurs when an innovation can be used for a variety of functions. Some innovations are, by their nature, limited to a single function (see chapter 2). However, the important factor here is whether, given an innovation that can be used for a variety of functions, the local agency has applied it in such a way that there is strong competition among applications. An example would be the competition among administrative and service functions for using a central computer. Such competition may retard routinization because:

1. Resources and support for the innovation may be divided among different constituencies within and outside the agency.
2. Passages and cycles in relation to one application may not be compatible, or, at the very least, will have to be coordinated among applications.
3. There is less likely to be a single supporter of the innovation who can marshal the necessary support for it—that is, each potential supporter of the innovation may believe that others will play the more prominent role.
4. The alternative applications will create instability in the everyday operation of the innovation as crises or other events may give reason for shifting emphasis from one application to another and back.

Naturally, this situation pertains only when the several applications are in competition with each other. In contrast, there may be any number of situations in which different applications are highly compatible and can all be accommodated easily by an innovation. In such situations, there will be more support for the innovation and the diversity of applications will serve as a positive influence on routinization.

Service payoffs from an innovation can be reflected in output measures, input measures, perceived satisfaction or convenience by key personnel, or other objective or subjective assessments. The more clearly an innovation has demonstrated such a payoff, even if in subjective terms, the more likely the innovation will become routinized (Berman et al., 1975). There may have been no formal evaluation of the payoff, or the payoff may not have produced an outcome that was considered central to the agency's purpose, such as educational achievement, public safety, or good health. The main characteristics of such a payoff are that it is of a specific nature, that it is perceivable by many people, and that there is some consensus that the payoff exists. The earlier and more sustained evidence of such a payoff, the better. The payoff is important for routinization because it allows advocates to argue more forcefully during key passages and cycles.

External Environment

An innovation may be initiated in relation to a prior need or crisis outside the agency or no problem or crisis—as in the distribution of a new technology, independent of need; it may be strongly or weakly supported by the users or clients of the agency's services or by the community at large. All these conditions are hypothesized to influence the degree to which an innovation becomes routinized.

The nature of the prior need can affect routinization in both directions. If a crisis were perceived as a single isolated occurrence, such as the need to innoculate people against the swine flu, and if an innovation were tailored specifically to serve that crisis, routinization would be less likely to occur because, when the crisis was over, the perceived need for the innovation would disappear.[9] In contrast, if the prior need were perceived as a prolonged or chronic affair, such as declining educational achievement scores or continued racial segregation, the innovation is more likely to be routinized. (This might occur even if the crisis eventually were to subside, for it would be difficult for the agency to return to its prior practice.) Naturally, as with the problem of defining a core function, it is not always clear what constitutes a crisis or prior need. The sense in which the term is used here, however, is that a prior need may be said to exist if it is only a perceived need rather than some objectively assessable condition.

Client support for an innovation can be a complex factor, because most service agencies have a variety of clients, such as students of different interests within a school as well as their parents, and not all clients may benefit equally from an innovation. Nevertheless, on balance, if there is active client support for an innovation, it is more likely to become routinized than if there is no such support or if there are conflicts among client groups. Such support could be made known informally, as when clients report their satisfaction with a situation to service practitioners, or it could be made known quite formally, as when students select courses in their pre-registration forms. This client support can obviously change over time, and it is difficult to determine which time period, if any, is more critical than other time periods. Suffice it to say that routinization will occur with greater certainty if client support is strong and sustained, or, if it is strong but intermittent, the peak support periods occur at the times that will most influence decisions concerning the key passages or cycles.

Community support for an innovation operates in much the same fashion, except that the support comes from the polity at large rather than from only those who are eligible to use the service. Strong and sustained support will have a positive effect on routinization (Costello, 1971), whereas little support or the existence of community conflicts may have detrimental effects. As with client support, community support can also be transmitted through formal and informal channels. The former ones include local referenda or votes on service-specific revenues;[10] the latter are expressed through the relationships between citizens and service officials, often mediated by local politicians.

Internal Characteristics

Internal characteristics cover conditions within the local service agency. In general, an innovation is hypothesized to be more likely to become routinized if it has greater support from the staff within an agency (Yin, Heald, and Vogel, 1977). Such support can come from a single innovator, who actively seeks to institutionalize the innovation by working on passages and cycles; agency administrators, who often make the key decisions concerning those passages and cycles; and service practitioners, who must incorporate the innovation into their own perception of "normal" practice. Such support can be challenged if the innovation has any adversary group, as would be the case if certain staff members had originally been opposed to the innovation or had lost status or power during implementation conflicts. The importance of internal support cannot be overstated. In many cases, an innovation can serve bureaucratic self-interests—such as growth rate of promotions, increased agency status—and thus become routinized even though there have been no distinct service payoffs (Yin, 1977).

The importance of a single, active innovator who protects the innovation and guides its progress through passages and cycles has been frequently noted in previous research on adoption (see Rothman, 1974). This innovator will most often be the one who best understands the innovation and who can—when necessary—provide the direct maintenance and repair services required by the innovation. Other agency staff who have questions about the innovation or who want to recommend revisions in its operation will refer first to this innovator. Finally, this person is also the one who initially helps to organize staff training programs and other orientation activities.

The same innovator may also be concerned about routinization and can take many actions to increase an innovation's success in passages and cycles. This may include generating client support for the innovation by creating a diverse set of functions for the innovation, initiating practitioner certification requirements, or pressing for conversion from soft to hard money whenever additional funds are available. Failure to take such actions will not always irreparably harm the routinization process. However, the absence of such a single, active innovator for some initial period of time will probably mean that an innovation will fail in a particular agency. Of course, over time, the innovation's ability to survive the turnover in this key position will be a positive sign that routinization is occurring.

The support of an innovation by agency administrators is important because these administrators: (1) define the initial circumstances under which an innovation will be used, such as its organizational location and resources available (Tansik and Radnor, 1971); and (2) are later involved in key decisions regarding passages and cycles. The existence of some support by agency administrators, whether it comes from the chief executive (Costello, 1971, and Perry and Kraemer, 1976), from the agency budget officer or comptroller (Bingham, 1976), or from a key line official, appears important to initial adoption. Recent evidence has also suggested, however, that top administrative support becomes even more important as an innovation becomes routinized (Lambright and Flynn, 1977). Thus, the innovation has the best chance of success if it maintains a coalition of supporters from the top administrators (House, 1976, and Lambright and Flynn, 1977).

An innovation will also not become routinized without widespread support among service practitioners. The extent of potential support is defined by the practitioners whose work can in theory be affected by the innovation. With some innovations, this involves all the practitioners within the agency; with others, however, only some practitioners are potentially affected, for example, nurses in a hospital but not doctors, detectives but not patrol officers, language teachers but not all teachers. The greater the actual support from whatever group is actually affected, the more likely an innovation will become routinized.

Lastly, every innovation can have an internal, active adversary group. Such a group may have formed during any stage of the innovative process from adoption to implementation. In particular, if the adoption and implementation stages involve internal conflict and produce strongly negative views toward the innovation, the persons with such views will continue to act to retard the routinization process (Tansik and Radnor, 1971).[11] In contrast, an innovation that had originally been adopted or implemented with relative ease, such as one in which there was a high degree of internal consensus all along, is not as likely to have an adversary group.

Federal or State Support

An important policy issue of recent decades has been the extent to which external support from federal or state governments can facilitate innovation in urban bureaucracies (Roessner, 1976). For this reason, it is necessary to examine the relationship between such support and routinization outcomes. However, the support may be considered an exogenous factor, not having the same role in organizational theory as the previously identified factors. Such support can take the form of direct funding for the innovation, funding of special projects prior to or following adoption that are related to the innovation, or technical assistance.[12]

Summary

Routinization consists of the achievement of certain passages and cycles, which are organizational events in the life history of an innovation. A passage occurs when an innovation makes a transition from one organizational state to another, such as the shift from soft to hard money. A cycle occurs when an innovation has survived a periodic organizational event such as turnover in personnel.

The important passages and cycles are based on the resources required by most innovations: budget, personnel, training for service practitioners, sanction through rules of organizational governance, and supply and maintenance operations. Ten specific passages and cycles have been identified for these resource areas, and the more passages and cycles an innovation has achieved, the more routinized it may be considered. Thus, if all passages and cycles have been achieved, an innovation should have become a part of an agency's regular operation, and the innovative practice indistinguishable from standard agency practice.

The framework of passages and cycles is an extensive elaboration of the organizational change approach to studying innovations. This, as well as three other prominent approaches to innovation, were reviewed briefly at the outset of the chapter. None of the approaches, however, has developed systematic operational criteria for assessing changes over time within an organization. In this respect, the passages and cycles framework represents a potentially significant advance for studying bureaucratic innovation. For this reason, the next three chapters attempt to describe in detail the empirical evidence from nineteen case studies in light of this framework.

Ten factors that may play a causal role in negotiating passages and cycles were also hypothesized in a preliminary manner. These will be examined briefly in chapter 7, in light of the evidence from the case studies and data from the telephone interviews.

Notes

1. Ronald Havelock (1969) has done an excellent job of reviewing the work for three of these approaches, all but the innovative organizations approach. He uses the label "problem-solving" in referring to the organizational change approach. This author has previously described these same approaches, but mainly in the context of problems of adoption and implementation, and not routinization. See Yin (1976) and Yin, Heald, and Vogel (1977).

2. For an excellent review of studies using organizational size as a variable, see Kimberly, 1976b.

3. In fact, the transition may be more important than if an innovation had

always been supported by hard money because a conscious decision had to be made to switch the innovation from soft to hard money. The decision itself might have been an occasion for arousing greater support for the innovation than would have occurred if there had been no decision (as in the case where the innovation had always been supported by hard money).

4. Many local service agencies have their own personnel systems that are not necessarily part of the local civil service. For discussion purposes, the comments here are intended to apply to the official personnel system of the local agency, whether it happens to be civil service or not.

5. This is a somewhat simplified description of the situation. The skills may initially be taught during these periodic training sessions but then may be incorporated by the professional school curriculum. As new practitioners are exposed to the new curriculum, the need for the original training sessions may be reduced, and these sessions may then cease. Cessation under these conditions would not be interpreted as a sign of a less routinized innovation.

6. These rules, embodied in statutes, regulations, and procedural manuals, were a major focus in Blau's classic study of bureaucratic change (1955). Blau found that new regulations frequently replaced old ones (p. 238), and he used these observations as evidence that the agency under study was continually changing rather than remaining stagnant.

7. A comparison among local services can lead to the interesting analogy between textbooks in education, which are the guidelines for the daily operations and standards, and the use of operating manuals in the other services. The textbooks, for instance, perform many of the same functions as "orders of the day" serve in police and fire departments. In this manner, textbooks do not merely convey the curriculum; they are also bureaucratic devices that define the relevant service practice.

8. The two passages or cycles were omitted because the budget cycles occur annually and hence were synonymous with the chronological age of the innovation, which is treated as a separate independent variable; and the training cycles vary considerably and are poorly documented in most agencies.

9. Note, however, that a single occurrence may be more than sufficient to result in adoption and implementation.

10. In one city in the case studies, the authors actually found an innovation-specific tax levy, with the local community voting every five years on whether to support the costs of the police computer system and its connection to the regional FBI computer network.

11. See Watson (1969) for a description of the development of adversary gropus and of the adversary process.

12. Studies of intergovernmental relations are just beginning to cope with the varied efforts—direct and indirect—of federal and state policies on local government behavior (e.g., see Pressman and Wildavsky, 1973). Until

further developed, however, it is impossible to specify the differential impacts of such initiatives as regulatory policies, transfer payment programs, direct aid, indirect aid programs, and technical assistance. Thus, only the most prevelant forms of innovation-related policies—i.e., direct funding and technical assistance—were examined in our own analysis.

4

Life Histories, Stage 1: The Improvisation Stage

The framework of passages and cycles guided the collection of evidence from nineteen case studies and ninety telephone interviews. In each of these efforts, the life history of an innovation at a specific site was recorded (Chapter 1 listed these sites). On the whole, the life histories sought to ascertain if and when the various passages and cycles had occurred. In addition, rudimentary questions were asked about the factors hypothesized to facilitate or hinder routinization.

The nineteen case studies provided the fuller set of data regarding the course of routinization over time. For this reason, this body of evidence was used in chapters 4, 5, and 6 to establish the basic outline of the routinization process. The use of the case studies, as pointed out in chapter 1, had followed an explicit chain of evidence. First, the data collected in the field had been dictated by an interviewer's guide that covered four general topics (background, description of the innovation, status of routinization, and reasons for routinization status) and that contained specific questions concerning passages and cycles. Second, each case study thus consisted of parallel types of information about each innovation at each site, and this allowed the uniform reporting of each case study, as illustrated by the narrative case studies in appendix C. Third, the narratives were then analyzed according to the key events that had occurred, and these events were listed in rough chronological order.[1]

From this chronological listing emerged the first finding from the case studies: each life history could be divided into three general stages—an *improvisation stage,* an *expansion stage,* and a *disappearance stage.* The distinctions among these three periods were not sharp ones. What was important was that the stages were conceptually useful and that there were clusters of activities associated with each stage, although the specific events that marked each period could vary from case to case. Thus, even though innovations may have matured at different rates and in a somewhat uneven manner, the three periods still gave some sense of stages of growth, with the stages following in a temporal sequence.

The improvisation stage was the initial period during which an innovation began to operate following adoption, and no passages or cycles had to occur during this period, although they often did in the various life histories. Instead, the main theme was merely to keep the innovation operating at some meaningful level and for some meaningful period of time. Usually, this meant that the innovation was used to perform at least one or two functions through a calendar year. The expansion stage was marked by both the continued growth of the innovation and the achievement of several passages or cycles. Finally, the disappearance stage involved the completion of the remaining passages and cycles, and the period was one in which the innovation continued to be used but eventually lost its recognition as an innovation. During this last period, in other words, an innovation achieved the status of standard agency practice.

The delineation of the three stages guided the grouping of chronological events in the life histories into three periods of time. The resulting table of events for each of the nineteen case studies are contained in tables 4-1 to 4-6. These tables were drawn directly from the case study narratives and represent the next step in the chain of evidence from the case studies; the tables thus serve as the basic source of evidence for the findings in this and the next two chapters. To understand the tables, the reader should note that the periods follow in chronological order, but each period may represent a different duration of calendar time. What distinguished the periods from each other was the occurrence of specific passages or cycles. Certain of these events tended to occur early in the life history, while other passages or cycles tended to occur late. This information became the basis for distinguishing among the three stages.

The remainder of this chapter and the following two chapters present the findings regarding these three stages in an innovation's life history. The chapters are based on specific citations from the case studies, as reflected by the key events listed in tables 4-1 to 4-6. Specific passages and cycles are discussed in chapters 5 and 6, and each discussion ends with a summary tabulation of the passages and cycles achieved by each case study. Because the events in the table constitute the raw data used in these tabulations, the key passages and cycles for each life history are indicated by a number in parentheses which refers to the passage or cycle number of the text. This notation will enable the reader to follow directly the chain of evidence from table of events to findings.

Chapter 7 then aggregates the passages and cycles achieved by each of the case studies and, depending upon the number achieved, categorizes the nineteen case studies according to their degree of routinization. A similar procedure was followed for establishing the routinization status for the innovations from the ninety telephone interviews. Most of chapter 7 is then dedicated to a summary discussion of the routinization process, taking into account an examination of the factors previously hypothesized to explain the routinization status of each innovation. The conclusions and their implications for future policy research are reported in chapter 8.

Overview of the Improvisation Stage

The main characteristic of the Improvisation Stage in an innovation's life was that major operations were undertaken for the first time. It was the first time that equipment was used and repaired, that practitioners and other employees

Table 4-1
Table of Events for Nineteen Case Studies. Police Computer Systems (N = 4)

Site	Improvisation Stage	Expansion Stage	Disappearance Stage	Current Status
Miami	New police chief hired $20 million bond issue approved; includes funds for second generation computer (6)[a] First generation computer (NCR Century 100) leased on local funds; batch processing only (2) External funds for special analyses Data processing established as separate organizational unit (3) UCR data submitted to state on tapes (1969-1973)	New chief hired (had helped plan data processing system) (8, 9) Second generation computers (PDPs) being installed (1) Data processing staff increases; new civil service classifications established (5) New computer capacity relieves competition among applications Expansion to dispatch and case entry applications will use mobile, on-line terminals New forms developed Continued support from assistant to city manager New chief reviews printouts himself (1974-	Data processing survives across-the-board budget cuts	Police department: about 1,200 persons City population: about 340,000 On-line terminals being installed No training yet for street officers
Indianapolis	First generation computer (IBM 1440) leased on local funds (2) Data processing established as separate organizational unit; county civil service positions used (3) Some technical assistance by a consultant group	Second generation computer (IBM 360) leased (1) Programmers recruited from sworn staff (5) First generation of terminals requires training procedures for clerks and officers Case entry application initiated	Data processing orientation offered in police academy (7) Second generation terminals leased New chief hired (had been head of data processing system); new department head (8, 9)	Police department: about 1,400 persons City population: about 740,000 About 70 on-line terminals, including some second generation terminals (10) External groups and agencies use terminals and data (10) No comprehensive manual

Table 4-1 – *Continued*

Site	Improvisation Stage	Expansion Stage	Disappearance Stage	Current Status
	Deliberate replacement of old forms as new applications are automated (1964-1968)	County-city government merger Third generation computer (IBM 370) leased; continued close service support from vendor (4) Data processing system and county data processing system share administrative applications and serve as backups to each other; data processing applications expanded (6) (1969-1974)	Data processing survives budget cut in department Dispatch application being added with new minicomputer (1975-	
Nashville	First generation computer leased on local funds and does batch processing only Deputy chief designs second generation system and applies for LEAA funds (1965-1970)	Second generation computer (Univac 418) consists of two cores, one for on-line and the other for batch; each is backup for other; leased on LEAA funds (1) Data processing established as separate division (3) New chief is hired and supports data processing system (former chief had opposed it) Vendor-provided service support is ended (4) On-the-job training for clerks and officers	Data processing supported on local funds; long-term lease is up for renewal (2) Civil service classifications for data processing staff being updated (5) New data processing head is hired (had been employed by vendor) (9) Data processing orientation offered in police academy (7) Training manual for using terminals is implemented (1976-	Police department: about 1,400 persons City population: about 450,000 About 95 on-line terminals (10) Computer system is used by other criminal justice agencies in metropolitan area (10) Competition from county computer

Table 4-1 — Continued

Site	Improvisation Stage	Expansion Stage	Disappearance Stage	Current Status
		Old forms are revised; data processing applications are expanded County computer performs administrative applications (1971-1975)		
Boston	First generation computer (IBM 360/30) leased on local funds (2) Data processing established as separate organizational unit (3) Civil service classifications all covered under state civil service system (5) New data processing head is hired Vendor provides maintenance service throughout (4) (1968-1972)	Second generation computer (IBM 360/135) leased on local funds; allows new applications and interface with state computer (1) Consultant firm helps on software On-the-job training for clerks Second new data processing head is hired (9) Old forms are revised Third generation computer (Systems III) replaces 360/135 and performs message switching to access city computer but implies no new applications Initiation of computer dispatch system (two mini-computers) purchased with LEAA funds; consultant firm helps on software and planning (1973-1976)	Data processing survives across-the-board budget cuts Computer dispatch system remains separate from city computer and is being implemented New chief is hired and reviews printouts himself (had helped implement IBM 360/135) (8) (1977-	Police department: about 3,000 persons City population: about 640,000 About 50 on-line terminals, but street officers have little direct contact yet All applications except dispatch are now processed by city computer Union continues to oppose data processing system No training yet for street officers

aNumbers refer to ten passages and cycles studied in actual life histories (see table 7-1).

Table 4-2
Table of Events for Nineteen Case Studies. Breath Testing for Driver Safety (N = 3)

Site	Improvisation Stage	Expansion Stage	Disappearance Stage	Current Status
Cincinnati	Traffic section participates in FARE program Cincinnati becomes site for $2.1 million ASAP grant; 3 Breathalyzers purchased and 12 traffic officers trained; videotapes also used; traffic commander coordinates equipment located in one subdistrict Some technical assistance from federal officials State board of health offers training and certification free of charge Revision in procedures manual and forms Use of videotapes discontinued State law does not mandate breath testing, but if such testing, Breathalyzers were only certified equipment at the time (1970-1974)	State board of health provides refresher training and recertification Officers in traffic section continue to provide all maintenance (4) Police department further decentralizes; breath-testing procedures incorporated into all subdistricts (3) (1975)	Police department initiates training in police academy, including senior operators and refresher course (5, 7) Five more Breathalyzers purchased with 50 percent state funds, one placed in each subdistrict; three old ones used for training or backup; all maintenance and supplies on local funds (1, 2) Breath-testing survives across-the-board budget cuts New police chief hired Traffic commander (coordinator) needs to spend less time on innovation (1976-	Police department: about 1,000 persons City population: about 450,000 About 140 officers (most outside of traffic) can operate and repair equipment (10) About 3,500 DWI arrests per year and rising; other payoffs identified in formal evaluation Maintenance and repair officers are still same incumbents No changes in civil service classifications or promotion incentives contemplated; but training and certification have internalized
Akron	Traffic commander and judge seek improvement over urinalysis	Coordinator initiates own training program for regular operators; state continues to provide	Breath-testing survives budget cuts; however, fewer DWI arrests because of fewer patrols	Police department: about 500 persons City population: about 270,000

Table 4-2 — *Continued*

Site	Improvisation Stage	Expansion Stage	Disappearance Stage	Current Status
	Chief decides to purchase two Breathalyzers; one is backup; nine officers trained; videotapes also used; lieutenant serves as coordinator (2)[a] State board of health offers training and certification free of charge State law does not mandate breath testing, but chief mandates that only Breathalyzer be used Videotape procedures entered into department's standard operating procedures (1968–1972)	training for senior operators and refresher course (and charges police department) Procedures for breath testing entered into department's standard operating procedures (3) Maintenance provided by traffic bureau (4) Breath-testing orientation in police academy Third Breathalyzer purchased with 50 percent state funds; is used as another backup (1) (1973–1976)	New coordinator (who does not train) is hired (9) (1977–	About 45 officers (most in traffic) can operate and repair (10) About 450 DWI arrests per year; decline from 800 in 1971 Location of training program uncertain Other jurisdictions receive training and make some use of Breathalyzer No civil service changes or promotion incentives contemplated
Memphis	Photo-electric breath-tester used (1953–1973); slow procedure, and instrument does not give BAC reading; only one stationary instrument Traffic committee reviews possible mobile units Innovation begins as joint police department–sheriff venture, with personnel costs shared and DWI unit placed in own metropolitan	New police department chief is hired; more supportive than predecessor Two additional vans and gas chromographs purchased (1) New officers continue to be assigned to DWI from regular police department ranks Technical assistance from vendor only occasionally needed DWI unit issues formal	Planning to trade in all five vans and replace all gas chromographs for new models Police department faces budget cuts, has difficulty paying for officer overtime in DWI unit (1977–	Police department: about 1,500 persons City population: about 630,000 Twenty-one officers, five vans, and three squad cars are all part of separate police department–sheriff unit About 8,000 DWI arrests and rising (10) Revenues from DWI fines (about $100 per case) go to city or county, but not used to explicitly offset budget expenditures for DWI unit

Table 4-2 – *Continued*

Site	Improvisation Stage	Expansion Stage	Disappearance Stage	Current Status
	organization; twelve men transferred and three gas chromographs purchased; delay in delivery of two mobile vans allows piecemeal orientation to new system; full procedure is to have vans arrive at a DWI stoppage on street by regular patrol officer and to conduct breath test on the spot; state funds used for equipment (2) Training and certification required by court; program run by university, augmented by statefunded course run by DWI unit Full-time DWI coordinator appointed (1972-1973)	procedures but not as part of department's standard operating procedures One additional van purchased and first two traded in; equipment purchases continue to use state funds or sheriff's office budget DWI unit gradually assumes all maintenance and repair responsibilities; many technical problems slowly overcome (4) (1974-1976)		Sheriff's office takes care of most administrative procedures No civil service changes or promotion incentives

[a]Numbers refer to ten passages and cycles studied in actual life histories (see table 7-1).

Table 4-3
Table of Events for Nineteen Case Studies. Mobile Intensive Care Units (N = 3)

Site	Improvisation Stage	Expansion Stage	Disappearance State	Current Status
Dallas	City had contracted with funeral homes for private ambulance service Ambulance committee (medical and municipal representatives) formed (1969) Proposal for countywide system defeated (1971) Mayor and council implement MICU in fire department with ordinance and revenue-sharing funds; 16 vehicles provide EMT transport only; 150 men trained by medical school; coordinated by officer who became chief of ambulance division (2, 6)[a] Ambulance division formed in fire department (3) MICU expansion with 120 paramedics trained from EMT; revenue-sharing funds for equipment Officers certified by state, receive extra pay for being MICU-trained City and vendor offer initial technical assistance (1972-1974)	Seven new units eventually added; one unit supported by private donation More fire officers given MICU training Fire department increases maintenance staff to repair MICU vehicles and equipment; worn-out parts replaced and updated New forms developed and updated Fire department no longer depends on external technical assistance (4) New chief hired and is more supportive (had been head of planning and research) (1975-1976)	MICU helps fire department avert across-the-board budget cuts Training program continues free of charge to fire department, expands to other municipalities by charging fee Revision in promotional structure for officers considered (1977-	Fire department: about 1,400 persons City population: about 850,000 About 17 active and 6 reserve MICU units cover entire city Forty-dollar charge for each MICU transport Other communities use system Original chief of ambulance division is still same incumbent; not all procedures formally documented

Table 4-3 – *Continued*

Site	Improvisation Stage	Expansion Stage	Disappearance Stage	Current Status
Birmingham	Advisory MICU committee formed (1968) by city ordinance Large federal MICU grant not funded (1969) MICU initiated with DHEW funds; one vehicle; local funds support after first year, as well as purchase of two more vehicles (1, 2, 3) Head of MICU committee (outside fire department) initiates training and coordinates with state Fire department chief and deputy chief are strong supporters, select exemplary trainees (1973-1974)	Training continues at university (76 certified paramedics, more being trained, although all units fully staffed) Three more vehicles purchased Civil service classifications established for paramedics (5) Fire department changes name to include "Rescue Service" (6) Paramedic assignment part of fire department promotion ladder; involves small additional pay (8) State MICU regulations incorporate fire department's experience (1975)	Second generation of Life-paks being installed Civil service classification being sought for MICU coordinator Full-time MICU coordinator established and new incumbent appointed; creates standard procedures bulletins (4, 9) Fire officers begin large-scale citizen training program in cardio-pulmonary resuscitation MICU helps fire department avert across-the-board budget cuts (1976)	Fire department: about 600 persons City population: about 300,000 About six active and one reserve MICU units cover entire city No public transport service; private transport service MICU responds to about half of all fire department calls Head of MICU committee is still same incumbent
Denver	General Hospital begins own MICU system (1973) Fire department is asked by General Hospital to initiate MICU to one outlying community; all training (14 officers) and equipment covered by federal funds and administered by General Hospital; paramedics	Fire department continues to consider MICU training for own personnel (1977-		Fire department: about 950 persons City population: about 520,000 No MICU units currently in operation under fire department General Hospital operates MICU with about 11 units

Table 4-3 — *Continued*

Site	Improvisation Stage	Expansion Stage	Disappearance Stage	Current Status
	receive extra pay covered by fire department funds Only low number of calls for this unit General Hospital withdraws training, certification, and support after one year; fire department service ends General Hospital, and not state, plays certification role (1975-1976)			

[a]Numbers refer to ten passages and cycles studied in actual life histories (see table 7-1).

Table 4-4
Table of Events for Nineteen Case Studies. Jet-Axe (N = 2)

Site	Improvisation Stage	Expansion Stage	Disappearance Stage	Current Status
Rochester	Commissioner (of fire bureau) has academy test Jet-Axe and decides to purchase ten Jet-Axes with local funds; six more Jet-Axes purchased shortly thereafter; fire officers trained in fire stations (1, 2)[a] New procedures incorporated into training manual (3) Trucks carry Jet-Axes but then transferred to chiefs' cars (1972-1973)	Fire bureau becomes department; new chief, who had direct experience with Jet-Axe, replaces commissioner Jet-Axes transferred from chiefs' cars to special equipment truck that responds to all fires (10) Six more Jet-Axes purchased (4) Training begins in academy (1976; had been no new trainees for 2 1/2 years); new head of academy appointed (1974-1976)	Training continues in fire stations and academy (7) (1977-	Fire department: about 675 persons City population: about 300,000 Sixteen Jet-Axes used in total (six for training, ten for fires) No maintenance, reorganization, or new forms needed Use of Jet-Axes declining
Omaha	Chief decides to purchase four Jet-Axes with local funds; fire officers trained in fire stations twice a year; film used to facilitate training (1) Training begins in academy Chiefs' cars carry Jet-Axes; assistant chief administers on daily basis Two more Jet-Axes purchased, limited to largest model (2) (1972-1974)	Use of Jet-Axes incorporated into fire department's standard operating procedures (3) Two more Jet-Axes purchased (1975) (4) Four more Jet-Axes purchased (1976) (1975-1976)	Training continues in fire stations and academy (7) (1977-	Fire department: about 525 persons City population: about 400,000 Six Jet-Axes used in total (two for training, four for fires) No maintenance, reorganization, or new forms needed No turnover of chief or assistant chief

Table 4-5
Table of Events for Nineteen Case Studies. Computer-Assisted Instruction (*N* = 4)

Site	Improvisation Stage	Expansion Stage	Disappearance Stage	Current Status
Dallas	NSF grant for CAI; ten terminals and computer time purchased from private company; data processing director coordinates (3)[a] First court-ordered school desegregation helps CAI First generation CAI computer (Burroughs 5500) acquired on lease-purchase with local funds (was second generation for administrative application); 18 CAI terminals purchased with external funds in relation to desegregation (2, 4) First CAI coordinator appointed First round of in-service training for CAI (1968–1973)	New comptroller hired (had been data processing director) (8) Second generation CAI computer (Burroughs 6700) acquired on lease-purchase with local funds; more terminals (1) Two other CAI computers (Hewlett-Packard and PDP) purchased with external funds; additional applications and terminals New CAI coordinator hired (9) First mathematics CAI supervisor appointed (5) State certifies advanced computer mathematics courses (6) Second court-ordered school desegregation: impact on CAI operation? (1974–1976)	CAI comptroller's position shifted to curriculum department (1977–	District: about 140,000 students City population: about 844,000 About 110 on-line CAI terminals; time oversubscribed (10) Drill-and-practice, problem-solving applications Considering CAI-oriented mathematics textbooks Competition with administrative application for computer time Adoption and use still at teacher's discretion In-service training not yet formalized
Oakland	Six high schools purchase programmable calculators on local funds State grant to 3 elementary schools for 15 terminals plagued by breakdowns and only operates for 6 months	Two new data-processing directors hired in quick succession In-service training offered sporadically by data processing directors Several individual CAI projects with external funds begin		District: about 65,000 students City population: about 360,000 About 13 terminals (same since 1971); time undersubscribed Main CAI application is computer programming No strong top administrative or practitioner support for CAI

Table 4-5 — *Continued*

Site	Improvisation Stage	Expansion Stage	Disappearance Stage	Current Status
	First generation CAI computer (Honeywell 6025) purchased with local funds (was third generation for administrative application); 13 terminals used to re-place programmable calculators (2, 4) Trial with computer pay-roll application is unsuccessful (1962-1972)	and end at individual teacher's initiative (1973-		
Tampa (Hillsborough County)	Mathematics teacher uses programmable calculator, becomes mathematics supervisor and encourages CAI First generation CAI computer (IBM 370/135) purchased on local funds (was fourth generation for administrative application); 9 terminals leased on curriculum funds; core is compatible with county computer (2, 3, 4) Mathematics supervisor co-ordinates CAI applications and offers one round of in-service training (5) Grants from LEAA and Title III support specific CAI	One school purchases minicomputers to add single terminal; funds from school building budget (6) No turnover in either data processing director or mathematics supervisor since outset New computer being con-sidered (1976-		District: about 120,000 students City population: about 280,000 About ten terminals (same since 1972); residual demand for computer time unclear Computer programming and computer mathematics only CAI applications Coordinator in curriculum department from beginning

Table 4-5 — *Continued*

Site	Improvisation Stage	Expansion Stage	Disappearance Stage	Current Status
San Diego	Pilot summer projects for CAI sponsored by data-processing department; other test projects on private funds New superintendent hired and district is decentralized Mathematics teachers convince data processing department to extend funds and principals to pool funds First generation CAI computer (HP 2000) acquired on 4-year lease-purchase from school funds; data processing department provides services; initial in-service training; each of 11 participating schools has time-share coordinator (2, 3, 4) (1969-1973)	Central computer (IBM 370) administrative application into its third or fourth generation but is separate from CAI Second and third CAI computers (HP 2000s) acquired on same arrangement as last; 60 terminals in all; external agencies buy time and use own terminals (1) Data processing department assigns full-time CAI coordinator Special CAI account was established within data processing department, facilitates use of some federal funds In-service training formalized with credits, extra pay, and maintenance/repair component (7) Bond issue approved; provides additional capital funds for CAI by including terminals as standard building equipment (6) Second generation of terminals purchased and applications expanded (1974-1975)	A few schools drop out, but hardware transferred to other schools CAI resource teacher hired with CETA funds; will eventually be funded from local sources CAI costs to decline because of completion of lease-purchase agreements Civil service classification for CAI coordinator updated (5) Curriculum department begins adoption of CAI-oriented textbooks Data-processing department enters formal service contracts with schools Teachers with CAI training given edge in transfers to new schools (8) (1976-	District: about 120,00 students City population: about 700,000 About 60 terminals (10) External agencies use CAI computer Drill-and-practice applications

[a]Numbers refer to ten passages and cycles studied in actual life histories (see table 7-1).

Table 4-6
Table of Events for Nineteen Case Studies. Closed-Circuit Television ($N = 3$)

Site	Improvisation Stage	Expansion Stage	Disappearance Stage	Current Status
Omaha	ESEA Title III grant for media center; university professor is innovator; CCTV programs with microwave transmission and dial-access system for three high schools; technical difficulties in installing system; position descriptions established for staff; not much in-service training for CCTV; CCTV is special project in television department (5) Local vocational education funds used to develop televison studio; CCTV staff turns over completely System modified to use ITFS, but delay in obtaining FCC approval to use ITFS channels for digital signals (needed to call specific programs to be shown) (1967-1972)	Maintenance difficulties (vendor located in distant city) Grant ends; local funds used until budget cuts eliminate system (1975); instead, district upgrades studio (2) Types of programs had increased e.g., library of 400-500 television programs had accumulated Few teachers exposed to system; little student incentive to use it (1973-		Distict: about 53,000 students City population: about 355,000 CCTV system served media centers in three high schools (including one parochial), but is no longer being used ITV in individual classrooms now Not core application (used for individual supplementary instruction in carrels of media center)

Table 4-6 — *Continued*

Site	Improvisational Stage	Expansion Stage	Disappearance Stage	Current Status
Portland	State-federal grant to improve education to disadvantaged students used in part for CCTV to nine elementary schools; television programs integrated with regular curriculum; CCTV coordinator appointed; in-service training for teachers (4) District decentralizes, original project discontinued; new coordinator appointed and operation assigned to central media department (3,5) (1967-1973)	Third coordinator appointed, develops ITV; classrooms use VTRs independently; vocational television production program initiated in magnet school; both state and local funds used; in-service training offered (2) ITV system becoming routinized with budget support, equipment updating, service expansion and civil service classifications; television production program now mandated by board of education (1974-		District: about 62,000 students City population: about 380,000 ITV, but no current CCTV system At peak, CCTV covered all classrooms in nine elementary schools; covered regular curriculum
Rochester	State grant for CCTV matched by local bond issue; about 1,300 television sets; operation administered by separate television department with part-time coordinator; takes several years to get all schools wired; contractor provides some initial technical assistance	Civil service classifications established for television personnel (5) Fifty-two schools receiving programs; not part of basic curriculum Superintendent and coordinator leave district New coordinator hired Transition to all local funds (2) Much equipment becoming outdated		District: about 41,000 students City population: about 300,000 A few schools use remnants of CCTV system that once served 52 schools Not core application (typing is main subject); always considered a special program Negligible teacher training; CCTV staff mainly recruited from outside district; no provision for equipment depreciation

Table 4-6 — *Continued*

Site	Improvisational Stage	Expansion Stage	Disappearance Stage	Current Status
	Full-time coordinator hired (1963-1966)	Continued union opposition and budget cutbacks force new superintendent to discontinue operation Television department and staff disbanded Individual schools continue to use CCTV on an intermittent basis (1967-		CCTV not integrated with curriculum department

^aNumbers refer to passages and cycles studied in actual life histories (see table 7-1)

received training in using the innovation, and that new organizational procedures for the innovation were developed. Because every local agency had its own unique tradition, staff, and situation within the municipal government, it was difficult to plan these activities precisely. Different factors were of slightly different importance from agency to agency. Supporters of the innovation therefore needed to remain flexible, resourceful, and patient as they established the initial routines. Above all, they had to be prepared to improvise. For instance, they had to know how to balance their reliance on outside consultants and vendors for technical assistance with their own ability to make on-the-spot repairs. Because there were few precedents, the initial period in the life of an innovation could thus be characterized as an improvisation stage.

Four features in particular marked this initial period: practitioner exposure, resource management, the nature of the key innovators, and the strategic choices made by the innovators. However, the improvisation stage did not have to involve any specific passages or cycles, even though some passages or cycles may have actually occurred in some case studies. The main goal of the improvisation stage, in other words, was the organizing of certain activities without regard to the formal organizational changes implied by specific passages and cycles. The activities were often organized in an ad hoc and transient manner. The following discussion therefore covers these improvisation activities.

Practitioner Exposure

Most innovations required knowledgeable initiatives on the part of service practitioners. In schools, the use of CAI and CCTV depended directly on the initiatives taken by teachers in individual classrooms, and not just on the actions carried out by administrators and coordinators. Adoption and implementation therefore took place at two levels, an administrative level that coordinated the entire system, and the classroom level, where some teachers might have simply chosen to avoid the innovation even though it had been adopted at the administrative level. With the Jet-Axe, breath testing, and MICU, practitioners had to learn how to use new techniques that in some cases totally displaced traditional procedures. Only in the case of police computers was it possible to initiate the innovation on the basis of functions that did not directly involve the street-level police officer, such as the statistical aggregation of the Uniform Crime Reports to be sent to state or federal agencies.

Because of the key role played by practitioners, the improvisation period had to include some opportunity for improvisation by practitioners. This frequently took the form of pilot projects and training that preceded the actual adoption of the innovation. In all the CAI cases, for instance, small groups of teachers had opportunities to experiment with CAI techniques. In Dallas, the opportunity was provided by a grant from the National Science Foundation that supported several CAI terminals and computer time leased from a computer firm. In San Diego, a similar opportunity was provided by summer projects funded by private sources. In Tampa and Oakland, practitioners themselves initiated requests to school administrators to purchase programmable calculators so that these could be tested in the classroom. These opportunities generally resulted in a small group of practitioners (usually mathematics teachers) gaining knowledge of CAI capabilities. The specific CAI applications, of course, were highly diverse and unstructured, but the experience was then used as feedback to central administrators who were contemplating the adoption of the larger and formal CAI system. In most cases, the teachers were able to provide specific information on the desirable characteristics of the core computer that would best accommodate CAI applications. In one case, San Diego, these early teacher experiences actually led to the main initiatives and support for purchasing a CAI system entirely separate from the computer system that served administrative functions.

With other innovations, early practitioner exposure played an equally important role. In the Birmingham experience, the MICU system was being installed for the first time and had been adopted on the basis of strong top administrative support. However, the initial coordinator carefully (and personally) selected the first class of fire officers who would receive paramedic training and operate the MICU units. The candidates were naturally selected from among the most talented officers; but, in addition, the new program deliberately involved officers who had several years' experience in the department rather than new recruits or those about to retire, so that the paramedic functions would be established at the outset as an important set of activities from the viewpoint of other officers in the department.

These initial practitioner opportunities were merely the beginning of the necessary longer-term support for the innovation by practitioner groups. Even though there was often a "creaming" effect—that is, the initial participants were the most highly motivated and skilled practitioners—the hope was that practitioner use would spread and implicit support for the innovation would gradually increase.

There were two innovations where, in part because of the nature of the innovation, such a process of practitioner exposure was not entirely possible. In one case, CCTV, the technical requirements for practitioner involvement were assumed to be minimal because television was thought to be an easy technology for most people to use. It was later found that teachers could even have difficulty in turning on and tuning their receivers. However, except for Portland, practitioners were not heavily involved in the central planning or implementation of the CCTV operation in the case studies. There was little in-service training for teachers, and the central operation was administered by technicians who were part of a media or television department and who had little contact with the formal school curriculum. As a result, the CCTV system tended to be seen as an outsiders' innovation, one that could even threaten the teachers' role in the classroom. At one site, (Rochester), such lack of integration of practitioners into the CCTV operation provided the basis for teacher opposition to the innovation, and the teachers' union argued against the innovation in budget negotiations over a period of years. This opposition eventually led to the demise of the CCTV operation, even though the system at one point had involved television programs being cabled over three channels and into over 1,000 television sets.

The other innovation where it was difficult to develop practitioner exposure was the Jet-Axe. This was because the explosive device is consumed during detonation and costs about $125 per unit. For demonstration or training purposes, fire departments were unwilling to detonate more than a few Jet-Axes. In actual firefighting, the need for the Jet-Axe only arises sporadically, because it is used only in fires where an especially impenetrable door or wall has to be opened. Therefore, even though formal training was widespread—in both Omaha and Rochester the experienced firefighters received instruction as part of their routine training in the firehouse and new recruits received training in the academy—the actual experience with the explosive device was limited to a few firefighters. Unless it is possible to provide practitioners with direct exposure to an innovation—an experience for which classroom instruction or the viewing of a film cannot serve as substitutes—it is difficult to allow practitioners the opportunity to test and improvise, much less to generate support for, such an innovation.

Resource Management

To support an innovation, funds were required to purchase or lease the appropriate equipment, to cover staff time to operate the innovation, and to cover training costs, including the costs of the training staff as well as the time allotted to the trainees. Flexibility and improvisation in the use of available funds were again dominant features of the early period of the innovation in our case studies. In fact, the most important feature was that there were few hard rules regarding the most effective procedures for resource management.

External versus Internal Funds

A pressing policy issue for federal officials has been whether the availability of external funds—provided by federal or state agencies—can facilitate the innovative process. Because this appears as such a crucial issue, table 4-7 enumerates the specific case study sites and the use, if any, of external funds to support the improvisation stage. This tabulation is independent of the question of whether

Table 4-7
Sources of Funds for Nineteen Case Studies

Type of Innovation/Site	Main Source of Initial Funds	Additional External Funds[a] before Adoption?	Additional External Funds[a] after Adoption?
Police computer			
Miami	Local	No	Yes
Indianapolis	Local	No	No
Nashville	Federal	No	No
Boston	Local	No	Yes
Breath testing			
Cincinnati	Federal	Yes	Yes
Akron	Local	No	Yes
Memphis	State	No	No
Mobile intensive care units			
Dallas	Federal	No	Yes
Birmingham	Federal	No	No
Denver	Federal	No	No
Jet-Axe			
Rochester	Local	No	No
Omaha	Local	No	No
Computer-assisted instruction			
Dallas	Local/Federal	Yes	Yes
Oakland	Local	No	Yes
Tampa	Local	No	No
San Diego	Local	Yes	Yes
Closed-circuit television			
Omaha	Federal	Yes	Yes
Portland	State/Federal	No	No
Rochester	State	No	Yes

[a]For example, specific projects or equipment purchases that were funded from state, federal, or private sources. These external funds did not provide the dominant support for the innovation, however.

the passage to local funding was later achieved or not. The table indicates the wide variety of patterns for using external funds. In two cases, Cincinnati and Rochester, the innovations were funded with amounts of external funds as part of high-visibility demonstration projects on breath testing (the Alcohol Safety Action Program of the U.S. Department of Transportation) and on CCTV (a state program to encourage educational applications of telecommunications). In both cases, the site was visited by many officials from other jurisdictions during the first few years of the innovation's lifetime. In other cases, federal or state funds were available as general revenue-sharing funds, as in the Dallas

MICU, or as categorical project funds, as in the Birmingham MICU and Memphis breath-testing. In about half of the cases, however, local funds were the entire source of support, whether from a bond issue, as in the Miami police computer, or from an agency's operating budget. Moreover, this mixed pattern was also true of small pilot projects or specific federal projects that may have preceded or followed the adoption of the larger innovation. Typically, these smaller projects were for specific applications of the larger innovation. For instance, in Tampa, specific CAI projects were initiated and completed with funds from the U.S. Law Enforcement Assistance Administration and the U.S. Office of Education, Title III, but these projects were only two applications in the larger CAI system.

Overall, chapter 7 will show that the availability of external funds was not related to the ultimate outcomes of these case studies—that is, to the number of passages and cycles achieved. There were cases where federal funds were associated with innovations that eventually changed radically (as in the Portland CCTV), as well as those that grew steadily to a routinized operation (for example, the Dallas MICU). There were also cases where there were similar outcomes, even though one had federal funding and the other did not, a contrast that appeared most strongly for two of the breath-testing cases, Cincinnati and Akron.

The reason that the use of external funds did not appear to make a difference in predicting any simple pattern of outcomes was that, where there was a local desire to innovate, the innovators acted in a resourceful manner and sought funds from the most readily available sources, whether external or internal. In most case studies, the funds used to support the initial operation came from more than one source—more than one local budget category or even more than one local agency. This approach was most easily illustrated by the diverse sources of financial support for the initial training of practitioners. With the two health-related innovations, MICU and breath testing, the state public health agency or a local hospital often performed the training function, with no charge to the relevant fire or police department. In other cases, departmental resources were used to implement on-the-job training or in-service training. In yet other cases, external funds were used either to reimburse the training staff or to cover the work time of the trainees. In all cases, the important objective was simply to establish an initial round of practitioner training, so that some small group of practitioners would be readily available to operate or to use the innovation.

External funds were often used to purchase equipment, which would reduce the initial outlay for the innovation by the local agency. However, even here there was no simple pattern. For computer systems, for instance, if funds for outright purchase were not available, a local agency did not have to rely on external funds but could consider an annual leasing arrangement, a long-term (for example, seven-year) lease, or a lease-purchase agreement. All of these alternatives were used in the various case studies. Furthermore, a computer terminal could be considered part of the standard equipment of a school building, and capital funds could be used when a building was being upgraded or a new wing constructed. In fact, the innovator who considered the only option to be a binary choice between external or internal funds severely limited his or her ability to improvise. The skilled innovator could always identify a variety of sources from which funds could be made available.

Management and Technical Resources

More important than the distinctions concerning the source of funding was the ability of an innovation to obtain another type of resource: managerial support at the administrative level where resources were allocated, and technical support at the level where the use of specific resources could be monitored. The administrative level involved a top policymaker—city council member, the municipal executive, or an agency head—who could allocate funds for a specific project or purchase. The successful innovation had the support of at least one such policymaker who was willing to take the risks and to approve budget expenditures at the outset, when there was little evidence concerning the potential success or failure of the innovation. This was true, for example, whether the outlays were for new Jet-Axes and were part of the routine purchasing procedures of an agency, or whether the outlays were for a minicomputer that had to go through the capital budget process.

Two other comments should be made about this top policymaker. First, "top" is a relative term. In a decentralized school district such as San Diego, the top policymakers were the principals of each school, as these were the administrators who had to make the key decisions for resource allocation. The innovators and interested practitioners in San Diego correctly concentrated on convincing the principals of various schools to pool their resources to acquire the first CAI computer. In centralized school districts, the appropriate policymaker was at the district, and not the school, level. For computer systems in school districts and police departments, for instance, the head of data processing or of administrative services fulfilled such a role. For other municipal agencies, the top policymaker was the agency head but could also be a person outside the agency. In Dallas, for example, the MICU program was initiated as a result of public and political concern over poor emergency services. The innovation began when the mayor and city council approved a new budget item on behalf of the fire department; the chief of the department, though supportive, did not necessarily play an active role in this major resource allocation decision.

Second, the support of the top policymaker, while necessary, was by no means a sufficient condition for ultimate success. In Rochester, the CCTV system was initiated both because of the availability of state funds as well as the enthusiastic support of the superintendent. In fact, the superintendent not only allocated the necessary resources but also actively used the CCTV system as part of his administrative functions. Nevertheless, the CCTV operation ceased a couple of years after the superintendent vacated his position. Although the presence of a top policymaker's support could not guarantee the success of an innovation, the absence of such support did debilitate it. This was especially true in Oakland, where the CAI system evolved without such support and without much central coordination; as a result, and for other reasons to be cited later, CAI was not widely used. In other cases (the Nashville police computer for example) lack of support by the agency head was offset by strong support by a deputy head. The main point was that there needed to be active support by some top administrator, whether an agency head, a deputy, or someone outside of the agency. When support was totally lacking among all these individuals, an innovation was in trouble.

Technical support at the operating level was a necessary complement to the role of the top policymaker. The operating level was where day-to-day decisions regarding the innovation were made, and the required support was much more of an ad hoc nature. The person who worked at this level, usually the coordinator of the innovation, needed to have a cooperative relationship with the top policymaker.

The technical support functions at this level covered a variety of tasks. First, the coordinator had to have immediate access to resources for repairing and maintaining the innovation. Often, this meant that the coordinator had to be able to make instant repairs for equipment malfunctions. CAI, police computer, CCTV, and breath-testing equipment specifically called for continual monitoring and maintenance. Where internal capabilities were lacking, an on-site vendor providing service as part of the original purchasing agreement served as a substitute. The vendor needed to be as accessible as possible, however, to avoid long periods of downtime. In several case studies, service representatives of the vendor either routinely contacted the agency on a daily basis or even had a desk in an agency office from which to work. In the cases of the Nashville and Indianapolis police computers, the vendors even assigned full-time personnel to work with the agency. Whether external assistance was used in this manner or not, the supervisor had to be sufficiently skilled and to have a flexible time schedule to attend to any malfunctions immediately.

Second, the supervisor had to estimate the need for supplies and replacement parts, taking special care not to over- or under-order. Here, the relationship with the top policymaker was important, for, if the supplies required substantial outlays, administrative approvals had to be obtained without delay. For the Jet-Axe, for instance, it seemed to be no coincidence that in both case studies the head of the agency was both the technical coordinator and the top policymaker. The cost of the Jet-Axe precluded maintenance of a large-scale inventory, and agencies generally kept only three or four extra explosives in stock; when the Jet-Axes were used for training or firefighting, replacements had to be obtained quickly, and the head of the agency was in the best position both to monitor the use of the Jet-Axes and to initiate the new purchase requests.

Third, backup equipment was set aside wherever possible, even if this meant that the innovation did not provide full coverage at the outset. In Akron, although two Breathalyzers were initially acquired, one was immediately defined as a backup for the other; for MICU and CCTV, reserve equipment was essential. For computer systems, however, the core unit could not easily be replaced for repair, and the entire system was sometimes inoperable for the duration of a repair.

Fourth, the supervisor often had to design and initiate the first round of practitioner training sessions and thus had to be able to identify resources to support such sessions. The assistance from other agencies in providing MICU and breath-testing training has already been noted. In relation to other innovations, however, the burden of developing the curriculum, scheduling the training sessions, and locating funds to pay for trainee work time all fell on the shoulders of the supervisor. In several CAI innovations (for example, Tampa, Dallas, and Oakland), the first round of practitioner training was organized on an informal basis and was not integrated into the formal in-service training curriculum. Such integration, if it was to occur at all, occurred during the later periods of the innovation's lifetime. During the improvisation stage, the main task was merely to organize and conduct an initial round of training.

In general, competent resource management involved a cooperative relationship between a top policymaker who controlled agency resources and a technical supervisor who dealt with the innovation on a daily basis. In some cases, these two roles may have been performed by the same person, whereas in other cases the roles may have been divided between the head of an agency, or even someone external to it, and a line officer in charge of the innovation. Both roles were important. One was needed for access to significant agency resources that required extended budget justifications and a certain amount of risk-taking in allocating resources before an innovation had a chance to prove itself; the other was needed so that these resources, as well as others that could be obtained from existing equipment pools and excess inventory items, could effectively serve the daily needs of the innovation. Once again, the key ability in performing these tasks was improvisation—to find the resources to maintain the innovation. During this early period, the innovation was kept operating at some visible level as much as possible, even though the outcomes were not yet assessable.

Nature of the Innovating Team

Previous research has repeatedly emphasized the importance of an active, dynamic, and charismatic person to serve as an innovator. However, the case studies showed that such a single person was not a necessary figure for most innovations. When respondents were asked to identify the person or persons who actively initiated support or put together the main elements for operating the innovation, the response was frequently more than one individual. As suggested by the discussion on resource management, although there were a number of specific functions that had to be served by a person involved with the innovation, these functions did not have to be served by the same person. These functions included:

1. Understanding the needs of an innovation and taking the initiative to identify and allocate specific resources for the innovation. This initiative may be taken by someone inside *or* outside of the agency.
2. Coordinating the use of the innovation with existing procedures and practices such as designing practitioner training, developing relevant applications for the innovation, or integrating new vehicles or equipment with existing facilities.
3. Technically mastering the innovation, whether for instructing others or for maintaining the operation of the innovation.

To this extent, the case studies revealed a much richer and detailed description of the innovative role than the stereotypic "charismatic and hardworking" person.

Table 4-8 identifies the person or persons associated with these innovative functions. The table shows that only in a few cases was the innovator a single individual. In most cases, there was an innovation team, although this does not imply that the team members made explicit alliances. For instance, for MICU, where medical expertise had to be combined with the functions of the fire department, it was essential in all cases to have some medical advisory committee or local hospital official working as part of the innovation team. This group or individual guided the technical implementation of the MICU units, arranged for paramedic training for fire officers, and developed the communication system between the fire department and the emergency medical facility. The presence of such a group or person is indicated by the check marks in the first column of the table. (In Denver, the external official actually dominated to the extent that fire officials played a passive role in the innovation.)

In most cases, an innovation team was composed of a top policymaker and a technical operator, whose roles have been described in the previous section. For police computers, an official external to the agency (for example, the mayor and a council member in Nashville) sometimes played the former role, while a deputy chief or division head played the latter. For CAI, the top policymaker was usually the director of the data processing section who made the major acquisitions and established the initial applications, whereas the technical operator was another official within either the curriculum department or the data processing section. This combination is indicated by the double check marks for Dallas and Tampa in the last column of table 4-8. In a small number

Table 4-8
Innovators Identified for Nineteen Case Studies

Type of Innovation/Site	Person(s) outside Agency	Head of Agency	Deputy Head or Other Major Bureau or Division Head	Official(s) within Agency
Persons Identified with Innovator-Functions[a]				
Police Computer				
Miami	x	x	x	
Indianapolis		x	x	
Nashville	xx			
Boston		x	x	
Breath-testing				
Cincinnati			x	x
Akron		x	x	x
Memphis	x			x
Mobile intensive care units				
Dallas	xx			x
Birmingham	x		x	
Denver	x			
Jet-Axe				
Rochester		x		
Omaha		x		
Computer-assisted instruction				
Dallas				xx
Oakland				x[b]
Tampa				xx
San Diego		x[c]		x
Closed-circuit television				
Omaha	x			x
Portland				x
Rochester		x[b]		

[a]Each x = an individual.

[b]Difficult to identify any innovator.

[c]Heads (principals) of decentralized units with full control over resource allocation.

of cases (Denver, MICU; Omaha and Rochester, Jet-Axe; Oakland, CAI; and Portland and Rochester, CCTV), the innovator was either a single individual or nonexistent.

The innovating role was a critical one, whether served by an individual or by a group. This was because the innovation was bound to encounter serious problems that could not be anticipated, and knowledgeable and resourceful individuals often had to be available to make fast, on-the-spot decisions. Until such problems had been encountered several times apiece, they could not be treated routinely; thus, it was best if there was little turnover among the incumbents who filled the innovator roles. Modified service applications, new equipment, and procedural changes could be implemented and monitored only if there was some continuity among the members of the innovation team. This need for continuity led to an important observation: When the improvisation stage for an innovation extended beyond the average period of an incumbent's tenure, leadership turnover was likely to occur, thereby creating difficulties for the innovation. An example was the highly qualified agency official, who might have remained in a specific position for only three years before being promoted; similarly, the terms of most elected officials usually did not exceed four years. From this perspective, the most easily incorporated new technology should probably require an improvisation stage of not more than two or three years.

Strategic Choices

The activities during the improvisation stage were guided by three strategies that appeared to be associated with case studies whose innovations later achieved more passages and cycles. These strategies were to maintain a narrow initial scope for an innovation; to deliberately and carefully eliminate the traditional practice, if any, displaced by the innovation; and to reduce the job threat to practitioners in using the innovation.

Scope of an Innovation

The previous sections have identified the need to avoid as much downtime as possible and to minimize the improvisation stage to two or three years. Both of these objectives were more easily served if the innovation had a narrow scope during this period. Narrow scope implied that the innovation was not used for all the possible applications or implemented for all the relevant districts in an agency.

In two cases, for instance (Birmingham and Denver), the operation of MICU began with a single vehicle. In the third case, the innovation began with several vehicles, but followed a deliberate, two-phase plan in which basic transport service (which was not previously provided by the agency) was first implemented, and paramedic services were then added about a year later. Similarly, even in the most successful cases, the breath-testing innovations were initiated on a subdistrict basis; only later was the innovation applied throughout the department.

For computer systems, narrow scope implied a limited number of applications as well as the selection of those applications that were easy to implement. The early applications of police computer systems, for example, included the automation of reported crime data and the storing of records for outstanding warrants, traffic violations, and stolen vehicles. Only later was it advisable to add records for stolen property, criminal histories, or even the department's own property management and personnel records, all of which involved much larger and more complex information bases. Naturally, individual police departments varied in the degree to which each of these files, previously maintained by manual entry and sorting, was suitable for automation or involved officers who would resist the use of the computer. The key task was to identify those files that had been adequately maintained manually, that were not difficult to transfer to computer formats, and that were under the supervision of a cooperative official, and to avoid those files that had the opposite characteristics. Such a strategy was followed in most of the case studies where, for example, the more difficult applications such as computerized dispatch, case entry, or criminal history systems did not appear until later, if at all.

There were several benefits from maintaining a narrow scope for the innovation. With a narrow scope, the innovation was more likely to be operated at a steady pace. The innovation was also not likely to overextend its resources or the capabilities of the innovator and technical staff in charge of maintaining the innovation. However, there was a psychological payoff as well. If narrowly defined, an innovation could be more quickly labeled as functional than if it were broadly defined. The Rochester CCTV case provided a negative illustration of this point: The CCTV system was defined so ambitiously at the outset that numerous schools and classrooms were included in the anticipated coverage. After three years from the start of a five-year grant, only 60 percent of the classrooms had even been wired; after four years, it was 90 percent. The innovation was thus still not fully operational after several years. Moreover, the major effort during this long period of time went into the physical implementation of the system, thereby potentially drawing resources away from other essential activities such as practitioner training or the integration of specific television programs into the formal curriculum. In contrast, an innovation whose scope was narrowly defined could initially consolidate support and later expand to other activities or subdistricts, which was the pattern followed by most of the successful case studies.

Deliberate Elimination of Superseded Procedures

This second strategy was often overlooked. Innovators attended to the development of new practices in relation to an innovation, but they forgot that conversion was facilitated if the superseded practices were simultaneously eliminated. With computer systems, the replacement-elimination procedure was perhaps best known. After a computer file had been established and provided information reliably, the old manual files could be destroyed. If the manual files were allowed to be maintained in parallel with the computer system, they could certainly serve as a backup system; however, their preservation also remained a threat to the routinization of the new computer system.

The elimination of superseded practices required a deliberate effort and did not automatically follow the installation of new practices. For instance, all innovations required new organizational procedures that were reflected in the use of new forms such as data entry forms, case report forms, or other organizational forms. When the new forms were satisfactorily being used, a few innovators systematically discarded the old ones. In Indianapolis, as new applications were automated and new forms created, specific orders were given to destroy the old forms still in inventory, and to cease printing the old forms. This was an explicit action that prevented the staff from returning to the previous practices. Similar actions included the removal of old equipment or the reassignment of specialized personnel associated with the superseded practice. For example, breath-testing innovations usually displaced traditional urinalysis procedures. Because breath testing did not require a chemist, which urinalysis did, the assignment of other responsibilities to the chemist made it more difficult for an agency to revive the urinalysis procedure on a full-time basis. In the long run, an effective displacement tactic was to encourage sufficient turnover among operating personnel so that few could recall how to carry out the superseded practice; alternatively, an ethos could be developed whereby few individuals desired to revert to the old practice.

Naturally there were some innovations such as the Jet-Axe that actually represented "add-on" services, and where no existing practice needed to be displaced. In these cases, the elimination procedures were not relevant, but other factors, especially the one discussed next, became more important.

Reduction of Job Threats to Practitioners

The importance of practitioner exposure has already been emphasized. For any innovation, practitioners need to gain direct experience in using the innovation. They need to understand its capabilities and implications for their everyday behavior and, in particular, to develop confidence that the innovation will not be a long-term threat to their jobs.

Many technological innovations for public services have, in fact, been promoted by federal agencies partly on the basis of potential job savings or reductions. The early development of CCTV and CAI, for instance, assumed the major payoff to be the provision of more individualized instruction for each student. This was presumed to relieve a teacher from spending too much time with a given student on tasks, such as drill and practice, that were valuable to the student but time-consuming to the teacher. In the short run, specific teaching jobs were not necessarily threatened; however, in the long run, these technologies could be interpreted as displacing the need to add new positions. Not surprisingly, teachers initially viewed CCTV or CAI with skepticism. Any such skepticism was overcome in the case studies wherever teachers had ample opportunities to use the innovation, (as in Dallas, Tampa, and San Diego, CAI; and Portland, CCTV). The teachers found that the innovations really did not displace their work but actually increased demands for their time and made some of their tasks easier. For instance, the major CAI application was the initiation of new courses—computer programming and advanced computer science. The expanded curriculum meant greater demands on teaching time and potentially more jobs. Moreover, in some of the courses, enthusiastic students developed programs to assist teachers in their regular mathematics courses. For instance, in one case study, advanced mathematics students wrote programs that altered the numbers for different problem sets, so that a teacher could have multiple versions of the same test. The teacher could then administer these versions to the same class and thereby reduce the opportunities for cheating, which had become an increasing problem. In fact, the successful use of CCTV and CAI generally expanded the teachers' resources, and these innovations did not necessarily reduce the need for teaching time. This observation may disappoint those policymakers who might have expected innovations to produce savings in manpower. However, the important point is that local innovators should strongly encourage practitioner use of the innovation, so that practitioners can learn about their own benefits from the innovation.

Some innovations, of course, actually displaced practitioner time. This was especially true of breath-testing operations. Under the traditional urinalysis procedure, an officer had to spend many hours on a single DWI suspect. The suspect would have to be brought into the station to produce a urine sample, during which time the officer was required to be present to observe the sample being given in order to prevent fraud. For female suspects, a matron had to be employed for the same purpose. The officer then had to deliver the specimen to the city laboratory, fill out the appropriate forms, and appear in court. The use of the Breathalyzer, whose test only takes a few minutes and entirely replaces the need for the trip to the city laboratory, markedly reduced the amount of officer time per DWI case. The innovation was thus a timesaving device and could, in theory, threaten job positions in the long run. However, this was not the outcome in any of the case studies, because the new convenience in using the Breathalyzer encouraged officers to make more DWI arrests. Although officers spent much less time per DWI case, they initiated many more cases. As a result, an officer could actually spend more time in court and away from patrol, a situation that even led to officer complaints about downtime at one site (Cincinnati). Nevertheless, the point is that even a timesaving innovation, especially if it eliminated duties that were unpleasant or boring, did not need to threaten jobs. The innovation could result in increased efficiency and thereby lead to new service applications or demands that more than offset the initial time saved. Acceptance of the innovation, however, was strongly facilitated by encouraging direct exposure and experience to the innovation on the part of practitioners.

Finally, some innovations were add-on services because they created new demands for practitioner time or skills without displacing any traditional practices. In such situations, encouragement of practitioner use helped to demonstrate that the innovation could actually preserve jobs in times of budget cuts. This was true in both MICU cases (Dallas and Birmingham) that ultimately became more routinized, where both fire departments averted budgetary cuts affecting all municipal agencies because of the added function. The installation of MICU services had increased the number of calls for the fire department and had given the officers an additional responsibility that the community valued. The Jet-Axe was also an add-on service because the traditional methods for breaking into a structure could not, and should not, be displaced. Because the Jet-Axe did not displace any previous practice, an innovator could not follow the strategy of eliminating the agency's ability to perform the previous practice. However, because the Jet-Axe was only used infrequently, practitioners could not gain much direct experience in using the innovation. Such conditions made it much more difficult to incorporate the innovation.

Summary

In summary, the improvisation stage marked the beginning of an innovation's life history. The decision to adopt the innovation occurred before the improvisation stage actually began, and hence has not been covered by the discussion. Instead, the aggregate pattern from the case studies has suggested some of the features of the improvisation stage: the need to expose practitioners to the innovation, the need to keep the innovation operating as consistently as possible, and the need for flexible management of resources. For all these requirements, it was important that the persons directing the innovation simply accomplish the tasks and be able to make on-the-spot decisions; it was not necessary for formal organizational procedures to be established or for major organizational changes—passages or cycles—to be made. These latter objectives, however, did increase in importance during the next two stages in an innovation's life history, as covered in chapters 5 and 6.

Note

1. The telephone interviews did not always contain specific dates and were thus less susceptible to this approach. The telephone interview data will be integrated into the discussion in chapter 7.

5 Life Histories, Stage 2: The Expansion Stage

Overview of the Expansion Stage

This middle period in the life of an innovation presented the first critical tests for routinization. Whereas the improvisation stage had been marked by activities associated with the initial operation of an innovation, no organizational passages or cycles had been required. In contrast, the expansion stage, as revealed by the case studies, included several critical passages and cycles; these involved the formal integration of the innovation into an agency's regular organization and procedures. For specific life histories, some of these passages actually occurred in the improvisation stage, and others were delayed until the final period in the life history. The main point was that, for any given case, *some* passages or cycles needed to be achieved during this middle period.

The most appropriate types of passages or cycles for this middle period appeared to be those that could be accomplished within a brief organizational time span—that is, less than a year. For instance, the development of new maintenance and supply procedures to serve an innovation could occur in most agencies within a few months. In contrast, a change involving a new training component in a police academy took more time to implement because the change had to be planned and approved, and then had to await the appropriate academic cycle before being initiated. The expansion stage, then, was marked by passages and cycles related to the continued growth of the innovation, such as the installation of a new generation of equipment, as well as to those that could organizationally be achieved quickly. Although it was still important for an innovation to remain operational throughout this period, the main attention of those supporting the innovation shifted from operational to organizational concerns. In short, there were several passages and one cycle that were generally achieved, and the expansion stage was thus characterized by the following types of events:

1. Increases in the number and scope of applications involving the innovation
2. Equipment turnover and updating (cycle)
3. Transition from external to internal funding and budgetary support for the innovation (passage)
4. Formal changes in the organizational identity of the innovation (passage)
5. Development of stable arrangements for the maintenance and supplies needed by the innovation (passage)

107

6. Initiation of internal personnel classifications or certification procedures to cover the new specializations associated with the innovation (passage)

The first type of event was the occasion for developing further support for the innovation and identifying potential service payoffs from it. The last five types represented five specific passages or cycles.

Increases in the Number and Scope of Applications

Most of the innovations in the case studies began by operating at a level less than their full capability. Most commonly, an innovation was applied to some subpart of an agency's operations to see whether it would first work on a smaller scale, and, if it did, expansion to all parts of a district or department generally followed. As pointed out in the previous chapter, a narrower scope was probably even wise at the outset. During the expansion stage, however, the innovations were extended and made available to all parts of the organization. Thus, where a breath-testing or MICU system had only been operating in one of several sub-districts, the expansion, even if phased over a period of time, eventually covered all subdistricts. In Cincinnati, for instance, such expansion not only took the form of coverage for all subdistricts, but the number of officers being trained as breath-testing operators was also increased, so that the officers in other parts of the department, and not merely in the traffic section, could use the breath-testing equipment and follow the full procedures for processing DWI cases. If such extension did not occur during this stage, the innovation was more likely to be considered a special project of some sort, and this reduced the chances for routinization.

There were at least two other ways in which an innovation's scope could be expanded. The first was applicable to all types of innovations: Once the initial procedures and applications had been established, the innovation could be used by agencies or parties outside the host agency. Thus, in Indianapolis and Nashville, the police computer systems were used by other criminal justice agencies in the metropolitan area besides the police department. In Indianapolis, one computer terminal was programmed to provide only crime analysis data and was actually used by neighborhood groups in conjunction with the city's neighborhood action program. Similarly, other jurisdictions used the Akron breath-testing equipment and shared the terminals in the San Diego system; for MICU, other agencies began to use the Dallas training program, and were charged for the training costs; and, in Birmingham, the fire officers began a wide-scale citizen training program for cardiopulmonary resuscitation, a technique that went beyond the standard notion of basic first aid. The use of the innovation by outside agencies and parties served several important purposes: Service demands for the innovation were increased; a broader base of support was developed; and the innovation itself began to be perceived by others as an integral function of the host agency.

The second way of expanding an innovation was more applicable to those innovations that have been labeled as "functionally flexible" (see chapter 2). For police computer and CAI systems in particular, once the initial applications had been successfully adopted, the computer system was then expanded and applied to other aspects of the agency's operations. In Miami, Indianapolis, and Boston, for instance, computer-assisted dispatching was a new application being installed at the time of the case study. This new application was more complex than earlier ones; however, the computer staff was mainly able to cope with the new application because of its experiences with earlier ones. The Dallas and San Diego CAI systems were likewise continually expanded to include new curriculum subjects and hence new groups of teachers and students, but this was not the situation in either Oakland or Tampa. In theory, such expansion to new applications was also relevant for CCTV and MICU systems, which have been defined as functionally flexible innovations. None of the innovations was able to accomplish such expansion in the CCTV case studies, however, partly because of the difficulties encountered with the first set of applications. The only exception was in Portland, where the applications for using classroom television increased— but in the context of a new instructional television (ITV) system that happened to displace the original CCTV system. Except for the expansion in Dallas and Birmingham already cited above, the basic innovation in the MICU systems was not as functionally flexible as the other types of innovations.

Once again, the Jet-Axe stood out as the single innovation that was so limited in its use that neither an expansion in scope nor in type of application occurred. Given the functional rigidity of the innovation, the only feasible goal at any site would have been to increase the use of the Jet-Axe in firefighting situations so that more firefighters could gain direct experience with the innovation. However, the actual frequency of application had leveled off in both Jet-Axe case studies.

In summary, increases in the number and scope of applications provided important opportunities for expanding the support for an innovation. The support was a result of additional clients or practitioners having the opportunity to use the innovation, as well as the identification of new service benefits beyond those, if any, associated with the initial round of applications. Together with the activities during the improvisation stage, the expansion in scope of applications thus formed the context within which several key passages were to be made. Five such passages or cycles are described in the remainder of this chapter. For each of the five, the discussion leads to a summary status list, indicating the actual status of each case study for the particular passage or cycle. The entire list may be found in table 5-1 at the end of the chapter. As previously noted, the descriptions reflect the aggregate pattern among the case studies (based on the summary table of events in tables 4-1 to 4-6 in the previous chapter), and specific passages or cycles for specific cases may have occurred chronologically earlier or later; these deviations, however, did not alter the conclusions to be drawn about the general life history patterns.

Equipment Turnover and Updating

Many innovations provided opportunities for expansion in relation to the updating and acquisition of specific pieces of equipment. Equipment turnover therefore served as an appropriate cycle in making progress toward routinization. Naturally, efforts had to be made to gain administrative support to update existing equipment or to acquire new pieces; but once such support had been generated, and, once the acquisition procedure had been used for one or more generations of equipment, the very practice of updating equipment became an integral part of an agency's operations.

No innovation facilitated the equipment turnover process more than computer systems, whether for police or for school use. All police computer systems in the case studies went through at least two and sometimes three or four generations of core computer equipment. Such changes usually relieved increasingly competing demands for computer time and were also linked to advances in the state of computer technology. Typically, but not always, the first generation of computers used by an organization had a small memory capacity and was only able to accommodate batch processing (for example, an IBM 1401); the second and third generation computers had larger memory capacities and were able to accommodate batch and on-line processing (for example, IBM 360 and 370 systems); and the fourth generation involved the acquisition of separate core computers for specialized functions (for example, minicomputers for message switching or for computer-assisted dispatch). By this definition of equipment turnover, the Nashville and Miami police computers had used two generations of computers; Boston, three; and Indianapolis, four. For the core computers in CAI systems, Oakland, Tampa, and San Diego had all implemented only one generation of CAI applications (though the computer system was in a later generation with regard to administrative applications), and Dallas, two. Thus, the CAI systems had not involved as many equipment cycles as their police counterparts.

In on-line computer systems, the terminals could also be updated as a result of increased demands and improvement in the state of the technology. Such turnover was difficult to assess because an agency was unlikely to change all its terminals at the same time; however, in a few cases (Indianapolis, police computer; San Diego and Dallas, CAI), significant numbers of new types of terminals had been acquired following the initiation of the computer system. For San Diego, the turnover in terminals had compensated in part for the lack of turnover in the core equipment, so that both the Dallas and San Diego CAI systems may be regarded as having fulfilled a prime requirement of the expansion stage, whereas the Tampa and Oakland CAI systems did not.

Innovations besides computer systems provided a more limited opportunity for equipment upgrading and turnover. In theory, CCTV systems could involve updating of receivers as well as recording and transmitting equipment. More efficient portable television cameras, for instance, have been continually developed and could be among the new equipment to be included for a CCTV system. However, because two case studies (those in Omaha and Rochester), did not survive their initial difficulties, such updating never became· an issue. In Portland, updating did occur to a limited extent, but the CCTV system was converted to an ITV system, and, for the purposes of this study did not qualify as a turnover in equipment. Similarly, MICU systems could also be subject to updating. New generations of vehicles were possible, as were changes in the life-support equipment carried within the vehicle. Such updating did occur in both Dallas and Birmingham; the latter involved the acquisition of a new generation of monitoring and telecommunications equipment, such as Life-Paks.

For the other technologies, breath-testing equipment and the Jet-Axe, no updated versions of equipment were relevant, although there were new models with minor modifications. The original equipment was generally suited to serve any expansion in service needs, and few improvements had occurred in the state of the technology. However, for such innovations, new equipment was nevertheless acquired in the form of additional units. Thus, in Cincinnati and Akron, purchases of new Breathalyzers occurred in the expansion stage, even though these new units were virtually identical with the original models. The new units were used to replace the older ones, which, in turn, were used for backup or training purposes. Similarly, the Memphis breath-testing operation involved successive purchases of new equipment and the original equipment was eventually traded in for credit toward those purchases. For the Jet-Axe, additional purchases were also made several times in the years that followed the initiation of the innovation. For the breath-testing and Jet-Axe innovations, the new acquisitions thus performed the same function of establishing the practice of updating equipment, even though the equipment itself did not represent a technologically new generation.

Table 5-1 includes a summary of the status of each case study for this first cycle. Wherever a new generation of equipment was installed, or wherever at least one sequential purchase of similar equipment was made, the case study was regarded as having achieved this particular cycle. (This table should also be referred to for summary tabulations for each of the remaining passages in this chapter).

Transition from External to Internal Budgetary Support

No passage has received more attention from federal policymakers than the transition from external to internal funding. Many federal policymakers have viewed the transition from soft to hard money as the major sign that an innovation has been routinized. Thus, the transition has been interpreted to mean that a local agency will support an innovation on a lasting and permanent basis. The transition appears appropriate for the middle period of a life history, because if there have been external sources of funding, such funding generally expires after three to five years, forcing a local agency to face the decision concerning local funding. However, the case studies indicated that this transition, although important, was only a part of a much more complex set of organizational changes. In other words, transition from soft to hard monies may have been a necessary but was not a sufficient condition for routinization. The other passages and cycles covered in this and the following chapter appear just as important to any operational definition of routinization.

It has already been noted that local funding support occurred at the outset in at least half of the case studies (see table 4-7) but that such support was not correlated with the ultimate success of the innovation in achieving passages and cycles. For those innovations that had been externally funded at the outset, all but one (Denver, MICU) eventually made the transition to internal funds. Thus, the costs of staff support, expenditures for supply and maintenance, and the acquisition of new equipment were all ultimately supported in some way out of an agency's own budget. In two cases (Nashville, police computer, and Dallas, MICU), the transition was made easier by the fact that the external funds (from LEAA in the first case and from general revenue-sharing in the second), had not ever been specifically identified as a separate part of the agency's budget; administratively, the expenditures for the innovation had been incorporated from the outset into the agency's regular budget, with the knowledge that the overall city budget was being reimbursed from an external source. This procedure helped to prevent the innovation from becoming overly identified as an externally funded project, even though in one case (Nashville), the external funds were part of a long-term, five-year grant.

Regardless of the budgetary mechanism, however, the main point is that all but one of the innovations in our case studies eventually received full local budgetary support. Such support tended to occur early in the life of the innovation (in many cases, during the improvisation stage) but did not preclude subsequent budget cuts or even cessation of the innovation. The three CCTV experiences may be most instructive in illustrating the reasons why the transition to hard money was not a sufficient condition to assure routinization.

In one case (Portland), a district-wide decentralization occurred after the CCTV innovation had been initiated. The original CCTV system had been organized on a centralized basis, and television programs had been transmitted to nine schools whose students had been predominantly from low-income families. In the decentralization, these nine schools became parts of different subdistricts, and each subdistrict had enough autonomy to determine its own priorities; the CCTV system was not sufficiently important for any single subdistrict to maintain the full system. As a result, even though the CCTV system was being supported by local funds, the innovation actually changed to an ITV system, whereby individual teachers could use over-the-air programs or videotapes for viewing in the classroom, but there was no transmission of programs from one classroom to another or from one school to another. Furthermore, a television production project was developed as part of a high school vocational education curriculum in which both state and local funds were used. The ITV system was thus more compatible with the decentralized organization of the Portland school district than was the original CCTV system. Changes in the innovation occurred, in short, independent of whether the innovation was supported by external or internal funds.

In Omaha, the CCTV system was originally supported by a federal grant and local funds were then used when the federal grant expired. The system, however, had encountered a series of difficulties throughout its improvisation stage, including technical difficulties in installation, early turnover among key CCTV staff, and delays in obtaining FCC approval to use certain channels for transmitting the digital signals needed to summon a television program. Moreover, the CCTV applications had not been highly integrated with classroom teaching; the main application was the installation of special carrels in the media centers of three schools, so that students could view television programs as a supplement to their classroom instruction. As a result, few students or teachers came into contact with the system. Those that did often encountered a system that was not functioning properly. Local funding for the project ceased when, under constrained budgetary conditions, the school district decided to use its resources to upgrade a television studio that had become part of the vocational education curriculum. The CCTV system thus had not achieved sufficient priority to avoid being affected by budgetary cutbacks.

In Rochester, the initial support for the CCTV system came from both state funds and a local bond issue. The proportion of state funding systematically declined over a five-year period, and, when the state funding was terminated, the entire system became locally funded. The initial conditions in Rochester were more auspicious than those in Omaha. The system was technically sound, reached numerous classrooms, and was strongly supported by the school superintendent. Nevertheless, under similar subsequent pressures to reduce budgets, as in Omaha, the CCTV system was discontinued. This appears to have been attributable to several factors: The CCTV system had not been used for core curriculum subjects (typing was the main subject); it had aroused practitioner and thus union opposition because it appeared as a job threat; it had not adequately accounted for the rapid depreciation of the television equipment; and the supportive superintendent was replaced. Moreover, observers at the site noted that the Rochester system had been initiated at an early time (in the mid-1960s), when there were few attractive educational television programs such as "Sesame Street" or "The Electric Company."

It may be argued that these case study experiences were inadvertently affected by the peculiar budgetary trends that have existed for the last 20 years. During this time, most local agencies first experienced significant budgetary growth, which was then frequently followed by severe cutbacks. The argument could be made that these conditions have made hard funding an exceptionally vulnerable characteristic; that under normal conditions of less rapid growth and contraction, the transition to hard money would be sufficient for routinization. The case studies suggest otherwise. They suggest that, on the contrary, budgetary cutbacks provided a strong and important test for routinization: If an innovation had become truly routinized, it should have achieved a sufficiently high priority to withstand even severe cutbacks. This was certainly the experience in several case studies, where police computer systems (for example, Miami, Indianapolis, and Boston), breath testing (for example, Memphis and Akron), and MICU systems (for example, Dallas and Birmingham) all survived budgetary cutbacks. Although operations were reduced in other agencies, or even in the same agency, the innovation remained largely unaffected.

In summary, local funding was an important early step in the routinization process. However, routinization requires an innovation to survive other organizational passages and cycles in addition to the transition to hard money (see table 5-1).

Formal Changes in the Organizational Identity of an Innovation

A third way in which organizational integration occurred was for an innovation and its staff to become a part of the appropriate organizational unit with an agency. Achievement of such organizational status was necessary if the innovation was ultimately to disappear as an innovation and to become part of "standard practice." Moreover, the creation of such organizational status frequently occurred when the innovation was initiated, so that the passage should at least have occurred during the expansion stage. However, the attainment of various organizational arrangements was a difficult transition to assess. The difficulty stemmed from the fact that there were at least four possible organizational arrangements:

1. The innovation became the basis for a new unit that *did not* achieve formal recognition as a standard organizational unit but remained a "special project."
2. The innovation became the basis for a new unit that *did* achieve formal recognition as a standard organizational unit.
3. The innovation became a formal responsibility of an existing unit or agency official who served as coordinator.
4. The innovation had no organizational status and no special coordinator.

The first problem was that, although the least desirable outcome for any innovation was to remain a "special project," it was often difficult to distinguish such status from the second organizational arrangement listed above—that is, from formal recognition as a standard organizational unit. Agencies had different procedures for making formal organizational changes, and some of these changes were artifactual (that is, in name only) and were reversible. Nevertheless, no matter what procedures were involved, it was important for an innovation to avoid "special project" status after the improvisation stage: again, the best examples of this shortcoming were the CCTV innovations in Rochester and Omaha, where there were no formal changes and where practitioners and administrators perceived the CCTV systems as special projects that were not part of the core organization. In Rochester, a formal television department had actually been created to administer the CCTV system, but was later disbanded.

A second problem was that different organizational arrangements were relevant for different innovations, depending upon the type of innovation and how it was used at a particular site. For breath testing, for instance, the appropriate arrangement was probably the integration of the innovation into the responsibilities of an existing unit, the traffic bureau or section. This was because the breath-testing innovation was intended to displace an old function, urinalysis, and was therefore located in the same organizational unit that had administered the old function; this was, indeed, the experience in two of the case studies on breath testing. In the third case (Memphis), however, a separate city-county unit had been established because the innovation served both the city and the metropolitan area; officers were assigned from both the police and the sheriff's departments to serve in this hybrid unit. Although adoption may have been made easier by developing a hybrid unit, and although the old function had been displaced, this organizational arrangement was now potentially vulnerable to problems in either the police or the sheriff's departments, and hence the appropriate passage was not regarded as having been fully achieved. In both Jet-Axe case studies, the innovation also provided an alternative to an existing function, the use of crowbars and axes, and was therefore organizationally placed at the same level, which involved practitioner adoption and use but no formal organizational unit; because the innovation created no new administrative demands, no formal coordinator position was needed.

Police computer systems, however, involved sufficient new equipment, skills, and procedures for a separate organizational unit to appear more appropriate. The formation of such a unit occurred in all four case studies on police computers and generally occurs in relation to the administrative functions of school computers. With MICU systems, the organizational issues were more complicated. MICU may be administered as a separate service within the fire department, in which case a separate organizational unit, such as the ambulance division in Dallas, appeared appropriate. MICU may also be administered, however, as a service provided within the context of existing ladder and engine companies, in which case integration into an existing organizational unit, as in Birmingham, was more appropriate.

For educational innovations, the problem of organizational arrangement raised an extremely sensitive issue. To the extent that both CAI and CCTV systems were considered innovations that would help classroom teachers, there needed to be some organizational integration of these systems into the central curriculum department of the school district. A CAI system, for instance, may be totally administered by the curriculum department, with technical assistance from the data processing unit, which was usually part of the district's administrative services. At a minimum, the CAI coordinator was frequently a member of the curriculum department, and not merely a member of the data processing unit. The reasons for such a close association were that lasting modifications in the curriculum, which mean the adoption of new practices and changes in the definition of what constitutes the core curriculum, appeared only to occur, but were not guaranteed, when the curriculum department had sanctioned the change and given it a high priority. In this regard, the four CAI case studies varied considerably: The San Diego and Tampa systems succeeded in integrating CAI with the curriculum department; Oakland had not; and Dallas had appointed a mathematics coordinator in the curriculum department and was also in the process of making the overall CAI coordinator a part of that department. The innovation was actually in a problematic situation in Oakland because CAI had no organizational status, even as a special project, nor was there any formal CAI coordinator.

In summary, formal changes in organizational identity were important to the long-term survival of an innovation (see table 5-1). Though such changes were difficult to assess, the following points appeared to be the most relevant:

1. Identity as a "special project" was curtailed as soon as possible after an innovation had been initiated.
2. The appropriate organizational arrangement for innovations that displaced older functions was integration into the existing organizational unit that administered the older function.
3. The appropriate arrangement for innovations that provided new functions was the creation of a new organizational unit.
4. For educational innovations that attempted to change classroom instruction, direct integration of the innovation into the curriculum department of a district was an important passage.

Stable Arrangements for Maintenance and Supply

Most of the innovations required some maintenance or supplies to keep the innovation operating. Maintenance involved routine preventive care and cleaning as well as the specific repairs needed by a piece of equipment. The supplies were the consumable items (such as special paper for computer systems, drugs for an MICU kit, or chemicals for a breath-testing device) that were an integral part of the innovation, and an agency had to make some provision for keeping such supplies in its inventory.

During the improvisation stage, the point has already been made that part of the innovator's key responsibilities was to insure that appropriate maintenance and supplies were available, whether through an outside vendor or through direct assistance by a person inside the agency. However, the main accomplishment during the improvisation stage was to keep the innovation operating, no matter what ad hoc procedures had to be used to obtain the necessary maintenance or supplies. In contrast, during the expansion stage, the procedural or organizational aspects rose in importance; the goal was not only to keep the innovation operating, but also to establish a dependable procedure for providing maintenance and supplies. The procedure did not take a long time to establish, and hence the transition was best handled during this part of an innovation's life history, although individual cases again varied.

Stable arrangements for maintenance and supply still frequently required outside assistance from a vendor or service company. Such assistance, however, was now part of a long-term arrangement that was not just linked to the initiation of the innovation. A typically unsatisfactory arrangement, in contrast, was one in which the service contract was for a relatively short-term—that is a one- or two-year "shakedown" period, with no assistance planned beyond that period. Alternatively, some stable arrangements were entirely based on internal resources, meaning that the maintenance responsibilities were assigned to some unit inside the agency—generally, but not always, the maintenance shop—and that supplies were acquired through the regular purchasing practices of the agency.

The development of internal capabilities was preferable over continued reliance on an outside vendor. However, certain types of innovations could only rely on long-term service agreements with external sources. Computer systems, for instance, presented the clearest case for continued external assistance. Whether the core computer had been purchased or leased, most local agencies did not have the capability for repairing computer equipment, and service contracts of some sort (for example, as part of the leasing arrangement) had to be negotiated. Thus, in all case studies involving CAI and police computers except for Miami, the routine use of such service contracts was evident. Some contracts covered the computing equipment; other contracts were with the telephone company and covered the maintenance of the lines connecting various terminals with the core computer. In all cases except Miami, the expenditures for the service contracts became readily accepted as part of the regular costs of operating the innovation, and the item was rarely questioned in budgetary reviews. In Miami, a major new generation of computer equipment had just been installed, and the service was still part of the initial installation agreement; however, there was no reason to believe that a satisfactory long-term arrangement would not emerge. For computer systems, then, the development of long-term service arrangements with outside vendors, even if renewable annually, constituted the appropriate passage for maintaining and supplying the innovation. Several case studies, however, went even one step further: the establishment of a compatible and complete backup computer. In Indianapolis (police computer) and Tampa (CAI), for instance, the agency's computer and the county computer were designed to be compatible; each could serve as a reserve unit for the other. Boston (police computer) had a similar arrangement with the city computer, and in Nashville (police computer), there were actually two core computers, one for on-line and the other for batch applications—but each core computer was capable of performing the other's functions.

For other types of innovation, including most of the remaining ones that were part of this study, internal capabilities were sufficient for servicing the innovation. For instance, in Dallas (MICU), where the MICU vehicles were repaired and maintained by the fire department's regular maintenance shop, specific increases in the maintenance staff were made by the agency to accommodate the new functions. Similar arrangements were established in Birmingham. However, not all case studies were able to establish regular procedures for using such internal capabilities. In CCTV systems, for instance, much of the repair and maintenance fell on the staff of the audio-visual department or special television production staff that had been hired in conjunction with the innovation. Staff turnover and inherent equipment defects led to the neglect of maintenance and repair in Rochester and Omaha.

For the three breath-testing case studies, maintenance and supplies were generally provided directly through the operating unit concerned with the innovation (for instance, an officer in the traffic department), and not through the agency's maintenance shop. In these cases, however, the agency had to be aware of the tradeoffs between having one officer conduct all service and repair (which ensures more consistent treatment of the equipment), and having a larger number of operators trained to perform such services (which ensures that the services would survive personnel turnover). In all three case studies, the agencies had actually done both: A single officer tended to have the main responsibility, but the training for new breath-testing operators included specific instruction regarding maintenance and repair, and these operators were therefore in a position to replace the active incumbent if he left the agency or took a new position. As for the Jet-Axe case studies, satisfactory arrangements only required that the fire departments establish adequate purchasing procedures because individual Jet-Axes were entirely consumed by use, and hence involved no maintenance or repair.

In summary, the expansion stage was the appropriate time for developing self-sufficient procedures for maintenance and supply. Although a key objective was still to make whatever repairs were needed to keep the innovation operating, a complementary organizational goal was now relevant: The procedures for maintenance and supply became a part of standard agency operations and were not merely based on ad hoc arrangements. Where such ad hoc arrangements were eliminated and replaced, the innovation successfully achieved another passage (see table 5-1).

Internal Personnel Classifications
or Certification Procedures

A fifth way in which innovations became integrated into local service agencies was through the development of new personnel examinations and classifications to cover the special skills related to the staffing requirements of the innovation. This change occurred either through civil service classifications or through formal training and certification procedures (see table 5-1). In either case, the middle period in the life history was an appropriate time to initiate such procedures on a permanent basis. This was because it could take two or three years to establish new personnel classifications, so an early start was helpful. At the same time, the initiatives were difficult to make during the improvisation stage because of the instability of different roles and the lack of time and experience needed to assemble the necessary documentation.

Civil Service Changes

In some cases, skills were new to an agency but might have existed in the employment market at large; in other cases, the skills reflected technological advances that had resulted in the creation of new personnel specialties. In a computer innovation, for instance, the staff included keypunch operators, programmers, and other technicians related to the operation of the computer system. For many cities, job classifications for these skills already existed in the county-wide (as in the Tampa CAI, and the Indianapolis police computer) or even state-wide (as in Boston, police computer) civil service system. Integration into a specific department was thus a matter of using these existing classifications. For other cities (the Miami and Nashville police computers; and the Dallas and San Diego CAI), new classifications were developed within the appropriate agency's civil service system. Advances in the state of the technology with computer systems, however, also required an ability to update classifications—for example, from keypunch operators to data entry clerks. This updating occurred at the city level if such skills were needed by several city agencies, or it occurred in relation to a specific department, such as the police.

The development of appropriate personnel classifications was necessary to the long-term survival of the innovation for two reasons. First, such classifications allowed an agency to make the skills related to an innovation part of the regular staff of the agency, facilitating the allocation of permanent positions for these staff. Secondly, these classifications provided the agency with an ability to compete in the employment market for persons with the relevant skills. In the CCTV cases, for instance, the establishment of the appropriate classifications allowed the CCTV systems to pay higher salaries to the necessary specialists. Conversely, in a computer system, if a systems analyst function could, for instance, only be filled by persons who were classified as programmers, it was less likely that the agency would be able to recruit the appropriately skilled person at a sufficiently high salary.

External Training and Certification

Some innovations called for an expansion in existing staff skills rather than for new civil service classifications. This occurred, for instance, with MICU or breath testing, where the innovation could be staffed by existing police or fire officers but where such officers required special training or certification beyond their initial civil service qualifications. In these cases, the certification procedure, usually established by the state, played a comparable role to that of developing a new civil service classification. It was thus important to formalize the certification procedure, and, in most of the case studies on these two innovations, not only had such formalization occurred but there was also a new procedure developed for refresher training and recertification. A paramedic for the Dallas MICU operation, for instance, received initial training from the medical school, was certified for a two-year period by the state department of public health (upon passing an examination), was given a two-week refresher course, and was then recertified for another two years (upon passing an examination again). In Birmingham, a paramedic not only had to follow these training and certification procedures, but the paramedic position had also been established as a civil service classification.

The need to rely on training and certification procedures, however, made the innovation somewhat more vulnerable than if civil service classifications were established. This was because training and certification were often provided by external agencies such as a public health department or a medical school, and there was no ready assurance that the external agency would continue its participation. For this reason, the internalization of certification procedures was considered a part of the definition of a satisfactory passage. This only occurred in one MICU case (Birmingham) and in one breath-testing case (Cincinnati). At the latter site, certification had become part of the regular program of the police academy; officers who served as teachers in the academy received their certification as teachers from the state public health department. In another breath-testing case (Akron), training was done internally, but not as part of the police academy curriculum. The officer who did the training had also been certified through public health agencies but had just retired at the time of the case study, and his replacement had not yet been certified to conduct the appropriate training. Thus, the nature of the training program's continuation was uncertain. Similarly, in the third breath-testing case (Memphis), the certification program was operated by a local university and had not been internalized. In one MICU case (Denver), the cessation of the innovation occurred with the withdrawal of the general hospital that had provided training and certification. The fire department actually had little choice, because there was no state training or certification program to use as an alternative.

Classification for the Coordinator

One position that usually required a new classification, whether through the civil service system or through formal training and certification from an external source, was the coordinator or supervisor of the innovation. This person had the day-to-day responsibility for the innovation, and, no matter how the innovation was organized, this coordinator position or its functions was generally new to the agency. Although an incumbent could begin serving in this capacity during the improvisation stage without an official personnel classification, such action had to occur in the long run. The coordinator role was sometimes defined as an entirely new position, as in Dallas and San Diego CAI, or it was integrated as a formal responsibility of an existing official (Cincinnati breath-testing). Because of the importance of formalizing the coordinator's position, a critical test of the first coordinator for an innovation, in fact, was whether he or she could establish the appropriate training, certification, or new classification procedures so that the next incumbent could be hired.

Summary

The expansion stage provided the first real tests for the routinization of an innovation. For innovations that were becoming routinized, the achievement of five passages or cycles generally occurred during this stage: equipment turnover and updating, transition from external to internal funding, changes in organizational identity, internalization of maintenance and supply capabilities, and initiation of personnel classifications and certification procedures. Although a particular innovation might not have accomplished all these passages or cycles during the expansion stage (and some of the innovations might have accomplished the passages and cycles earlier), subsequent routinization was more likely to be achieved if more of these events had taken place. Conversely, an innovation that had expanded without accomplishing any of these organizational tasks was not likely to achieve status as a part of an agency's "standard practice."

Table 5-1
Summary of Passages or Cycles During the Expansion Stage

Type of Innovation/Site	Passage or Cycle 1. Achieved Equipment Turnover or Sequential Purchases		Passage or Cycle 2. Achieved Transition to Support by Local Funds		Passage or Cycle 3. Achieved Appropriate Organizational Status		Passage or Cycle 4. Achieved Stable Arrangement for Maintenance and Supply		Passage or Cycle 5. Internalized Personnel Classification or Certification	
	Yes	No	Yes	No	Yes	No	Yes	No	Yes	No
Police computer										
Miami	X		X		X				X	
Indianapolis	X		X		X			X	X	
Nashville	X		X		X		X		X	
Boston	X		X		X		X		X	
Breath-testing										
Cincinnati	X		X		X		X		X	
Akron	X		X		X		X			X
Memphis	X		X			X	X			X
Mobile-intensive care units										
Dallas	X		X		X		X			X
Birmingham	X		X		X		X		X	
Denver		X		X		X		X		X
Jet-Axe										
Rochester	X		X		X		X			X
Omaha	X		X		X		X			X
Computer-assisted instruction										
Dallas	X		X		X		X		X	
Oakland		X	X			X	X			X
Tampa		X	X		X		X		X	
San Diego	X		X		X		X		X	
Closed-circuit television										
Omaha		X	X			X		X	X	
Portland		X	X		X		X		X	
Rochester		X	X			X		X	X	

6

Life Histories, Stage 3: The Disappearance Stage

Overview of the Disappearance Stage

The main theme of the final period in the innovation life histories was the cessation of the innovations' identity as an innovation. This meant that the functions involving the innovation continued, but they were no longer regarded as peculiar, special, or ad hoc. Where routinization was achieved, the functions were established as a standard part of agency practice. Thus, "disappearance" connoted a final shift in the innovation's perceived status; it did not mean that the innovative functions had been terminated by the agency.

It is obviously very difficult to define this final shift. In general, if one were tracking the life history of an innovation from its inception, there might always be a tendency to find some remnant of the innovation that could continue to be labeled as a new function. An insight into the process is provided, however, if one examines an agency's current practices and, retrospectively, attempts to identify those functions that were once innovations. Such a retrospective view makes the shift more apparent. An example may be helpful. In most urban police departments, the use of walkie-talkies by patrol officers would now be perceived as a regular part of police practice. The walkie-talkies are a standard part of the patrol officer's equipment; the procedures for using the walkie-talkie are taught as part of every patrol officer's basic training; and the communications functions served by the walkie-talkies are an integral part of everyday procedures. If police departments were now precluded from having walkie-talkies, the entire department, including both the top administrators and the patrol officers, would probably object to the removal of part of its "normal" service capabilities. This entire array of conditions constitutes a routinized practice. Yet, walkie-talkies were clearly once an innovation; most police departments only began using such equipment about 20 years ago. Moreover, a new type of walkie-talkie, a minicomputer that allows both voice and digital communication, would now be considered a "new" innovation.

Similar examples may be found in other local service agencies. Specific practices for using such items as audio-visual equipment in schools, call boxes and patrol cars in police departments, or any number of fire extinguishing instruments in fire departments, were all once innovations. They all now appear as part of standard practice, often accepted not only by agency officials but also by the public as a standard part of the definition of a contemporary service agency. In other words, the retrospective view provides clear evidence that

125

numerous innovations have now become incorporated into the functions of an agency such as a police department. Taking a very long-term perspective, a standard textbook on police operations has summarized many law enforcement changes in a way that best illustrates the retrospective view (Wilson and McLaren, 1972):

> Police methods have changed greatly during the past hundred years. The police today use almost every conceivable means of transportation and communication. The horse patrol and nightstick gave way to automobiles containing teleprinters, helicopters with television, and jet flying belts. Modern communication centers tape-record telephone messages and complaints as well as radio dispatches . . . . Police dispatchers now have access to computer-based visual-display terminals giving identification data, records of wanted property, and other information of great tactical value. Telephonic devices can automatically record onto dictating machines reports made by officers from any telephone, and these reports can be transcribed onto a master from which any desired number of copies of the report may be reproduced. These systems are gradually replacing the typing of reports by the officers themselves as well as eliminating the frequently illegible copies of reports that resulted from the use of carbon paper. Television-based filing and retrieval systems now permit nearly instantaneous capture, storage, and random-access retrieval of documents with resolution high enough to permit classification of fingerprints transmitted by the system.

Examples of this final shift, or "disappearance" of an innovation, are thus readily apparent retrospectively. The problem posed when tracking specific life histories, however, is to identify the operational changes that are associated with the shift. Once again, the notion of specific passages and cycles was relevant; the more passages that had been achieved by an innovation in this final stage of its life history and the more cycles that had passed, the more that disappearance appeared to have occurred. Based on the case studies, at least five types of passages and cycles were relevant:

1. Changes in organizational governance—that is, the rules affecting the basic definition of the service agency's functions and responsibilities (passages)
2. Internalization of all training procedures so that new practitioners continually learn how to use the innovation (passages)
3. Promotion of personnel who are acquainted with and support the innovation (cycles)
4. Eventual turnover in the key personnel directly coordinating the innovation (cycles)
5. Expansion of the use of the innovation to the full range of possible service users (cycles)

The remainder of this chapter elaborates on each of these passages and cycles and the experiences found in the case studies. As in the previous chapter, a summary status table (table 6-1) is presented at the end of this chapter.

Changes in Organizational Governance

The role of any agency is defined by certain rules of governance—that is, the language in state legislation or city ordinances, an agency's own standard operating procedures, a provision in a collective bargaining agreement, or a public mandate such as a bond issue. Although such rules can be changed and reversed, the time needed to make such changes is often a period of years. In the case studies, innovations were integrated into agency practice by becoming part of such rules. This change could require much time and effort, but, once an innovation was integrated in this manner, further reversal could take even more time and effort, and hence routinization was much more likely to occur. The lengthy period needed to make such a passage meant that changes in organizational governance could occur late in an innovation's life. However, it sometimes occurred as part of the improvisation stage because such changes were part of the initial adoption of the innovation.

In most of the case studies, the use of the innovation resulted in changes in standard operating procedures. Revisions in the procedural manual of the agency, for instance, were part of the implementation of the breath-testing innovations in Cincinnati and Akron. Such changes, however, can often be ignored or revised without great difficulty; thus, other governance changes were more potent, and only these were counted as sufficient for a passage to have been achieved (see table 6-1). A city ordinance, for instance, defined the role of the police computer system in Indianapolis and the MICU systems in Dallas and Birmingham, and provided the basis for budget requests for these innovations; a bond issue explicitly included support of the police computer system in Miami, and Miami also instituted an arrangement whereby its regular crime reports to the state were physically conveyed in the delivery of a computer tape, and not merely reports or printouts; and CAI terminals in Dallas were purchased as part of the school district's compliance with court-ordered desegregation, establishing CAI as an integral part of the school system—the terminals could not be used for non-CAI purposes nor could CAI be allowed to fall into general disuse without raising issues of noncompliance with the desegregation order.

Other variations existed as well. In San Diego, CAI terminals were made part of the standard equipment for new school buildings, so that the terminals could be purchased with funds from a bond issue. A similar change occurred in Tampa, where CAI terminals, and hence minicomputers, were purchased with capital funds in conjunction with the construction of a new wing to an existing school building. In school districts, other changes in governance involved the certification of specific courses in the curriculum (for example, Dallas's advanced computer mathematics course received state certification), and, ultimately, the adoption of new textbooks that were in part based on the innovation (for example, CAI-based textbooks were being considered by the San Diego district).

For most MICU and breath-testing innovations, state certification procedures and standards reinforced the use of the innovation. New state laws, for instance, set certain standards for using breath-testing equipment, mainly by establishing the BAC level for defining an intoxicated condition. Perhaps the most dramatic change, however, occurred in Birmingham, where the success of the MICU system caused the fire department to change its name to "fire and rescue squad," in explicit recognition of the new functions being performed as a result of the innovation; subsequent review of the agency's budget automatically assumed the additional workload imposed by the MICU service, and not merely that associated with firefighting.

Unlike some previously described passages and cycles such as equipment turnover, external to internal budget support, formal organizational identity, and stable supply and maintenance procedures, all of which tended to be necessary but not sufficient conditions for routinization, these changes in organizational governance appeared to serve as an important component of routinization. Unfortunately, a particular innovation did not always have an opportunity to be part of a revision in a rule for organizational governance. Most innovations, in fact, may not have such opportunities and will have to rely on the aggregate effect of other factors to attain routinization. Nevertheless, innovators concerned with establishing an innovation on a long-term basis constantly sought opportunities to change the rules of governance as an effective means of achieving routinization.

Internalized Practitioner Training

The improvisation stage stressed the need for some initial practitioner training to use the innovation. An important objective then was merely to expose as many practitioners as possible to the innovation and to be certain that sufficient staff personnel could properly use the innovation. As a result, an important step during the improvisation stage was the establishment of some training sessions, either conducted by the agency itself or even conducted with the assistance of an outside vendor.

In contrast to the training needs of the improvisation stage, there was a need during the later stages in the innovation life histories to develop a regular, ongoing training program. No matter how many times a training program had been repeated, there were certain transitions needed before routinization could occur. For fire and police departments, the bulk of the practitioner's initial training took place in the fire or police academy. Therefore, training requirements associated with an innovation had to become part of the academy's curriculum in order to routinize the training. In addition, fire departments offered regular training sessions in the firehouse, usually to keep certain fire-fighting skills in practice and up-to-date. Training requirements in relation to an innovation were therefore also integrated with these other activities in the firehouse. For school districts, the initital practitioner training occurred during the practitioner's formal college or graduate education. Because such university programs were not directly linked to specific school districts, as was the academy to a police or fire department, it was difficult to expect university curricula to change quickly in relation to the training requirements for an innovation, although such change in the curriculum would probably constitute a potent transition for routinizing an innovation. A more frequent outcome was that in-service training programs, allowing a teacher to update and broaden his or her skills once on the job, gradually reflected the training related to an innovation. Such integration was an important passage. Whether training involved the academy or in-service programs, the incorporation of specific curricula tended not to occur until late in an innovation's life history; time was needed to identify the training resources, to organize the specific training lessons, and to gain approval for such activities. Furthermore, the process could be prolonged because the governing board and the teaching staff often drew their memberships from the older practitioners in an agency, and such persons were not always likely to adopt positive attitudes toward new practices. For these reasons, the transition from ad hoc to regular training programs typically occurred during the disappearance stage.

The two Jet-Axe case studies both accomplished the transition into the fire academy and the firehouse curricula. In Rochester, the training in the academy had actually been delayed because there were no classes for new trainees for two years due to budgetary constraints. As soon as enough new students were admitted to constitute a class, however, the academy program was enhanced to include a few hours of training concerning the use of the Jet-Axe. To the extent that movies, lectures, and manuals sufficed, all new firefighters were taught about the Jet-Axe and its operation; of course, as previously mentioned, little actual practice was possible because of the few Jet-Axes that could be detonated in training demonstrations.

Similarly, other types of innovations also resulted in changes in the training program in the police or fire academies, but in a less organized manner. For police computers, Indianapolis and Nashville (but not Miami or Boston) established orientation programs for data processing, so that all new officers in the academy would be able to use available terminals or otherwise take advantage of the computer resources of the department. For breath testing, Cincinnati and Akron were both able to install orientation programs for all new officers in the academy so that all new officers would be aware of the procedures even if they were not to become actual breath testing operators; Cincinnati also provided the formal training for breath testing operators as part of the academy's curriculum. Training for breath testing operators in both Akron and Memphis, however, continued to be provided by external groups—a state health department in one case and a university in the other. Such external training, which was also used in the MICU cases, can often be adequate in the long run. However, there is always the possibility that the external source, especially if not a city agency, will be unable to provide the training, or may change the ground rules for providing the training at some future date, and thus the passage to internal training programs was still considered to be essential for routinization and was not considered as having been achieved in these cases.

With the educational innovations, in only one case (San Diego) was there any evidence of formal changes in in-service programs. In all other cases, although some in-service sessions were held, and in some cases were even conducted regularly, the formal program appeared not to have been affected. In contrast, the San Diego system provided CAI training as a formal part of the in-service program, with specific credits given that could also result in increased salaries. The training program, incidentally, also included some lessons on the maintenance and repair of the CAI terminals.

Without successful passage into internal training programs, it is difficult to conceive of an innovation becoming a part of "standard practice." The very notion of such a body of standard practice implies that practitioners learn to do things a particular way in their intitial training that enables them to become practitioners. If an innovation demands some special skills, and if learning these skills is not part of the regular curriculum, the skills may always be considered somewhat external to standard practice. Hence, the use of the innovation may also be perceived as falling outside the core activities of an agency. In summary, some significant portion of the training ultimately had to become part of the practitioner's initial education, either in a fire or police academy or in a school of education, for the use of an innovation to become fully routinized (see table 6-1).

Promotion of Personnel

A major cyclic activity in organizations is the promotion of personnel from one rank to another. Most employees may have three or four promotions during their careers. For local service agencies, these promotions were the main sources of new recruits for all but the entry-level positions. This is due to the existence of personnel policies that disfavor lateral entry and that instead rely heavily on promotion from within the ranks. The consequent closed nature of local service agencies is a characteristic shared by police departments, fire departments, and school districts alike; persons outside the agency are only likely to be recruited at the very beginning of their service careers, usually qualifying by taking a civil service entrance examination, or at the top of the agency, where new appointees are usually selected by the mayor or city council and hence frequently involve candidates from outside the agency.

Due to the general pattern of vertical mobility, promotions of persons directly familiar with the innovation were quite likely to occur during the later stages of an innovation's life history. Such promotions were important to the innovation's routinization for two reasons. First, if an official that had been using the innovation and had been pleased with it was promoted, such an official was likely to support the innovation from the vantage point of his or her new position. Often, this new position involved greater managerial power, and support for the innovation consequently became more solidified. Thus, in three of the four police computer case studies (all but Nashville), a new police chief was appointed after the innovation had been operating for several years. In each of these three cases, the new police chief had previously been an officer within the department, and had directly helped to plan or implement the police computer system. In one case (Indianapolis), the new chief had actually been the coordinator of the computer system in his prior position. In these three cases, the promotions meant that the top executive in the agency was more supportive of the innovation, more likely to make personal use of it by reviewing computer printouts, and more sophisticated in seeking new service applications for it; of course, a concomitant development was that the agency head could also be more careful and critical in budget and other reviews of the innovation's services. However, on balance, promotion meant increased support for an acceptance of the innovation.

Similar promotions to executive level positions of persons who had direct contact with an innovation were potentially possible with the other types of innovation, but only occurred in one case study besides the police computer cases. This was a CAI innovation (Dallas), where the incumbent originally involved with the data processing system then became the comptroller of the school district. From this new vantage point, the comptroller made more supportive decisions concerning the use of the school computer, both for administrative and for CAI applications.

The second way in which promotions were important to an innovation's routinization involved the practitioner rather than the top executive; practitioner promotions or transfers from one subdistrict to another could incorporate the skills in using the innovation as criteria for promotion or transfer. In only two case studies did this occur to any degree. In Birmingham (MICU), the paramedic position was integrated into the general promotion ladder from one officer rank to another. In other words, service as a paramedic gave an incumbent additional credentials for being promoted into the next higher rank.

In San Diego (CAI), teachers were transferred to new schools in part on the basis of their CAI experience. Although such transfers did not require a CAI background, at least the function was perceived as part of the desirable credentials for the transfers. In a third case study (the Dallas MICU), a modified promotion ladder, integrating the paramedic position with regular fire officer ranks, was under consideration but no action had taken place by the end of the case study.

The occurrence of both types of promotional changes—of individuals to top-level positions and of practitioner-level promotions or transfers—clearly put an innovation into an advantageous situation. Moreover, these promotions were cyclic events, so that the longer an innovaton was in use, the more likely that individuals acquainted with the innovation were to be promoted. After a long period of time, the systematic promotion procedures can, of course, result in the replacement of nearly the entire staff of an agency. This will not only produce broader support and familiarity with the innovation, but, in the long run, it may lead to the elimination of any knowledge of agency practice before the innovation was initiated. Because this is clearly a long-term development, survival over promotion cycles was regarded as a characteristic of the disappearance stage of an innovation (see table 6-1).

Eventual Turnover of Key Personnel

At some point in an innovation's life history, the key personnel who initially supported or implemented the innovation may leave their positions. Such turnover in the agency head's position or the coordinator's position represented a critical event in an innovation's life history. If turnover occurred too early, before an innovation had been operating properly, the innovation's survival in the agency was severely threatened, and the innovation could fail to achieve later passages or cycles. If turnover failed to occur at all, however, this was also detrimental, because the innovation could have become permanently associated with a specific group of persons rather than with the agency as a whole. This latter situation strikes at the heart of the "institutionalization" problem, for institutionalization or routinization ultimately means that an innovation can survive in an organization without the continued support of the same individual or group of incumbents. Too often in recent years, for instance, an innovative mayor or police chief has taken office and initiated many new practices. When the term of office of this person has expired, the incumbent has taken a position in another city, and the innovations in the original city have ceased. The innovations, in short, were only associated with a particular incumbent and not with the general role of the mayor's or police chief's office.

Turnover in the role of the innovation's key personnel, therefore, represented another important organizational cycle; two, three, or more incumbents could sequentially replace each other in a given position. For routinization, the turnover issue is a complex one. There must be very little turnover at the outset, during the improvisation stage, but it was desirable to have some turnover in the later periods, during the disappearance stage. The later turnover was often associated with other important organizational changes. For instance, if there had been no turnover, it was less likely that all key procedures had been fully documented. Only when a new coordinator took over was an agency put to the real test of showing that it could keep the innovation operating without the assistance of the initial coordinator. What was therefore important in assessing turnover was not merely to record the number of turnovers, but also to note when such turnover occurred in relation to an innovation's life history (see table 6-1).

Turnover in the data processing coordinator's position was found in all police computer case studies. Moreover, the turnover was not disruptive; the core computer continued to increase in size or to add applications, and the computer system continued to achieve other important organizational passages. The new data processing coordinators were all persons who had previously served in more junior capacities, like assistant coordinator, in relation to the innovation. In one case (Nashville), the new coordinator had been a member of the vending company that had provided the computer equipment to the police department. Naturally, the turnover in all cases was marked by some transition problems and adjustments in personal relationships. However, the main accomplishment was that the innovation was no longer identified with the original incumbent alone. Moreover, the new coordinator often brought new ideas for expanding the use of the innovation. In short, the turnover showed that the innovation was now a part of the agency's practice independent of any single incumbent, and, furthermore, that a line of succession had been established for providing future coordinators.

Turnover did not occur as uniformly in the other innovations in the case studies. A new coordinator was appointed in the later phases of the Akron breath-testing innovation, but no such turnover occurred in either of the other breath-testing cases. In Cincinnati, however, the success of the innovation had gradually allowed the traffic commander, who was doubling as coordinator, to spend less time on the innovation. Similarly, new coordinators were appointed in the later period of two other innovations (Birmingham, MICU, and Dallas, CAI), but not in any of the other cases. In a few of those other cases (Oakland, CAI, and Omaha, Portland, and Rochester, CCTV), turnover among key personnel occurred early in the life history and appeared to have negatively affected the operation of the innovation.

Expansion to Full Range of Potential Users

A final characteristic of the disappearance stage was for an innovation to be adopted by the full range of potential users. This characteristic again strikes at the heart of routinization: If an innovation is only being used by some special subset of practitioners even though its functions are theoretically applicable to all practitioners, the innovation will continue to be regarded as special and not part of standard practice. "Standard practice," in short, implies practice by all.

Unfortunately, without a detailed analysis of specific organizational practices that would demand far more fieldwork than was possible, it was extremely difficult to determine whether an innovation had reached its full set of potential users. The propositions reflecting full use, if it could be measured, might be as follows:

1. For police computers, the computer system is used for a large number of applications; for each application, such as traffic citations, all practitioners involved in processing new entries or reports use the computer system and do not rely on any manual system that duplicates what the computer can do.
2. For breath testing, all tests for DWI are conducted with breath-testing equipment, with urinalysis or other older practices used as a supplement but only for specially defined situations.
3. For MICU, an MICU unit responds to all calls for fire and non-fire emergencies.
4. For Jet-Axe, the equipment is ued wherever barriers of a certain type (which, however, are extremely difficult to define) are encountered in firefighting.
5. For CAI, all teachers for a given subject, such as mathematics, integrate CAI into their classroom activities if CAI programs have been developed for that subject; more desirably, CAI programs are developed for numerous subjects, and all teachers for these subjects use CAI.
6. For CCTV, the conditions are the same as those just mentioned for CAI.

In lieu of assessing the extent to which any site had achieved these conditions, certain proxy or substitute indicators had to be developed. The general notion was to assess the size of the innovation at the time of the case study in relation to the size of the innovating agency or its clients. If an innovation involved an on-line police computer system, for instance, it was assumed that, regardless of the types of computer applications, some minimal number of on-line terminals would have to be present for the innovation to be regarded as having achieved full or near-full use.

The field observations for each case study led to specific impressions concerning the level of use of an innovation. Although these impressions were initially subjective ones, the case studies were then categorized according to whether widespread or partial use, or no use, had been observed. These observations are summarized in table 6-1, and represent the final judgments regarding the attainment of widespread use for the innovation in each case study. These subjective judgments were then made operational by observing that, if certain features of each innovation were selected, the following cut-off points appeared to characterize the fully utilized cases:

1. For police computers, the ratio of on-line terminals to police employees was one terminal for about every forty employees in the police department.
2. For breath testing, the number of trained breath-testing operators was about one trained operator for every hundred employees in the police department.
3. For MICUs, there was about one MICU vehicle for every hundred employees in the fire department.
4. For Jet-Axes, there was an average of about three Jet-Axes used per year by the fire department for the duration of the life of the innovation.
5. For CAI, the ratio of computer terminals for CAI use was one terminal for about every twenty-five hundred students in the school district.
6. For CCTV, the ratio of television receivers connected to the CCTV system was about one receiver for every three-hundred students in the school district.

Among the police computer case studies, two sites (Indianapolis and Nashville) had achieved full use, but two (Miami and Boston) had not. In Miami, on-line applications were just being implemented at the time of the case study in conjunction with the acquisition of a new computer system; in Boston, the computer system had been fully utilized at one point in its life history, but the Boston city government had taken over the major computational responsibilities several years ago, leaving the police department with two functions: a computational ability to perform message switching and therefore to act as a user of the city's system, and an emerging computerized-dispatching application that was being implemented at the time of the case study.

Similar contrasts were found for four of the five remaining types of innovations. The Denver MICU case never involved more than two vehicles under the control of the fire department; only six Jet-Axes had ever been detonated in total by the Omaha fire department over a five-year period; the Oakland and Tampa CAI systems had not expanded to more than about a dozen classrooms throughout the whole school district (Oakland had thirteen CAI terminals and Tampa had ten); and none of the three CCTV systems were currently being used as CCTV systems, although full utilization had been achieved at one time in Rochester and the Portland system was being fully used, but as an ITV, and not a CCTV, system. For the last innovation, breath-testing, all three sites were operating at a full level. In all, ten of the nineteen sites had attained widespread use at the time the case study observations were made (see table 6-1).

Table 6-1
Summary of Passages or Cycles During the Disappearance Stage

Type of Innovation/Site	Passage or Cycle 6. Changes in Organizational Governance		Passage or Cycle 7. Internal Training Program		Passage or Cycle 8. Promotion of Personnel Acquainted with Innovation		Passage or Cycle 9. Eventual (Late) Turnover in Key Personnel		Passage or Cycle 10. Attainment of Widespread Use	
	Yes	No	Yes	No	Yes	No	Yes	No	Yes	No
Police computer										
Miami	x			x	x		x			x
Indianapolis	x			x	x		x		x	
Nashville		x	x			x	x		x	
Boston		x	x		x		x			x
Breath-testing										
Cincinnati		x	x			x		x	x	
Akron		x		x		x	x		x	
Memphis		x		x		x		x	x	
Mobile intensive care units										
Dallas	x			x	x			x	x	
Birmingham	x			x		x	x		x	
Denver		x		x		x		x		x
Jet-Axe										
Rochester		x	x			x		x	x	
Omaha		x	x			x		x		x
Computer-assisted instruction										
Dallas	x			x	x		x		x	
Oakland		x		x		x		x		x
Tampa	x			x		x		x		x
San Diego	x		x		x			x	x	
Closed-circuit television										
Omaha		x		x		x		x		x
Portland		x		x		x		x		x

Summary

The disappearance stage was the final period in an innovation's life history. During this period, the remaining passages and cycles occurred that ultimately led to the full incorporation of an innovation. Innovative practice had become standard practice.

Five passages or cycles have been discussed: changes in organizational governance, internalization of training programs, promotion of personnel acquainted with the innovation, turnover of key personnel, and attainment of widespread use of the innovation. Most of the passages involved multiyear time lags between the initiation and completion of the passage; similarly, most of the cycles occurred less frequently than on an annual basis. Thus, it was considered appropriate that these passages and cycles were characteristic of the disappearance stage. If one compares table 5-1 with table 6-1, noting the degree to which the passages and cycles had been achieved by the nineteen case studies, the proportion successfully attaining any given passage or cycle for the expansion stage was generally higher than the proportion for the passages and cycles in the disappearance stage. To this extent, the observations from the case studies illustrate the distinction between the two stages.

A fully routinized innovation was, therefore, characterized by the attainment of all ten passages and cycles—five in the middle period and five in this last period. If all ten had been attained, the innovation was no longer likely to be considered an innovation, and its functions had been established as standard practice. In other words, an outsider analyzing the agency's operations would now regard such functions as an integral part of the agency's work.[1]

Note

1. This assertion can, of course, be easily tested by assessing the perceptions of new practitioners entering an agency or those of other persons acquainted with the agency; however, such testing was beyond the scope of the present inquiry. In general, it would be predicted that practitioner and administrator perceptions would acknowledge the practice as standard.

7 Explaining Routinization

Assessing the Degree of Routinization

What does it mean for a new service practice to become routinized? The preceding chapters have described nineteen life histories that have emphasized the occurrence of specific passages and cycles. These organizational events have been used to assess the degree of routinization, with the process appearing to progress through three stages—an improvisation stage, and expansion stage, and a disappearance stage. Table 7-1 shows these three stages and the total passages and cycles achieved in the nineteen life histories.

The more passages or cycles that a given innovation has achieved or survived, the more routinized the innovation has become. In other words, if one examines specific agency practices and distinguishes subjectively according to the degree to which each practice appears to be part of an agency's everyday, or routine, business, the subjective impression appears to be confirmed by accounting for the number of passages or cycles achieved in relation to each practice. Under the specific conditions governing any given agency and innovation, some passages and cycles may be more important than others. However, for the aggregate analytic purposes of the present study, each of the ten passages or cycles has been assumed to carry an equal weight in defining the degree of routinization of an innovation.

This framwork for assessing routinization is essentially a structural one, reflecting the organizational status of a particular innovation or practice. The passages and cycles are specific organizational activities that are observable and that define the organizational status of a practice. Such activities have been largely ignored in previous research, and thus the main focus of the present study has been to define—perhaps for the first time—such explicit and discrete organizational events. At the same time, no attempt has been made to develop corroboratory perceptual or attitudinal evidence. Yet, in the final analysis, a routinized practice is one that has achieved a certain organizational status as well as one that is perceived as "standard" or "normal." The accumulation of relevant perceptual evidence may be seen as a task for further research.

Routinization Scores and Ratings

Given this structural approach, the degree of routinization of the nineteen innovations was summarized in terms of a routinization score and rating, based

139

Table 7-1

Summary of Passages and Cycles in an Innovation's Life History

Passage or Cycle Number	Life History Stage	Number of Case Studies Achieving Each Passage or Cycle
	Improvisation Stage	
	(no necessary passages or cycles)	
	Expansion Stage	
1	Equipment turnover	13
2	Transition to support by local funds	18
3	Establishment of appropriate organizational status	14
4	Establishment of stable arrangement for supply and maintenance	15
5	Establishment of personnel classifications or certification	12
	Disappearance Stage	
6	Changes in organizational governance	7
7	Internalization of training program	6
8	Promotion of personnel acquainted with the innovation	6
9	Turnover in key personnel	7
10	Attainment of widespread use	10

on the number of passages and cycles achieved by each innovation. This score was simply a summary tabulation of the passages or cycles achieved by each innovation, as presented in tables 5-1 and 6-1 of the previous two chapters. The final tabulation is shown in table 7-2. The ratings were created by assigning the innovations to three groups, based simply on a one-third division among the scores: 7 to 10 passages or cycles (highly routinized); 4 to 6 passages or cycles (moderately routinized); and 0 to 3 passages or cycles (marginally routinized).

The summary scores indicated that many of the nineteen innovations (all four police computer systems; Birmingham MICU; Cincinnati breath testing; and Dallas and San Diego CAI) had already achieved a rating of highly routinized. At the same time, several other innovations (the Denver MICU; Oakland CAI; and two of the three CCTV innovations) had only begun to be routinized and were rated as marginally routinized. The remaining innovations all fell in the middle range and were rated as moderately routinized. This distribution of the scores, it should be remembered, was in part a result of the procedure used for selecting the nineteen case studies, because the selection process had deliberately screened for a stratified sample according to the age and use of various innovations; see chapter 1.

Table 7-2
Ratings and Routinization Scores for Nineteen Innovations (Case Studies)

Case Study	Type of Innovation	Rating/Routinization Score
		Highly routinized
Indianapolis	Police computer	10
Birmingham	MICU	9
Dallas	CAI	9
San Diego	CAI	9
Nashville	Police computer	8
Miami	Police computer	7
Boston	Police computer	7
Cincinnati	Breath testing	7
		Moderately routinized
Akron	Breath testing	6
Dallas	MICU	6
Rochester	Jet-Axe	6
Omaha	Jet-Axe	6
Tampa	CAI	5
Memphis	Breath testing	4
Portland	CCTV	4
		Marginally routinized
Oakland	CAI	2
Omaha	CCTV	2
Rochester	CCTV	2
Denver	MICU	0

A similar procedure was applied to the ninety innovations covered by the telephone interviews. The telephone questionnaire included the same ten passages or cycles, but the responses to three could not be used because of ambiguous or inaccurate wording in several questions.[1] For instance, although a detailed question was included concerning turnover in key personnel (passage or cycle No. 9), the specific dates of such turnover were not identified, and it was impossible to say when the turnover had occurred in the life history of the innovation. For this particular cycle, the time of occurrence is extremely important to routinization—that is, turnover that occurs too early in the life history may have negative effects. For the seven remaining passages or cycles, however, the ninety innovations were similarly ranked according to the total number of passages or cycles that had been achieved.

There were variations in the application of the passages and cycles to each type of innovation due to the fact that different questionnaires had to be used for each innovation. For MICU and CCTV, all seven remaining passages or cycles were used in constructing the routinization score. For police computers and CAI, the maintenance and supply measure (No. 4) was not precise enough to distinguish initial versus longer-standing arrangements; thus, these two innovations had routinization scores based on six passages and cycles. The equipment turnover—that is, dates of new purchases (number one)—and maintenance and supply (number four) questions were not included in the Jet-Axe interviews, and the personnel classification (number five) and operating funds (number two) questions were inadvertently omitted from the breath-testing interviews. As a result, the routinization scores for these two innovations were based on five passages and cycles. Despite these differences, however, the scores for the six innovations were all weighted to a 7-point scale for purposes of comparison. These scores, ranging from zero to 7, were then used as the basis for dividing the innovations into the three rating categories—highly routinized (5, 6, or 7), moderately routinized (3 or 4), and marginally routinized (zero, 1, or 2). Table 7-3 shows the numbers of innovations in each of these three groups, by type of innovation.

The data indicate that about 34.4 percent of the telephone cases fell into the highly routinized category, 45.6 percent into the moderately routinized category, and 20.0 percent into the marginally routinized category. Among the types of innovations, the breath-testing and Jet-Axe cases tended to be more routinized, and the police computer and CAI cases tended to be less routinized. In contrast to the case studies, it should be remembered that these telephone interview results were based on a random sample of innovations. Thus, the distribution of routinization outcomes may be considered representative of the universe of innovations adopted, as defined in chapter 1.

Routinization and the Age of an Innovation

The first question that followed the assembling of these routinization scores and ratings was whether there was a simple relationship between

Table 7-3
Routinization Ratings for Ninety Innovations (Telephone Interviews)

| Type of Innovation | Rating | | |
	Highly Routinized	Moderately Routinized	Marginally Routinized
Police computer	3	7	3
Mobile intensive care units	4	8	4
Computer-assisted instruction	5	5	6
Closed-circuit television	5	6	3
Jet-Axe	6	8	1
Breath testing	8	7	1
Total	31	41	18

routinization and the chronological age of an innovation. The older innovations might have been the more routinized ones, and this alone might have accounted for the pattern of scores.

In order to examine this proposition, the data from the case studies and telephone interviews were both arrayed along two dimensions: the median age of all the innovations versus the degree of routinization.[2] Table 7-4 shows that the hypothesized relationship did not exist. For the case studies, the age of innovation made no difference in predicting the degree of routinization; for the telephone interviews, there was even a slight tendency in the opposite direction; the younger innovations tended to be more routinized. In sum, the degree of routinization was not related to the chronological age of the innovation.

Routinization and Different Types of Innovations

Relationship to Six Types of Innovations

A preliminary examination of these scores and ratings from both the case studies and the telephone interviews revealed that there were no systematic variations among routinization outcomes when the six different types of innovations—police computer, MICU, CAI, CCTV, Jet-Axe, and breath testing—were compared with each other. This is an important observation, because a potential conceptual limitation of the passages and cycles framework was the degree to which certain passages or cycles might have been irrelevant for some types of innovations. If certain passages or cycles were irrelevant to the use of Jet-Axe, for instance, the Jet-Axe scores would have been artificially lower than those of the other innovations. An item analysis for each of the ten passages or cycles,

Table 7-4
Age of Innovation by Degree of Routinization

Source of Evidence	Degree of Routinization		
	High	Moderate	Marginal
Case Studies ($n = 19$)			
Above median age[a]	4	3	2
Below median age	4	4	2
Telephone Interviews ($n = 82$)[b]			
Above median age[a]	13	20	12
Below median age	15	17	5

[a]Median defined independently for each type of innovation.

[b]No information on age for eight cases.

however, showed no such irrelevancies, with one exception—rules of organizational governance may not be expected to change as a result of the use of the Jet-Axe, and indeed, this passage was not achieved by the two Jet-Axe case studies. However, even if the routinization scores for these two case studies were to be adjusted for this irrelevant passage (see table 7-2), the overall rating of the innovations would not be different.[3]

Another potential example of this problem might be incorrectly inferred from the case-study data in table 7-2 where, for instance, there was a tendency for the police computer cases to be among the highly routinized and the CCTV cases to be among the marginally routinized innovations. Such a result could have reflected some inherent bias in applying the passages and cycles framework to these two types of innovations, independent of the actual degree of routinization that had occurred in each case. However, this pattern tended to be reversed in the telephone interview data shown in table 7-3, so that there is little support for the original inference. Moreover, the overall association between the type of innovation and degree of routinization in the telephone interviews was weak and not statistically significant. It therefore seems that the passages and cycles framework did not create any artificial and undesirable discrimination among different types of innovations. Nevertheless, a distinction should be made between the conceptual biases (which, it is argued, are few) and the measurement problems (which, as indicated by the difficulties in defining some of the passages and cycles in the telephone interviews, need to be overcome in a more effective manner in future studies).

Where the types of innovations did make a difference was in explaining how routinization occurred. Thus, although there was no distinctive variation in routinization outcomes according to the six types of innovation, the degree of routinization appeared to have been achieved for each type for slightly different reasons. These differences were suggested in the previous three chapters. However, the major generalizations seem to be related to the three groups of innovations described in chapter 2:

1. Task-specific innovations
2. Task-diverse (service-only) innovations
3. Task-diverse (service and administrative) innovations

(It should be recalled that the Jet-Axe and breath-testing innovations were intended to represent the first group; the MICU and CCTV innovations, the second; and the CAI and police computer innovations, the third.)

Task-Specific Innovations

What is important about the three groups is that different factors were predicted to be important for each group. Thus, the three groups were not by themselves predicted to be differentially associated with routinization. Rather, within each group, a full range of routinization scores and ratings was possible. The main predictions were that different organizational conditions would be important in accounting for the degree of routinization within each group. For the task-specific innovations, the general conditions were hypothesized in chapter 2 to include: widespread practitioner acceptance, visible service payoffs, and minimal retraining needed for practitioners. The findings are consistent with these initial hypotheses.

Widespread Practitioner Acceptance. First, a major limitation of task-specific innovations was that they could not, by definition, be used for a variety of applications to promote widespread practitioner acceptance. In fact, the Jet-Axe and breath-testing innovations were each used to perform only a single major task—blasting through an especially difficult wall or barrier in one case, and testing DWI arrestees in the other. Because of this limitation, it was important that, for routinization to proceed, such tasks were performed as frequently as possible in an agency's daily work activities. Thus, the innovation's inherent limitations in performing a diverse array of applications was compensated by a repetitive number of occasions upon which the single relevant application was performed. Many of the limitations of the Jet-Axe appeared to stem from the fact that the innovation could not be used for a diverse set of applications, but the single application for which it is relevant also did not occur very frequently in fire-fighting activities. Under such conditions, it was difficult to establish widespread practitioner acceptance simply because few practitioners had opportunities to use the innovation. Breath-testing innovations, in contrast, were also limited to a single application, but DWI arrests occurred frequently in a police department's everyday activities.

Visible Service Payoffs. Second, the experiences with the two task-specific innovations showed that the important characteristic of service payoffs was that they be "visible" from the practitioner's viewpoint. The payoffs did not have to be reflected in the measures commonly used by evaluation researchers. For instance, cost-savings may be a significant payoff identified by an external evaluator, but such savings are not necessarily the relevant measures for practitioners. (Among other things, cost-savings by a public agency may not be visible to the individual practitioner.) What was more important was that, in the eyes of practitioners, the innovation produced a concrete improvement in performing a specific task—whether by improving performance or by reducing the time, physical effort, inconvenience, or even distastefulness involved in performing the task. Thus, the adoption and implementation of a task-specific innovation is actually the collective result of individual decisions made by individual practitioners; each practitioner may even be regarded as a separate adopter, whose actions can undermine or facilitate an agency's initial decision to adopt an innovation.

Retraining for Practitioners. The case study results did not strongly support the hypothesis that, for task-specific innovations, routinization would more likely occur if the needs for practitioner training were minimal. The breath testing innovation, for instance, involved considerable training, certification, retraining, and recertification requirements; furthermore, individual practitioners also became senior operators—that is, persons certified to teach others to become breath testing operators. A task-specific innovation could, in short, involve complex and extended retraining. Practitioners enthusiastically undertook such retraining where the perceived payoffs were sufficient and where ample time and opportunity were set aside for the retraining experience.

Task-Diverse Innovations

The two remaining groups of innovations were clustered together because of the finding that competition for an innovation's resources by different applications did not appear to play an important role in the routinization process. It had been hypothesized that, for task-diverse (service and administrative) innovations, strong competition between the service and administrative applications would reduce the tendency toward routinization. This group of innovations was therefore to be distinguished from task-diverse (service-only) innovations. However, the case study evidence indicated that competition could also occur among the service applications, even where no administrative applications existed. Such competition did not differ from that between service and administrative applications. Similarly, analysis of the telephone interviews also indicated no differences on this point. For this reason, the two groups of task-diverse innovations did not appear to be as different as originally postulated, and they are treated as a single group in all subsequent discussions.[4]

For the task-diverse innovations, the general conditions that appear to influence the routinization process were hypothesized in chapter 2 to include: support from agency administrators, a large number of service applications, support from a core group of practitioners, an active innovator to promote applications, and ample opportunities for practitioner training. In general, these conditions overlap with the ten hypotheses suggested as important for all types of innovations, and these conditions are therefore covered in the next subsection. However, several conclusions that appear to be specific to task-diverse innovations can be made at this point.

Role of the Coordinator. First, although all types of innovations may benefit from a strong and capable coordinator, the role was more important for task-diverse than for task-specific innovations. This is because the former, by definition, involved a variety of potential applications, and hence a variety of organizational actors and procedures that needed to be coordinated. Thus, whereas the need to coordinate a task-specific innovation such as the Jet-Axe could be accommodated within the everyday duties of the chief of a fire department, and breath testing innovations could be coordinated by an officer such as the commander of the traffic division who also had many other duties, task-diverse innovations such as CCTV or CAI all required a senior official whose full-time duties were the coordination of the particular innovation. The coordinator did not have to be the same person as the innovator, who had initially garnered the support needed to adopt and implement the innovation; the coordinator, however, was likely to fill a new role within the organization. This meant that the successful passage related to new personnel classifications was more important for task-diverse rather than task-specific innovations.

Practitioner Support. Second, because the task-diverse innovations involved a number of applications, and because a different group of practitioners was likely to be connected with each application, the task-diverse innovation could ultimately derive support from a variety of practitioner groups. Such support occurred if the practitioners were pleased by their experiences with the innovation, and if new job assignments and professional development opportunities were increased. (Note that these payoffs were still not those generally used by external evaluators.) Thus, the task-diverse innovations had a potentially different base of support from that of task-specific innovations. For instance, CAI systems derived support from mathematics teachers, science teachers, or other school staff, depending upon which applications were attempted in any given school district. What was important was the intensity of support from the relevant subgroup rather than, as in the case of task-specific innovation, widespread support throughout the agency.

Increase in Applications. Third, task-diverse innovations had a greater possibility for diversification and growth than task-specific innovations. This meant that purchases of new generations of equipment had to be planned carefully to anticipate increased needs. At the same time, premature purchases had to be avoided, and new generations of equipment could not be added so fast that agency personnel had little chance to get accustomed to the new equipment. In general, the addition of new applications had to be continually balanced against the acquisition of new equipment, and this activity required a continued attention and skill that was not needed for task-specific innovations.

Summary

The results showed that no simple relationships existed between the six types of innovation and the degree of routinization. The type of innovation did make a difference, however, in explaining how routinization took place, and here the key distinction was between task-specific and task-diverse innovations. The task-specific innovations were much more heavily dependent upon a high frequency of use, visible payoffs to individual practitioners (which were not necessarily the same types of payoffs identified by managers or evaluation research teams), and somewhat independent adoption decisions by individual practitioners. The task-diverse innovations, in contrast, relied more heavily on the role of a full-time coordinator, needed to draw intensive practitioner support but from smaller groups of practitioners, and needed to be carefully managed in relation to the acquisition of new equipment. The research implications of these two different experiences with task-specific and task-diverse innovations will be described in chapter 8.

Factors Associated with Routinization

The earlier description of the passages and cycles framework included ten factors that were hypothesized to facilitate routinization (see chapter 3). Briefly, the ten factors were that an innovation covered or had:

1. Core application in an agency's activities
2. Minimal competition for resources among different applications
3. Service payoffs
4. Prior need, either from crisis conditions or chronic service deficiencies
5. Client support (support from residents who directly benefited from the innovation's output)
6. Community support (support from residents in the community as a whole)
7. Top administrative support within the agency
8. Practitioner support within the agency
9. Active innovator support
10. No adversary group that specifically opposed the innovation

All ten of these factors were examined as part of each of the nineteen case studies. In addition, questions concerning most of the ten were included in the telephone interviews. Throughout, the analysis consisted of simple associations between each factor and the degree of routinization. Because of the crude measures used (most were nominal or ordinal scales), no attempt was made to conduct any multivariate analysis, which generally requires ordinal and integral scales.[5] The findings should therefore be considered as forming the basis for further testing when better measures have been developed.

Case Study Results

Review of Individual Hypotheses

The results may first be discussed for the case studies. To facilitate the discussion, table 7-5 summarizes the presence or absence of each factor for the nineteen case studies. For two of the factors, minimal competition and active innovator, there was not much variation among the case studies, with most having both conditions present (sixteen out of nineteen case studies for the former, and seventeen out of nineteen for the latter). Thus, nothing conclusive can be drawn about these two factors in distinguishing among the three degrees of routinization, but it may be that both factors must be present in all cases to facilitate any type of routinization.

Three other factors had sufficient variation but no apparent relationship to the degree of routinization. These included the presence of service payoffs and client support, and the absence of an adversary group. Of these factors, it should be pointed out that in only one case study (Cincinnati, breath testing) was there a formal evaluation effort to define the service payoff. In all the other cases that had a payoff, the presence of the factor was based on informal reports to the case study team of the perceived savings or gains that had been made.

Of the remaining factors, two had a weak relationship to the degree of routinization: prior need and community support. The prior need factor could have been based on either a crisis or emergency situation (such as Birmingham's fatalities that led to increased demand for an MICU system) or a chronic and gradually eroding situation (such as the rising crime rate in Indianapolis that increased the need for a computer-based reporting system, or the slowly rising rate of traffic accidents in Akron that led to increased concern with drunken driving). However defined, the prior need factor was only important because it was notably absent among the marginally routinized cases; it was not a frequently present factor in the highly routinized cases. The community support factor appeared only weakly related to routinization because of the small number of case studies for which this factor was relevant. Residents in general, it should be recalled, were not found to be aware of such innovations as police computers, CAI, or even breath testing. Given a low level of awareness of an innovation, little support from a community can be expected.

Finally, three factors appeared to have a substantial relationship to the degree of routinization. These were the use of the innovation for a core application, the presence of top administrative support, and the presence of practitioner support. For the core application factor, the case studies are almost arrayed precisely, with the exception of the Boston police computer and Memphis (breath-testing) cases. In Boston, the computer system was not regarded as hav-

Table 7-5
Presence of Ten Factors Hypothesized to Facilitate Routinization (Case Studies)

Degree of Routinization/Site[a]	Type of Innovation	Ten Factors Hypothesized to Facilitate Routinization				Strong Support for Innovation by:					
		Core Application	Marginal Competition	Payoffs[b]	Prior Need	Clients	Community	Administrators	Practitioners	Active Innovator	No Adversary Group
High											
Indianapolis (10)[c]	PC	+	+	+	+		+	+	+		+
Birmingham (9)	MICU	+	+	+	+		+	+	+	+	
Dallas (9)	CAI	+				+		+	+	+	+
San Diego (9)	CAI	+		+		+		+	+	+	+
Nashville (8)	PC	+	+	+			+		+	+	
Miami (7)	PC	+	+		+	+	+			+	+
Boston (7)	PC		+	+				+		+	
Cincinnati (7)	BT	+	+	+	+			+	+	+	+
Moderate											
Akron (6)	BT	+	+	+	+	+		+	+	+	+
Dallas (6)	MICU	+	+	+	+	+			+	+	
Rochester (6)	J-A		+	+			+			+	+
Omaha (5)	J-A		+	+	+			+		+	+
Tampa (5)	CAI							+			+
Memphis (4)	BT	+	+	+		+			+	+	+
Portland (4)	CCTV		+							+	+
Marginal											
Oakland (2)	CAI		+							+	
Omaha (2)	CCTV		+			+					
Rochester (2)	CCTV		+				+	+			+
Denver (0)	MICU		+	+						+	

[a]The routinization score for each site is shown in parentheses.

[b]"Perceived" payoffs, not the result of any evaluation (see text).

[c]

ing involved core applications because most of the computer applications did not affect the everyday operation of the agency; in Memphis, a core application had evolved, but the situation was only marginally routinized, perhaps because the breath testing operation was not formally a part of either the police department or the sheriff's department, but was shared by the two.

For the administrative support factor, the case study results were also in the predicted direction, but with three exceptions: Nashville (police computer), Dallas (MICU), and Rochester (CCTV). In both Nashville and Dallas, agency officials were not enthusiastic about the innovation at first. However, there was considerable support for the innovation by officials in the executive or legislative branches outside the agency, and officials within the agency eventually accommodated it. In the Rochester case, the CCTV system received extremely strong support, although the system only became marginally routinized.

For the practitioner support factor, there were also three case studies that were exceptions to the predicted relationship: Miami and Boston (police computer), and Memphis (breath testing). In Miami and Boston, neither site developed extensive on-line use of the computer system at the time of the case study; hence, few practitioners had opportunities to use the system. However, in both cases there were reasons to believe that this situation would change, because both sites were installing newer computer systems. The Memphis exception reflected the same condition previously described—the innovation appeared to have had many factors facilitating routinization but such an outcome was perhaps delayed by the hybrid organizational status of the breath testing unit.

Summary Interpretation

The relationships of these individual factors to the routinization outcomes supported the conclusion that, for routinization to occur, every innovation needed some person(s) in the agency to serve as an active innovator. The importance of the innovator was reflected by the fact that the majority of the case studies (seventeen out of nineteen) had a person(s) who brought information about the innovation into an agency, developed internal support, and helped to promote the conditions necessary for the agency's initial use of the innovation. The innovator was not necessarily the adopter (who made the decision to try the innovation); or the coordinator (who ultimately guided the actual use of the innovation); or a single individual (several people often shared the role). The innovator or innovative team was, nevertheless, the initial point of entry into an agency for initiating a new practice.

Given an active innovator, an innovation was more likely to become routinized if it involved a core application and had the support of other persons within the agency such as the top administrators and some practitioner group. Some external conditions, such as the prior need for the innovation or community support for it, only weakly affected routinization; other external conditions, such as client support, did not appear to affect routinization. The general pattern of results, therefore, supported the overall interpretation that, as long as an innovation covered a core application, the main factors facilitating or retarding routinization were internal and not external to the agency. Innovations appeared not to become routinized without acceptance by practitioners and support from top administrators.[6]

The potential importance of the core application attribute should not be overlooked. An innovation covered a core application if it displaced some existing function, such as substitution of computer for manual operations, or if it was a new function that publicly redefined the basic mission of an agency, such as expansion to firefighting services supplemented by emergency rescue. If a policymaker is interested in encouraging innovation, the first task should thus be to focus on those innovations that involve core applications. Many innovations, such as CCTV, may only *potentially* involve core applications and must therefore be explicitly designed at any given site to cover such applications. This might be done by integrating the use of CCTV with the mandated curriculum, such as the regular English classes that cover reading, spelling, or grammar. If explicit attempts are not made, the innovation may only involve elective courses—or worse yet, no formal courses at all—and is less likely to become routinized.

Telephone Interview Results

The telephone interviews also included questions covering six of these ten factors.[7] This allowed a further checking of the preceding findings but through the use of the ninety telephone sites rather than the nineteen case studies.

The analysis involved the coding of the six factors as present or absent for the innovation at each site, based on the relevant questions in the telephone interview. The results were then arrayed in a 2 X 3 matrix for each factor (presence or absence of the factor versus the three degrees of routinization as previously defined in table 7-3). The arrays or contingency tables were subjected to associational analysis, with gamma scores (which can range from —1.00 to 1.00) used to measure the strength of the relationship between the factor and routinization.[8] These gamma scores are shown in table 7-6.

The pattern of scores indicated general agreement with the case study findings. Basically, those findings had shown that three factors—the use of the innovation as a core application, top administrative support, and practitioner support—were most closely associated with increased routinization. The telephone interview results in table 7-6 were similar to the case study findings because two of these same factors had the strongest relationship to routinization, even though one of the statistical differences was only significant at the

Table 7-6
Relationship Between Ten Factors and Degree of Routinization
(Telephone Interviews)

| | Association between Factor and Routinization Rating | | |
Factor	Gamma Score[a]	Degrees of Freedom	X^{2a}
Core application	.59	2	5.30[b]
Minimal competition	−.37	2	4.21
Service payoffs	−.15	4	2.85
Prior need	n.a.	−	−
Client support	n.a.	−	−
Community support	.11	10	8.97
Administrative support	n.a.	−	−
Practitioner support	.58	2	7.16[c]
Active innovator	n.a.	−	−
No adversary group	.20	2	1.66

[a]The gamma score indicates the strength and direction of the relationship between two variables, with the possible scores ranging from 1.00 (perfect positive association) to −1.00 (perfect negative association). The X^2 is used to give the reader some idea of the level of statistical significance of the gamma score, even though the collection of telephone interviews was not a random sample. The X^2 levels should therefore only be used as a guideline for interpreting the data.

[b]$p < 0.10$

[c]$p < 0.05$

n.a. = no available data (see text for explanation)

$p < 0.10$ level, while the third factor was one of those that had no applicable data. In short, the data from the ninety sites also showed that the core application and practitioner support factors were related—albeit weakly—to increased routinization, and that none of the other factors appeared to have made much of a difference.[9]

Routinization and External Support

The main conclusion from the case studies and the telephone interviews has been that routinization was largely affected by internal rather than external factors. This general theme was reinforced by an examination of two other external factors that policymakers have typically hoped would facilitate the use of innovations: external financial and technical assistance.

Among the case studies, external financial assistance was defined in three ways. The first covered the use of federal or state, but not local, funds where such funds were the main support in initiating the innovation; the second, funds for discrete projects preceding adoption; and the third, funds for discrete projects after adoption. The distribution of the case studies according to these three definitions was shown in chapter 4 (see table 4-7), and these same data are repeated in table 7-7 but with the case studies now arrayed according to their degree of routinization. The data show that there was little relationship between the use of external funds, for whichever of the three definitions, and the degree of routinization. A similar analysis was conducted for technical assistance, with no relationship formed between the presence of such assistance and routinization. This is not to say that either funding or technical assistance was unimportant in individual cases, but just that it made no difference in the pattern of scores for the entire group of cases.

Table 7-7
Relationship Between Presence of External Funds and Routinization Outcomes

		Use of External (State or Federal) Funds		
Degree of Routinization/Site[a]	Type of Innovation	External Funds Used as Main Source of Initial Funds	External Funds for Specific Projects before Adoption	External Funds for Specific Projects after Adoption
High				
Indianapolis (10)	PC			
Birmingham (9)	MICU	+		
Dallas (9)	CAI	+		+
San Diego (9)	CAI		+	+
Nashville (8)	PC	+		
Miami (7)	PC			+
Boston (7)	PC			+
Cincinnati (7)	BT	+	+	+
Moderate				
Akron (6)	BT			+
Dallas (6)	MICU	+		+
Rochester (6)	J-A			
Omaha (5)	J-A			
Tampa (5)	CAI			
Memphis (4)	BT	+		+
Portland (4)	CCTV	+		
Marginal				
Oakland	CAI			+
Omaha	CCTV	+	+	+
Rochester (2)	CCTV	+		+
Denver (0)	MICU	+		

[a]The routinization score for each site is shown in parentheses.

Among the telephone interviews, there were also questions covering external financial support and external technical assistance. The gamma scores indicating the association between these factors and the routinization outcomes are shown in table 7-8. The results show that there was no statistically significant relationship between either of these external factors and routinization. The use of external funds was defined in terms of the presence of funds at any time in the innovation's life history; technical assistance was defined in two ways—initial and continuing technical assistance.

The findings from both the case studies and the telephone interviews indicated that external assistance—whether in the form of financial or technical assistance—was unrelated to the degree of routinization. This finding was congruent with the conclusions regarding the importance of internal factors from the previous discussion covering the ten hypotheses.

One possible explanation for why the external factors may not be a significant correlate of routinization comes from the case studies. In the case studies, it was observed that some external assistance resulted from requests, proposals, or other initiatives taken by local officials; on some occasions, as in the Birmingham (MICU) case, the officials even actively and continually sought such support, although an initial grant request had been turned down. Other external assistance (financial and technical), however, resulted from initiatives made by a person outside the agency. Such an outsider could have been a federal official, a state or county official, or a member of a private vendor, such as a computer firm. Whether external assistance followed from local or external initiatives might have had strongly contrasting effects on routinization. Yet, it was very

Table 7-8
Relationship Between External Factors and Degree of Routinization (Telephone Interviews)

Factor	Association between Factor and Routinization Rating		
	Gamma Score[a]	Degrees of Freedom	X^{2} [a]
Presence of external funds at any time in the innovation's life history	−.05	2	1.67
Presence of external technical assistance to initiate the innovation only	−.22	2	1.20
Presence of external technical assistance on a continuing basis	−.05	2	0.07

[a]See table 7-6 for definition. None of the X^{2} scores is statistically significant.

difficult to establish the actual facts regarding who had initiated what. The data-collection measures merely noted the presence or absence of external assistance but did not distinguish among the initiating agents, which may therefore account for the failure to find any relationship.

Routinization: What It All Means

The Meaning and Incidence of Routinization

Organizational change ultimately involves the process by which new practices become standard business in a local agency. Whether the process is called routinization, institutionalization, incorporation, or some other term, it is central to all organizations, not just local agencies. Moreover, any attempt to deal seriously with organizational change must be concerned with this long-term perspective. In the past, too much attention has been paid to the initial phases of adoption and implementation in the change process, often to the detriment of an organization, which may have suffered many short-term disruptions but gained no long-term benefits. It has also been argued that the routinization of new practices has become a particular concern of local agencies because of the changing urban conditions in this country. Many traditional agency practices in education, public safety, and other neighborhood services have been made obsolete, and both local and federal officials have pressed for change. But in dealing with local agencies and their political and social environment, it is doubly important to be concerned with long- and not just short-term effects.

The main contribution of this study has been to describe, in operational terms, the routinization process. Because this has not been done before, the study has necessarily relied more on observations from a set of nineteen case studies, but corroborating evidence has also been presented from a set of ninety telephone interviews with local officials. The case-study observations allowed for a more flexible probing of local conditions, even though each case study followed the same basic outline, which was necessary for later aggregation. The operational terms in which routinization has been described are based on ten passages and cycles—the key events in the life history of a specific, innovative practice.

The point at which a practice becomes "routinized" cannot be defined in any absolute sense. In fact, any organizational practice, no matter how long-standing, is always susceptible to replacement by some innovative procedure. This is both the dynamic and frustrating nature of organizational life. Rather than search for an absolute definition, this study's approach has been to distinguish among three relative degrees of routinization—innovations that have become highly, moderately, and only marginally routinized. The innovations that were defined as highly routinized were those that developed local budgetary support, formed appropriate personnel classifications and organizational identities to sustain the innovation, established supply and maintenance procedures, and coped with the inevitable process of equipment replacement and upgrading as innovative practices expanded. Such innovations also accomplished other passages and cycles not generally achieved by the moderately or marginally routinized innovations. For instance, regular training programs to teach practitioners to use the innovation were established; personnel who supported the innovation were promoted into the higher ranks of the organization; rules of organizational governance were frequently changed to accord the innovation an integral role in the agency's mission; and there was even turnover among the key personnel operating the innovation, indicating that the new practice had not been dependent on a specific set of individuals. These were the conditions—that is, passages and cycles —that characterized routinization.

In addition to the creation of the passages and cycles framework, another key to the study has been the identification of a specific set of innovations, and the tracing of the life histories of these innovations in individual agencies. The life histories have been divided into three periods of time: the improvisation stage, during which the innovation becomes operational and new practices are actually established in the local agency; the expansion stage, during which the first set of key passages and cycles occur; and the disappearance stage, during which the innovative practice remains but becomes so much a part of normal practice that it is no longer regarded as an innovation. The life histories in our sample of case studies often extended over a period of ten to fifteen years to cover all three stages. For this reason, a deliberate choice made in the study design was to identify and select a sample of "old" innovations, and then to trace life histories in a post hoc or historical manner. Although organizational memories may be difficult to tap, this procedure avoided the even greater uncertainties that follow from tracing "new" innovations forward in time.

On balance, it was found that a large percentage of the innovations had attained the status of being "highly routinized." Eight out of nineteen case studies (42.1 percent) and thirty-one out of ninety telephone sites (34.4 percent) fell into this category; conversely, 21.1 percent of the case studies and only 20.0 percent of the telephone sites fell into the opposite category of "marginal" routinization. These results are notable in two respects. First, they indicate that many innovations in these two samples (the case-studies sample was stratified deliberately to create variation in routinization outcomes, and the telephone interview sample was random) have lasted and become a virtual part of standard practice. Such encouraging results mean that local agencies can innovate and may not be the bastions of "resistance to change" that they have been typically construed to be.

Second, the percentage of highly routinized innovations is much higher than that found in a recent study of federal innovations in education (Berman and McLaughlin, 1977 and 1978). That study found that none of the innovations had lasted longer than the period of initial federal funding, thereby leaving a much more pessimistic view of innovation. The apparent discrepancy in findings may have two rather simple explanations. First, the present study has focused on technological innovations, whose hardware components were easier to trace than the organizational innovations that marked the Berman and McLaughlin study. The choice of technological innovations, as described in chapter 2, was deliberately made to facilitate the life-history approach.[10] Second, this study has also sampled from innovations that had not necessarily been initially supported by federal funds. In fact, about half of the innovations in the case studies were locally initiated and supported. From the local perspective, then, many innovations can be and have been adopted, implemented, and routinized. These simply may not be the innovations included on the agendas of federal agencies.

The Conditions that Lead to Routinization

The major conditions that lead an innovation to become routinized all appear to be internal to the specific local agency. This is not necessarily an unexpected outcome, but it does suggest that external initiatives, as in a federally initiated agenda, are either limited or will have to be designed with a greater degree of sophistication.

The specific internal conditions involve the role of an innovator or innovator-team, who must develop agency support for the innovation and establish the appropriate skills and resources for initially operating it. Among the other important initial conditions, some group of agency practitioners must be trained to use the innovation and to begin using it as frequently as possible, preferably in relation to regular agency practices rather than as a special project.

Routinization is now likely to proceed further if the innovation becomes part of a core agency practice. One way of defining a core practice is that the innovation displaces an old practice. Under this definition, the new practice can be routinized more effectively if the capability for carrying out the old practice is systematically removed after the new practice has been installed. This dual tactic is often forgotten by those supporting an innovation; they rightly focus on installing new practices, but negligently fail to attend to the policies needed to terminate the old practices. Another way a core practice is established is that the innovation expands the agency's original array of services. Under this definition, the new practice can be routinized more effectively if the expanded array is formally recognized in a revised version of the agency's mandate. Thus, those supporting the innovation must work for changes in an agency's rules of governance as reflected in a city ordinance, a bond issue's definition of the standard practices that may be financed, or even in a perceptual shift reflected in a new agency name or defense in municipal budgetary reviews.

Throughout its early life history, an innovation must continually gain increased support from agency practitioners. This support will result in part if the innovation covers a core practice. However, the innovation must also operate effectively. Here it may be important to distinguish between task-specific and task-diverse innovations. For the former, an effective operation must usually be proven in terms of the individual practitioner's own use of the innovation. Furthermore, some of the criteria by which the practitioner judges an innovation—such as convenience, reduced physical effort, additional sense of safety on the job, or elimination of distasteful tasks—are different from those typically held by external evaluators. Thus, for task-specific innovations, external evaluators will not always predict correctly whether there are service payoffs. For task-diverse innovations, the role of the coordinator becomes critical; one of the major objectives of the coordinator is to identify specific applications and practitioner groups to which the innovation can be directed. Practitioner support may thus come from any number of subgroups in an agency but is still not likely to be based on the programmatic criteria—that is, response time, lives saved, changes in student achievement—typically used by external evaluators. The findings showed that these types of service payoffs and any external evaluations played a negligible role in routinization. One possibility is that the task-diverse innovations draw practitioner support to the extent that the innovation provides an expanded employment base, such as more jobs or job assignments. Naturally, the new work must be compatible with the practitioner's professional status and aspirations. The main point is that there may be bureaucratic rather than service efficiency incentives at work, and little is known about the bureaucratic incentive system.

Finally, an important internal condition is the specific support of top agency administrators. These administrators are usually an essential part of the key decisions about an innovation—for instance, to adopt and undertake it, to make staff available on some ad hoc arrangement such as overtime or special hours, or to make budgetary funds available each year. Without administrative support, most innovations will fail to become routinized. The main exceptions are the task-specific innovations that may initially be adopted by individual practitioners at no cost to an agency. The administrators appear also to respond to bureaucratic incentives. If an innovation permits an expanded agency budget, for instance, the administrator may have a strong incentive for routinizing the innovation. However, again little is known about the bureaucratic incentive system of top administrators, especially given the confluence of actors such as union representatives, staff from the municipal executive's office, and local legislators who are involved in determining agency policies.

In contrast to these internal conditions, external financial and technical assistance were consistently found to be unrelated to the degree of routinization. This does not mean, however, that local agencies can or will innovate as easily without such external assistance. More likely, the lack of relationship was due to the inability to distinguish between two very different conditions—where local officials actively pursue external assistance and where such assistance is the result of initiatives by a federal granting agency of other external agent. External assistance may, in fact, be important to routinization if such assistance matches local needs and agendas. Further research is needed, however, to identify the initiating official and the extent of match between external and local agendas.

Overall, these findings and observations may lead to an improved basis for dealing with routinization in the future. In particular, there may be some ways in which federal policymakers can avoid the extreme positions of appearing to impose federal agendas on local agencies, or merely distributing funds on a formula and revenue-sharing basis. The first extreme can lead to undesired clashes and a failure to deal with local needs in the long run. However, the second extreme can lead to a failure to innovate at all, even where innovation appears needed. Further research on the design of more effective strategies is the subject of the final chapter.

Notes

1. Of the original ten passages and cycles, questions on changes in organizational governance (number six), promotion of personnel acquainted with the innovation (number eight), and turnover in key personnel (number nine), were eliminated from the analysis because of this problem. If these same passages or cycles were eliminated from the case study data, the results for the case studies would have been altered, but only slightly: The Miami and Boston police computer cases would have dropped from highly to moderately routinized, and the Rochester and Omaha Jet-Axe cases would have increased from moderately to highly routinized; all the remaining cases would have remained in their original rankings.

2. The median age was defined separately for case studies and telephone interviews and for each type of innovation. Thus, for instance, the age of a particular telephone Jet-Axe interview was compared to the median age of all telephone Jet-Axe interviews. Other definitions of age were also tested (e.g., simply comparing all innovations four years or older versus those younger than four years), but these did not alter the results. The reader may wish to further examine the age dimension by tabulating the age of the nineteen case studies as presented in tables 4-1 to 4-6.

3. It should be remembered from note 1 of this chapter that the governance passage was one of three omitted from the routinization scores for the telephone interviews for *all* types of innovations, due to measurement difficulties. Thus, the Jet-Axe cases were no different from the other innovations in the final routinization score.

4. This finding may still need further testing. It may be that the

distinction becomes important when more than one agency or jurisdiction is involved with the innovation. However, because such cross-agency or cross-jurisdictional arrangements were deliberately excluded from the present study, the distinction between the two groups of task-diverse innovations may not have been given a fair chance to emerge.

5. For an example of the multivariate regression or correlational techniques that can be applied to organizational studies when the appropriate measures have been developed, see Yin, Heald, and Vogel (1977).

6. It should be noted that the study has only been concerned with routinization. Thus, no inferences should be made regarding the factors facilitating adoption. There may have been any number of such factors, but these were not examined as part of the present study.

7. The other four factors could not be covered due to the problems of defining the factors adequately in a telephone interview.

8. A gamma score can vary from 1.00 (perfect positive association) to -1.00 (perfect negative association), and thus has the same interpretation as a correlation coefficient (r). The gamma statistic, however, is used whenever data involve ordinal and nominal scales, as in the present study.

9. As previously noted, no multivariate analysis was attempted because of the weakness of the measures. However, simple associational analysis (independent variable X independent variable) was conducted and showed that this basic result—the importance of the core application and practitioner support factors—appeared not to be an artifact of strong collinearity between the two factors. In this case, one might argue that only one factor was really important.

10. Unfortunately, the Berman and McLaughlin study included few technological innovations, so there was almost no overlap in the sample of that study and this one.

8 Directions for Future Policy Research

The discovery of how new practices become routinized by local service agencies can potentially lead to more effective public policies—whether to facilitate or inhibit routinization. To the extent that the present study has broken new ground, however, the main findings still require corroboration by further research. New studies should especially focus on the passages and cycles framework with regard to other innovations and life histories; this and other specific suggestions for future research are the topic of this chapter.

The main purpose of further research would ultimately be to provide advice to improve public policy. Thus, the general direction of future research should be to sharpen the key conclusions and to apply them to specific policymaking needs. The following discussion covers the dual nature of the policy audience, further research on routinization strategies, and further research to facilitate the role of federal mission agencies.

Dual Nature of the Policy Audience

Public policy regarding local services has traditionally been a strictly local matter determined by the political and administrative priorities within each local jurisdiction. Any policy lessons on routinization would thus ordinarily be directed to municipal executives and legislators, local agency heads, and staff persons who serve as coordinators for specific innovations. Because local services are still controlled by such decisionmakers, this is the main audience for whom new policy research must continue to be designed.

A second policy audience, however, has become more important with the increased participation of federal agencies, and, to a lesser extent, state agencies, in local service delivery. In some fields, such as highway construction, this type of participation has existed for some time. In other fields, such as education, law enforcement, and fire-suppression, federal participation has been relatively new and has followed the enactment of major legislative initiatives such as federal aid to education (1965), federal law enforcement assistance (1968), and recently enacted legislation on fire safety administration like the National Fire Prevention and Control Administration in the Department of Commerce. As a result, there are now any number of federal decisionmakers who are also concerned with improving the delivery of local services. Moreover, local service practices can now be substantially affected—though not always in predictable ways—by the actions of these federal officials. Future policy research should therefore also attempt to serve this second group of decisionmakers, who may include federal mission agency heads and their staffs.

These two policy audiences operate from two different perspectives.[1] For this reason, two somewhat different research agendas need to be developed. In general, further elaboration of specific routinization strategies is likely to be directly relevant to a local service agency, and local decisionmaking needs to be only indirectly relevant to federal decisionmakers. The latter group will need to modify its own bureaucratic routinization processes through the use of federal policies in order to implement changes at the local level. Thus, the needs of this second policy audience also require further research on the efficacy of various federal policies. Such research is dealt with separately after the discussion on routinization itself.

Further Research on Routinization Strategies

The findings in chapter 7 have already been summarized in terms of the meaning of routinization and the conditions that lead to its occurrence. These findings may now be integrated into a broader depiction of the innovative process, to identify directions for future policy research. From the point of view of a local service agency, the key policy questions for adopting and routinizing an innovation might be framed in the following order:

1. When should innovative practices be considered? In other words, what service problems are most likely to be successfully dealt with by the initiation of new practices?
2. How should an innovation, once adopted, be used in order to increase the likelihood of routinization?
3. What organizational procedures must be explicitly changed in order to accommodate an innovation in increasing the likelihood of routinization?
4. What is the range of situations or innovations to which any of these guidelines can be generalized?

The research needs are presented according to this sequence of questions.

Research on the Adoption of Innovation

Local agencies are continually confronted with a wide range of problems, some dealing with basic service deficiencies, such as declining educational achievement scores, and others dealing with administrative management, such as a work overload in a clerical operation. At the same time, intermediary organizations like professional associations or extension and change agents, federal agencies, and industrial groups have identified a wide array of innovations, or presumed "solutions" to local problems. The local agency decisionmaker thus has a complex priority-setting problem: How should he or she determine what types of innovations are appropriate for what types of problems?

These initial questions regarding the criteria for adopting an innovation were largely ignored by the present study. This was a deliberate omission in the research design, because so much previous research had already focused on the adoption process. Such existing research has generally concluded that the adoption of an innovation is most appropriate when (see Rothman, 1974, pp. 417-483):

1. The adopting agency has a professional staff structure, is less formally organized, and is decentralized
2. The innovation being adopted has a perceived relative advantage over and is less complex than other innovations or the status quo, is compatible with the adopting agency, and is easy to communicate
3. The use of the innovation is supported by opinion leaders and peers (practitioners) outside the adopting agency

Further research on adoption is nevertheless needed. In particular, studies of adoption behavior have usually focused on the diffusion of specific innovations; what is needed instead is further study of local agencies and the situations or problems that give rise to the need to innovate. In short, whereas the typical adoption study has focused on solutions, or innovations, more work is needed from the perspective of problems, or needs.

Once a problem framework has been developed, one facet of the present study that might be explored in further studies of adoption is the distinction between task-specific and task-diverse innovations. When local needs have led to a task-specific innovation being considered for adoption, such as an innovation limited to a single service application, the more important criteria may have to do with practitioner receptivity and support. Research should focus on the importance of the following factors, which have been suggested by the findings in the previous chapter:

1. The degree to which the innovation matches the priorities perceived by practitioners
2. The informal reaction of small groups of practitioners in the agency who have been given an opportunity to test the innovation
3. Evidence that the innovation was previously well received by practitioners in other jurisdictions

A task-specific innovation is likely to go unused, even if agency management has "adopted" the innovation, if these factors tend to be negative.

In contrast, when a task-diverse innovation is considered for adoption, such as an innovation that is potentially relevant to a variety of service applications, the more important criteria may have to do with the staff capabilities for coordinating the innovation. Thus, research should focus on the following factors:

1. The presence of a staff person who can serve as coordinator, which includes the ability to manage as well as to assist in repairing the innovation
2. The degree to which the innovation is of sufficient organizational significance that a coordinator who does well can be rewarded with one or more promotions while still working with the innovation
3. The presence of someone who can work with the coordinator, if not the coordinator himself, to identify the best array of initial service applications for the innovation, and who is sensitive to the development of intense, but not necessarily widespread, practitioner support for the innovation

The supposition from the present study is that a task-diverse innovation is likely to fail if there is no capable coordinator or coordinating team, and if, as a consequence, there is heavy turnover in this role during the first few years in the innovation's life. Conversely, highly significant innovations can attract talented coordinators, who may be able to grow with the innovation and to make substantial career advances based on success with the innovation.[2]

Research on Strategies for Routinization: Ways of Using the Innovation

No research can address the issue of whether, and under what circumstances, local agencies should seek to routinize a new practice. Thus, the present study has provided no information about the "appropriateness" of such a course of action; moreover, there are certainly many situations when the initial experiences with an innovation might be sufficiently negative that routinization should not be allowed to occur. At the same time, it is very difficult to specify for any given situation those innovations that should or should not be routinized. The diversity of local conditions and innovations precludes any general statements, and research can therefore offer few normative guidelines. Instead, the assumption throughout the text has been that agency decisionmakers have already deemed routinization desirable—that is, that they have already decided to make an innovation part of standard agency practice. Given this decision, several findings from the present study appear worth corroborating in further research.

First, the findings have suggested that, at the outset, it is essential for the innovation to become fully operational for at least a few complete tasks, so that agency personnel can learn what the innovation can do. Only when an innovation is operational can it develop an identity that others, even if peripherally involved, can describe and to which existing agency practices can be related. Chapter 4 pointed out that one way of better assuring that the innovation became operational was to limit its initial scope, so that only a subset of activities was performed or only a small portion of the agency was initially involved. This strategy has been referred to elsewhere as "under-innovating."[3] The limited scope, however, did include some completed tasks, so that the use of the innovation was associated with concrete outputs, even if they were not the ultimate payoffs by which the innovation was formally evaluated.

Second, the findings have suggested that the initial use of the innovation should involve as much direct contact with practitioners as possible. Here it is again useful to distinguish between task-specific and task-diverse innovations. For the task-specific innovations, direct contact appeared to be facilitated if the innovation was related to a highly repetitive agency function. If the opportunity for using the innovation only occurred infrequently, practitioners had little practice in using the innovation, and few people had direct contact with it or were able to learn its functions. For task-diverse innovations, direct contact appeared to be facilitated if the coordinator identified several service applications that involved an enthusiastic subgroup of agency practitioners. Often, these applications had emerged because some subgroup had supported the innovation's adoption in the first place. Under such circumstances, this subgroup was likely to be highly motivated to help make the innovation become operational.

Third, as the innovation becomes operational, close attention should be given to the possible ways for expanding its use. Even a task-specific innovation presented some flexibility in this regard, for an agency did have some discretion in performing certain activities more often than in the past, such as more stringent enforcement of laws pertaining to persons who drive while intoxicated or issuance of parking violations. Where such flexibility existed, those supporting the innovation could press for the highest frequency of service use. A task-diverse innovation, of course, presented a wide variety of opportunities for increasing the number or frequency of service applications. Coordinators of the innovation sought to identify these new applications and to extend the innovation's functions to cover them. Each new application did require additional effort and resources, but these requirements were more than offset by the additional practitioner support that occurred.

A critical consideration throughout these initial and expanded activities was whether the innovation could be used as part of the agency's core practices. The "core," as noted in chapter 7, covered situations in which an innovation displaced a traditional function or created a new function that was then associated with a redefinition of the agency's basic mission. An innovation could also cover a core practice by serving a well-established need that had previously gone unfulfilled. Certain innovations lend themselves to becoming a part of core practice, simply by virtue of their inherent functions. However, other innovations, mainly of the task-diverse type, presented certain choices among applications. In such cases, the coordinator or other supporters of the innovations could direct the use of the innovation to core applications. Actions were also taken to eliminate the superceded practice, where relevant, as effectively as possible.

Finally, throughout the initial and expanded use of the innovation, explicit attempts should be made to identify payoffs in terms that practitioners can directly experience. In the case studies, these included convenience, reduced time and effort, job safety, service changes that may make a job more stimulating, and other outcomes that were not necessarily the types of payoffs significant to formal evaluations. The more that practitioners could experience these payoffs, the more they supported the innovation. Sometimes the payoffs to the practitioner were similar to and correlated positively with formal evaluative outcomes, such as a speedier and more effective response to health emergencies, an outcome which practitioners can directly experience and will find rewarding. This response was related to an increase in lives saved, an outcome with which formal evaluations are likely to be concerned. There were occasions, however, when the practitioner payoffs were unrelated to evaluation outcomes. For example, an educational innovation might make a teacher's work easier or more convenient—or more fun—but might produce no service benefits such as students' educational achievement or other educational outcomes. Under such circumstances, the findings suggested that the routinization process could still continue.

Research on Strategies for Routinization: Organizational Changes

The use of an innovation in the various ways described above should lead to its growing support among practitioners and agency leaders alike. The argument, in short, has been that when an innovation is used frequently, performs a core practice, and has payoffs meaningful to practitioners, both the practitioners and higher officials within an agency will try to make the innovation an integral part of agency operations. The routinization process was further facilitated, however, if certain organizational changes were also explicitly pursued. These changes were not important during the early period in an innovation's life history, when the main goal was to make the innovation operational by whatever improvisation was necessary. The organizational changes did increase in importance, though, after the initial improvisation period had transpired. Again, the findings suggested the need for further corroboration along the following lines.

The key organizational changes were related to the resources needed by most innovations. Most innovations required budgetary support, maintenance and supplies, trained personnel to administer and operate the innovation, and explicit organizational procedures for linking the innovation to other aspects of agency operations. In general, the innovator or others seeking to routinize the innovation attempted to implement the specific organizational changes that would provide the innovation with these resources. At the outset of an innovation's life history, ad hoc or temporary changes, such as a special in-service training program, sufficed. In the long run, however, the changes had to be integrated with existing agency procedures. The goal, in short, was to establish budgetary support for the innovation that was no different from the budgetary support for the rest of the agency's operations, to establish training programs that were a part of the practitioner's regular training, to have the innovation included in procedural manuals or other rules of governance that also covered all other agency practices, and so on. In some cases, the innovation not only needed to be incorporated into such procedures but also affected them, such as a computer innovation that affected the way an agency organized its budgeting system. In such cases, the routinization process was more complicated, and innovators had to deal with a dual task— that is, incorporating an innovation into a set of organizational procedures but also changing the basis for such procedures.

A major distinction throughout all these organizational changes was that some changes required more lead time than others. (This refers simply to the procedural mechanics of making organizational changes, and not necessarily to the time needed to develop political or bureaucratic support for such changes.) The fastest changes often involved maintenance and supply procedures or formal reorganizations of an agency's structure. Changes that required more time to implement were the establishment of personnel classifications, the creation of major modifications in an agency's rules of governance (as reflected in the passage of a city ordinance or a new bond issue), and the eventual promotion of personnel acquainted with the innovation. Chapters 5 and 6 have distinguished between these faster and slower organizational changes by differentiating between the expansion stage in an innovation's life history and the disappearance stage in the same history. Because of the long lead time, certain organizational initiatives had to be made as early as possible during the innovation's life history; to ignore the development of personnel reclassification actions, for instance, only delayed the eventual creation of the appropriate personnel positions and classifications needed by the innovation.

For innovations that attempted to affect educational practices, it was especially important that, above and beyond the development of support among practitioners, the organizational changes were made in collaboration with the curriculum department or its equivalent in the school district. Few changes in core educational practices appear to be made without such collaboration, and most innovations requiring teacher retraining or the redefinition of teaching assignments must also be approved by the curriculum department. In addition, the curriculum department usually had close links with agencies in higher levels of government, such as state agencies, that regulated the governance of the school district by granting accreditation, establishing standards, or developing lists of specific textbooks for teachers to adopt. Although these observations regarding the role of the curriculum department may appear obvious, the findings of the present study showed that, in many instances, supporters of an educational innovation were unaware of the critical role played by the curriculum department, and many efforts were wasted because they were not directed at the curriculum department.

Whatever organizational changes were pursued, those supporting the innovation had to deal with a varied group of agency personnel. Each organizational area—such as budgeting, personnel, maintenance and supply—had a slightly different power and staff structure even within the same agency, and had to be confronted separately. To this extent, the negotiation of each organizational change was best regarded as an independent task. The composition of the innovating team needed to be enhanced during the expansion stage to include sufficient expertise to deal with each task.

In summary, these preceding organizational changes were found to be important elements of any routinization strategy. Further research, testing these notions with other kinds of innovations and in agency settings different from the ones in the present study, would be helpful in corroborating or disproving these findings.

Research on Strategies for Routinization: Perceptual and Attitudinal Changes

As previously noted, routinization finally occurs when both organizational and perceptual changes have been accomplished. The organizational changes are reflected in the passages and cycles and have been the main concern of the present study. However, further research is needed to investigate the perceptions and attitudes of various groups—practitioners, administrators, and the citizenry—with regard to a range of service practices.

In a longitudinal research design, perceptual norms might be assessed when a practice was new and then compared to those norms prevalent when the practice, on the basis of organizational characteristics, appeared to be routinized. The predicted outcome would be that the perceptions would change over the course of the innovation's life history, and that there would be a perceptual counterpart to the progression through the improvisation, expansion, and disappearance stages. An alternative design would be a cross-sectional one, in which perceptions of various practices would be assessed. There, the predicted outcome would be that those practices that had already achieved the appropriate passages and cycles would be perceived as "standard practice." Whatever the design, the main point would be to assess perceptions toward practices whose organizational status had also been explicitly defined according to the passages and cycles framework.

Research on the Role of Federal Mission Agencies

The policy implications of this further research on routinization have been cast in a form that is presumed to be directly applicable to the needs of local decisionmakers. Thus, any corroboratory evidence from new research will hopefully give direct guidance to a local agency head, staff person, or coordinator of some innovation.

The research on routinization as described, however, does not provide explicit guidance for action by federal decisionmakers. For federal officials to take advantage of any new knowledge regarding the routinization process in local agencies, the general relationship of federal mission agencies to local service agencies must first be taken into account.[4] The revelant federal mission agencies are those federal departments that encourage and support local innovation. These include:

1. The Department of Housing and Urban Development, which administers programs to support local government innovation in general
2. The Department of Health, Education, and Welfare, which administers programs to encourage educational and health innovations
3. The Department of Justice, which administers programs to assist law enforcement agencies and support innovations in criminal justice practice
4. The Department of Commerce, which administers programs to support innovations in the fire service
5. The Department of Transportation, which administers programs to improve local transportation services

Because of their position in the intergovernmental structure, the federal mission agencies can only work indirectly to influence the routinization process in local services.

The Role of Federal Agencies

Any attempt to describe the policy implications for federal mission agencies must be introduced by a discussion of the rationale for federal intervention. This is because local service problems and practices are essentially the purview of local, and, in some cases, state, governments and agencies, and the federal role in this context has not always been clear and has frequently been challenged. However, it may be claimed that federal mission agencies do in fact have a major responsibility in supporting innovation—and hence for selectively promoting or discouraging routinization—in local government practice. This responsibility is based on several needs created by the innovative process that cannot be fulfilled by state and local governments acting alone, namely the need for:

1. Supporting research and development (R&D) on innovations that may be applicable to local needs
2. Promoting transference and diffusion from site to site, including the creation of networks of technology agents
3. Conducting evaluations
4. Assisting local jurisdictions to deal with problems deemed national in significance

Supporting Research and Development. Successful use of innovations by local governments depends first and foremost on high-quality and responsive research and development (R&D). Federal laboratories, field agents, and technology centers, as well as federally sponsored university research, constitute a nationwide R&D resource. Although these resources may primarily serve other objectives, as in the case of NASA installations, the R&D expertise can often provide essential technical guidance for state and local efforts.

In this regard, it should be noted that the Jet-Axe innovation was a direct spinoff from technology originally developed for aerospace functions. Similarly, there have been any number of "hardware" and "software" innovations that have received initial federal support and have then been found to be useful by local service agencies. A primary function of federal mission agencies therefore continues to be the support of specific R&D efforts that will produce innovations for local service agencies.

Promoting Transference and Diffusion. Many local governments share similar problems and experiences. Yet, there are so many governmental units at the local level that communications among these units is often haphazard. One community may already have developed a basic approach to a problem that can also benefit another community, even though the second community will still have to modify the approach to suit its unique needs. Without a good communications network, the transference and diffusion of ideas and solutions will be minimal. A second role of federal mission agencies is therefore to support and improve the transference and diffusion of ideas from one local site to another.

Federal support for diffusion can take either of two forms. First, the federal government can encourage the dissemination of information on specific innovative ideas and technologies. An information clearinghouse or the sponsorship of conferences and workshops would be examples. Second, the federal government can explicitly support the development of communications networks. This can take the form of support for extension agents[5] or for professional associations, such as the International City Management Association and the International Association of Chiefs of Police. Support can also be given to emerging groups, such as the emergency medical professions, that deal with new local functions.

Whether for disseminating information on specific technologies or for network-building, the rationale for federal support is based directly on federal, and not local, concerns. This is because, presumably, there is a shared set of problems that goes beyond the boundaries of an individual city. In other cases, there may be a communications system that is actually a national network, involving officials from many cities or states. The network is therefore a resource that only the federal government can nurture.

Conducting Evaluations. Evaluative information is needed to provide feedback on project performance and accomplishments. Such feedback may be used to allocate resources in the future. However, most local governments are not equipped to perform such functions as evaluation research. Nor would it be appropriate for every local unit to have its own evaluation staff. Such a resource would be difficult to develop and would be poorly used. Because very specialized skills are often required and are not frequently available, it is equally appropriate for federal agencies to support the evaluation of local service practices.

For evaluation, federal agencies can serve as an information resource to local governments, recommending specific evaluators or providing guidance on the latest state-of-the-art in evaluation research. In addition, federal agencies can support specific evaluative efforts that cover more than a single city agency. Such efforts can make more economic use of special evaluation skills. Thus, evaluative feedback can be made available to many cities that participate in a single, larger-scale evaluation supported by the federal government. Finally, federal mission agencies can support research on improved evaluation methods. Such methods are needed to assess both organizational and service impacts, as well as to assure that evaluations are conducted as efficiently and effectively as possible.

Dealing with Problems of National Significance. A fourth rationale for federal intervention is based on the federal role in assuring that services are responsive to national needs such as health care, compensatory education, new mass transit facilities, or prevention of crime in the streets, because of their national significance. Even though the problems can only be confronted at the local level, federal resources can nevertheless be mandated by the Congress, and large-scale programs can be mounted by the executive branch.

Among the innovations covered by the present study, it has already been noted that three—MICU, CAI and CCTV—were in part supported by federal funds under just such a rationale. In addition, federal involvement in the breath-testing innovation has also been based on a|similar rationale—that is, the rising national rate of automobile accidents due to drunken driving.

Summary of Federal Role in Relation to Routinization. These four rationales for federal intervention in agency practices can all be related to the routinization process. Where the federal mission agencies are concerned with the implementation of a specific innovation, for instance, the concern should extend to the point of routinization or institutionalization. Otherwise, a local agency may be unnecessarily disrupted by having to adopt an innovation that is later discarded out of negligence. Naturally, the policy implications that draw from the process are dual-edged. There may be some occasions where routinization should be disrupted, and federal mission agencies can use the same knowledge about the routinization process to create such a disruption. The point of research on routinization would be to provide guidance on how the process can be facilitated or retarded once decisionmakers have selected the desired outcome, rather than to indicate when and where routinization was appropriate, or from whose point of view.[6]

Research on Federal Intervention Strategies

On the surface, federal mission agencies have a variety of policy mechanisms to influence innovation both positively and negatively. These mechanisms include, but are not limited to:

1. Revenue-sharing or noncategorical funds to local agencies
2. Funds for extension agents or professional associations to encourage innovation among practitioners
3. Funds for developing specific innovations
4. Funds for testing specific innovations at specific sites such as a demonstration project

Federal agencies may also set specific performance standards for local practice, thereby providing an indirect incentive for innovation, and any number of federal regulatory actions, such as school desegregation, can affect both innovation and routinization.

Political reality probably demands that the entire array of mechanisms continues to be used. Some may receive more emphasis than others, but it is difficult to imagine a whole type of mechanism being completely eliminated. Thus, although there has been a shift from categorical to noncategorical programs in the last decade, beginning with the Nixon administration, the categorical programs are unlikely to be dropped entirely. In other words, the realistic policy alternatives are not to choose among the mechanisms, but to improve each mechanism in its own way to facilitate the adoption and routinization of new practices. Any improvements in using these mechanisms will require policy research on such topics as: the synthesizing of lessons from various local experiences; allocating and monitoring the use of federal funds as routinization occurs or fails to occur; and developing a better understanding of local agency processes rather than merely supporting specific innovations.

Synthesizing the Lessons from Local Experiences. Local governments may each operate in unique historical and political settings, but this does not preclude them from having numerous common experiences. For instance, as a result of the energy crisis of 1973-74 and the continually rising costs of energy since then, many school districts discovered that they shared common problems in operating school buildings and attempting to conserve energy.[7] Clearly, many different agencies—as our case studies only begin to suggest—have also had common experiences with the routinization of specific innovations.

Federal agencies need to develop new but simple ways of synthesizing the lessons from these experiences and using them in designing any federal programs aimed at improving local services. For routinization, the issues to be covered might include the development of:

1. *A policy-typology of innovations* extending far beyond the simple distinction between task-specific and task-diverse innovations, which would allow officials to understand what policy implications, if any, have been consistently associated with different types of innovations.
2. *A refined understanding of the career paths of local innovators and coordinators* to determine what types of paths are most closely associated with successful routinization. (For instance, the findings of this study suggested that the stereotypic urban innovator who moves too rapidly from one jurisdiction to another will facilitate the adoption of many innovations but may fail to promote routinization.)
3. *Insights into the most (and least) transigent cycles and passages in local agencies* so that future innovators may be forewarned about the need to make early plans for certain types of organizational changes.

These and other topics should be explicitly examined by synthesizing existing research. Ultimately, the lessons drawn can be incorporated by federal agencies into their own programs—for instance, by making new awards for demonstration projects, promoting, to the extent necessary, R&D on certain types of innovations, or encouraging professional associations to undertake innovative activities.

Unfortunately, recent research on federal management practices has suggested that federal agencies have had difficulty in synthesizing lessons from the past. Totally new demonstration programs, for instance, have been initiated in one federal department without any reference to experiences with similar programs in other departments. High rates of personnel turnover among federal officials have also helped to create a degree of inconsistency within the same program. How these and other problems of federal management are resolved remains to be seen. However, it may be that greater burdens than in the past will be placed on those federal agencies, such as the U.S. Office of Management and Budget or the National Science Foundation, that cut horizontally across substantive program areas.

Allocating and Monitoring the Use of Federal Funds. Previous research has differed in drawing conclusions about the role of federal funds in local service innovation. Many studies, including the present one, have concluded that there is no consistent pattern between the availability of federal funds for a project and the outcomes of that project.[8] Other studies, examining different federal programs or a different sample of projects, have, in contrast, found federal funds to facilitate desirable outcomes.[9]

These conflicting results can be explained if one distinguishes between indiscriminate and impotent effects. Indiscriminate effects occur when there is no discernible pattern across an array of projects; impotent effects occur when there is no measurable effect for any single project. The conflicting results from previous studies, as well as the case study examples in the present research, suggest that the main discovery has been one of indiscriminate, but not of impotent, effects. In other words, there have been numerous instances in which a specific innovative experience was critically assisted by some federal funds, so that the funds were hardly impotent. The negative findings that often emerge are of the aggregate patterns across numerous projects (which include many situations in which federal funds were indiscriminately applied) as the negative or null experiences served to statistically offset the positive or successful experiences. An important question for further research is, therefore, to identify those situations in which federal funds can have a potent effect on local innovations.

For routinization, this could lead to major advances in applying federal funds more discriminately. Presently, most awards of federal funds (where funds are not distributed on a strictly formula basis) are based on grant or contract applications that only emphasize the early steps in the innovative process. For instance, applications may provide considerable detail about how a project is to be started and implemented but give no clue as to any routinization plans even when a multi-year award is involved. The only long-term concern, if any, is whether there is a plan for local funds to eventually substitute for the initial federal funds in supporting the innovation. The present findings have suggested that federal agencies should alert applicants to the need for achieving certain tasks that we have called passages and cycles, and that applicants should present preliminary plans for achieving these tasks. At the outset, the plans may be no more than a sketchy outline. However, after the first six to nine months of a project have passed, these plans could be described in greater detail.

Some of the questions that might be raised from the perspective of a federal official in evaluating an application and in monitoring subsequent progress might include the following:

Initial Factors

1. Does the type of innovation suggest the need for a full-time coordinating role? If so,
2. What is the proposed coordinator's background, turnover history, and relationship to agency practitioners?
3. Is there any evidence that the proposed project fits the unique needs of the local agency at this point in time?
4. Is there an adequate training program for the first cohort of users of the innovation?
5. Does the proposed project staff have a technical grasp of the innovation, and is there a plan for dealing with maintenance, repair, upgrading, and depreciation problems?

Organizational Factors

1. What steps have been taken to avoid status as a special project (e.g., avoiding special budget lines, temporary personnel appointments, or a special organizational unit that does not match existing agency units)?
2. How is the innovative practice to be assessed, and do these criteria include meaningful payoffs in terms of practitioner needs?
3. How does the innovative practice compare with other agency priorities for ultimately using local funds?
4. How is the innovative practice to be integrated with existing personnel classification and certification procedures?
5. What are the possibilities for personnel promotions as a result of using or administering the innovation?
6. What is the plan for making changes in the regular practitioner training program to incorporate whatever new skills are needed to use the innovation?

A dilemma that arises in applying these questions to any award or monitoring procedure, however, is that federal intervention can become so cumbersome that local projects will have difficulty in simply getting started. Thus, further research is needed to show how the concerns reflected in these illustrative questions can be addressed without such interference. For example, the routinization questions might not be considered in detail at the outset of a new project. The main point is that federal officials should have a complete agenda to guide themselves as a project progresses. The federal officials will have to think in longitudinal terms to develop a series of changing criteria for monitoring local progress, clearly going beyond the current attention to writing effective Requests for Proposals (RFPs).[10]

Developing a Better Understanding of Local Agency Processes. Skepticism has continued to grow about the benefits of federal intervention for local services.[11] This is partly because the large-scale federal programs of the 1960s were accompanied by unreasonably high expectations (which, one author has pointed out, have not been typically applied to defense expenditures where many federal dollars may be wasted in testing a new system such as the B-1 bomber).[12] In addition, federal programs have often entailed long delays and bureaucratic harassment, to the point that capable local agencies are now "capable" not only in the sense of being able to provide service but also in being able to obtain federal grants.

More disappointing, the Washington view of urban service problems is still poorly informed about local agency processes—that is, the way that local agencies conduct their everyday business. For instance, the importance of the textbood adoption process, which usually involves a state and local educational agency, went unappreciated throughout early attempts to reform education.[13] No matter what reform measures might be considered by federal officials or outside experts, the implementation of new service practices can only occur through the use of existing organizational procedures such as the textbook adoption process.

Any federal intervention program must therefore be designed around the existing context of local agency operations. This context includes the observation that local agency operations:

1. Are often designed to serve patronage and not performance criteria;
2. Have low rates of lateral entry, so that the senior officials of an agency have often spent their entire careers within the agency;
3. Are vertically connected to the intergovernmental system through a maze of county, regional, state, and federal agencies; and yet
4. Retain certain functional similarities across different local jurisdictions, as when police departments in two different jurisdictions retain a basic resemblance to each other).

In addition to improved synthesizing of local experiences and use of federal funds, federal mission agencies can also support new research that will improve knowledge about this context and about local agency services. For the routinization process, research is needed for at least four purposes:

1. To corroborate the present findings in an independent study or studies
2. To determine the degree to which the findings can be generalized to other types of innovations and public or private organizations

3. To elaborate the routinization process in greater detail, covering both the various outcomes and causal factors
4. To develop more refined measures of organizational change, so that multivariate analysis can be conducted in the future

The first two purposes could both be served by the same study or series of studies. The research design should include explicit attempts to replicate a portion of the present findings by selecting at least one or two of the same innovations, as well as attempts to extend the findings by selecting other innovations and other types of organizations for study. It would be particularly useful to know whether: (a) the routinization process that has been described here is limited to local services—and is found in private local services as well as public local services like private police, private schools, private sanitation collection; (b) the routinization process is a characteristic of public organizations—and is found in federal as well as local agencies; or (c) the process is even more generalizable to a wide variety of organizations and innovations.[14]

For the third and fourth purposes of elaborating the routinization process in greater detail and developing better measures of organizational change, a schematic drawing can provide a common basis for discussing specific types of further research. Figure 8-1 shows the main stages in the life history of an innovation, as the innovation changes over time from a new to a standard agency practice. The highlights of the life history are the three stages shown in the three boxes, with each stage defined according to the achievement of certain passages or cycles. Most of the relevant organizational forces that move an innovation from one stage to another are briefly listed next to the arrows supporting each stage, and a circle is used to represent those situations in which a traditional practice has been displaced by the innovative practice. Of course, the fully routinized practice, represented by the disappearance stage, can itself become a potential candidate for displacement by yet another innovation at some later date.

A major priority for further research would be to determine the general mutability or immutability of the routinization process in greater detail, with interval measures that would facilitate multivariate analysis. It may be, for instance, that certain early conditions during the decision to adopt will supportively facilitate the ultimate routinization outcomes. If so, policymakers would have a potent instrument for change because the conditions surrounding the adoption step might be easily manipulated. There is an interesting problem that arises from this mutability issue. On the one hand, routinization appears to be a fragile process, with many innovation life histories becoming abortive before full routinization has been achieved. On the other hand, many service practices appear to be extremely difficult to supplant or terminate once they have become routinized.[15] These apparently disparate organizational phenomena may ultimately be explained by the same set of factors; that is, the same

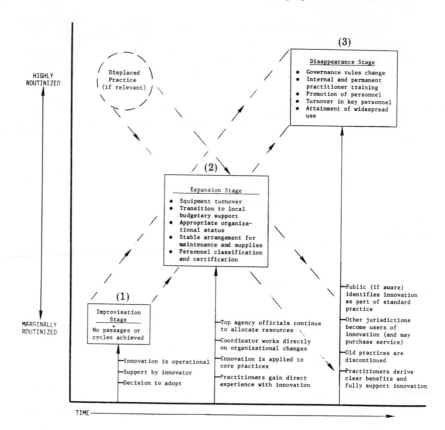

Figure 8-1. Complete Life History of a Local Service Innovation

new knowledge that will make routinization a less fragile process is also likely to make program termination an easier achievement for policymakers.

Research should also focus on the specific importance of individual passages and cycles and the factors that lead to their achievement. Because the present study was the first to explore the routinization process, an explicit assumption had to be made regarding the equal importance of each passage and cycle. However, certain passages or cycles may in fact be more critical than others, given specific types of innovations or agency settings. Wherever this is the case, intervention techniques can be designed to be more precise and effective. Taking but one example, the life history of an innovation during the expansion stage may be critically impeded or advanced by the degree to which the appropriate personnel classification and certification procedures can be established. Because personnel systems in most municipal civil services operate very slowly, it may therefore be essential that some groundwork be conducted during the improvisation stage; further, federal agencies or other supporters of the innovation may want to have early signals that such personnel changes are possible and might want to include information about the existing personnel procedures in early reviews of the innovation's progress. If an agency has had chronic difficulties in obtaining new classifications of any sort, the supporters of the innovation will have been forewarned that extra efforts will have to be made or that routinization is not likely to occur.

Conclusions on Further Policy Research

The findings of the present study should be regarded as but one source of new information for policy guidance. Other research and experiences will also have to be integrated to develop a firmer set of directives. Nevertheless, the study has suggested many steps that, if confirmed by further research, will allow local policy officials to assess and influence routinization.

For federal mission agencies concerned with improving local services, policy implementation will involve both the substantive steps directly related to routinization as well as improvements in federal program management itself. Regardless of the firmness of our knowledge about routinization, no routinization strategies can be pursued unless federal agencies are also prepared to organize themselves more effectively to synthesize the lessons from local experiences, to become more sophisticated in allocating and monitoring the use of federal funds, and to support further research on local organizatons.

The problem of delivering neighborhood services to residents—services like ensuring public safety, increasing environmental safety, and providing adequate educational, public health, sanitation, and recreational services—has now become a problem for governments at all levels. It is impossible to return to the simplistic era when municipal governments alone could manage these services. Intergovernmental coordination has become a fact of life, but the design of effective policies can only be based on an improved understanding of how actual service practices emerge and become routinized.

Notes

1. A brief description of these differences is found in McLaughlin and Berman (1975).

2. The extreme claim would be that some practitioners' major career advancement has often been based on a successful experience with a single, significant innovation. Often, such an individual can rise to the very top of an agency, as in the recent trend for data processing officers to advance to the heads of law enforcement agencies.

3. See Lambright and Flynn (1977). However, an important difference is that the present study only regarded "under-innovation" as an interim strategy; ultimately, the innovation must achieve full utilization (passage or cycle number ten); otherwise it will always be regarded as a special situation (e.g., a demonstration project) and not as a standard practice.

4. Increasing attention has been given to problems of implementing federal programs at the local level. See, for example, McLaughlin and Berman (1975), Hargrove (1975), Rein and Rabinowitz (1977), and Bardach (1977).

5. For example, the National Institute of Education is currently assessing the development of educational extension agents and the Department of Energy is examining the role of energy extension agents; both developments generally follow the model of the existing agricultural extension service.

6. The text does not deal with the potentially conflicting situations that may arise when it is in the interest of some parties to routinize a practice but contrary to the interests of other parties.

7. For a fuller description of local service experiences related to energy consumption, see Yin and Gwaltney (1977).

8. For example, see Lambright and Flynn (1977).

9. For example, see Bingham (1976).

10. For an illustrative discussion of how to improve RFPs for soliciting evaluation research, see Weidman (1977).

11. For instance, see Pressman and Wildavsky (1973) and Bardach (1977).

12. See Lambright (1976).

13. For a description of the local educational policy context, see Quick (1978).

14. One easily implemented research strategy to test these notions would be to develop a cross-sectional design, in which "standard practices" are analyzed in operational terms in a wide variety of organizations and with a wide variety of practices that had once been innovations. If the simple descriptive results were similar to the present findings, the basic argument for a highly generalizable routinization theory would have been established, and further studies could explore the actual process in each type of organization.

15. See the special issue of *Policy Sciences*, vol. 7, June 1976, for several articles on the topic of program termination.

Appendixes
Introduction

Each of the appendixes serves as supplementary material to the text, with appendixes A-D providing the procedures and raw data cited in chapter 1, and with Appendix E providing a review of the literature cited in chapter 3. The appendixes were prepared by the following persons: Appendix A, Robert Yin and Ellen Marks; Appendix B, Ellen Marks; Appendix C, Peter Bateman (the case studies on Cincinnati, Dallas, Miami, and San Diego); Suzanne Quick (the case studies on Birmingham, Oakland, and Portland), and Robert Yin (the case study on Hillsborough County); Appendix D, Ellen Marks; and Appendix E, Robert Yin.

Appendix A
Comparison of On-Site
Case Studies with
Telephone Interviews

Distinctive Features

There are many well-known differences between telephone and personal interviewing as methods of data collection. The use of telephone interviews fell into great disfavor following the disastrous results of the *Literary Digest* poll in 1936, but the use has increased sharply over the last ten years or so. The use of personal interviews has always been the most common technique for collecting data from households, and it has also been a mainstay of organizational research (Hyman et al., 1954; Festinger and Katz, 1966; and Selltiz et al., 1976). When used in the context of organizational research, personal interviews often form the basis for a case study. However, the data collection method using personal interviews should not be confused with the research design using an organizational setting as a case study. The discussion that follows focuses on the relative advantages between telephone and personal interviews as methods of data collection.

Most of the comparisons between telephone and personal interviews, and comparisons of both with mail surveys, have dealt with situations in which a member of a household is the main respondent. The study of routinization, however, involves members of local service agencies as respondents, and therefore falls into the category of interviewing known as *elite* interviewing (Dexter, 1970). For interviewing agency officials, the major trade-offs between the two methods have to do with costs, amount of information, and length of interview. For other considerations, such as the accuracy of the information and the response rate, the differences between the two methods appear minimal.

Costs

Mail surveys have always been the least costly method of collecting data; telephone interviews and personal interviews are more costly. One set of comparative cost figures was assembled by Boyd and Westfall (1972) and is reproduced in table A-1. The table shows that the pattern of cost differences remains the same whether household or elite interviews are involved. Moreover, the costs of the personal interviews will be much higher than those shown in the table if the interviews require trips to several different cities. If a research plan calls for no other consideration than maximizing the number of interviews

Table A-1
Cost Comparisons for Different Methods of Data Collection, for Households and Elite Respondents

Item	Method of Data Collection				
	Telephone	Mail	Personal	Telephone	Personal
Subject of survey	Health	Unknown	Health	Health	Health
Respondents	General U.S. population	Urban households	Urban households	Doctors	Doctors
Completed questionnaires	456	750	1,298	24	40
Administrative costs	$ 506	$ –	$ 5,900	$ –	$ –
Interviewer costs	584	–	10,700	160	645
Telephone tolls	1,259	–	–	125	–
Mailing expense	–	153	–	–	–
Travel expense	–	–	800	–	–
Inducements	–	493	–	–	–
Miscellaneous costs	275	295	300	–	–
Total costs	$2,626	$941	$17,700	$285	$645
Costs per completed interview	$ 5.78	$ 1.25	13.65	$ 11.87	$ 16.12

Source: Harper W. Boyd and Ralph Westfall, *Marketing Research*, 3d. ed., Richard D. Irwin, Homewood, Ill., 1972.

per unit cost, personal interviews should not be considered as an option. The use of Wide Area Telecommunications Service (WATS) lines in recent years has further reduced telephone costs to the point that the costs of telephone interviews may be quite competitive with those of mail surveys.

Amount of Information

At the same time, personal interviews allow for the collection of the greatest amount of information (Boyd and Westfall, 1972). The personal interview allows for observations of nonverbal behavior, observations of other conditions in an agency, the collection of documents or other artifacts while on the scene, and greater flexibility in asking questions that might be needed to reconcile contradictory responses. Moreover, a single respondent may be interviewed several times, with the interview situation varying from formal to informal settings (Becker and Meyers, 1974). In this regard, the mail survey is the poorest method, but telephone interviews are not much better. Certain kinds of information, covering spatial arrangements, the newness of different equipment, and other critical factors that surround the use of an innovation, simply cannot be obtained over the telephone. Finally, it has been argued that personal interviews, with their concomitant observational opportunities, are more appropriate than telephone interviews when a study tends to be exploratory, hypothesis-generating rather than hypothesis-confirming, or is on a topic of organizational process rather than outcome (see Aberbach et al., 1975; and Eveland, Rogers, and Klepper, 1976).

Length of Interview

Along with additional types of information, the personal interview also has the advantage of yielding much longer interviews. This means that the same questions can often be asked several times or with slightly different words, so that the meaning or consistency of a respondent's answers can be checked. The reverse concern actually exists with telephone interviews, where elite interviews have tended to be of short duration—10 to 20 minutes (Zamoff et al., 1974; and Wolfson, 1976)—and where even mail surveys may be better suited for long questionnaires (Boyd and Westfall, 1972). Thus, independent of the comparative advantage of personal over telephone interviews in terms of interview length, a secondary question is whether the maximum time for a telephone interview is sufficient.

Accuracy of Information

In contrast to the strong differences in costs, amount of information, and length of interview, there are no major differences in accuracy of information or response rates. One study of responses by physicians found "essentially no differences between the responses of physicians interviewed in person and those interviewed by telephone" (Colombotos, 1969). This general lack of differences has also been found in household surveys (see Hochstim, 1967; and Rogers, 1976), although personal interviews appear to produce slightly greater biases when the interview questions involve the reporting of socially undesirable behavior. Surveys of such issues as abortion, drunken driving, and failure to register to vote, for instance, tend to produce answers of a more socially desirable nature if personal rather than telephone interviews are used, with mail surveys producing the least bias (Wiseman, 1972; and Locander et al., 1974).

Response Rates

There appear to be no major differences between personal and telephone interviews in terms of response rates from elites. For households, too, the differences appear to be diminishing. Traditionally, it has been thought that mail surveys produce much lower response rates than either personal or telephone interviews, and that telephone interviews produce a slightly higher response rate than personal interviews because callbacks are easier to make (see Boyd and Westfall, 1972). However, recent methodological experiments have shown that response rates can be boosted to the point where all three produce fairly similar rates; responses to mail surveys are boosted by prior telephone notification (Wiseman, 1972), and responses to telephone interviews, by a prior letter (Dillman et al., 1976).

Summary

In spite of the great disparity in costs, personal interviewing appears to be a necessary method for collecting data on routinization. This is because:

1. The routinization study involves both hypothesis generation as well as hypothesis testing;
2. Routinization is a complex phenomenon whose study requires a data collection method that yields as much information as possible; and
3. Personal interviews allow for on-site observations that provide important clues for understanding the use and nature of an innovation.

Because of the high costs, however, the personal interviews need to be conducted in conjunction with telephone interviews. The telephone interviews can give some indication of the extent to which innovations have been operating in various local agencies, even though the causal links in the routinization process cannot be investigated. In this manner, the information from the telephone interviews provides a broader perspective for the personal interviews and can potentially strengthen the external validity of the sample of personal interviews. Thus, our study of routinization used both methods. Personal interviews and visits were made to a selected group of sites; telephone interviews were made for the unvisited sites, or the bulk of such sites, where the same type of innovation has been used. This use of multiple methods appears to be particularly relevant to studies of organizational structure and change (see Pennings, 1973).

Methods Used in Previous Studies
of Agency Innovations

The comparative advantages and disadvantages of mail surveys and personal and telephone interviewing have been reflected by previous studies on innovations by local agencies. In general, the more that a study has focused on organizational processes, the more that the data collection has relied on personal and open-ended interviewing. In contrast, the more that a study has focused on comparisons between characteristics of cities or of organizations, the more that the data collection has relied on mail surveys, telephone interviews, and closed-ended interviewing.

At one extreme, Baer et al. (1976) examined the reasons for success or failure among federal demonstration projects. Neither the full array of reasons nor a definitive measure of success and failure was obvious at the outset of the study. The study therefore consisted of 24 projects, all of which were examined through personal interviews. One group of projects was selected and conducted with an explicit hypothesis-testing objective. The conduct of the study did not follow a uniform set of procedures, so that different types of respondents and questions were used. However, the nature of the demonstration projects was sufficiently diverse that a uniform set of procedures would probably have placed too great a constraint on the collection of the evidence relevant for each case. Nevertheless, despite the diversity of cases and procedures, the Baer et al. study is distinctive because it attempted to aggregate the lessons from the twenty-four projects according to several rudimentary, nonparametric scales, and the outcome of the study—a fuller understanding of the life of a demonstration project—appeared to justify fully the choice of methods.

A similar type of objective—to develop a new model of organizational innovation—underlies a recent study by Eveland, Rogers, and Klepper (1976).

The study focused on the process by which a new computer application, the geocoding of street-address files, was implemented by regional agencies and used by local agencies. Again, because the nature of the relevant questions could not be fully known before the research began, the study consisted of eight sets of personal interviews at the regional level, with each set consisting of numerous interviews of regional officials and personnel in the local user agencies.

At the other extreme, Nelson (1975) used the data from closed-ended questionnaires to study the adoption of innovations by local schools. The questionnaires were mailed to school principals, with supporting materials also provided by mail by superintendents and central office administrators. The closed-ended questions were appropriate because the main objective of the study was: (a) to determine the number and type of innovations adopted by each school, and (b) to correlate school and community characteristics with the adoption results. In this type of study, many of the school and community characteristics may be derived from existing records, such as census or municipal data, as well as from the mail survey itself. The results of the study involved the identification of the correlates of innovation, thereby following the same general approach that we have described elsewhere as the "innovative organizations approach" (see chapter 3). There are many other studies that have followed the same approach and used the same method. Corwin (1975), for instance, analyzed the correlates of school innovativeness based on a mail survey to principals of schools employing graduates of the Teacher Corps. In all such studies, the identification of such correlates is only an indirect way of studying the organizational change process, and this remains a limitation of both the approach and the use of mail surveys.

These contrasting uses of methods suggest that there is an inherent tradeoff between the value of having wide-ranging descriptive data, indicating the extent and nature of adoptions by agencies across the country, and the value of having in-depth personal interviews, indicating the possible explanatory factors for the events at a single site. Not surprisingly, several studies have attempted to combine the advantages of both methods. In two different studies (Bingham, 1976; and Feller, Menzel, and Kozak, 1976), mail surveys were first used to determine the extent of adoption of innovations by different local agencies in all major cities (cities of over 50,000 population in the first study and of over 25,000 in the second study). These were closed-ended surveys and generally brief, and additional data were obtained from census and other municipal sources so that cross-city comparisons could be made. Both studies also included, however, a series of personal interviews using thirteen cities and thirty innovations as the subjects of the first study, and twenty sites and several manufacturers in the second. The results of these interviews allowed the investigators to gain insight into the innovative process and to interpret the original set of correlative data. The use of multiple methods in these as well as other studies (see Jones et al., 1974) further confirms the relative advantages and disadvantages of the methods. Some topics, such as marketing strategies used by manufacturers in promoting an innovation, simply cannot be studied through telephone interviews or mail surveys if the basic process is not well understood at the outset. The simple reliance on intensive personal interviews at a small set of sites, however, fails to provide an adequate perspective for generalizing to a larger number of sites.

Appendix B
Data Collection
Instruments

This appendix contains copies of the instruments used in the study. These include the guidelines for face-to-face interviewing (case studies) as well as the instruments for telephone interviews.

The instruments are grouped in the following manner:

Case Studies

COMPUTER-ASSISTED INSTRUCTION
Site Screening

School District/City: _____   Date of Call: _____

Respondent's Name: _____   Screener: _____

Title: _____

Phone #: _____

1. *Have the schools in your district ever used computer-assisted instruction?*
                    Yes _____   No _____

2. *When was computer-assisted instruction first used in your district?* _____ (year)

3. *Is computer-assisted instruction still in use?* Yes _____   No _____

   [IF NO] *When was it last used?* _____ (year)

4. *How many of the schools in your district use CAI?*

                    _____ of _____ elementary schools
                    _____ of _____ junior high schools
                    _____ of _____ senior high schools

5. *What classes use CAI?*

   Algebra _____   Trigonometry _____   Special Ed _____
   Geometry _____   Biology _____   Other (list) _____
   Calculus _____   Chemistry _____   Other (list) _____
   General Math _____   Language _____

6. *How many staff are involved in administering the CAI operation?* _____

7. *Has your CAI budget always been as large as it is now?*

                    Growing or same _____
                    Reduced   _____

8. *Does the school district use the same computer for administrative purposes?*
                    Yes _____   No _____

   [IF YES] *What administrative functions is it used for?*

   Teacher scheduling _____   Payroll _____   Other (list) _____
   Grades   _____   Reports _____   Other (list) _____

   [IF YES] *When did your school district first use this computer for
            administrative functions?* _____ (year)

*Thank you very much for your help. As I indicated, these are preliminary questions to
guide our research. Whom should we contact later if we would like to arrange for a
site visit?* _____

POLICE COMPUTERS

Site Screening

Date of Call: _____

Agency Name/City: _____

Respondent Name: _____

Title: _____

Tel. #: _____

1. *Has your department ever used a computer?* Yes _____ No _____

2. *Is the computer still being used?* Yes _____ No _____

3. *When did your department first use a computer?* _____

4. *Is this the same computer that is in use today?* Yes _____ No _____

   (IF YES) *Is the department planning on installing a new computer in the near future?* Yes _____ No _____

   (IF NO) *When was the current computer brought in?*_____

5. *Is the computer owned _____ or leased ____?*

6. *Does the money to pay for the computer itself come from:*
   department funds _____?
   another city agency _____?
   the county _____?

7. *Does the department employ its own computer programmer?* Yes _____ No _____

   (IF YES) *About how large is the computer staff?* _____

   (IF NO) *Who updates the computer programs?* _____

8. *What is the computer used for?*

Administrative	Service	
Attendance _____	NCIC	_____
Paper processing _____	Processing the UCR report _____	
Officer performance	Dispatching officers _____	
evaluation _____	Traffic control or analysis _____	
Inventory _____	Listing property or M.O. _____	
Budget analysis _____	Case status report _____	
Other (list) _____	On-line officer inquiries _____	
	Other (list) _____	

9. *We are also interested in the use of breathalyzers by police departments.*

   a. *Does your department use one?* Yes _____ No _____

      (IF NO) *Has it ever used one?* Yes _____ No _____

   b. *When did the department first use a breathalyzer?* _____

      (IF RESPONDENT UNABLE TO ANSWER, ASK FOR REFERRAL) _____

Thank you very much for your help. As I indicated, these are preliminary questions to guide our research. Whom should we contact later if we would like to arrange for a site visit? _____

<u>MOBILE INTENSIVE CARE UNITS</u>
Site Screening

Agency Name/City: _____ Date of Call: _____

Respondent's Name: _____ Screener: _____

Title: _____

Phone #: _____

1. *Has your department ever used a mobile intensive care unit?* (OTHER ACCEPTABLE TERMS: ADVANCED EMT, CORONARY CARE UNIT, PARAMEDIC)

                                                Yes_____   No_____

2. *Is it still in use?*   Yes_____   No_____

   (IF NO) *When was it last used?*   _____(year)

3. *When did your city first use a mobile intensive care unit?* _____ (year)

4. *Has this operation always been under [agency's] jurisdiction?*

                                                Yes_____   No_____

   (IF NO) *Where was it located before and when did it move to [agency]?*

   _____

5. *How many mobile intensive care units do you have in operation?* _____

   (IF MORE THAN ONE) *When did you acquire the most recent unit?* _____(year)

6. *What are the titles of the personnel who staff the units?*

   How many [title] are there?

Paramedic _____	Firemen _____
EMT-Advanced _____	Police Officers _____
Mobile Intensive	Volunteers _____
Care Personnel _____	Other (list): _____

7. *Have the number of units or the number of personnel always been as large as it is now?*

   Number of units grown or same _____ Number of staff grown or same _____
   Number of units decreased _____ Number of staff decreased _____

8. *What prehospital functions are the personnel trained to provide?*

Cardiac defibrillation _____	Drug administration _____
I.V. therapy _____	Ventilation techniques _____
Recognition of cardiac	Basic life support _____
arrhythmias _____	Other (list) _____
ECG transmission _____	Other (list) _____

Thank you very much for your help. As I indicated, these are preliminary questions to guide our research. Whom should we contact later if we would like to arrange for a site visit? _____

CLOSED CIRCUIT TELEVISION[*]

Site Screening

School District/City: _____ Date of Call: _____

Respondent's Name: _____ Screener: _____

Title: _____

Tel. #: _____

1. *Have the schools in your district ever used instructional television?*
                         Yes _____   No _____

2. *Can that same program be received in several different classrooms at the same time?*   Yes _____   No _____

3. *Does the school district operate the facilities that transmit these programs?*
                         Yes _____   No _____

   (IF YES): *When were these facilities first used?* _____(Year)

               How does transmission take place? _____
               (cable, dedicated channel, or other)

4. *What proportion of the schools in your district use the closed circuit system?*

High Schools	Elementary Schools
___0-25%	___0-25%
___26-50%	___26-50%
___over 50%	___over 50%

5. *Has the number of programs on the closed circuit system always been as large as it is now?*
               _____ YES, number is growing or same
               _____ NO, number has been reduced

6. *We are also interested in the use of computer-assisted instruction by school districts.*

   a. *Does your district use CAI?*   Yes _____   No _____

   b. (IF NO): *Has it ever used CAI?* Yes _____   No _____

      *When did the schools first use CAI?*_____

      (IF RESPONDENT UNABLE TO ANSWER, ASK FOR REFERRAL) _____

Thank you very much for your help. As I indicated, these are preliminary questions to guide our research. Whom should we contact later if we would like to arrange for a site visit? _____

_____

[*]Make sure the screener's introduction clearly mentions CCTV, not just educational TV.

BREATH TESTING
Site Screening

Agency Name/City: _____ Date of Call:_____
Respondent's Name: _____ Screener: _____
            Title: _____
            Tel. #: _____

1. *Has your department ever used a breathalyzer?* Yes _____   No _____

2. *When was it first used?* _____ (year)

3. *Is it still in use?* Yes _____   No _____
    [IF NO] *When was a breathalyzer last used?* _____ (year)

4. *Are any tests performed other than by a breathalyzer to determine blood
    alcohol concentration?*   Yes _____   No _____
    [IF YES] *What else is used?*

    *What proportion of suspects stopped for driving under the influence receive
    [means of test]?*

                        Test   Proportion
                  Breathalyzer   _____
                  Urinalysis   _____
                  Blood test   _____
             _____   _____

5. *Do you tend to use breathalyzers as a normal procedure, occasionally, or rarely?*
                  Normal procedure   _____
                  Occasionally   _____
                  Rarely   _____

6. [IF STILL IN USE] *Has the extent of using the breathalyzer grown, declined, or
    remained the same since it was first used?*
                  Grown   _____
                  Declined   _____
                  Remained the same   _____

7. *Where are your breathalyzers located? How many are at [location]?*
    [IF PRECINCT STATIONS] *How many precinct stations are in [city]?*
                  Precinct station   _____
                  Headquarters   _____
                  Mobile   _____
             _____   _____

*Thank you very much for your help. As I indicated, these are preliminary questions
to guide our research. Whom should we contact later if we would like to arrange for
a site visit?*
_____

JET-AXE

Site Screening

Agency Name/City: _____ Date of Call: _____

Respondent's Name: _____ Screener: _____

Title: _____

Phone #: _____

1. *Has your department ever used a jet-axe?*   Yes _____   No _____.

2. *When was it first used?* _____ (year)

3. *Is it still in use?*   Yes _____   No _____

    [IF NO] *When was the jet-axe last used?* _____ (year)

4. *During the year of its most extensive use, about how many jet-axes were used?*

    _____

5. *Do/did you tend to use jet-axes as a normal procedure, occasionally, or rarely?*

    Normal procedure _____
    Occasionally   _____
    Rarely   _____

6. [IF STILL IN USE] *Has the extent of using the jet-axe grown, declined, or remained the same since it was first used?*

    Grown   _____
    Declined _____
    Same   _____

7. *What proportion of the ladder companies use(d) a jet-axe?* _____

8. *In your opinion, what is a widely used piece of new hardware that your department has acquired within the past 10 years?* _____

    [PROBE] *Has your department ever used hand-held walkie-talkies?*

    Yes _____   No _____

NOTES:

Thank you very much for your help. As I indicated, these are preliminary questions to guide our research. Whom should we contact later if we would like to arrange for a site visit? _____

GUIDELINES FOR SITE VISITS

- The following are simple reminders for our site visit procedures.
Also attached is a final set of the topics to be covered by the site
visit and to be included in the case study.

1. While on site, keep your eyes open for relevant reports,
   documents, and artifacts that can be obtained.

2. When the visit is done by a pair of fieldworkers, leave
   the question of how to divide the write-up until after
   the site work is completed. (Cases needn't be divided
   the same way every time.)

3. In writing up the cases, be sure to mention each of the
   ten hypotheses (marked on the following pages with
   brackets) even though a hypothesis may have turned out
   to be irrelevant.

4. In writing up the cases, make the list of informants a
   separate attachment to the case. Do not use names of
   individuals in the cases themselves, and avoid attrib-
   uting specific comments to specific informants.

5. The general order of topics for each case should be:

   I.   Background (about 2-3 pages)

   II. Status of Routinization (cover all passages and
        cycles and use three subtopics as subheads if
        possible--about 6-8 pages)

   III. Reasons for Routinization Status (cover hypoth-
        eses in your priority order of their importance
        --about 6-8 pages)

I. BACKGROUND

A. NATURE OF THE AGENCY/INNOVATION

1. General structure/function/domain of influence.

2. Number of employees and annual operating budget; budget history including anticipated expansion or cuts.

3. Dominant types of personnel organizations;

    --Civil service

    --Unions

    --"Natural" employee groupings

4. Any salient recent events affecting the agency,

    --e.g., personnel turnover due to elections, restructuring, unusual publicity.

5. Where does the innovation fall within the agency?

    --Who is involved in the day-to-day operation of the innovation (i.e., key personnel and titles--current).

    --How important is the innovation for the day-to-day operation of that subdivision.

6. How did the agency come to use the innovation?

    --Why was it thought to be a good idea?

    --Initial funding?

    --Who was the initiator, main supporter, continued supporters?

    --Was there ever opposition to the innovation?

7. Has the innovation changed at all since it was first introduced? How flexible is the innovation?

8. What hardware/equipment is currently used in the innovation? Which of this is minimally necessary for the innovation to operate?

B. NATURE OF THE COMMUNITY (all information from secondary sources except questions 5 and 6)

1. Population

2. SES and demographic data

3. Local government employees/1000 population

4. Geographic location and type of government

5. Has the community changed much in the last ten years?

6. What are the pressing current problems/concerns/hopes of the agency with respect to community needs?

II. STATUS OF ROUTINIZATION

A. BUDGET AND PURCHASING

1. The annual cost of the innovation in $\begin{vmatrix} \text{money} \\ \text{personnel} \end{vmatrix}$

    --Budget history?

2. Is the budget support $\begin{vmatrix} \text{money} \\ \text{personnel} \end{vmatrix}$ part of the regular budget?

    --If so, when and how did it occur?

    --If not, for how many years have requests been made for regular funds or permanent positions?

3. To what extent has equipment been rented or purchased?

    --Significant dates, if purchased. $\Big[$ If not purchased at time of
    --Long-term contracts? $\Big\{$ adoption, why the decision
    $\Big[$ to do so later?

4. If there were budget cuts, would the innovation be treated as a typical agency program, or would it be given special treatment? (Or: are budget decisions pertinent to the innovation made in the same way as budget decisions about other agency programs?)

5. Has the use of the innovation been associated with any reductions in budget for personnel or other agency programs?

    --If so, when did reductions take place?

B. PERSONNEL AND TRAINING

1. How many people are involved full-time only in operating the innovation?

    --Civil service status and position?

    --Are there special job classifications, with own exams? When established?

2. How many practitioners use the innovation as part of their job?

    --A new function? When?

    --New job descriptions?

3. What kind of training program is associated with the use of the innovation?

    --Special vs. ongoing programs

    --Field training versus basic training in service academies

    --When started (and how many cycles)

    --Part of any training manuals?

4. Has the agency brought in any new staff in connection with the innovation whose qualifications or background differed from that of the existing staff?

5. Since the innovation was implemented have any individuals outside the agency ever provided assistance with the innovation?

6. Has the innovation survived a round (how many cycles) of turnover among key personnel or among practitioners who use the innovation?

7. Is there any evidence of formal changes in practitioner certification procedures or performance standards that reflect the use of the innovation?

C. ORGANIZATIONAL GOVERNANCE AND MAINTENANCE

Operations

1. Has the use of the innovation led to specific revisions in operating manuals or organizational forms and paperwork?

2. Is the use of the innovation mandated by:

    --Legislative act or executive order

    --Reference to specific service standards

    --Judicial decisions

3. Does the innovation involve new maintenance or purchasing procedures?

    --Revised purchasing specifications

    --Training and part of maintenance crew's work (internal or external service)

4. Are there any specific old functions that have been replaced by the innovation?

    --If so, how and when was replacement operationally established?

5. Has the use of the innovation been part of any collective bargaining negotiations?

6. Has there been any reorganization of organizational units or sections in order to use the innovation? When?

Equipment

1. Have any aspects of the equipment involved in the innovation changed since it was first introduced?

    --New equipment purchased.

    --Second generation materials (more cycles?)

    --Equipment improvement or redesign (if so, who was involved in the effort?)

2. Has the equipment involved in the innovation been used for any function other than that for which it was originally intended?

III. REASONS FOR ROUTINIZATION STATUS

A. HYPOTHESES (SERVICE APPLICATIONS AND OUTCOMES)

H_1, H_3

1. General function and range of specific applications. Is it a core application?

--What services are provided to whom?

--Who benefits, directly or indirectly? Any specific measures of service payoffs or improvement?

H_1

2. In what ways is the innovation different from what preceded it?

--New function/services | Another definition

--New equipment | of core application

H_3

3. What are the perceived benefits of this innovation?

--Who has benefitted most?

--Has the innovation created any problems, anticipated or otherwise?

H_2

4. Is there more than one application for which the innovation can be used? If so, how are priorities set and resources shared? Is there evidence of competition among the applications?

B. HYPOTHESES (EXTERNAL ENVIRONMENT)

H_5, H_6

1. Outside the agency and local government, who have been the most enthusiastic supporters of the innovation?

H_5

2. Are the users of the innovation (clients) organized into supporting the innovation?

3. Are there potential clients who serve as a larger pool from which community support is derived?

H_6

4. Who in the community is likely to be aware of innovation?

5. Has there been any publicity about the innovation in recent months?

6. Who in the community benefits most from innovation? Who is likely to support it; oppose it?

H_4

7. Did the use of the innovation begin as a result of:

--Crisis condition

--Chronic service needs

C. HYPOTHESES (INTERNAL ENVIRONMENT)

h_9, H_{10} {
1. Do older personnel teach newer personnel how to use the innovation?

2. Is there apparent resistance or acceptance by practitioners in in using the innovation?

3. Would practitioners now resist removal or dropping of the innovation?
}

H_{7-9} {
4. For those involved, is career advancement and reward a likely positive incentive or irrelevant (or negative)?
}

H_7 {
5. To what extent do top agency administrators (e.g., chief, deputy chief, comptroller) support the innovation? How is their support indicated?
}

H_8 {
6. To what extent has there been an active innovator who:

    --Coordinates activities

    --Can make repairs if necessary

    --Seeks to institutionalize the use of the innovation
}

H_{10} {
7. Are there any groups within the local agency or government who oppose the innovation (and who might support some other innovation)?
}

Keypuncher: Go to
new card--punch 6
in col. 1, dupli-
cate cols. 2-10

METHODOLOGICAL CHARACTERISTICS OF THE INTERVIEW

1. Interviewer _____   ☐   *11/*

2. Date(s) of interview _____   ☐☐☐☐☐☐   *12-17/*

3. What is the respondent's relationship to the innovation?

                          Director of innovation........   1   *18/*
                          Assistant to director of
                            innovation...................   2
                          Staff person who knew most
                            about innovation.............   3
                          Only person in department
                            who knew about innovation....   4
                          Other (list) _____   5

4. What was the length of the interview?   Minutes
                                                      ☐☐☐   *19-21/*
5. What was the respondent's attitude toward the interview?

                          Friendly......................   1   *22/*
                          Accepting.....................   2
                          Indifferent...................   3
                          Hostile.......................   4
                          No response...................   9

6. Did the respondent appear willing to talk at greater length?

                          Yes...........................   1   *23/*
                          No............................   2
                          No response...................   9

7. After contacting the respondent, was it necessary to set up an
    appointment to conduct the interview at a later date?

                          Yes...........................   1   *24/*
                          No............................   2

8. Was the interview interrupted and completed at a later time?

                          Yes...(ANSWER Q.9A)...........   1   *25/*
                          No............................   2

    8A. Why? _____

         _____   ☐   *26/*

9. Was more than one respondent interviewed?

                          Yes...(ANSWER Q.10A)..........   1   *27/*
                          No............................   2

    9A. Why? _____

         _____   ☐   *28/*

10. Did the respondent voluntarily offer the names of other people
    with whom we might wish to speak?

Yes..........................	1	*29/*
No...........................	2	
No response..................	9	

11. What appeared to be the extent of the respondent's knowledge
    of the innovation?

Knowledgeable.................	1	*30/*
Somewhat informed.............	2	
Not well informed.............	3	
No response...................	9	

12. Did the respondent ask for Rand to clear the interview with his
    superior?

Yes..........................	1	*31/*
No...........................	2	

13. Did the respondent request confidentiality?

Yes..........................	1	*32/*
No...........................	2	

14. What was the cost of this interview, including preliminary
    telephone calls?

33-36/

COMPUTER-ASSISTED INSTRUCTION

City and State _____

Respondent's Name _____
            Title _____
Telephone Number _____
Interview Dates   _____

Secondary Respondent's Name _____
                     Title _____
Telephone Number   _____

Appointment set for (day) _____
    (time) _____ (with) _____

If School District was called previously for any innovation:

Respondent's Name _____
            Title _____
Telephone Number _____
Date of Call   _____
Innovation   _____
Rand Screeners   _____

A. EQUIPMENT

____ 1. *Has your district ever had its own computer that included instructional applications?* [PROBE WITH FIRST FIVE APPLICATIONS ON P. 5]

Yes................................. 1   *11/*
No.................................. 2
No response......................... 9

____ 2. *How is the computer operation administered?*

School district alone.................. 1   *12/*
School district and other agency.... 2
Other agency, with school district
consulted as users (name agency)

_____ 3
No response........................ 9

____ 3. *Are there any full-time computer operators on the school district staff?*

Yes................................. 1   *13/*
No.................................. 2
No response......................... 9

IF Q.1 = 2,9; OR Q.2 = 3,9; AND Q.3 = 2,9, GO TO Q.46, THEN TERMINATE
INTERVIEW.

____ 4. *Have you ever had more than one computer for instructional purposes?*

Yes...(GO TO Q.4A AND 4B)........... 1   *14/*
No...(GO TO Q.4A ONLY).............. 2
No response......................... 9

____ 4A. *Please name the computer (core) model(s).*
[IF ONE ONLY, GO TO Q.5; NOTE "NOT SURE" RESPONSES WITH
ASTERISK]

#1 (list) _____   *15/*

#2 (list) _____

#3 (list) _____

____ 4B. *Which of these models has served the most students over time?*
[THIS IS THE FOCUS FOR ALL REMAINING QUESTIONS]

Fill in number from Q.4A (1,2, or 3) ⬚   *16/*

____ 5. *Is the computer still in use?*

Yes................................. 1   *17/*
No...(GO TO Q.5A)................... 2
No response......................... 9

____ 5A. *What was the last year it was used?*
[ENTER TWO-DIGIT YEAR; ENTER 99 IF NO RESPONSE]

Year   ⬚⬚   *18-19/*

_____ 6. *How many models of core computers preceded this one?*
[ENTER NUMBER OF MODELS; ENTER 9 IF NO RESPONSE]

$\qquad$ # models preceding current one   ☐   *20/*

_____ 7. *What year was the first core computer used?*
[ENTER TWO-DIGIT YEAR; ENTER 99 IF NO RESPONSE]

Year   ☐☐   *21-22/*

_____ 8. *How many on-line terminals are connected to this computer?*
[ENTER THREE-DIGIT NUMBER; ENTER 999 IF NO RESPONSE]

terminals   ☐☐☐   *23-25/*

_____ 8A. *How many of these terminals are used for instructional*
applications?
[ENTER THREE-DIGIT NUMBER; ENTER 999 IF NO RESPONSE]

terminals   ☐☐☐   *26-28/*

_____ 9. *Is the core computer purchased, leased, or on a lease-purchase*
option?

Purchased...(ANSWER Q.9A)...........	1
Leased...(ANSWER Q.10)..............	2
Lease-purchase...(GO TO Q.11).......	3
Other (list)_____	4
No response...(GO TO Q.11)..........	9

29/

_____ 9A. *When was this core computer purchased?*
[ENTER TWO-DIGIT YEAR; ENTER 99 IF NO RESPONSE]

Year   ☐☐   *30-31/*

_____10. *How many years is the lease for?*
[ENTER ONE DIGIT; ENTER 9 IF NO RESPONSE]

# of years   ☐   *32/*

_____11. *Is there a service contract for repair and maintenance of the*
computer?

[IF YES] *With whom?*

[IF NO] *Who provides repair and maintenance?*

Yes, contract with manufacturer.....	1
Yes, contract with other outside....	
group (list)_____	2
Yes, no response for by whom........	3
No, service provided by district....	4
No, service provided by other	
agency (list)_____	5
No, no response for by whom.........	6
No response.........................	9

33/

____12. *Was there any technical assistance from outside the district in order to begin the computer-assisted instructional applications?*

[IF YES] *From what source?*

Yes, manufacturer...................	1	*34/*
Yes, other education agency.........	2	
Yes, local university...............	3	
Yes, other (list)..................	4	
Yes, combination (list)_____	5	
No.................................	6	
No response........................	9	

____13. *Has there been any <u>continuing</u> technical assistance from outside the district for the computer-assisted instructional applications?*

[IF YES] *From what source?*

Yes, manufacturer...................	1	*35/*
Yes, other education agency.........	2	
Yes, local university...............	3	
Yes, other (list)_____	4	
Yes, combination (list)_____	5	
No.................................	6	
No response........................	9	

B. SERVICES

USE THE FOLLOWING CHART FOR QUESTIONS 14-19; NOTE "NOT SURE" RESPONSES BY PLACING ASTERISK IN BOX WITH CHECK MARK.

14. *What are the main applications or functions of the computer operation?* [PROBE WITH LIST]

15. *What year was (application) first performed by a computer?*

16. *Of these applications, were any <u>not</u> performed before the computer operation began?*

[IF YES] *Which ones?*

17. *If the computer could not be used for a week, which of the applications could <u>not</u> be performed <u>any</u> other way?*

18. *Of the applications that the computer provides, which are the top three that are responsible for most of the operating time of the core computer?*

19. *Have there been any problems in setting priorities among different applications because of limitations on computer time or capacity?*

[IF YES] *Which applications?*

[IF YES] *How has the department dealt with such problems?* (list)

_____

_____

ENTER 1 IF YES, IF NO, 9 IN NO RESPONSE FOR ALL QUESTIONS EXCEPT Q.15;
FOR Q.15, ENTER TWO-DIGIT YEAR OR 99 IF NO RESPONSE; NOTE "NOT SURE"
RESPONSES BY PLACING ASTERISK IN BOX NEXT TO ENTERED NUMBER.

APPLICATION	Q.14	Q.15	Q.16	Q.17	Q.18	Q.19	
Computer math courses							36-42/
Programming in regular math							43-49/
CAI for all students in regular courses							50-56/
Special projects for advanced students							57-63/
Remedial practice							64-70/
						Keypuncher: Go to new card--punch 2 in col. 1, duplicate cols. 2-10.	
Other:							11-17/
Other:							18-24/
Other:							25-31/
Student scheduling							32-38/
Test scoring, evaluations, or research							39-45/
Grade reporting							46-52/
						Keypuncher: Go to new card--punch 3 in col. 1, duplicate cols. 2-10.	
Budget or accounts							11-17/
Payroll							18-24/
School personnel							25-31/
Student records							32-38/
Property inventory							39-45/
Other:							46-52/
Other:							53-59/

C. STAFF AND ADMINISTRATION

USE FOLLOWING CHART FOR QUESTIONS 20-22; NOTE "NOT SURE" RESPONSES BY
PLACING ASTERISK TO RIGHT OF CIRCLED NUMBER.

20. *Does the district have (personnel) associated with the computer-
     assisted instructional applications in its current budget?*

     [IF YES] *How many full-time equivalent (personnel) are there?*
               [ENTER TWO-DIGIT NUMBER; ENTER 99 IF NO RESPONSE]

     [IF NO, ENTER 00]

21. *Is (personnel) a* permanent *position in the district's budget?*

22. *Does the specific civil service or other official personnel classi-
     fication include CAI-qualifications for (personnel)?*

```
Keypuncher: Go to
new card--punch 4
in col. 1, dupli-
cate cols. 2-10.
```

Personnel	Q.20 # FTE?	Q.21 POSITION PERMANENT?			Q.22 CLASSIFICATION?			
		Yes	No	No Response	Yes	No	No Response	
General Coordinator		1	2	9	1	2	9	*11-14/*
Curriculum Supervisor (any subject)		1	2	9	1	2	9	*15-18/*
Teaching Staff		1	2	9	1	2	9	*19-22/*
Other: (list)		1	2	9	1	2	9	*23-26/*
Other: (list)		1	2	9	1	2	9	*27-30/*

____23. *For the teaching staff, what kind of* formal *computer training is
        routinely provided by the district?*

Informal assistance................	1	*31/*
Special classes run by district.....	2	
Classes at local college or manufacturer......................	3	
Other (list)_____	4	
Combination (list)_____	5	
None...(GO TO Q.25)................	6	
No response...(GO TO Q.25).........	9	

____24. *What proportion of the eligible teaching staff has participated in this training?*

Most or all......................... 1   *32/*
About half.......................... 2
Few or a small minority............. 3
None................................ 4
No response......................... 9

____25. *In order for a new teacher to qualify for computer-assisted instruction subjects, must he or she have had formal computer training?*

Yes................................. 1   *33/*
No.................................. 2
No response......................... 9

____26. *How many individuals have filled the coordinator position, including the present one?*
[ENTER TWO-DIGIT NUMBER; ENTER 99 IF NO RESPONSE]

coordinators   ☐☐   *34-35/*

[IF MORE THAN ONE] *What position does the previous coordinator now hold?*   (list)
_____   ☐   *36/*

____27. *Was the coordinator ever a teacher in the district and what position does the coordinator have?*   [PROBE WITH LIST]

Not teacher, in data processing unit 1   *37/*
Yes, teacher, in data processing
unit................................ 2
Yes, teacher, in curriculum depart-
ment................................ 3
Other (list)_____ 4
No response......................... 9

____28. *Does any member of the curriculum (instructional) department assist in the CAI operation?*   [PROBE WITH LIST]

Serves as main coordinator......... 1   *38/*
Collaborates with data processing
unit in coordinating computer use.. 2
Other (list)_____ 3
Combination (list)_____ 4
None................................ 5
No response......................... 9

____29. *Who was responsible for first introducing computer-assisted instruction into the district?*

Superintendent...(ANSWER Q.29A).....	1
Staff person within data processing unit (ANSWER Q.29A).................	2
Staff person within curriculum department...(ANSWER Q.29A).........	3
Person outside district.............	4
Group of persons (e.g., city council, agency consortium).............	5
Combination of above (list)	
_____	6
Other (list)_____	7
No response........................	9

39/

____ 29A. *Is this person still with the district?*

Yes...(ANSWER Q.29B)................	1
No.................................	2
No response........................	9

40/

____ 29B. *In what position? (list)_____*

41/

____30. *Why was computer-assisted instruction initiated?*

Growing demands from teachers or students............................	1
Rising enrollment..................	2
Specific need or crisis (list)	
_____	3
All of above.......................	4
Combination of above (list)_____	5
Other (list)_____	6
No response........................	9

42/

____31. *What is the source of most of the software used for instructional applications?*

Own programming staff within district	1
Programming staff in other city agency.............................	2
Consultants or external programmers.	3
Prepackaged programs...............	4
Students or teachers in the district	5
Other (list)_____	6
No response........................	9

43/

____32. *Where do most of the operating funds for CAI come from?*
[USE LIST AS PROBE]

Regular part of district budget..... 1   *44/*
Some other part of municipal budget 2
Federal grants or funds............ 3
Special bond issue or other levy.... 4
State grants or funds.............. 5
Combination (list)_____ 6
Other (list)_____ 7
No response....................... 9

____33. *Were there ever any federal, state, or foundation funds used to support CAI?*

Yes, federal....................... 1   *45/*
Yes, state........................ 2
Yes, foundation.................... 3
Yes, combination (list)_____ 4
No...(GO TO Q.34).................. 5
No response....................... 9

33A. *Where did these funds come from?* [ENTER 9 IF NO RESPONSE]

33B. *During what years?* [ENTER 99-99 IF NO RESPONSE]

33C. *What was the amount?* [ENTER 99 IF NO RESPONSE; MAY ROUND
TO NEAREST $100,000 OR LIST RANGE]

[PLACE ASTERISK NEXT TO ANY "NOT SURE" RESPONSE]

Source	Years	Amount
_____	_____	_____	*46-52/*
_____	_____	_____	*53-59/*
_____	_____	_____	*60-66/*

Keypuncher: Go to
new card--punch 5
in col. 1, dupli-
cate cols. 2-10.

34. *What was the annual budget for CAI during 1976, excluding personnel
and salaries? 1975? 1974?*
[ENTER AMOUNT; ENTER 999 IF NO RESPONSE; MAY ROUND TO NEAREST
$100,000 OR LIST RANGE; NOTE "NOT SURE" RESPONSE WITH ASTERISK]

1976 _____   *11-14/*

1975 _____   *15-18/*

1974 _____   *19-22/*

_____35. *Have any changes in textbook adoptions been made due to the use of CAI?* [USE HIGHEST]

New texts with CAI sections for all
relevant classes..................... 1   *23/*
New texts with CAI sections for
some classes........................ 2
Supplementary CAI materials......... 3
Texts for special computer courses.. 4
None................................ 5
Other (list)_____ 6
No response......................... 9

_____36. *Are there any state or local laws or regulations that call for the existence of CAI?*

Yes (list)_____ 1   *24/*
No.................................. 2
No response......................... 9

_____37. *Are any of the instructional applications of the computer linked to some state or local law or regulation?*

Yes (list)_____ 1   *25/*
No.................................. 2
No response......................... 9

D. INTERNAL FACTORS

USE FOLLOWING CHART FOR QUESTION 38; NOTE "NOT SURE" RESPONSES BY PLACING
ASTERISK TO RIGHT OF CIRCLED NUMBER.

38. *To what extent do teachers in different subjects use CAI?*

Subject	Most	Few	None	No Response	
Math	1	2	3	9	*26/*
Reading	1	2	3	9	*27/*
Chemistry	1	2	3	9	*28/*
Biology	1	2	3	9	*29/*
Social Science	1	2	3	9	*30/*
Other:	1	2	3	9	*31/*

_____39. *Are the CAI terminals used in a classroom while class is in progress?*

Yes, more than one terminal......... 1   *32/*
Yes, usually one terminal only...... 2
No, special time or classroom
for terminals...................... 3
No response......................... 9

_____40. *Is the amount of available terminal time about right to serve*
        student demands?

                              Yes............................... 1   *33/*
                              No, some terminal time is unused.... 2
                              No, more time is in continual
                              demand............................ 3
                              No, more time is in continual demand
                              <u>and</u> there is a formal waiting list.. 4
                              No response....................... 9

_____41. *Have any service benefits from the instructional applications been*
        recognized?

                              Yes...(ANSWER Q.41A)............... 1   *34/*
                              No................................ 2
                              No response....................... 9

_____ 41A. *How have these service benefits been recognized--reported*
          in the budget, discussed in budget justifications, special
          studies or evaluations, or some other way?

                              Specific savings or efficiencies
                              reported in budget................ 1   *35/*
                              Specific savings or efficiencies....
                              discussed in budget justifications.. 2
                              Special studies or evaluations...... 3
                              Combination of above (list)
                              _____
                                                                 4
                              Other (list)_____ 5
                              None of above...(GO TO Q.42)....... 6
                              No response...(GO TO Q.42)......... 9

_____ 41B. *What is one example of a service benefit?* (list)   *36/*

          _____

          _____

_____42. *In your opinion, has there been resistance of <u>any</u> sort by district*
        personnel in using the computer for instructional applications?

                              Yes...(ANSWER Q.42A)............... 1   *37/*
                              No................................ 2
                              No response....................... 9

_____ 42A. *What was the nature of the resistance?*

                              Over specific applications only..... 1   *38/*
                              Over initial adoption   2
                              Over use of the entire system   3
                              Other (list)_____ 4
                              Combination (list)_____ 5
                              No response....................... 9

E. EXTERNAL FACTORS

___43. *Has there been any publicity regarding the instructional applications?*

Yes, local media or press...........	1	*39/*
Yes, national media or press........	2	
Yes, both...........................	3	
No...(GO TO Q.44)...................	4	
No response...(GO TO Q.44)..........	9	

___43A. *Has the publicity generally been favorable, mixed, or unfavorable?*

Favorable...........................	1	*40/*
Mixed...............................	2	
Unfavorable.........................	3	
No response.........................	9	

USE FOLLOWING CHART FOR QUESTIONS 44-45; NOTE "NOT SURE" RESPONSES BY PLACING ASTERISK TO RIGHT OF CIRCLED NUMBER.

44. *Have there been any active supporters of the instructional applications outside of the school district?*

45. *Have there been any active opposers of the instructional applications outside of the school district?*

	Q.44			Q.45			
	SUPPORTERS OR USERS			OPPOSERS			
Activists	Yes	No	No Response	Yes	No	No Response	
Municipal executive	1	2	9	1	2	9	*41-42/*
Other municipal officers	1	2	9	1	2	9	*43-44/*
Local legislators	1	2	9	1	2	9	*45-46/*
Citizen groups	1	2	9	1	2	9	*47-48/*
Parents	1	2	9	1	2	9	*49-50/*
Other:	1	2	9	1	2	9	*51-52/*

___46. *In the next year or so, do you see any difficulties affecting the overall instructional applications other than budget?*

Yes...(ANSWER Q.46A)................	1	*53/*
No..................................	2	
No response.........................	9	

___46A. *What are these difficulties?* (list)   *54/*

_____

_____

<u>POLICE COMPUTERS</u>

City and State _____

Respondent's Name _____
                    Title _____
Telephone Number _____

Interview Dates _____

Secondary Respondent's Name _____
                    Title _____
Telephone Number _____

Appointment set for (day) _____
      (time) _____ (with) _____

If Police Department was called previously for any innovation:

Respondent's Name _____
                    Title _____
Telephone Number _____

Date of Call _____

Innovation _____

Rand Screeners _____

A. EQUIPMENT

____ 1. *Does your department currently have its own computer?* [A MACHINE REQUIRING PROGRAMMING, NOT JUST ADP]

                    Yes...(GO TO Q.2)...................... 1   *11/*
                    No...................................... 2
                    No response............................ 9

____ 1A. *Did it ever have its own computer?*

                    Yes.................................... 1   *12/*
                    No..................................... 2
                    No response............................ 9

____ 2. *How is the computer operation administered?*

                    Police department alone................ 1   *13/*
                    Police department and other agency..... 2
                    Other agency, with police department
                    consulted as users (name agency
                    _____)......... 3
                    No response............................ 9

____ 3. *Are there any full-time computer operators on the Police Department staff?*

                    Yes.................................... 1   *14/*
                    No..................................... 2
                    No response............................ 9

____ 4. *What model computer (core) do you use today?*

                    #1 (list) _____
                    #2 (list) _____

        IF ALL ANSWERS ARE NEGATIVE--i.e., Q.1 = 2,9; Q.1A = 2,9;
        Q.2 = 3,9; Q.3 = 2,9; <u>or</u> if Q.4 = non-computer--GO TO Q.47,
        THEN TERMINATE INTERVIEW.

____ 5. *How many models of core computers have preceded the current one?*
        [ENTER NUMBER OF MODELS; ENTER 9 IF NO RESPONSE]

                    # models preceding current one   ☐   *15/*

____ 6. *What year was the first core computer used?*
        [ENTER TWO-DIGIT YEAR; ENTER 99 IF NO RESPONSE]

                    Year   ☐☐   *16-17/*

____ 7. *How many on-line terminals are now located within the department?*
        [ENTER THREE-DIGIT NUMBER; ENTER 999 IF NO RESPONSE]

                    # terminals·   ☐☐☐   *18-20/*

____ 8. *Is the core computer currently purchased, leased, or on a lease-purchase option?*

$$\begin{array}{ll}
\text{Purchased...(ANSWER Q.8.A)...............} & 1 \\
\text{Leased...(ANSWER Q.9)...................} & 2 \\
\text{Lease-purchase...(GO TO Q.10)...........} & 3 \\
\text{Other (list)} \rule{3cm}{0.4pt} & 4 \\
\text{No response...(GO TO Q.10).............} & 9
\end{array}$$

21/

____   8A. *When was this core computer purchased?*
         [ENTER TWO-DIGIT YEAR; ENTER 99 IF NO RESPONSE]

                                              Year   ☐☐   22-23/

____ 9. *How many years is the lease for?*
         [ENTER ONE DIGIT; ENTER 9 IF NO RESPONSE]
                                              # of years   ☐   24/

____10. *Was there any technical assistance from outside the department in order to begin the computer operation?*
         [IF YES] *From what source?*

$$\begin{array}{ll}
\text{Yes, manufacturer.......................} & 1 \\
\text{Yes, other law enforcement agency......} & 2 \\
\text{Yes, local university..................} & 3 \\
\text{Yes, other (list)} \rule{2cm}{0.4pt} & 4 \\
\text{Yes, combination (list)} \rule{2cm}{0.4pt} & 5 \\
\text{No...(GO TO Q.12).....................} & 6 \\
\text{No response...........................} & 9
\end{array}$$

25/

____11. *Did any of the individuals who provided this assistance become employees of the Police Department?*

$$\begin{array}{ll}
\text{Yes...................} & 1 \\
\text{No....................} & 2 \\
\text{No response...........} & 9
\end{array}$$

26/

____12. *Has there been any* <u>continuing</u> *technical assistance from outside the department in operating the computer?*
         [IF YES] *From what source?*

$$\begin{array}{ll}
\text{Yes, manufacturer.......................} & 1 \\
\text{Yes, other law enforcement agency......} & 2 \\
\text{Yes, local university..................} & 3 \\
\text{Yes, other (list)} \rule{2cm}{0.4pt} & 4 \\
\text{Yes, combination (list)} \rule{2cm}{0.4pt} & 5 \\
\text{No....................................} & 6 \\
\text{No response...........................} & 9
\end{array}$$

27/

____13. *Is there a service contract for repair and maintenance of the computer?*
         [IF YES] *With whom?*
         [IF NO] *Who provides repair and maintenance?*

$$\begin{array}{ll}
\text{Yes, contract with manufacturer........} & 1 \\
\text{Yes, contract with other outside} & \\
\text{group (list)} \rule{2cm}{0.4pt} & 2 \\
\text{Yes, no response for by whom...........} & 3 \\
\text{No, service provided by department.....} & 4 \\
\text{No, service provided by other agency} & \\
\text{(list)} \rule{2.5cm}{0.4pt} & 5 \\
\text{No, no response for by whom............} & 6 \\
\text{No response...........................} & 9
\end{array}$$

28/

B. <u>SERVICES</u>

      USE FOLLOWING CHART FOR QUESTIONS 14-21; NOTE "NOT SURE" RESPONSES
      BY PLACING ASTERISK IN BOX WITH CHECK MARK.

14. *What are the main applications or functions of the computer operation?*
    [PROBE WITH LIST]

15. *What year was (application) first performed by a computer?*

16. *Of these applications, were any <u>not</u> performed before the computer
    operation began?*

    [IF YES] Which ones?

17. *If the computer could not be used for a week, which of the applications
    could <u>not</u> be performed <u>any</u> other way?*

18. *Of the applications that the computer provides, which are the top
    three that are responsible for most of the operating time of the
    core computer?*

19. *Have there been any problems in setting priorities among different
    applications because of limitations on computer time or capacity?*

    [IF YES] Which applications?

    [IF YES] How has the department dealt with such problems? (list)

_____

20. *Are there any applications that were once tried or used that are no
    longer part of the computer operation?*

    [IF YES] Which applications?

    *[IF YES] What are the main reasons that these applications are no
    longer part of the computer operation? (list)*

_____

21. *In your opinion, if there were severe budget cutbacks, which applica-
    tions would probably have to be discontinued?*

CODING FORM FOR QUESTIONS 14-21

ENTER 1 IF YES, 2 IF NO, 9 IF NO RESPONSE FOR ALL QUESTIONS EXCEPT Q.15; FOR
Q.15, ENTER TWO-DIGIT YEAR OR 99 IF NO RESPONSE; NOTE "NOT SURE" RESPONSES BY
PLACING ASTERISK IN BOX NEXT TO ENTERED NUMBER.

APPLICATION	Q.14	Q.15	Q.16	Q.17	Q.18	Q.19	Q.20	Q.21	
UCR									*29-37/*
Payroll									*38-46/*
Personnel									*47-55/*
Inventory									*56-64/*
Budget or accounts									*65-73/*

Keypuncher: Go to new card--punch 2 in col. 1, duplicate cols. 2-10.

	Q.14	Q.15	Q.16	Q.17	Q.18	Q.19	Q.20	Q.21	
Other:									*11-19/*
Other:									*20-28/*
Other:									*29-37/*
Dispatching									*38-46/*
Case entry									*47-55/*
Traffic									*56-64/*

Keypuncher: Go to new card--punch 3 in col. 1, duplicate cols. 2-10.

	Q.14	Q.15	Q.16	Q.17	Q.18	Q.19	Q.20	Q.21	
Crime analysis									*11-19/*
Search for plates									*20-28/*
Search for stolen property									*29-37/*
Warrants									*38-46/*
Other:									*47-55/*
Other:									*56-64/*
Other:									*65-73/*

C. STAFF AND ADMINISTRATION

USE FOLLOWING CHART FOR QUESTIONS 22-24; NOTE "NOT SURE" RESPONSES
BY PLACING ASTERISK TO RIGHT OF CIRCLED NUMBER.

22. *Does the department have (personnel) associated with operating the
    computer in its current budget?*

    [IF YES] *How many full-time equivalent (personnel) are there?*
          [ENTER TWO-DIGIT NUMBER; ENTER 99 IF NO RESPONSE]

    [IF NO, ENTER 00]

23. *Is (personnel) a* permanent *position in the department's budget?*

24. *Is there a specific civil service or other official personnel classi-
    fication for (personnel)?*

```
Keypuncher: Go to
new .card--punch 4
in col. 1, dupli-
cate cols. 2-10.
```

Personnel	Q.22 NUMBER FTE?			Q.23 POSITION PERMANENT? Yes	No	No Response	Q.24 CLASSIFICATION? Yes	No	No Response	
Coordinator				1	2	9	1	2	9	*11-14/*
Programmer				1	2	9	1	2	9	*15-18/*
Clerical				1	2	9	1	2	9	*19-22/*
Other (list)				1	2	9	1	2	9	*23-26/*
Other (list)				1	2	9	1	2	9	*27-30/*

[SKIP Q.25 IF THERE ARE NO PROGRAMMERS IN DEPARTMENT]
____25. *For new programmers, what kind of* formal *computer training is routinely
    provided by the department?*

Special training sessions by manufacturer.........................	1 *31/*
Formal training classes run by department...........................	2
Training in police academy...........	3
Other (list)_____	4
Combination (list)_____	5
None.................................	6
No response..........................	9

____26. *In order for a person to qualify as a programmer in this department,*
        must he or she pass an exam?

____27. [IS YES] *What agency gives the exam?*
        [PROBE TO DETERMINE IF CIVIL SERVICE]

                          Yes, civil service.................. 1   *32/*
                          Yes, test by Department............. 2
                          Yes, test by other agency (name
                          agency)_____ 3
                          Yes, combination (list)_____ 4
                          No................................. 5
                          No response........................ 9

____28. *How many individuals have filled the coordinator position, including*
        the present one?
        [ENTER TWO-DIGIT NUMBER; ENTER 99 IF NO RESPONSE]

                          # coordinators   ☐☐   *36-37/*

        [IF MORE THAN ONE] *What position does the previous coordinator*
        now hold? (list) _____ ☐   *38/*

____29. *Who was responsible for first introducing the computer into the*
        department?
                          Chief of Department.(ANSWER Q.29A) 1   *39/*
                          Staff person within department...
                          (ANSWER Q.29A)................... 2
                          Staff person in other agency
                          (give position)_____ 3
                          Person outside city government... 4
                          Group of persons (e.g., city
                          council, agency consortium)...... 5
                          Combination of above (list)
                          _____ 6
                          Other (list)_____ 7
                          No response..................... 9

____   29A. *Is this person still with the department?*
                          Yes...(ANSWER Q.29B)............. 1   *40/*
                          No 2
                          No response..................... 9

____   29B. *In what position?*
        (list) _____ ☐   *41/*

____30. *Why was the computer operation initiated?*
                          Growing demands for recordkeeping 1   *42/*
                          Rising incidence of crime........ 2
                          Specific need or crisis (list)
                          _____ 3
                          All of the above................. 4
                          Combination of above (list)
                          _____ 5
                          Other (list)_____ 6
                          No response..................... 9

____31. *What is the source of most of the software used by the computer operation?*

Own programming staff within
department......................... 1   *43/*
Programming staff in other city
agency............................. 2
Consultants or external programmers 3
Prepackaged programs............... 4
Other (list)_____ 5
No response........................ 9

____32. *Where do most of the operating funds for the computer come from?*
[USE LIST AS PROBE]

Regular part of Department budget.. 1   *44/*
Some other part of municipal budget 2
Federal grants or funds............ 3
Special bond issue or other levy... 4
State grants or funds.............. 5
Combination (list)_____ 6
Other (list)_____ 7
No response........................ 9

____33. *Within the police department's organization, is the computer operation a separate section or part of another section?*

Separate section................... 1   *45/*
Part of another section (list)
_____ 2
Other (list)_____ 3
No response........................ 9

____34. *Were there ever any federal, state, or foundation funds used to support the computer operation?*

Yes, federal....................... 1   *46/*
Yes, state......................... 2
Yes, foundation.................... 3
Yes, combination (list)_____ 4
No...(GO TO Q.35).................. 5
No response........................ 9

34A. *Where did these funds come from?* [ENTER 9 IF NO RESPONSE]

34B. *During what years?* [ENTER 99-99 IF NO RESPONSE]

34C. *What was the amount?* [ENTER 99 IF NO RESPONSE; MAY ROUND TO NEAREST $100,000 OR LIST RANGE]

[PLACE ASTERISK NEXT TO ANY "NOT SURE" RESPONSE]

Source	Years	Amount								
_____	_____	_____								*47-53/*
_____	_____	_____								*54-60/*
_____	_____	_____								*61-67/*

35. *What was the annual budget for the computer operation during 1976,*
excluding personnel and salaries? 1975? 1974?
[ENTER AMOUNT; ENTER 999 IF NO RESPONSE; MAY ROUND TO NEAREST
$100,000 OR LIST RANGE; NOTE "NOT SURE" RESPONSE WITH ASTERISK]

    1976 _____   □□□□   *11-14/*

    1975 _____   □□□□   *15-18/*

    1974 _____   □□□□   *19-22/*

____36. *What formal changes in organizational procedures have been made due*
to the use of the computer?

Creation of new organizational
units............................. 1 *23/*
Creation of new forms for report-
ing information to the computer....
(ANSWER Q. 36A)................... 2
Both...(ANSWER Q.36A).............. 3
Neither........................... 4
Other (list)_____ 5
No response....................... 9

36A. *Are any of the old forms still available?*

They never existed................ 1 *24/*
They are still available in the
department........................ 2
They are still available outside
the department.................... 3
They are no longer available...... 4
No response....................... 9

____37. *Are there any state or local laws or regulations that call for the*
existence of the computer operation?

Yes (list)_____ 1 *25/*
No................................ 2
No response....................... 9

____38. *Are any of the services the computer provides called for by some*
state or local law or regulations?

Yes (list)_____ 1 *26/*
No................................ 2
No response....................... 9

D. INTERNAL FACTORS

USE FOLLOWING CHART FOR QUESTIONS 39-40; NOTE "NOT SURE" RESPONSES
BY PLACING ASTERISK TO RIGHT OF CIRCLED NUMBER.

39. *Does (personnel) use the computer's* printouts *on a regular basis?*

40. *Does (personnel) use the computer* on-line *on a regular basis?*

	Q.39			Q.40			
	USES PRINTOUTS?			USES ON-LINE?			
Personnel	Yes	No	No Response	Yes	No	No Response	
Top Administrators	1	2	9	1	2	9	*27-28/*
Police supervisors	1	2	9	1	2	9	*29-30/*
Dispatching staff	1	2	9	1	2	9	*31-32/*
Officers on the street, excluding traffic	1	2	9	1	2	9	*33-34/*
Other:	1	2	9	1	2	9	*35-36/*
Other:	1	2	9	1	2	9	*37-38/*

____41. *What kind of computer training does the department provide for any police officers who are users?*

On the job only...(ANSWER Q.41A)...	1	*39/*
Some special classes...............	2	
Some class offered by police academy...........................	3	
Other (list)_____	4	
No training.......................	5	
No response.......................	9	

____41A. *If a user were to leave, who is responsible for training his replacement?*

Employee being replaced............	1	*40/*
Employee's supervisor..............	2	
Computer operations staff, providing some on the job training....		
Other (list)_____	4	
No one............................	5	
No response.......................	9	

____42. *Have any service benefits from the computer been recognized?*

                              Yes...(ANSWER Q.42A)............... 1   *41/*
                              No................................. 2
                              No response........................ 9

____   42A. *How have these service benefits been recognized--reported in*
                    the budget, discussed in budget justifications, special
                    studies or evaluations, or some other way?

                              Specific savings or efficiencies
                              reported in budget................. 1   *42/*
                              Specific savings or efficiencies
                              discussed in budget justifications. 2
                              Special studies or evaluations..... 3
                              Combination of above (list)

                              _____
                                                              4
                              Other (list)_____ 5
                              None of above...(GO TO Q.43)....... 6
                              No response...(GO TO Q.43)......... 9

____   42B. *What is one example of a service benefit?* (list)   *43/*

              _____

              _____

____43. *In your opinion, has there been resistance of any sort by depart-*
        mental personnel in using the computer?

                              Yes...(ANSWER Q.43A)............... 1   *44/*
                              No................................. 2
                              No response........................ 9

____   43A. *What was the nature of the resistance?*

                              Over specific applications only.... 1   *45/*
                              Over initial adoption.............. 2
                              Over use of the entire system...... 3
                              Other (list)_____ 4
                              Combination (list)_____ 5
                              No response........................ 9

E. **EXTERNAL FACTORS**

____ 44. *Has there been any publicity regarding the department's computer?*

Yes, local media or press..........	1	*46/*
Yes, national media or press.......	2	
Yes, both.........................	3	
No...(GO TO Q.45).................	4	
No response...(GO TO Q.45).........	9	

____ 44A. *Has the publicity generally been favorable, mixed, or un-favorable?*

Favorable.........................	1	*47/*
Mixed.............................	2	
Unfavorable.......................	3	
No response.......................	9	

USE FOLLOWING CHART FOR QUESTIONS 45-46; NOTE "NOT SURE" RESPONSES
BY PLACING ASTERISK TO RIGHT OF CIRCLED NUMBER

45. *Have there been any active supporters or users of the computer out-side of the Police Department?* [USE LIST AS PROBE]

46. *Have there been any active opposers of the computer outside of the Police Department?* [USE LIST AS PROBE]

	Q.45			Q.46			
	SUPPORTERS OR USERS			OPPOSERS			
Activists	Yes	No	No Response	Yes	No	No Response	
Municipal executive	1	2	9	1	2	9	*48-49/*
Other municipal officers	1	2	9	1	2	9	*50-51/*
Local legislators	1	2	9	1	2	9	*52-53/*
Citizen groups	1	2	9	1	2	9	*54-55/*
Other:	1	2	9	1	2	9	*56-57/*

____ 47. *In the next year or so, do you see any difficulties affecting the computer operation other than budget?*

Yes...(ANSWER Q.47A)..............	1	*58/*
No................................	2	
No response.......................	9	

____ 47A. *What are these difficulties?* (list)   *59/*

_____

_____

MOBILE INTENSIVE CARE UNITS

City and State _____

Respondent's Name _____

Title _____

Telephone Number _____

Interview Dates _____

Secondary Respondent's Name _____

Title _____

Telephone Number _____

Appointment set for (day) _____

(time) _____ (with) _____

If Fire Department was called previously for any innovation:

Respondent's Name _____

Title _____

Telephone Number _____

Date of Call _____

Innovation _____

Rand Screeners _____

A. EQUIPMENT

_____ 1. *Does your department currently have a mobile intensive care unit?*

                                        Yes...(GO TO Q.2)............. 1   *11/*
                                        No........................... 2
                                        No response.................. 9

_____   1A. *Did it ever have one?*

                                        Yes.......................... 1   *12/*
                                        No...:....................... 2
                                        No response.................. 9

_____ 2. *Are the personnel who are part of your emergency medical service trained to provide (service)?*

	Yes	No	No response	
Cardiac defibrillation	1	2	9	*13/*
ECG transmission	1	2	9	*14/*
Drug administration	1	2	9	*15/*

_____ 3. *What department supervises the personnel of the emergency medical service operation?*

                                        Fire department alone......... 1   *16/*
                                        Fire department and other
                                          agency...................... 2
                                        Other agency, with fire depart-
                                          ment consulted (name agency)
                                        _____
                                                                       3
                                        Other agency (list)
                                        _____
                                                                       4
                                        No response.................. 9

IF ALL ANSWERS ARE NEGATIVE--i.e., Q.1 = 2,9; Q.1A = 2,9; Q.2 = 2,9 ON
TWO OF THREE SERVICES; OR Q.3 = 3,4,9--GO TO Q.35, THEN TERMINATE
INTERVIEW

_____ 4. *Does your emergency medical service operation use specially equipped mobile intensive care vehicles?*

     [IF NO] *How is the equipment carried to the scene of an emergency?*

                                        Yes, special vehicle........... 1   *17/*
                                        No, added to existing fire
                                          trucks....................... 2
                                        No, carried in a car........... 3
                                        No, other (list)_____ 4
                                        No, combination (list)_____ 5
                                        No, no response................ 6
                                        No response.................... 9

_____   4A. *How many mobile intensive care units are currently in operation?*
               [ENTER NUMBER OF UNITS; ENTER 9 IF NO RESPONSE]

                                        # units   ☐   *18/*

_____ 5. *What year was the first unit acquired?*
[ENTER TWO-DIGIT YEAR; ENTER 99 IF NO RESPONSE]

Year   ☐☐   *19-20/*

_____ 6. *Have any of the units currently in operation replaced older models?*

Yes........................... 1   *21/*
No...(GO TO Q.7).............. 2
No response................... 9

6A. *How many models of units preceded the current ones?*
[ENTER NUMBER OF MODELS; ENTER 9 IF NO RESPONSE]

models preceding current ones   ☐   *22/*

_____ 7. *Have any units either been removed from service or moved to another agency* [WITHOUT BEING REPLACED]?

Yes........................... 1   *23/*
No...(GO TO Q.8).............. 2
No response................... 9

7A. *How many were removed or moved?*

During what years?

[IF MOVED] *To what agency?*

Why did this change occur?

[NOTE "NOT SURE" RESPONSES WITH ASTERISK]

Number	Year	Agency	Reason

_____ _____ _____ _____   ☐☐☐☐☐☐   *24-29/*

_____ _____ _____ _____   ☐☐☐☐☐☐   *30-35/*

_____ _____ _____ _____   ☐☐☐☐☐☐   *36-41/*

_____ 8. *Was there any technical assistance from outside your department in order to begin the mobile intensive care unit?*

Yes, manufacturer............. 1   *42/*
Yes, other fire department.... 2
Yes, local university......... 3
Yes, other (list)_____ 4
Yes, combination (list)

_____ 5
No...(GO TO Q.9).............. 6
No response................... 9

_____ 8A. *Did any of the individuals who provided this assistance become employees of the fire department or mobile intensive care unit?*

Yes........................... 1   *43/*
No............................ 2
No response................... 9

_____ 9. *Has there been any <u>continuing</u> technical assistance from outside
          the department for this operation?*

```
Yes, manufacturer.............  1     44/
Yes, other fire department....  2
Yes, local university.........  3
Yes, other (list)_____    4
Yes, combination (list)
_____ 5
No...........................   6
No response..................   9
```

_____ 10. *Is there a service contract for repair and maintenance of the
           emergency medical equipment?*

     [IF YES]   *With whom?*

     [IF NO]   *Who provides repair and maintenance?*

```
Yes, contract with manufacturer.  1    45/
Yes, contract with other out-
   side group (list)_____   2
Yes, no response for by whom....   3
No, service provided by de-
   partment.....................   4
No, service provided by other
   agency (list)_____    5
No, no response for by whom.....   6
No response.....................   9
```

B. SERVICES

     USE FOLLOWING CHART FOR QUESTIONS 11-14; NOTE "NOT SURE" RESPONSES
     BY PLACING ASTERISK IN BOX WITH CHECK MARK.

11. *What are the prehospital services the emergency medical personnel
     provide?*

12. *What year was (service) first performed by a member of your staff?*

13. *Of the services you have mentioned, what are the top three that are
     performed most often?*

14. *Are there any prehospital services that were once provided but are
     no longer?*

     [IF YES]   *Which services?*

     [IF YES]   *What are the main reasons that these services are no longer
     part of the emergency medical operation?*   (list)

_____

_____

CODING FORM FOR QUESTIONS 11-14

ENTER 1 IF YES, 2 IF NO, 9 IF NO RESPONSE FOR ALL QUESTIONS EXCEPT Q.12;
FOR Q.12, ENTER TWO-DIGIT YEAR OR 99 IF NO RESPONSE; NOTE "NOT SURE"
RESPONSES BY PLACING ASTERISK IN BOX NEXT TO ENTERED NUMBER.

Service	Q.11	Q.12	Q.13	Q.14	
Basic first aid					46-50/
Cardio-pulmonary resuscitation					51-55/
I.V. therapy					56-60/
Drug administration					61-65/
Ventilation techniques					66-70/

> Keypuncher: Go to new card--punch 2 in col. 1, dupli-cate cols. 2-10

Recognition of cardiac arrhythmias					11-15/
Cardiac defibrillation					16-20/
ECG transmission					21-25/
Other:					26-30/
Other:					31-35/
Other:					36-40/

14A. Are there any other city agencies that offer on-site emergency
medical services like those provided by your department?
[NOTE: SOPHISTICATED TECHNIQUES, NOT JUST FIRST AID]

Yes, local hospital.......... 1   41/
Yes, police department........ 2
Yes, other (list)_____ 3
Yes, combination (list) _____ 4
Yes, no response............. 5
No........................... 6
No response.................. 9

15. *Does the department provide transport for victims when hospital care is deemed necessary?*

[IF YES] *In what vehicle?*

[IF NO] *Who provides transport?*

Yes, mobile intensive care unit.	1	42/
Yes, ambulance...................	2	
Yes, other (list)_____	3	
Yes, combination (list)		
_____	4	
No, private ambulance firm......	5	
No, city ambulance..............	6	
No, other (list)_____	7	
No, combination (list)		
_____	8	
No response.....................	9	

[IF YES] *What year did the department first provide transport?*
[ENTER TWO-DIGIT YEAR; ENTER 99 IF NO RESPONSE]

Year ☐☐ 43-44/

C. STAFF AND ADMINISTRATION

    USE FOLLOWING CHART FOR QUESTIONS 16-18; NOTE "NOT SURE" RESPONSES
BY PLACING ASTERISK TO RIGHT OF CIRCLED NUMBER.

16. *Does the department have (personnel) associated with the mobile
intensive care unit operation in its current budget?*

    [IF YES] *How many full-time equivalent (personnel) are there?*
        [ENTER TWO-DIGIT NUMBER; ENTER 99 IF NO RESPONSE]

    [IF NO, ENTER 00]

17. *Is (personnel) a permanent position in the department's budget?*

18. *Is there a specific civil service or other official personnel
classification for (personnel)?*

Personnel	Q.16 NUMBER FTE?		Q.17 POSITION PERMANENT? Yes	No	No Response	Q.18 CLASSIFICATION? Yes	No	No Response	
Coordinator			1	2	9	1	2	9	*45-48/*
MICU staff: Paramedics			1	2	9	1	2	9	*49-52/*
MICU staff: EMT-advanced			1	2	9	1	2	9	*53-56/*
MICU staff: EMT-basic			1	2	9	1	2	9	*57-60/*
MICU-staff: Other			1	2	9	1	2	9	*61-64/*
Civilian medical personnel			1	2	9	1	2	9	*65-68/*
Firemen			1	2	9	1	2	9	*69-72/*
Other (list):			1	2	9	1	2	9	*73-76/*

Keypuncher: Go to new card--punch 3 in col. 1, duplicate cols. 2-10.

USE MOST SOPHISTICATED PERSONNEL TITLE MENTIONED ABOVE, EXCEPT
COORDINATOR, FOR QUESTIONS 19-20.

____19. *For new (personnel), what kind of formal training is routinely
provided by the department?*

Special training sessions by manufacturer........................	1
Formal training classes run by department.........................	2
Training in fire academy............	3
Other (list)_____	4
Combination (list)_____	5
None...(GO TO Q.20).................	6
No response.........................	9

11/

19A. *How many classes of (personnel) have gone through the initial
training program?*
[ENTER TWO-DIGIT NUMBER; ENTER 99 IF NO RESPONSE]

classes   ☐☐   *12-13/*

____20. *In order for a person to qualify as a (personnel), must he or she
pass a special exam and/or be a fire officer?*

Yes exam and yes employee...........	1
Yes exam and no employee............	2
No exam and yes employee...(GO TO Q.20B)..............................	3
No exam and no employee...(GO TO Q.20B)..............................	4
No response.........................	9

14/

____ 20A. *What agency gives the exam?*
[PROBE TO DETERMINE IF CIVIL SERVICE]

Yes, civil service...................	1
Yes, test by department.............	2
Yes, test by local health department or hospital........................	3
Yes, test by other agency (name agency)_____	4
Yes, combination (list)_____	5
No response.........................	9

15/

____ 20B. *For (personnel) who have been initially trained, what kind of
update training is routinely provided by the department?*

Special training sessions by manufacturer........................	1
Formal training classes run by department.........................	2
Training in fire academy............	3
Other (list)_____	4
Combination (list)_____	5
None...(GO TO Q.21).................	6
No response.........................	9

16/

____ 20C. *About how often are these training sessions held?*

Once every two years........... 1   *17/*
Once every 18 months........... 2
Once a year.................... 3
Once every 6 months............ 4
Other (list)_____ 5
No response.................... 9

____21. *How many individuals have filled the coordinator position,*
including the present one?
[ENTER TWO-DIGIT NUMBER; ENTER 99 IF NO RESPONSE]

coordinators   ☐☐   *18-19/*

[IF MORE THAN ONE] *What position does the previous coordinator*
now hold? (list) _____   ☐   *20/*

____22. *Who was responsible for first introducing the mobile intensive*
care unit operation into the department?

Chief of Department...(ANSWER
   Q.22A)....................... 1   *21/*
Staff person within department
   ...(ANSWER Q.22A)............. 2
Staff person in other agency
   (give position)_____ 3
Person outside city government 4
Group of persons (e.g., city
   council, agency consortium).. 5
Combination (list)_____ 6
Other (list)_____ 7
No response... 9

22A. *Is this person still with the department?*

Yes...(ANSWER Q.22B).......... 1   *22/*
No........................... 2
No response.................. 9

22B. *In what position?*
     (list) _____   ☐   *23/*

____23. *Why was the mobile intensive care unit operation initiated?*

Growing demands for better pre-hospital care............	1	24/
Rising incidence of deaths that might have been prevented......................	2	
Specific need or crisis (list) _____	3	
All of the above.............	4	
Combination of above (list) _____	5	
Other (list)_____	6	
No response................	9	

____24. *Where do most of the operating funds for the operation come from?*

Regular part of Department budget......................	1	25/
Some other part of municipal budget......................	2	
Federal grants or funds.......	3	
Special bond issue or other levy........................	4	
State grants or funds.........	5	
Combination (list)_____	6	
Other (list)_____	7	
No response..................	9	

____25. *Within the fire department's organization, is the mobile intensive care unit operation a separate section or part of another section?*

Separate section.............	1	26/
Part of another section (list) _____	2	
Other (list)_____	3	
No response..................	9	

____26. *Were there ever any federal, state, or foundation funds used to*
       support the mobile intensive care unit operation?

                                          Yes, federal.................. 1   *27/*
                                          Yes, state................... 2
                                          Yes, foundation.............. 3
                                          Yes, combination (list)
                                          _____
                                          _____   4
                                          No...(GO TO Q.27)............ 5
                                          No response.................. 9

   26A. *Where did these funds come from?*   [ENTER 9 IF NO RESPONSE]

   26B. *During what years?*   [ENTER 99-99 IF NO RESPONSE]

   26C. *What was the amount?*   [ENTER 99 IF NO RESPONSE; MAY ROUND
         TO NEAREST $100,000 OR LIST RANGE]

   [PLACE ASTERISK NEXT TO ANY "NOT SURE" RESPONSE]

        Source   Years   Amount

   _____ _____ _____   [ ][ ][ ][ ][ ][ ][ ]   *28-34/*

   _____ _____ _____   [ ][ ][ ][ ][ ][ ][ ]   *35-41/*

   _____ _____ _____   [ ][ ][ ][ ][ ][ ][ ]   *42-48/*

   _____ _____ _____   [ ][ ][ ][ ][ ][ ][ ]   *49-55/*

   _____ _____ _____   [ ][ ][ ][ ][ ][ ][ ]   *56-62/*

27. *What was the annual budget for the operation during 1976, excluding*
     personnel and salaries? 1975? 1974?
     [ENTER AMOUNT; ENTER 999 IF NO RESPONSE; MAY ROUND TO NEAREST
     $100,000 OR LIST RANGE; NOTE "NOT SURE" RESPONSES WITH ASTERISK]

        1976 _____   [ ][ ][ ][ ]   *63-66/*

        1975 _____   [ ][ ][ ][ ]   *67-70/*

        1974 _____   [ ][ ][ ][ ]   *71-74/*

____28. *Are there any state or local laws or regulations that call for the*
       existence of the mobile intensive care unit operation?

                                          Yes (list)_____ 1   *75/*
                                          No........................... 2
                                          No response.................. 9

____29. *Are any of the services the personnel provide called for or regulated*
       by some state or local law or regulation?

                                          Yes (list)_____ 1   *76/*
                                          No........................... 2
                                          No response.................. 9

Keypuncher: Go to
new card--punch 4
in col. 1, dupli-
cate cols. 2-10.

D. INTERNAL FACTORS

____30. *Have any service benefits from the mobile intensive care unit
         operation been recognized within the fire department?*

                    Yes...(ANSWER Q.30A).......... 1   *11/*
                    No............................ 2
                    No response................... 9

____   30A. *How have these service benefits been recognized--reported
               in the budget, discussed in budget justifications, special
               studies or evaluations, or some other way?*

                    Specific savings or efficien-
                    cies reported in budget...... 1   *12/*
                    Specific savings or efficien-
                    cies discussed in budget
                    justifications............... 2
                    Special studies or evaluations 3
                    Combination of above (list)
                    _____
                                                  4
                    Other (list)_____   5
                    None of above...(GO TO Q.31).. 6
                    No response...(GO TO Q.31).... 9

____   30B. *What is one example of a service benefit? (list)*

         _____   ☐   *13./*
         _____

____31. *In your opinion, has there been resistance of _any_ sort by depart-
         mental personnel regarding the mobile intensive care unit operation?*

                    Yes...(ANSWER Q.31A).......... 1   *14/*
                    No............................ 2
                    No response................... 9

____   31A. *What was the nature of the resistance?*

                    Over specific services only... 1   *15/*
                    Over initial adoption......... 2
                    Over entire program........... 3
                    Other (list)_____   4
                    Combination (list)_____   5
                    No response................... 9

E. EXTERNAL FACTORS

_____32. *Has there been any publicity regarding the department's mobile
          intensive care unit operation?*

                                    Yes, local media or press..... 1   *16/*
                                    Yes, national media or press.. 2
                                    Yes, both..................... 3
                                    No...(GO TO Q.33)............. 4
                                    No response...(GO TO Q.33).... 9

_____ 32A. *Has the publicity generally been favorable, mixed, or
             unfavorable?*

                                    Favorable..................... 1   *17/*
                                    Mixed......................... 2
                                    Unfavorable................... 3
                                    No response................... 9

USE FOLLOWING CHART FOR QUESTIONS 33-34; NOTE "NOT SURE" RESPONSES
BY PLACING ASTERISK TO RIGHT OF CIRCLED NUMBER.

33. *Have there been any active supporters of the operation outside of
     the fire department?* [USE LIST AS PROBE]

34. *Have there been any active opposers of the operation outside of
     the fire department?* [USE LIST AS PROBE]

Activists	Q.33			Q.34			
	SUPPORTERS			OPPOSERS			
	Yes	No	No Response	Yes	No	No Response	
Municipal executive	1	2	9	1	2	9	*18-19/*
Other municipal officers	1	2	9	1	2	9	*20-21/*
Local legislators	1	2	9	1	2	9	*22-23/*
Citizen groups	1	2	9	1	2	9	*24-25/*
Local hospital	1	2	9	1	2	9	*26-27/*
Other:	1	2	9	1	2	9	*28-29/*

_____35. *In the next year or so, do you see any difficulties affecting the
          operation other than budget?*

                                    Yes...(ANSWER Q.35A).......... 1   *30/*
                                    No............................ 2
                                    No response................... 9

_____ 35A. *What are these difficulties?* (list)

_____   *31/*

_____

CLOSED-CIRCUIT TELEVISION

City and State _____

Respondent's Name _____

          Title _____

Telephone Number _____

Interview Dates _____

Secondary Respondent's Name _____

          Title _____

Telephone Number _____

Appointment set for (day) _____

   (time) _____ (with) _____

If School District was called previously for any innovation:

Respondent's Name _____

          Title _____

Telephone Number _____

Date of Call _____

Innovation _____

Rand Screeners _____

A. EQUIPMENT

____ 1. *Have the schools in your district ever used instructional television?*

                              Yes...(GO TO Q.2)................... 1   *11/*
                              No...(GO TO Q.45)................... 2
                              No response........................ 9

____ 2. *Can the school district (or any part of it) transmit the same tele-*
        vision program to several different classrooms at the same time?

                              Yes...(GO TO Q.2A AND 2B).......... 1   *12/*
                              No................................. 2
                              No response........................ 9

____ 2A. *How does transmission take place?*

                              Cable.............................. 1   *13/*
                              Dedicated channel.................. 2
                              Microwave.......................... 3
                              Other (list)_____ 4
                              Combination of above (list)_____ 5
                              Regular over-the-air television
                              broadcast by local TV station....... 6
                              No response........................ 9

____ 2B. *Does the school district operate the central facility that*
         transmits these programs?

                              School district alone.............. 1   *14/*
                              School district and other agency.... 2
                              Other agency, with school district
                              consulted as users (name agency)
                              _____ 3
                              No response........................ 9

IF Q.1 = 2,9; OR Q.2 = 2,9; OR Q.2A = 6,9; OR Q.2B = 3,9; GO TO Q.45,
THEN TERMINATE INTERVIEW.

____ 3. *Please describe the basic equipment used for actually transmitting*
        programs from the central facility (e.g., amplifiers, antenna, other
        transmitting equipment).

        _____
        _____ [|]   *15-16/*

____ 4. *Is the central facility's transmitting equipment still in use?*

                              Yes................................ 1   *17/*
                              No...(GO TO Q.4A).................. 2
                              No response........................ 9

____ 4A. *What was the last year it was used?*
         [ENTER TWO-DIGIT YEAR; ENTER 99 IF NO RESPONSE]

                              Year   [|]   *18-19/*

_____ 5. *Does this facility serve the entire district, a group of schools, or a single school only?*

                                  District-wide....................... 1   *20/*
                                  More than one school................ 2
                                  One school only..................... 3
                                  No response......................... 9

_____ 6. *Has any of the transmitting equipment been updated, and if so, how many times?*
[ENTER NUMBER OF TIMES; ENTER 9 IF NO RESPONSE]

                                  # times updated   ☐   *21/*

_____ 7. *What was the first year in which programs were transmitted?*
[ENTER TWO-DIGIT YEAR; ENTER 99 IF NO RESPONSE]

                                  Year   ☐☐   *22-23/*

_____ 8. *How many television receivers can receive the programs that are transmitted?*
[ENTER THREE-DIGIT NUMBER; ENTER 999 IF NO RESPONSE]

                                  # television sets   ☐☐☐   *24-26/*

_____ 9. *Is the main transmitting equipment purchased, leased, or on a lease-purchase option?*

                                  Purchased...(ANSWER Q.9A)........... 1   *27/*
                                  Leased...(ANSWER Q.10).............. 2
                                  Lease-purchase...(GO TO Q.11)....... 3
                                  Other (list)_____ 4
                                  No response...(GO TO Q.11).......... 9

_____ 9A. *When was it purchased?*
[ENTER TWO-DIGIT YEAR; ENTER 99 IF NO RESPONSE]

                                  Year   ☐☐   *28-29/*

_____10. *How many years is the lease for?*
[ENTER ONE DIGIT; ENTER 9 IF NO RESPONSE]

                                  # of years   ☐   *30/*

_____11. *Is there a service contract for repair and maintenance of the transmitting equipment?*

[IF YES] *With whom?*

[IF NO]   *Who provides repair and maintenance?*

                                  Yes, contract with manufacturer..... 1   *31/*
                                  Yes, contract with other outside
                                  group (list)_____ 2
                                  Yes, no response for by whom........ 3
                                  No, service provided by district.... 4
                                  No, service provided by other
                                  agency (list)_____ 5
                                  No, no response for by whom......... 6
                                  No response......................... 9

_____12. *Was there any technical assistance from outside the district in order*
        to begin transmitting the instructional programs?

        [IF YES] *From what source?*

                                        Yes, manufacturer................... 1   *32/*
                                        Yes, other education agency......... 2
                                        Yes, local university............... 3
                                        Yes, other (list)_____ 4
                                        Yes, combination (list)_____ 5
                                        No.................................. 6
                                        No response......................... 9

_____13. *Has there been any* *continuing* *technical assistance from outside the*
        district in transmitting the instructional programs?

        [IF YES] *From what source?*

                                        Yes, manufacturer................... 1   *33/*
                                        Yes, other education agency......... 2
                                        Yes, local university............... 3
                                        Yes, other (list)_____ 4
                                        Yes, combination (list)_____ 5
                                        No.................................. 6
                                        No response......................... 9

B. SERVICES

    USE THE FOLLOWING CHART FOR QUESTIONS 14-17; NOTE "NOT SURE" RESPONSES BY
    PLACING ASTERISK IN BOX WITH CHECK MARK.

    14. *How do teachers in elementary/secondary schools use the main programs*
         transmitted by the central facility? [PROBE WITH LIST]

    15. *What year was (program) first transmitted?*

    16. *Of the programs that the central facility provides, which are the*
         top three that are responsible for most of the television time in
         the schools?

    17. *Have there been any problems in setting priorities among different*
         programs because of limitations on the capacity of the central
         facility?

         [IF YES] *Which programs?*

         [IF YES] *How has the district dealt with such problems?* (list)

         _____

         _____

ENTER 1 IF YES, 2 IF NO, 9 IF NO RESPONSE FOR ALL QUESTIONS EXCEPT Q.15;
FOR Q.15, ENTER TWO-DIGIT YEAR OR 99 IF NO RESPONSE; NOTE "NOT SURE"
RESPONSES BY PLACING ASTERISK IN BOX NEXT TO ENTERED NUMBER.

ELEMENTARY SCHOOL PROGRAMS	Q.14	Q.15	Q.16	Q.17	
Math (discretionary or remedial)					34-38/
Math (mandatory for regular classes)					39-43/
Reading (discretionary or remedial)					44-48/
Reading (mandatory for regular classes)					49-53/
Science (discretionary or remedial)					54-58/
Science (mandatory for regular classes)					59-63/

Keypuncher: Go to new card--punch 2 in col. 1, duplicate cols. 2-10.

Social studies (discretionary or remedial)					11-15/
Social studies (mandatory for regular classes)					16-20/
Other:					21-25/

JUNIOR HIGH OR HIGH SCHOOL PROGRAMS					
Math (discretionary or remedial)					26-30/
Math (mandatory for regular classes)					31-35/
Reading (discretionary or remedial)					36-40/
Reading (mandatory for regular classes)					41-45/
Science (discretionary or remedial)					46-50/
Science (mandatory for regular classes)					51-55/
Social studies (discretionary or remedial)					56-60/
Social studies (mandatory for regular classes)					61-65/
Other:					66-70/

C. STAFF AND ADMINISTRATION

USE FOLLOWING CHART FOR QUESTIONS 18-20; NOTE "NOT SURE" RESPONSES BY
PLACING ASTERISK TO RIGHT OF CIRCLED NUMBER.

____18. *Does the district have (personnel) associated with the television
facilities in its current budget?*

[IF YES] *How many full-time equivalent (personnel) are there?*
[ENTER TWO-DIGIT NUMBER; ENTER 99 IF NO RESPONSE]

[IF NO, ENTER 00]

____19. *Is (personnel) a* permanent *position in the district's budget?*

____20. *Does the specific civil service or other official personnel classi-
fication include television-related qualifications for (personnel)?*

> Keypuncher: Go to
> new card--punch 3
> in col. 1, dupli-
> cate cols. 2-10.

Personnel	Q.18 #FTE?	Q.19 POSITION PERMANENT?			Q.20 CLASSIFICATION?			
		Yes	No	No Response	Yes	No	No Response	
General Coordinator		1	2	9	1	2	9	*11-14/*
Production Staff		1	2	9	1	2	9	*15-18/*
Engineering and Technical		1	2	9	1	2	9	*19-22/*
Other:		1	2	9	1	2	9	*23-26/*
Other:		1	2	9	1	2	9	*27-30/*

____21. *For the teaching staff, what kind of* formal *training is routinely
provided by the district in order to use the television programs?*

Informal assistance................. 1   *31/*
Special classes run by district..... 2
Classes at local college or
manufacturer....................... 3
Other (list)_____ 4
Combination (list)_____ 5
None...(GO TO Q.23)................. 6
No response...(GO TO Q.23).......... 9

____22. *What proportion of the eligible teaching staff has participated in this training?*

Most or all......................... 1   *32/*
About half.......................... 2
Few or a small minority............. 3
None................................ 4
No response......................... 9

____23. *In order for a new person to qualify for teaching positions that use television programs, must he or she have had formal training in using television in the classroom?*

Yes................................. 1   *33/*
No.................................. 2
No response......................... 9

____24. *How many individuals have filled the coordinator position, including the present one?*
[ENTER TWO-DIGIT NUMBER; ENTER 99 IF NO RESPONSE]

coordinators   ☐☐   *34-35/*

[IF MORE THAN ONE] *What position does the previous coordinator now hold?* (list)
_____   ☐   *36/*

____25. *Was the coordinator ever a teacher in the district and what position does the coordinator have?* [PROBE WITH LIST]

Not teacher, in television or AV
unit................................ 1   *37/*
Yes, teacher, in television or
AV unit............................. 2
Yes, teacher, on other instructional
staff............................... 3
Other (list)_____ 4
No response......................... 9

____26. *Does any member of the curriculum (instructional) department assist in the television operations?* [PROBE WITH LIST]

Serves as main coordinator.......... 1   *38/*
Collaborates with television unit
in coordinating television use...... 2
Other (list)_____ 3
Combination (list)_____ 4
None................................ 5
No response......................... 9

_____27. *Who was responsible for initiating the transmission of television
          programs into the district?*

> Superintendent...(ANSWER Q.27A)..... 1   *39/*
> Staff person within television or
> AV units (ANSWER Q.27A)............. 2
> Staff person within other instruc-
> tional staff (ANSWER Q.27A)......... 3
> Person outside district............ 4
> Group of persons (e.g., city
> council, agency consortium)........ 5
> Combination of above (list)
> _____ 6
> Other (list)_____ 7
> No response........................ 9

_____ 27A. *Is this person still with the district?*

> Yes..,(ANSWER Q.27B)............... 1   *40/*
> No................................. 2
> No response........................ 9

_____ 27B. *In what position?* (list)_____ [   ]   *41/*

_____28. *Why was the transmission of programs initiated?*

> Growing demands from teachers
> or students........................ 1   *42/*
> Rising enrollment.................. 2
> Specific need or crisis (list)
> _____ 3
> All of above....................... 4
> Combination of above (list)_____ 5
> Other (list)_____ 6
> No response........................ 9

_____29. *Was over-the-air television used in the classroom before the central
          facility was introduced?*

> Yes................................ 1   *43/*
> No................................. 2
> No response........................ 9

_____30. *Do classrooms currently receive over-the-air programs directly?*

> Yes................................ 1   *44/*
> No................................. 2
> No response........................ 9

_____31. *Where do most of the television programs that are transmitted from
          the central facility come from?*

> Produce own programs............... 1   *45/*
> Tape over-the-air programs and
> retransmit......................... 2
> Purchase programs separately....... 3
> Other (list)_____ 4
> No response........................ 9

____32. *Where do most of the operating funds for the central facilities and*
         television equipment come from?   [USE LIST AS PROBE]

                              Regular part of district budget..... 1   *46/*
                              Some other part of municipal budget   2
                              Federal grants or funds............ 3
                              Special bond issue or other levy.... 4
                              State grants or funds.............. 5
                              Combination (list)_____ 6
                              Other (list)_____ 7
                              No response....................... 9

____33. *Were there ever any federal, state, or foundation funds used to*
         support these activities?

                              Yes, federal....................... 1   *47/*
                              Yes, state......................... 2
                              Yes, foundation.................... 3
                              Yes, combination (list)_____ 4
                              No...(GO TO Q.34).................. 5
                              No response....................... 9

   33A. *Where did these funds come from?* [ENTER 9 IF NO RESPONSE]

   33B. *During what years?* [ENTER 99-99 IF NO RESPONSE]

   33C. *What was the amount?* [ENTER 99 IF NO RESPONSE; MAY ROUND
         TO NEAREST $100,000 OR LIST RANGE]

   [PLACE ASTERISK NEXT TO ANY "NOT SURE" RESPONSE]

Source   Years   Amount

_____   _____   _____ | | | | | | | | *48-54/*

_____   _____   _____ | | | | | | | | *55-61/*

_____   _____   _____ | | | | | | | | *62-68/*

Keypuncher: Go to
new card--punch 4
in col. 1, dupli-
cate cols. 2-10.

34. *What was the annual budget for the central operation and the television*
     equipment during 1976, excluding personnel and salaries? 1975? 1974?
     [ENTER AMOUNT; ENTER 999 IF NO RESPONSE; MAY ROUND TO NEAREST
     $100,000 OR LIST RANGE; NOTE "NOT SURE" RESPONSE WITH ASTERISK]

              1976 _____ | | | | | *11-14/*

              1975 _____ | | | | | *15-18/*

              1974 _____ | | | | | *19-22/*

_____35. *Have any changes in textbook adoptions been made due to the use of the television programs?* [USE HIGHEST]

New texts with special sections for
all relevant classes................ 1   *23/*
New texts with special sections
for some classes.................... 2
Supplementary television-related
materials........................... 3
Texts for special television courses 4
None................................ 5
Other (list)_____ 6
No response......................... 9

_____36. *Are there any state or local laws or regulations that call for the existence of the central facility or television programs?*

Yes (list)_____ 1   *24/*
No.................................. 2
No response......................... 9

_____37. *Are any of the television programs linked to some state or local law or regulation?*

Yes (list)_____ 1   *25/*
No.................................. 2
No response......................... 9

D. INTERNAL FACTORS

USING FOLLOWING CHART FOR Q.38, NOTE "NOT SURE" RESPONSES BY PLACING
ASTERISK TO RIGHT OF CIRCLED NUMBER.

38. *To what extent do teachers in different subjects use the television programs that are transmitted by the central facility?*

Subject	Most	Few	None	No Response	
Math	1	2	3	9	*26/*
Reading	1	2	3	9	*27/*
Science	1	2	3	9	*28/*
Social science	1	2	3	9	*29/*
Other:	1	2	3	9	*30/*

____39. *Are the television receivers used in the teacher's own classroom?*

Yes.................................. 1 *31/*
No, special classroom (e.g.,
library) for television sets........ 2
No response........................ 9

____40. *Have any service benefits from the programs transmitted by the central facility been recognized?*

Yes...(ANSWER Q.40A)................ 1 *32/*
No.................................. 2
No response........................ 9

____40A. *How have these service benefits been recognized--reported in the budget, discussed in budget justifications, special studies or evaluations, or some other way?*

Specific savings or efficiencies
reported in budget.................. 1 *33/*
Specific savings or efficiencies
discussed in budget justifications.. 2
Special studies or evaluations...... 3
Combination of above (list)
_____ 4
Other (list)_____ 5
None of above...(GO TO Q.41)........ 6
No response...(GO TO Q.41).......... 9

____40B. *What is one example of a service benefit? (list)*

_____ ☐ *34/*
_____

____41. *In your opinion, has there been resistance of any sort by district personnel in using the programs that are transmitted?*

Yes...(ANSWER Q.41A)................ 1 *35/*
No.................................. 2
No response........................ 9

____41A. *What was the nature of the resistance?*

Over specific applications only..... 1 *36/*
Over initial adoption............... 2
Over use of the entire system....... 3
Other (list)_____ 4
Combination (list)_____ 5
No response........................ 9

E. EXTERNAL FACTORS

___42. *Has there been any publicity regarding the central facility or the programs that are transmitted?*

                              Yes, local media or press.......... 1   *37/*
                              Yes, national media or press....... 2
                              Yes, both.......................... 3
                              No...(GO TO Q.43).................. 4
                              No response...(GO TO Q.43)......... 9

___42A. *Has the publicity generally been favorable, mixed, or un-favorable?*

                              Favorable.......................... 1   *38/*
                              Mixed.............................. 2
                              Unfavorable........................ 3
                              No response........................ 9

USE FOLLOWING CHART FOR QUESTIONS 43-44; NOTE "NOT SURE" RESPONSES BY PLACING ASTERISK TO RIGHT OF CIRCLED NUMBER.

43. *Have there been any active supporters of the central facility and its television programs outside of the school district?*

44. *Have there been any active opposers outside of the school district?*

| | Q.43 | | | Q.44 | | | |
| | SUPPORTERS OR USERS | | | OPPOSERS | | | |
Activists	Yes	No	No Response	Yes	No	No Response	
Municipal executive	1	2	9	1	2	9	*39-40/*
Other municipal officers	1	2	9	1	2	9	*41-42/*
Local legislators	1	2	9	1	2	9	*43-44/*
Citizen groups	1	2	9	1	2	9	*45-46/*
Parents	1	2	9	1	2	9	*47-48/*
Other:	1	2	9	1	2	9	*49-50/*

___45. *In the next year or so, do you see any difficulties affecting your educational television operation other than budget?*

                              Yes...(ANSWER Q.45A)............... 1   *51/*
                              No................................. 2
                              No response........................ 9

45A. *What are these difficulties? (list)*

_____   ☐   *52/*

_____

BREATH TESTING

City and State _____

Respondent's Name _____

            Title _____

Telephone Number _____

Interview Dates   _____

Secondary Respondent's Name _____

                    Title _____

Telephone Number   _____

Appointment set for (day) _____

  (time) _____ (with) _____

If Police Department was called previously for any innovation:

Respondent's Name _____

            Title _____

  Telephone Number _____

Date of Call _____

Innovation   _____

Rand Screeners _____

A. EQUIPMENT

_____ 1. *How does your department currently test persons suspected of driving under the influence of alcohol?*

Breath analysis (or breath testing) ...(GO TO Q.2).....................	1	11/
Breath screening only (balloon).....	2	
Urinalysis..........................	3	
Blood analysis......................	4	
Other (list)_____	5	
Combination (list)...(GO TO Q.2		
IF BREATH ANALYSIS IS INCLUDED)		
_____	6	
No response.........................	9	

_____ 1A. *Has your department ever used any kind of breath-analysis equipment in its routine operations?*

Yes...(GO TO Q.2)....................	1	12/
No, demonstration only..............	2	
No, never...........................	3	
No response.........................	9	

_____ 1B. *What have been the main reasons for not using any breath analysis equipment in routine operations?*

_____

_____   13/

[TERMINATE INTERVIEW AFTER Q.1B]

_____ 2. *What is the major piece of breath-analysis equipment you use?*

Breathalyzer........................	1	14/
Other (list)_____	2	
Combination (list)_____	3	
No response.........................	9	

_____ 3. *How many are actually in everyday operation? How many serve as backup equipment?*
[ENTER TWO-DIGIT NUMBER; ENTER 99 IF NO RESPONSE]

in operation   15-16/

of backups   17-18/

_____ 4. *When was the equipment first used in everyday operation?*
[ENTER TWO-DIGIT YEAR; ENTER 99 IF NO RESPONSE]

Year   19-20/

_____ 5. *Is the current equipment purchased, leased, or on a lease-purchase option?*

            Purchased...(ANSWER Q.5A)........... 1   *21/*
            Leased...(ANSWER Q.6).............. 2
            Lease-purchase...(GO TO Q.6)........ 3
            Other (list)_____ 4
            No response...(GO TO Q.7).......... 9

_____ 5A. *When was this equipment purchased?*
[ENTER TWO-DIGIT YEAR; ENTER 99 IF NO RESPONSE]

            Year   [|]   *22-23/*

_____ 6. *How many years is the lease for?*
[ENTER ONE DIGIT; ENTER 9 IF NO RESPONSE]

            # of years   [   ]   *24/*

_____ 7. *Has any of the original equipment been replaced by new equipment?*
[IF YES] How many models followed the original one?
[ENTER 0 IF NO; ENTER 9 IF NO RESPONSE]

            # models following original   [   ]   *25/*

_____ 8. *Have you ever used videotapes for persons suspected of driving under the influence?*

            Yes...(GO TO Q.8A).................. 1   *26/*
            No................................. 2
            No response........................ 9

_____ 8A. *When were videotapes first used for this purpose?*
[ENTER TWO-DIGIT YEAR; ENTER 99 IF NO RESPONSE]

            Year   [|]   *27-28/*

_____ 8B. *When were they last used?*
[ENTER TWO-DIGIT YEAR; ENTER 99 IF NO RESPONSE]

            Year   [|]   *29-30/*

_____ 8C. *Are the videotapes used to record the suspect's motor skills or to record the taking of the breath-analysis test (or both)?*

            Motor skills only................... 1   *31/*
            Breath analysis test only........... 2
            Both............................... 3
            Neither............................ 4
            Other (list)_____ 5
            Combination (list)_____ 6
            No response........................ 9

____ 9. *Before the breath-analysis equipment was used, how did the department test persons suspected of driving under the influence of alcohol?*

                    Breath screening.................... 1   *32/*
                    Urinalysis.......................... 2
                    Blood analysis...................... 3
                    Other (list)_____ 4
                    Combination (list)_____ 5
                    None...(GO TO Q.10)................. 6
                    No response...(GO TO Q.10).......... 9

   9A. *Is this procedure still used at all, and if so, how frequently?*
        [PERCENTAGE; INDICATE IF EMERGENCY ONLY]

        _____

        _____   [ ]   *33/*

____10. *How did your department first hear about the breath-analysis equipment?*

                    From another police department...... 1   *34/*
                    From another agency in the city..... 2
                    From a manufacturer................. 3
                    From an outside group (e.g., PTI,
                    university or consultant)........... 4
                    From a report or magazine article... 5
                    Other (list)_____ 6
                    No response......................... 9

____11. *What were the main reasons for deciding to use the equipment?*

        _____

        _____   [ ]   *35/*

____12. *Is there a service contract for repair and maintenance of the breath-analysis equipment?*
        [IF YES] *With whom?*

        [IF NO]   *Who provides repair and maintenance?*

                    Yes, contract with manufacturer..... 1   *36/*
                    Yes, contract with other outside
                    group (list)_____ 2
                    Yes, no response for by whom........ 3
                    No, service provided by department.. 4
                    No, service provided by other agency
                    (list)_____ 5
                    No, no response for by whom......... 6
                    No response......................... 9

____13. *Where is the breath-analysis equipment located?*
        [USE LIST AS PROBE]

In a dedicated room (one building only)...............................	1	*37/*
In a dedicated room (several sites-- e.g., precincts)....................	2	
No dedicated room (one building only)...............................	3	
No dedicated room (several sites)...	4	
Other (list)_____	5	
Combination (list)_____	6	
No response.........................	9	

B. SERVICES

____14. *Following a suspect's apprehension, what is the maximum time period within which the suspect must be given a breath test?*

        _____   *38-39/*

____15. *Is the time period specified by law, police regulations, or common practice?*

Law...................................	1	*40/*
Regulations...........................	2	
Practice..............................	3	
Other (list)_____	4	
Combination (list)_____	5	
None..................................	6	
No response...........................	9	

____16. *Has there been a standard for deciding what BAC range represents a state of intoxication?*

Yes...................................	1	*41/*
No...(GO TO Q.17)....................	2	
No response...........................	9	

____16A. *What is the standard?*

        _____   *42/*

____16B. *Is this standard specified by law, police regulations, or common practice?*

Law...................................	1	*43/*
Regulations...........................	2	
Practice..............................	3	
Other (list)_____	4	
Combination (list)_____	5	
None..................................	6	
No response...........................	9	

____17. *About how many persons have been given the breath-analysis test in the last year? How about for each of the two preceding years?*

_____ (1976)   `[ | | | ]`   *44-47/*

_____ (1975)   `[ | | | ]`   *48-51/*

_____ (1974)   `[ | | | ]`   *52-55/*

____18. *About how many persons refused to take the breath-analysis test during 1976?*

_____   `[ | | ]`   *56-58/*

____19. *What are the penalties, if any, for refusing to take the test?*

_____   `[ ]`   *59/*

____20. *Was there any technical assistance from outside your department in order to begin the breath-analysis operation?*

           Yes, manufacturer.................... 1   *60/*
           Yes, other police department........ 2
           Yes, local university............... 3
           Yes, other (list)_____ 4
           Yes, combination (list)_____ 5
           No.................................. 6
           No response......................... 9

____21. *Has there been any <u>continuing</u> technical assistance from outside the department for this operation?*

           Yes, manufacturer.................... 1   *61/*
           Yes, other police department........ 2
           Yes, local university............... 3
           Yes, other (list)_____ 4
           Yes, combination (list)_____ 5
           No.................................. 6
           No response......................... 9

```
Keypuncher: Go to
new card--punch 2
in col. 1, dupli-
cate cols. 2-10
```

C. STAFF AND ADMINISTRATION

_____22. *Who was responsible for first introducing breath-analysis into*
         the department?

Chief of Department...(ANSWER Q.22A)	1	*11/*
Staff person within department (ANSWER Q.22A)......................	2	
Staff person in other agency (give position)_____	3	
Person outside city government......	4	
Group of persons (e.g., city council, agency consortium).........	5	
Combination (list)_____	6	
Other (list)_____	7	
No response.........................	9	

_____ 22A. *Is this person still with the department?*

Yes...(ANSWER Q.22B)................	1	*12/*
No.................................	2	
No response.........................	9	

_____ 22B. *In what position?* (list)_____   ☐ *13/*

_____23. *Within the police department's organization, is the breath-*
         analysis operation a separate section or part of another
         section?

Separate section....................	1	*14/*
Part of another section (list) _____	2	
Other (list)_____	3	
No response.........................	9	

_____24. *How many men are trained to operate and repair the breath-analysis*
         equipment?

         How many men are trained only to operate the equipment?

         \# trained as operators
           & repair   ☐☐☐   *15-17/*

         \# trained as operators only   ☐☐☐   *18-20/*

_____25. *Do the operators also carry out other assignments or do they operate*
         the breath-analysis equipment all the time?

Operate equipment only..............	1	*21/*
Operate equipment for a shift or two, then do other assignments......	2	
Operate equipment as one of several assignments during same shift.......	3	
Other (list)_____	4	
Combination (list)_____	5	
No response.........................	9	

_____26. *Do the operators also run the videotape equipment?*
[IF Q.8 WAS ANSWERED YES]

Yes................................. 1   *22/*
No.................................. 2
Other (list)_____ 3
No response......................... 9

_____27. *Are there any men in the department who once operated the breath-analysis equipment, but who no longer do so?*

Yes................................. 1   *23/*
No.................................. 2
No response......................... 9

_____28. *Is there a supervisor who coordinates the breath-analysis operation?*

Yes................................. 1   *24/*
No...(GO TO Q.29)................... 2
No response......................... 9

_____ 28A. *How many individuals have filled the supervisory role, including the present one?*
[ENTER TWO-DIGIT NUMBER; ENTER 99 IF NO RESPONSE]

coordinators   *25-26/*

_____ 28B. [IF MORE THAN ONE] *What position does the previous supervisor now hold? (list)*
_____   *27/*

_____29. *For the new operators, what kind of training programs are provided?*

Special training sessions by
manufacturer........................ 1   *28/*
Formal training classes run by
department.......................... 2
Training in police academy.......... 3
State health department............. 4
Other (list)_____ 5
Combination (list)_____ 6
None...(GO TO Q.30)................. 7
No response......................... 9

_____ 29A. *How much time does the training take?*

One day or less..................... 1   *29/*
More than one day but less than
one week............................ 2
More than one week.................. 3
No response......................... 9

_____ 29B. *How many classes of officers have gone through the training program since the breath-analysis equipment was first used?*
[ENTER TWO-DIGIT NUMBER; ENTER 99 IF NO RESPONSE]

classes   *30-31/*

____ 30. *In order for a person to qualify as an operator, must he or she pass an exam?*

[IF YES] *What agency gives the exam?*
[PROBE TO DETERMINE IF CIVIL SERVICE]

Yes, civil service................... 1   *32/*
Yes, test by department............. 2
Yes, test by other agency (name
agency)_____ 3
Yes, combination (list)_____ 4
No.................................... 5
No response.......................... 9

____ 31. *Must operators also be formally certified?*

[IF YES] *By whom?*

Yes, state health department........ 1   *33/*
Yes, other (list)_____ 2
Yes, combination (list)_____ 3
No.................................... 4
No response.......................... 9

____ 32. *For equipment operators who have been initially trained, is there any update training?*

Special training sessions by
manufacturer........................ 1   *34/*
Training sessions in police
precinct or headquarters............ 2
Training sessions in police academy. 3
Other (list)_____ 4
Combination (list)_____ 5
None................................ 6
No response......................... 9

____ 33. *Who transports a suspect from the street to the site of the breath-analysis equipment?*

Regular police officers............. 1   *35/*
Traffic division only............... 2
Mobile unit arrives at street site
(no transport) 3
Other (list)_____ 4
Combination (list)_____ 5
No response......................... 9

____ 34. *Do regular patrol officers receive any training about the breath-analysis operation?*

Yes, on the job..................... 1   *36/*
Yes, in police academy.............. 2
Yes, other (list)_____ 3
Combination (list)_____ 4
None................................ 5
No response......................... 9

____35. *Were there ever any federal, state, or external funds used to support the breath-analysis equipment?*

Yes, federal........................	1	37/
Yes, state..........................	2	
Yes, other (list)_____	3	
Yes, combination (list)_____	4	
No...(GO TO Q.36)...................	5	
No response........................	9	

    35A. *Where did these funds come from?* [ENTER 9 IF NO RESPONSE]

    35B. *During what years?* [ENTER 99-99 IF NO RESPONSE]

    35C. *What was the amount?* [ENTER 99 IF NO RESPONSE; MAY ROUND TO NEAREST $100,000 OR LIST RANGE]

[PLACE ASTERISK NEXT TO ANY "NOT SURE" RESPONSE]

Source	Years	Amount		
_____	_____	_____	☐☐☐☐☐☐☐	38-44/
_____	_____	_____	☐☐☐☐☐☐☐	45-51/
_____	_____	_____	☐☐☐☐☐☐☐	52-58/

____36. *Has the specific use of breath-analysis equipment been linked to any state or local law or regulation?*

Yes (list)_____	1	59/
No.................................	2	
No response........................	9	

____37. *What formal changes in organizational procedures have been made due to the breath-analysis operation?*
[PROBE WITH LIST]

Creation of new organizational units	1	60/
Creation of new forms (e.g., for reporting results of alcohol test) (ANSWER Q.38)......................	2	
Both (ANSWER Q.38)..................	3	
Neither............................	4	
Other (list)_____	5	
No response........................	9	

____38. *Are any of the old forms still available?*

They never existed..................	1	61/
They are still available in the department.........................	2	
They are still available outside the department......................	3	
They are no longer available........	4	
No response........................	9	

D. INTERNAL FACTORS

___39. *Have there been any service benefits from using the breath-analysis equipment?*

Yes...(ANSWER Q.39A)................ 1   *11/*
No................................... 2
No response......................... 9

___39A. *How have these service benefits been recognized--reported in the budget, discussed in budget justifications, special studies or evaluations, or some other way?*

Specific savings or efficiencies
reported in budget.................. 1   *12/*
Specific savings or efficiencies
discussed in budget justifications.. 2
Special studies or evaluations...... 3
Other (list)_____ 4
Combination (list)_____ 5
None...(GO TO Q.40)................. 6
No response...(GO TO Q.40).......... 9

___39B. *What is one example of a service benefit?* (list)

_____
_____   *13/*

___40. *In your opinion, has there been resistance of any sort by departmental personnel regarding the breath-analysis operation?*

Yes...(ANSWER Q.40A)................ 1   *14/*
No................................... 2
No response......................... 9

___40A. *What was the nature of the resistance?*

Over specific services only......... 1   *15/*
Over initial adoption............... 2
Over entire program................. 3
Other (list)_____ 4
Combination (list)_____ 5
No response......................... 9

___41. *What kind of support has the chief of the department given to the use of the breath-analysis operation?*

Introduced the operation............ 1   *16/*
At least some support............... 2
Neutral............................. 3
Some opposition..................... 4
No response......................... 9

E. EXTERNAL FACTORS

____42. *Has there been any publicity regarding the department's use of*
        breath-analysis?

Yes, local media or press	1	*17/*
Yes, national media or press	2	
Yes, both	3	
No..(GO TO Q.43)	4	
No response...(GO TO Q.43)	9	

____42A. *Has the publicity generally been favorable, mixed, or*
         unfavorable?

Favorable	1	*18/*
Mixed	2	
Unfavorable	3	
No response	9	

USE FOLLOWING CHART FOR QUESTIONS 43-44; NOTE "NOT SURE" RESPONSES BY
PLACING ASTERISK TO RIGHT OF CIRCLED NUMBER.

43. *Have there been any active supporters of the breath-analysis opera-*
     tion outside of the department?

44. *Have there been any active opposers of the breath-analysis operation*
     outside of the department?

Activists	Q.43			Q.44			
	SUPPORTERS OR USERS			OPPOSERS			
	Yes	No	No Response	Yes	No	No Response	
Municipal executive	1	2	9	1	2	9	*19-20/*
Other municipal officers	1	2	9	1	2	9	*21-22/*
Local legislators	1	2	9	1	2	9	*23-24/*
Citizen groups	1	2	9	1	2	9	*25-26/*
Other:	1	2	9	1	2	9	*27-28/*

____45. *In the next year or so, do you see any difficulties affecting the*
        breath-analysis operation other than budget?

Yes...(ANSWER Q.45A)	1	*29/*
No	2	
No response	9	

____45A. *What are these difficulties?* (list)

_____

_____   ☐ *30/*

JET-AXE

City and State _____

Respondent's Name _____

Title _____

Telephone Number _____

Interview Dates _____

Secondary Respondent's Name _____

Title _____

Telephone Number _____

Appointment set for (day) _____

(time) _____ (with) _____

If Fire Department was called previously for any innovation:

Respondent's Name _____

Title _____

Telephone Number _____

Date of Call _____

Innovation _____

Rand Screeners _____

A. EQUIPMENT

_____ 1. *Has your department ever used the Jet-Axe for firefighting?*

                                    Yes...(GO TO Q.2)................... 1   *11/*
                                    No...(GO TO Q.1A).................. 2
                                    No response...(GO TO Q.1A)......... 9

_____ 1A. *Has your department ever purchased the Jet-Axe?*

                                    Yes...(GO TO Q.2)................... 1   *12/*
                                    No...(GO TO Q.1B).................. 2
                                    No response...(GO TO Q.1B)......... 9

_____ 1B. *Has your department ever heard of the Jet-Axe?*

                                    Yes...(GO TO Q.1C, 1D, & 1E)....... 1   *13/*
                                    No...(TERMINATE INTERVIEW)......... 2
                                    No response...(TERMINATE INTERVIEW). 9

_____ 1C. *How did your department first hear about the Jet-Axe?*

                                    From another fire department....... 1   *14/*
                                    From another agency in the city..... 2
                                    From a manufacturer................ 3
                                    From an outside group (e.g., PTI,
                                    university or consultant).......... 4
                                    From a report or magazine article... 5
                                    Other (list)_____ 6
                                    No response........................ 9

_____ 1D. *Did your department consider using the Jet-Axe?*

                                    Yes................................ 1   *15/*
                                    No................................. 2
                                    No response........................ 9

_____ 1E. *What were the main reasons for deciding not to use the Jet-Axe?*

          _____

          _____   ☐   *16/*

          [TERMINATE INTERVIEW AFTER Q.1E]

_____ 2. *When was the first Jet-Axe purchased?*

                                    Year   ☐☐ *17-18/*
*
_____ 3. *When was the Jet-Axe first used in a fire?*

                                    Year   ☐☐ *19-20/*
*
_____ 4. *When was the Jet-Axe last used in a fire?*

                                    Year   ☐☐ *21-22/*
*
_____ 5. *About how many Jet-Axes have been used by the department in actual
          firefighting, for all years?*

_____   # used   ☐☐ *23-24/*
*
Skip if Q.1A was answered

____ 6. *About how many Jet-Axes have been used by the department for training or demonstration purposes, for all years?*

used   ☐☐   *25-26/*

____ 7. *About how many Jet-Axes are in vehicles or in storage today?*

in vehicles or storage   ☐☐   *27-28/*

____ 8. *How did your department first hear about the Jet-Axe?*

From another fire department........	1	*29/*
From another agency in the city.....	2	
From a manufacturer.................	3	
From an outside group (e.g., PTI, university, or consultant).........	4	
From a report or magazine article...	5	
Other (list)_____	6	
No response........................	9	

____ 9. *What were the main reasons for deciding to use the Jet-Axe?*
[FOR Q.1A: *For what reasons has the Jet-Axe not been used in firefighting?*]

_____

_____   ☐   *30/*

B. SERVICES

____10. *How is the Jet-Axe transported to the scene of an alarm?*

Chief's car.........................	1	*31/*
Ladder or truck.....................	2	
Engine or pumper....................	3	
Other vehicle (list)_____	4	
Combination (list)_____	5	
No response........................	9	

____11. *What proportion of these vehicles (of all in this category that are operated by the department) carry the Jet-Axe?*

One or two only.....................	1	*32/*
A minor portion....................	2	
Most or all........................	3	
No response........................	9	

____12. *Who actually places the Jet-Axe to be detonated?*

Chief..............................	1	*33/*
Chief's aide.......................	2	
Fire officer.......................	3	
Other (list)_____	4	
Combination (list)_____	5	
No response.......................	9	

_____13. *Was there any technical assistance from outside your department in order to begin using the Jet-Axe?*

        Yes, manufacturer.................... 1   *34/*
        Yes, other fire department.......... 2
        Yes, local university............... 3
        Yes, other (list)_____ 4
        Yes, combination (list)_____ 5
        No.................................. 6
        No response......................... 9

_____14. *Has there been any <u>continuing</u> technical assistance from outside the department for this operation?*

        Yes, manufacturer.................... 1   *35/*
        Yes, other fire department.......... 2
        Yes, local university............... 3
        Yes, other (list)_____ 4
        Yes, combination (list)_____ 5
        No.................................. 6

_____15. *When are new Jet-Axes purchased to replenish the supply?*

        Whenever an existing Jet Axe is used 1   *36/*
        Whenever two Jet Axes are used...... 2
        Whenever several Jet Axes are used.. 3
        Other (list)_____ 4
        No response......................... 9

_____16. *Who decides* [NOT APPROVES] *when to repurchase the Jet-Axe for the department?*

        Chief............................... 1   *37/*
        Assistant Chief..................... 2
        Supply/maintenance officer.......... 3
        Other (list)_____ 4
        No response......................... 9

_____17. *How many individuals have filled this role, including the present one?*
[ENTER TWO-DIGIT NUMBER; ENTER 99 IF NO RESPONSE]

        # coordinators   [|]   *38-39/*

[IF MORE THAN ONE] *What position does the previous decisionmaker now hold?* (list) _____ [ ] *40/*

_____18. *How many models (e.g., sizes) of Jet-Axes are kept in supply?*
[ANSWER SHOULD VARY BETWEEN 1 AND 5; ENTER 99 IF NO RESPONSE]

        # models   [|]   *41-42/*

_____ 18A. *How many Jet-Axes are kept in reserve or in inventory within the department but not on any vehicle?*
[ENTER TWO-DIGIT NUMBER; 00 IF NONE; 99 IF NO RESPONSE]

        # in reserve or inventory   [|]   *43-44/*

*_____19. *For what types of firefighting tactics has the Jet-Axe been used?*
[USE LIST AS PROBE]

Blasting for ventilation............	1	*45/*
Blasting for access................	2	
Both...............................	3	
Neither............................	4	
Other (list)_____	5	
Combination (list)_____	6	
No response........................	9	

C. STAFFING AND ADMINISTRATION

_____20. *Who was responsible for first introducing the Jet-Axe into the department?*

Chief of Department...(ANSWER Q.20A)	1	*46/*
Staff person within department (ANSWER Q.20A).......................	2	
Staff person in other agency (give position)_____	3	
Person outside city government......	4	
Group of persons (e.g., city council, agency consortium).........	5	
Other (list)_____	6	
Combination (list)_____	7	
No response........................	9	

20A. *Is this person still with the department?*

Yes...(ANSWER Q.20B)................	1	*47/*
No.................................	2	
No response........................	9	

20B. *In what position?* (list)_____ ☐ *48/*

_____21. *What proportion of the firemen are trained to use the Jet-Axe?*

A few only (less than six)..........	1	*49/*
A minor portion (less than 50%).....	2	
Most or all of the firemen..........	3	
No response........................	9	

*_____22. *What proportion of the firemen have actually used the Jet-Axe in a fire?*

A few only (less than six)..........	1	*50/*
A minor portion (less than 50%).....	2	
Most or all of the firemen..........	3	
No response........................	9	

_____23. *For new firemen, what kind of formal training for using the Jet-Axe is routinely provided by the department?*

Special training sessions by manufacturer.........................	1	*51/*
Formal training classes run by department..........................	2	
Training in fire academy............	3	
Other (list)_____	4	
Combination (list)_____	5	
None...(GO TO Q.24).................	6	
No response.........................	9	

_____ 23A. *How much time does the training take?*

Less than half an hour..............	1	*52/*
Half an hour to an hour.............	2	
Over an hour........................	3	
No response.........................	9	

_____ 23B. *How many classes of firemen have gone through the training program since a Jet-Axe was first purchased?*
[ENTER TWO-DIGIT NUMBER; ENTER 99 IF NO RESPONSE]

classes   ☐☐   *53-54/*

_____24. *For firemen who have been initially trained, what kind of update training is routinely provided by the department?*

Special training sessions by manufacturer.........................	1	*55/*
Training sessions in the fire house.	2	
Training in fire academy............	3	
Other (list)_____	4	
Combination (list)_____	5	
None................................	6	
No response.........................	9	

_____25. *Where do the funds for purchasing Jet-Axes come from?*

Regular part of department budget...	1	*56/*
Some other part of municipal budget.	2	
Federal grants or funds.............	3	
Special bond issue or other levy....	4	
State grants or funds...............	5	
Other (list)_____	6	
Combination (list)_____	7	
No response.........................	9	

_____26. *Who determines how much to set aside in each year's budget for new Jet-Axe purchases?*

Chief...............................	1	*57/*
Deputy or Assistant.................	2	
Budget officer......................	3	
Other (specify)_____	4	
No response.........................	9	

____27. *Were there ever any federal, state, or external funds used to
         support the Jet-Axe?*

                              Yes, federal........................ 1   58/
                              Yes, state.......................... 2
                              Yes, external....................... 3
                              Yes, combination (list)_____ 4
                              No.................................. 5
                              No response......................... 9

____28. *Has the use of the Jet-Axe been linked to any state or local law
         or regulation?*

                              Yes (list)_____ 1   59/
                              No.................................. 2
                              No response......................... 9

                              ┌──────────────────────┐
                              │ Keypuncher: Go to   │
                              │ new card--punch 2   │
                              │ in col. 1, dupli-   │
                              │ cate cols. 2-10.   │
                              └──────────────────────┘

D.   INTERNAL FACTORS

* ____29. *Have there been any service benefits from using the Jet-Axe?*

                              Yes...(ANSWER Q.29A)................ 1   11/
                              No..:............................... 2
                              No response......................... 9

*   ____ 29A. *What is one example of a service benefit?* (list)

         _____
         _____   ☐   12/

____30. *In your opinion, has there been resistance of <u>any</u> sort by depart-
         mental personnel regarding the use of the Jet-Axe?*

                              Yes...(ANSWER Q.30A)................ 1   13/
                              No.................................. 2
                              No response......................... 9

    ____ 30A. *What was the nature of the resistance?*

                              Over specific services only......... 1   14/
                              Over initial adoption............... 2
                              Over entire program................. 3
                              Other (list)_____ 4
                              Combination (list)_____ 5
                              No response......................... 9

____31. *What kind of support has the chief of the department given to the*
         use of the Jet-Axe?

                              Introduced the Jet-Axe.............. 1   *15/*
                              At least some support............... 2
                              Neutral............................. 3
                              Some opposition..................... 4
                              No response......................... 9

E. EXTERNAL FACTORS

____32. *Has there been any publicity regarding the department's use of the*
         Jet-Axe?

                              Yes, local media or press........... 1   *16/*
                              Yes, national media or press........ 2
                              Yes, both........................... 3
                              No...(GO TO Q.33)................... 4
                              No response...(GO TO Q.33).......... 9

____ 32A. *Has the publicity generally been favorable, mixed, or*
           unfavorable?

                              Favorable........................... 1   *17/*
                              Mixed............................... 2
                              Unfavorable......................... 3
                              No response......................... 9

USE FOLLOWING CHART FOR QUESTIONS 33-34; NOTE "NOT SURE" RESPONSES BY
PLACING ASTERISK TO RIGHT OF CIRCLED NUMBER.

33. *Have there been any active supporters of the Jet-Axe outside of*
     the fire department?

34. *Have there been any active opposers of the Jet-Axe outside of*
     the fire department?

	Q.33			Q.34			
	SUPPORTERS			OPPOSERS			
Activists	Yes	No	No Response	Yes	No	No Response	
Municipal executive	1	2	9	1	2	9	*18-19/*
Other municipal officials	1	2	9	1	2	9	*20-21/*
Local legislators	1	2	9	1	2	9	*22-23/*
Citizen groups	1	2	9	1	2	9	*24-25/*
Other:	1	2	9	1	2	9	*26-27/*

_____ 35. *In the next year or so, do you see any difficulties affecting
the use of the Jet-Axe, other than budget problems?*

                                   Yes...(ANSWER Q.35A)................ 1   *28/*

                                     No................................. 2

                                     No response........................ 9

_____ 35A. *What are these difficulties?* (list)

_____

_____   ☐   *29/*

Appendix C
Case Studies of
Innovations

Introduction to the Case Studies

This appendix contains eight of the case studies that were developed from the fieldwork. All eight have been reviewed and approved by the service agencies involved with each innovation. The eight therefore serve as illustrative examples of the basic information that was available for each of the case studies. Reviews and approvals were also obtained from the remaining eleven case studies, but in each of these cases the relevant service agency requested that the case studies not be identified with a particular city or site (all agencies were given this option). Therefore, these latter case studies are available from the author but have not been reproduced in the present report.

Each of the case studies in this appendix follows the same basic format from the fieldwork guidelines (see the instrument in appendix B). For each narrative, sections A and B describe the background and the nature of the innovation; section C covers the current status of routinization as of the time of the case study (i.e., passages and cycles as described in chapter 3); and section D reviews the ten hypotheses that had previously been given as possible reasons for routinization status (also see chapter 3):

Service Applications and Outcomes

H_1 :   The innovation involved a core application

H_2 :   There was minimal competition among applications

H_3 :   There were service-related payoffs

External Environment

H_4 :   The innovation arose from crisis conditions

H_5 :   There was client support

H_6 :   There was community support

Internal Factors

H_7 :   There was administrative support

H_8 :   There was a single, active innovator

H_9 :   There was practitioner support

H_{10} :   There were no adversary groups

Although such a standard outline allows for aggregate case analysis by facilitating comparisons across cases, it should nevertheless be remembered that the outline was imposed on each case and does not purport to cover the case information from every point of view.

All case studies were conducted during the winter, 1976-77 and early spring, 1977.

Birmingham Fire and Rescue Service, Birmingham, Alabama

Persons Interviewed

Assistant Fire Chief

Coordinator, EMS activities

Mayor of Birmingham

Executive Secretary to the Mayor

Two EMT-III instructors at the Regional Technical Institute (RTI)

Two dispatchers

EMT-III paramedic

Chairman of Birmingham EMS Committee and Alabama EMS Board

Member of Chairman's staff

Director of Emergency Services at University Hospital

Fire Maintenance Bureau superintendent

Background

Birmingham is Alabama's largest city, with a population of approximately 350,000. The mayor is the chief executive and shares responsibility for governance with a nine-member city council. Some 30 independent municipalities surround Birmingham and bring the population of the metropolitan area to over 770,000.

The several steel mills and nearly one thousand manufacturing establishments that fall within the city limits are the basis of Birmingham's reputation as an industrial metropolis. However, the city has also acquired a national reputation as an outstanding center for medical care. This is largely due to the growth of the University of Alabama medical complex, which has expanded rapidly in the past fifteen years. The downtown area boasts many specialty hospitals, clinics, and medical training facilities associated with the university, and, in addition, there are more than a dozen private hospitals within the city's borders.

The Birmingham Fire and Rescue Service (BF&RS) employs over six hundred persons, approximately one-fifth the total number of municipal employees. The number of employees on the department's payroll has remained fairly constant over the past five years, and the budget has increased slightly. In 1976-77, the department's budget was $9 million, which represented roughly 10 percent of the overall city expenditures.

A distinctive feature of the BF&RS is the strong emphasis that departmental leaders place on professional development. Members of the force are actively encouraged to attend conferences and other functions aimed at improving services. In addition, BF&RS officials have assumed an active leadership role in various matters related to the fire service. For example, the current department chief will serve as next year's president of the International Association of Fire Chiefs. Similarly, the supervisor of the maintenance program recently served on a national panel convened by the federal government to develop recommendations for firefighting vehicles.

The Innovation

The emergency medical services (EMS) program officially began in early 1973 with the purchase of a single emergency vehicle and the training of seventeen firefighters to serve as EMT-IIIs (advanced level paramedics). The availability of funds from a one-year grant for an EMS pilot effort was directly responsible for the introduction of the service at that time. However, the impetus for an EMS program had been growing since the late 1960s, when an industrial accident drew widespread public attention to the shortcomings of the city's existing methods of dealing with emergency situations. In 1967, a furnace exploded in a local factory, spewing forth molten iron. Ambulances were called to the scene to transport victims to local hospitals, but of the eleven men who were burned, only two survived. Subsequent investigation indicated that the men might have been saved had appropriate on-site medical attention been available.

This incident, coupled with a growing dissatisfaction with the limited services provided by private ambulance companies, motivated the city council to issue an ordinance that established an advisory EMS committee. The committee was broadly based, with representation from such groups as the police department, the fire department, the Red Cross, the Heart Association, the Bar Association, and medical practitioners. The members were charged with keeping abreast of and making recommendations to the council with respect to the needs for emergency medical services in the city.

In 1969, the committee advised the council to join with surrounding municipalities to seek a $3.6 million three-year federal grant to establish an EMS demonstration project in the Birmingham metropolitan area. The council concurred and over seventy-five people were recruited to develop a proposal which outlined plans for: (1) the purchase of emergency medical vehicles for placement in fire departments, and (2) the training of fire personnel to operate the vehicles.

The federal government eventually decided against using Birmingham as an EMS demonstration site and rejected the request for funds. However, the process of developing the proposal had the secondary effect of generating support for a local EMS operation. Support intensified after a second tragic accident in 1972 that resulted in the allegedly preventable deaths of two young high school coaches. These events precipitated the city's 1973 decision to participate in a one-year EMS program. The program was supported by federal money from the DHEW's Regional Medical Program, but at a level far below the $3.6 million originally anticipated. The $300,000 grrant was used to purchase three emergency vehicles (one for Birmingham and two for neighboring municipalities), to develop and institute a training program for paramedics, and to pay a portion of the salaries of the fire fighters who temporarily left their posts to work in the program. Municipalities that participated in the program were required to offer matching funds.

The pilot program proceeded well and was transferred to local funds in 1974. The program has undergone substantial expansion in its four years of operation, and BF&RS currently operates six emergency vehicles (rescue units). Seventy-three men have received EMT-III certification. A team of two EMT-IIIs, a lieutenant and a firefighter, typically operate a vehicle (although occasionally there are three men on duty), and there are three such paramedic teams associated with each vehicle. The vehicles are equipped with an assortment of rescue apparatus, in addition to radio and telemetric equipment that enables the paramedic to transmit verbal and physiologic information about patient status to a hospital's emergency room. Two UHF channels have been reserved for rescue unit use, and communications between the vehicles and participating hospitals are coordinated through the department's communications center.

The BF&RS operation does not transport patients and therefore has not replaced the private ambulance service. A rescue unit responds to any call for help received through the communications center. Where necessary, a private ambulance is also dispatched to the scene. If continuous emergency care is required during transport to a hospital, an EMT-III will leave the rescue unit and ride with the patient in the ambulance.

There has been a steadily rising demand for EMS service in Birmingham. In 1975, nearly half of the 10,250 fire and other emergency alarms involved the EMS service. The program has attracted considerable public interest, and the fire officers are frequently asked to speak about their activities at public functions. In addition, the mayor recently made city funds available for the fire officers to begin a large-scale citizen training program in cardiopulmonary resuscitation. The Birmingham EMS committee meets monthly and attracts the participation of about two dozen individuals in addition to the officially designated membership. The individual who heads the committee also serves as chairman of the state and national EMS committees.

Status of Routinization

Budget and Equipment. The Birmingham EMS operation was initiated with federal money funneled through a state agency. The operation was transferred to local funding in 1974 at the end of a one-year pilot period and has continued to be supported by city funds since that time. Thus, the innovation has survived three budget cycles. Expenditures for the program are not explicitly distinguished from expenditures for other BF&RS activities. The budget submitted to the mayor and council requests money for personnel, but there is no formal indication of what proportion of the requested funds will be used for the rescue as opposed to firefighting operations. This arrangement has enabled the fire department to maintain its established level of staffing while other city agencies have experienced sharp personnel cutbacks because of budgetary restrictions. Instead of reducing BF&RS funds in the same way as other agency funds, the council decided to maintain a stable level of funding for the BF&RS, with the expressed intent of encouraging the expansion of the EMS operations. In other words, rather than release "extra" officers who had been on the BF&RS's payroll, the council voted to maintain the existing levels so department staff could be redistributed to increase the number of paramedics in the city. This action has served to establish the EMS program as an essential part of the overall department operations.

The largest equipment expenditures in the innovation have been for EMS vehicles. In addition to the pilot vehicle purchased with federal money, the department received funding approval for the purchase of two additional EMS vehicles in 1974 and three more in 1976. Moreover, funds were allocated for a replacement vehicle in 1975, with the intention of using it as a substitute for the pilot vehicle, which in turn has been held in reserve for use whenever any of the newer vehicles require maintenance or repair.

The other major piece of equipment used in the EMS program is the

"Lifepak." It is used for transmitting data such as electrocardiograms (ECGs) via radio telemetry. Since the EMS program began, the original Lifepak has been succeeded by the more streamlined Lifepak-5. In 1977, the BF&RS requested funds to replace all its models with the newer equipment, and it expects little difficulty in obtaining approval.

Procedures for purchasing equipment and supplies for the EMS operation are the same as those used by the department for other operations. Requests are forwarded to a city purchasing agent who oversees the purchase and approves the transfer of funds to pay for the desired items. This is a routine procedure, but it requires considerable paperwork. However, the procedure has been made somewhat easier for the EMS program because the purchasing agent has taken an EMT-III course and is better informed regarding how the EMS program operates.

Personnel and Training. Seventy-six BF&RS personnel have received EMT-III status since 1973. All have completed a rigorous training program at the Regional Technical Institute (RTI) of the University of Alabama. This training program, which combines about 81 hours of classroom instruction in each level with approximately 450 hours of experience in the hospital wards, grew out of the pilot EMS program. The federal grant required the training program, and the medical director of the EMS committee took the initiative to develop the necessary curriculum. Seventeen firefighters enrolled in the pilot class, which subsequently became a standard course at RTI. Five groups of firefighters, ranging in size from nine to eighteen officers, enrolled in subsequent EMT-III courses.

Although only forty-eight of the BF&RS personnel who have achieved EMT-III status are currently assigned to one of the six EMS units, the department continues to permit firefighters to begin EMT-III training. This, in part, is due to the department's commitment to the EMS program. Agency officials repeatedly emphasize the advantages of having as many officers as possible trained in paramedic procedures. They also point out that this enables officers with firefighting assignments to better appreciate and thus cooperate with the officers on EMS assignments.

The EMS program has been deliberately structured so the paramedic assignment will not be a dead-end job. One paramedic and one lieutenant typically comprise an EMS unit. When the lieutenant is promoted to captain, he leaves the unit and thus creates room for others to move into the paramedic corps. This arrangement is important for routinization because it institutionalizes a procedure that allows individuals who are likely to be knowledgeable about and sympathetic to the EMS operation to enter the higher ranks of the department.

Birmingham operates under a civil service system. Any new position or job classification must be approved by the mayor before the salary is established by the civil service system. There have been two new job classifications created in connection with the EMS program. Shortly after the program was transferred to local funds, the job of paramedic was given civil service status. More recently, the department created and informally filled a full-time EMS coordinator position. Procedures are now under way to obtain a civil service designation for this job. (The coordinating activities had previously been carried out by the assistant chief, along with his other administrative duties.)

Any account of the EMS personnel would be incomplete without mentioning the role of the chairman of the EMS committee, an individual outside the department who oversees the EMS activities. The chairman has assumed responsibility for ongoing oversight of the level of medical expertise of the department's EMT-IIIs. He frequently requires them to attend special sessions to update or refresh their medical knowledge and skills. In addition, he has worked to establish a model EMT program at RTI that includes the BF&RS personnel as instructors and thus assures a continuing link between the medical and fire service communities.

Organizational Governance. The operation of the EMS program is not mandated by executive or legislative order, but there have been several directives that bear on its operation. The first was the creation by city ordinance of the Birmingham EMS committee. As was mentioned earlier, this ordinance assures continuing attention by prominent local citizens to Birmingham's needs for emergency medical services.

Other initiatives have come from the state and are primarily related to the training of EMS personnel. The state established an EMT-III licensing requirement in 1973-74 that is based on a state board examination. The state has also passed a law that requires all EMT-IIIs to attend a 40-hour refresher course every three years. In addition, the EMT-III curriculum is now mandated by the state board of health.

None of these initiatives has had a great effect on the EMS operation. This is largely because the chairman of the EMS committee is also head of the state EMS board, which plays a major role in developing the regulations in support of the legislative mandates. In effect, he has used the Birmingham operation as the model program on which the regulations are built. Yet, the regulations are important to the continued operation of the Birmingham EMS program. They assure that the groundwork in paramedic training laid by the current EMS committee chairman will be retained, even if he were to cease being active in the Birmingham EMS program.

Within the BF&RS, there has been steady progress toward refining and standardizing the EMS operation. When the current EMS coordinator assumed his position in September 1976, there was a lack of uniformity in the various units' operations. A major responsibility of the new coordinator has therefore been to establish detailed standard procedures for all six EMS units. A special procedures bulletin is now issued each time there is an incident that points to some uncertainty or conflict in the current operations. Standard supply lists recently have been issued for all units. Careful records are now kept on the use of supplies by each unit; expendable items are restocked weekly.

Reasons for Routinization Status

Service Applications and Outcomes.

H_1 *core application.* Although the provision of on-site emergency medical care was not a core function of the BF&RS when the EMS program began, it has rapidly evolved into a central activity of the department. The importance of the EMS operation is reflected by the fact that nearly half of the calls answered by the department in 1975 involved the EMS program. Moreover, there has been an annual increase in the number of requests made for EMS aid. Another indication of the core status of the EMS operation is the department's stationery, which shows the formal title of the agency as the "Birmingham Fire and Rescue Service Department."

H_2 *competition.* The different applications provided by the EMS program are highly compatible, with no opportunity for competition among applications. When the program began, it was decided that the vehicles would respond to all calls for help, no matter how large or small the "emergency." Because of this, the innovation provides a wide range of medical services. Instead of creating competition among applications, the decision to operate in this way has resulted in more frequent use of the service by the public, and it appears to have broadened the base of support in the community.

H_3 *service-related payoffs.* Although there have been no formal evaluations of the effectiveness or productivity of the EMS program in the BF&RS, the strong consensus among all respondents is that the program is an extremely successful and productive one. The consistent annual growth in the number of citizens using the service was cited by respondents as one measure of the program's success. Other indirect measures of service-related payoffs have been the mayor's decision to include continued support of the EMS program in his election platform, as well as continued press and constituency enthusiasm for the operation (see H_5-H_6, client-community support).

In addition to having payoffs related to the provision of needed services to clients, the program appears to have benefited the BF&RS in several ways. As a result of the EMS program, the BF&RS has gained greater visibility and status in the community. As one respondent pointed out, prior to the involvement in EMS, members of the public rarely had contact with the fire department and were likely to question how firefighters filled their time. The high level of service of the EMS program focuses attention on fire department activity as opposed to inactivity. Moreover, as was noted in the budget section, the EMS program has been largely responsible for a sustained level of budgetary support of the fire department at times when other local agencies were experiencing cutbacks.

External Environment.

H_4 *crisis conditions.* The EMS program was initiated in response to what was perceived as a chronic need of the Birmingham community—the need for immediate on-site medical care for victims of emergency situations. However, it is not obvious that this perceived need was strongly felt by the majority of community members prior to the onset of EMS activities in the city. Rather, it appears that those with reason to use or be familiar with the existing services were aware of the shortcomings of those services, while the public at large was only exposed to the limitations of the existing arrangements for emergency medical care when an incident was extensively covered by the media.

H_5, H_6 *client-community support.* The EMS program enjoys widespread support from both private citizens and public officials outside the department. Each week, the department receives several unsolicited invitations from various citizen groups to speak about the EMS operation. In addition, some groups have expressed a desire to contribute to the financial support of EMS; in one case, proceeds from a local group were used to purchase equipment for a vehicle. The mayor attributes his support of the program to the widespread public satisfaction it has elicited, and, when running for election, he included continued support of the EMS program as part of his election platform. Since he has been in office, the mayor has approved budget requests for the program and recently made additional funds available for the EMT-IIIs to begin a citizen training program in cardiopulmonary resuscitation.

There are at least three factors that contribute to the public's enthusiasm for EMS. The first centers on the very nature of the services offered. The EMS operation provides needed and previously unavailable assistance during crisis situations. Unless such assistance were poorly administered (which is not the case in Birmingham, where the medical community clearly respects the level of competence of the EMT-IIIs), one would expect to find a high level of enthusiasm among those who had benefited from the service.

The second factor is the breadth and visibility of the operation. When one examines maps of Birmingham that show the number of emergency runs completed since the innovation's adoption, it is apparent that at least one household on every block in the city has used the service during any given year. Moreover, the department estimates that every family in the city will call in an EMS vehicle at least once in eight years. The appearance of any emergency medical vehicle, like that of a fire truck or police car at any location, attracts the attention of neighbors and passersby.

Finally, community support has grown because of conscious efforts on the part of the BF&RS administrators to draw public attention to the EMS operation. Thus, when the first EMT-IIIs graduated, the stars of the television program "Emergency" were invited to Birmingham for the ceremonies. Similarly, the media are kept informed of any program activities that may be of interest to the public. Only one article critical of the program has appeared since the EMS program began, and the public outcry was so intense that the paper re-examined the incident and subsequently retracted the critical comments.

Internal Characteristics.

H_7 *administrators.* The EMS program has enjoyed the strong support of administrators in the fire department. The chief has been enthusiastic about the program, and the most active proponent is the administrator with rank second only to that of the chief. The assistant chief has put a premium on the medical training of the paramedics and arranged for release time for the trainees during the most demanding six months of the EMT training program. He did this because he was convinced that the continued success of the EMS program was inexplicably tied to the quality of medical treatment provided by the paramedics. His notion was that well-trained fire practitioners would draw support from both the medical community and the public, whereas mediocre paramedics would antagonize both.

In addition, his high rank has enabled the assistant chief to have direct access to key individuals outside the agency, such as the mayor or hospital administrators, whose decisions have directly affected many aspects of the EMS operation. Thus, the assistant chief has been in a position to discuss budget priorities with the mayor on a casual basis and to arrange a reciprocal training agreement with the hospital.

H_8 *innovator.* Until September, 1976, when a special EMS coordinator's position was designated and filled by a captain in the department, the EMS activities were coordinated by the assistant chief, a man who appears to command the respect and support of department administrators and practitioners.

From the outset, the assistant chief viewed the EMS operation as a means through which the BF&RS could provide the community with vitally needed services and thus enhance the importance of the fire department as a whole for the community. As a long-time and skilled administrator, he acted in a cautious but deliberate manner to ensure that the EMS operation continued to meet the ambitious expectations held for it from its inception. For instance, he carefully screened the first group of practitioners for personality traits that would lend themselves to building rapport in the community as well as for the intellectual abilities necessary to meet the EMT-III training demands. He also decided that only firefighters with at least four years of experience would be permitted to enter paramedic training, thus ensuring the selection of seasoned firefighters who would be likely to work well with non-paramedic colleagues. These decisions appear to have contributed to the continued enthusiasm for the EMS service.

H_9 *practitioners.* EMS is a distinctive innovation in that its operation relies on the coordination of efforts by practitioners from more than one local agency. For the innovation to be successfully routinized, practitioners from both the fire service and the cooperating medical facilities must come to view EMS as part of their "normal" practice.

This has been the case in Birmingham. On the one hand, the practitioners from the fire department who are involved (the EMT-IIIs) typically consider it a privilege to serve in the paramedic corps. All are firefighters who have volunteered for the paramedic service, and there have consistently been far more applications for the paramedic jobs than there have been positions available. The large number of applications has enabled department officials to screen potential paramedics carefully for ability, commitment, and other characteristics they believe to be associated with quality service.

On the other hand, coordinators of the EMS program have given careful attention to the need for health practitioners such as nurses and doctors to understand the nature of the field operations. Thus, emergency room nurses who communicate with paramedics in the field are encouraged to spend time answering calls with an emergency medical team so they can become fully familiar with the EMS operation. This not only helps the nurses understand the conditions under which the paramedics operate, but it also enables the nurses to build rapport with the paramedic staff. Similarly, the paramedics conduct rounds at various hospitals in Birmingham, thereby allowing the hospital staff to be exposed to and gain confidence in the level of competence of the paramedics.

H_9, H_{10} *adversary group.* There appears to be little personal opposition and no organized opposition to the EMS operation from the BF&RS staff. On the contrary, the innovation appears to have brought a prestige to the department that benefits the entire staff. The staff for the EMS operation is selected from volunteers among the regular firefighters, and thus the officers serving as paramedics have been working colleagues of those responsible for the firefighting operations of the department. The paramedics receive a slightly higher salary than that of the regular firefighters to compensate for the responsibilities they assume and the larger number of calls to which they respond, but the difference is sufficiently small that resentment on the part of the firefighters is unlikely.

The only resistance to the EMS from the community derives from the private ambulance companies serving Birmingham. Although the companies do not operate as an adversary group per se, their existence has to some extent restricted the EMS operation. The fact that the inclusion of patient transport in the EMS operation would have interfered with privately owned businesses influenced the initial decision not to provide transport services. Despite sporadic dissatisfaction with the quality of service provided by the private companies, the BF&RS administrators have been reluctant to expand their operation to include transport as well as on-site treatment of patients.

Cincinnati Police Division, Cincinnati, Ohio

Persons interviewed

Lieutenant, commander of CPD Traffic Bureau

Police Officer, CPD Traffic Bureau

Instructor, Regional Training Academy

Police Officer, Office of Program Management, CPD

Coordinator, Alcohol Safety Action Program, Department of Safety

Background

The city of Cincinnati is governed by one of the oldest council/manager systems in the country and has a single department of safety containing both police and fire services. Although the city's population has declined from a peak of 502,550 in the late 1960s, the Cincinnati Police Division (CPD) has slowly expanded from 906 positions in 1970 to its present complement of about one thousand sworn officers. CPD administrators have continued to seek improvements in the agency's operations and have implemented such new systems as team polic- ing, a regional crime information center, decentralization of support services, and a building program for several new stations. A growing agency budget has supported many of these changes, as has the receipt of large amounts of federal assistance. For example, the agency budget in 1975 was $22 million, an increase of $4.1 million over the previous year; additional funds were made available through the LEAA and the National Highway Safety Administration.

The decentralization of the CPD and reorganization of operating units have been the major focus of the division since 1969. In that year, the CPD began regrouping sections and bureaus. The following year, consolidation reduced the number of districts from seven to six. In 1975, consolidation again reduced the number of districts to five and established the new position of assistant chief to coordinate all bureaus. Also created that year was the operations bureau, which included almost all of the field operations, such as criminal investigation and traffic. The new bureau had a budget of over $13 million and had 75 percent of the CPD assigned to it. The reorganization had a major effect on the traffic enforcement program, for the previously separate traffic section was first placed under the operations bureau and then totally decentralized to all of the five stations.

In 1976, the CPD suffered a major disruption when the chief of police, who had been in office for five years, and several other top administrators were indicted. This created a large turnover in personnel and altered the direction of the agency.

The Innovation

In 1970, the traffic section began participating in the federally sponsored program "Fatal Accident Reduction Enforcement" (FARE). In 1971, Cincinnati was selected as one of the 35 national test sites for the newly conceived Alcohol Safety Action Program (ASAP); the city was awarded $2.1 million to cover the costs of the project for 1972-74. Included in the grant were funds to purchase three breath-testing instruments (Breathalyzers), ten patrol vehicles, and salaries for ten officers and two sergeants. The extra funding was a substantial boost to the more informal FARE program.

During the three years the ASAP was active, the CPD had ten officers and two sergeants assigned to the project. There were another fifteen men in the traffic section headquarters to assist regular CPD officers in accident investigation and in the processing of DWI cases. The twelve ASAP officers would handle virtually all of the DWI arrests, responding to the scene at the request of regular patrol officers. When the project was terminated, the twelve ASAP men and the other fifteen support officers were reassigned to the various district stations.

Under ASAP, patrolling officers would arrest a driver for a traffic offense and, if there were reason to suspect the driver, for DWI. The driver would be taken to the traffic section offices to be processed. The station was equipped with three Breathalyzers running twenty-four hours a day. The driver would be asked to take a breath test; if he refused, then the state's "implied consent" law required that he forfeit his license for a period of six months. The Breathalyzer operator would read the suspect his rights, including his right to refuse the test, and would then ask the person to blow into a small tube attached to the instrument.

While the sample was being processed, the officer proceeded to interview the driver, using the Alcohol Influence Report as a checklist. The results of the breath test were noted on the form, and the case was forwarded to the prosecutor's office.

When ASAP first started, the CPD intended to videotape all offenders during the testing and interviewing. The grant enabled the CPD to purchase two video cameras, three recorders, and three video monitors; all equipment, except for one monitor in the prosecutor's office, was kept at traffic headquarters. But the videotapes were less than satisfactory. First, the tape was effective only if the subject was moving around. Second, the conviction rate, even without the tape, was 85 to 90 percent. Third, the whole trial usually took only fifteen minutes—the same amount of time it would take to play back the tape. Finally, the judges objected to the tape being used in some cases but not in others. Not surprisingly, the CPD phased out the videotapes in 1973, after having used them several times in court.

The Breathalyzer itself represented a major change for the traffic section. Previously, all offenders had to be tested by urinalysis, which took a great deal of time and was sometimes ineffective. Although the ASAP grant specified only that the program would use breath testing in place of urinalysis, the choice of instrument was left to the jurisdiction. With the Breathalyzer, an offender of either sex could be tested in a few minutes and could not give the excuse of being unable to provide a sample. The Breathalyzer also removed the need to involve the city chemist in each incident and trial.

In 1976, the Ohio Department of Transportation approached the CPD with an offer to help purchase any additional breath-testing instruments. The CPD had wanted to acquire several additional instruments for two years but could not get the administration to allocate the funds. The state offer of 50-percent reimbursement was a strong incentive, and so the traffic section was able to get five Breathalyzer 900-As.

Today, the traffic section utilizes all eight instruments. The original three instruments are used as the regional police academy for training and as backup for the other five. The five new instruments are located in each of the five station houses and are kept in a secured room under the supervision of a sergeant at each station. There are 139 trained operators spread throughout the districts and over the shifts to handle all testing.

Status of Routinization

Budget and Equipment. From 1972-74, the Breathalyzer operation was funded from the $2.1 million federal grant. The costs included the purchase of the first three instruments, salaries for ten officers and two sergeants, overtime pay, ten patrol vehicles, and supplies. As with most federal grants, there had to be matching local funds; however, these funds were allocated for the whole project and not just for the innovation. When the project was phased out, the CPD assumed the continuing costs: the twelve men who were on the project and who were originally on the division payroll were put back on the payroll, overtime was budgeted but at a much lesser amount, and regular CPD vehicles were utilized. The annual cost of supplies for the Breathalyzer was incorporated as a part of the regular CPD supply budget.

Similarly, the five new instruments purchased in 1976 were paid for with local funds. Although the state was to reimburse the city for 50 percent of the cost of the instruments, the CPD had to cover the full amount (five Breathalyzer 900-As at $1,000 each including simulator cost $5,000) in its own budget. The state reimbursement funds went to the city treasury and not to the CPD. However, because the instruments have been purchased, the annual costs of the innovation are relatively small compared to other supplies and especially to personnel costs. Test ampules cost $.70 each; the costs for other supplies amount to a few hundred dollars more per year. Thus, budget cutbacks similar to those that have already occurred do not affect the innovation directly. It should also be noted that in 1976 the CPD went through an economy program in which ninety-four men were laid off and large cutbacks were made in all budgetary categories.

The low operating costs for the Breathalyzer have enabled the city to save the money hitherto spent on expensive chemical analyses of blood, urine, or saliva. These tests, done by the city chemist and his staff, required a full-time assistant and overtime pay for the long hours spent testifying in court. Thus, the purchase of the instruments has been from soft funds, first from federal grant money and later from discretionary division funds. But the annual operating costs have made the necessary passage from the federal money to regular department funds, even though Breathalyzer supplies are not a separate line item in the annual budget. In both purchasing cycles, the initiative was from outside the division and the choice of instruments was constrained by the state.

Purchasing specifications and procedures, as well as the procedures for budget preparation, have remained unchanged by the use of the Breathalyzer. The purchasing specifications, prepared by the traffic section commander, were simply those listed by the manufacturer or the terms of the state grant. The purchasing procedures are the same as for any other piece of equipment: the maintenance technician calls the chief's office to request that the supplies be purchased; the chief's office fills out a purchase requisition and forwards it to the city purchasing office; and the supplies are ordered.

Personnel and Training. Breath testing requires the presence of a trained operator to calibrate the instrument, process the breath sample, and perform any maintenance/repair procedures necessary. The division currently has 130 trained operators to run the five instruments; three of the operators are in the traffic section, and the rest are distributed throughout the five stations. All but eight are senior operators, meaning they are capable of running breath tests and of doing all the maintenance procedures. The other eight will be trained as senior operators in the near future.

In the CPD, the operators are regular division officers who have undergone a forty-hour training period and have been certified by the state board of health. In 1972, the state board came to the division to train the operators in a special eighty-hour course on the instrument, its repair, and the videotape system. As turnover occurred among the twelve operators, the new officers would be sent to the regular training programs sponsored by the state board in Columbus. The state provided the training free of charge.

As the end of the ASAP grant drew near, the division realized it was going to need a larger number of part-time operators to substitute for the full-time ASAP officers. It was at this point that the CPD internalized its training program. The CPD made a request to the state board-of-health instructor that it be allowed to establish its own training program just for Cincinnati police. The state agreed, and in 1975 the division started to train senior operators at the regional police academy. The training has been available to all law enforcement agencies in Hamilton County. Classes of up to twenty-four officers have been trained as the need has arisen, which has usually been three or four times a year.

The officers to be trained have been chosen from among those who have volunteered, and there has usually been a short waiting list. The course used at the academy was developed by the state board and is mandated as the course of instruction. The instructor can design his own schedule and can add extra material, but he must follow the state's outline and materials. The state supplies only twenty-four copies of "Basic Training Program for Breath Examiner Specialist" to be used by the students and returned at the end of the course. The instructor is also given an "Instructor's Lesson Plan" to follow.

The Cincinnati instructors have tried to give the officers as much material as possible on the Breathalyzer. The current book for the course is a revised edition, which is not as good as the original, from the CPD's viewpoint. It covers only the instrument and does not discuss the history or principles involved in chemical testing. Therefore, the division assumed the task of reprinting the original text for the course and now provides each operator with his own copy. In addition to the old manual given the students, the new manual loaned to them, and the oral instruction, the students also receive other instructional materials: handouts on the CPD's procedures, federal rules governing DWI arrests, and recent court decisions.

The title of "operator" or "senior operator" is not connected with the CPD's or city's civil service system; that is, it is not a formal CPD classification or rank. Instead, the title is conferred by the state board of health after the officer has taken the course and passed the certifying examination. At the end of the forty-hour course, an examiner from the board comes to the class to give each student a written and practice test. Upon passing the examination, the officer is certified as an operator for a period of two years. The title and the examination process existed in the state prior to the implementation of the innovation in Cincinnati. At the end of the two years, the operator must take another certifying examination. To prepare for the examination, the operator returns to the academy for an eight-hour refresher course focused on the state's textbook. At the end of the course, the examination is given by the state examiner. Those who pass are recertified for another two years; those that fail are sent for training in the next class. In addition to the recertification examinations, the state also gives each operator an annual proficiency examination. The state examiner will give the officer a solution with an unknown alcohol concentration and ask the operator to test it. As the operator runs through the steps, the examiner checks them off his list and verifies the answer.

By setting up its own training program, the CPD has internalized its own training staff as well. The instructors for the course are employed by the agency or other government offices. Thus, the CPD no longer relies on an outside agency for its training. New operators can be trained as the need arises by in-house staff using the CPD materials; refresher training can be handled in a similar manner.

The innovation has consequently been operated for five years without the need to bring in specialized personnel. All operators have been regular CPD officers, and almost all have received their necessary training while in the agency. The Breathalyzer has also been a sufficiently simple and self-contained instrument that little external technical assistance was necessary. State board officials helped to design the training program and conducted the early training, and federal National Highway Safety Administration (NHSA) representatives provided information on the instrument. The city chemist has helped to explain the nature of the chemical testing involved and has served as an "expert" in establishing the validity of the Breathalyzer. However, such assistance has been mainly administrative in nature; the technical problems have been handled entirely on an internal basis.

Organizational Governance. The intensive ASAP program prompted the revision of the CPD's procedure manual to include five pages of procedures for handling DWI arrests. These procedures delineate the steps to be followed from the time of arrest until appearance in court, but do not include a detailed discussion of how to operate the Breathalyzer. The procedures specify that all alcohol safety unit personnel must be senior operators to use the Breathalyzer and video equipment. Also required is the use of the Breathalyzer "operational checklist" whenever a test is being conducted. Because the procedures specifically mention the videotaping, it appears that the manual had not been revised since 1973, when the taping was last done. A note in the manual, however, indicates that a supplemental information bulletin from the chief authorized elimination of the videotaping.

The use of the Breathalyzer has also necessitated the revision of one CPD form and the adoption of a state form. The division uses an intoxication report form to record the findings of the psychomotor tests, information on the driver, and the results of the chemical test. Prior to the innovation, the form did not include space for recording information on breath testing. Since the adoption of the Breathalyzer, the form has been revised to include the time, date, operator's name, and the instrument used to conduct the breath test. The form specifically names the Breathalyzer, although there is also space to indicate if another kind of chemical test was used. The state board of health also requires that if the CPD is going to use the Breathalyzer, it must test the instrument for accuracy at specified intervals. Each time the Breathalyzer is calibrated, which must occur after every ten tests or nine days, the operator must fill out a state Breathalyzer test report.

Ohio state law supports the use of breath testing in the prosecution of DWI incidents, but does not mandate its use. The law simply requires that a person arrested for DWI must submit to a chemical test of some kind or automatically forfeit his license for a period of six months. Chemical tests are permitted on blood, urine, breath, or saliva. It is up to the local jurisdiction to decide which test is to be used, as long as the testing instrument has been approved by the state board of health.

Cincinnati has no formal policy requiring that only the breath test be used. The Breathalyzer is generally used, but its selection may be tempered by the situation (for example, an unconscious driver cannot give a breath sample). However, the training, procedures, and supervisory process clearly emphasize the breath test.

The Cincinnati police are not represented by a regular union in labor negotiations; therefore, the innovation has not been part of any collective bargaining.

Maintenance and Repair. Traffic section personnel maintain and service the Breathalyzers. If the instruments cannot be repaired, they are sent to an outside company to be serviced. All senior operators are capable of making repairs, but experience has proven that the best results are obtained when a minimum number of persons is involved, to reduce inconsistent treatment of the equipment.

If an operator accidentally spills acid on the instrument, he will immediately disassemble and clean the instrument. Otherwise, if an instrument needs attention, the operator will call the traffic section to send over a replacement. Ninety percent of the repairs can be done on the scene, while the other 10 percent are done at a work bench in the traffic section. The section has spent about $300 on spare parts, and one technician has supplied his own tools for the repair operation.

The innovation has replaced one type of chemical testing with a newer, more convenient type. As such, it has not replaced any of the old functions for the traffic section, nor has it changed many of the procedures. The changes that have been made, assigning DWI enforcement to ASAP or decentralizing manpower to the districts, have been the result of administrative reforms separate from the innovation.

Except for the videotape system that was used for two years and then dropped, the equipment involved in the innovation has essentially remained the same since implementation. The Breathalyzer instrument and its accompanying simulator are the basic components of the innovation. They are both self-contained, and there is almost nothing that can be done to modify their operation. The five new Breathalyzers purchased in 1976 were an updated model (but not second generation) of the three purchased in 1972; the primary difference was that the newer models had a ninety-second timer. The other characteristics of the instrument were identical.

Reasons for Routinization Status

Service Applications and Outcomes.

H_1 *core application.* The innovation has made several important changes in the processing of DWI arrests in Cincinnati. First, it has replaced urinalysis with breath testing as the primary chemical test. Second, it allows the chemical test to be done at the police station at the time of booking instead of being done several days later at a city laboratory. Third, it allows the officer/operator to perform the test himself rather than relying on a chemist in another city agency. Fourth, it replaces a several-step analytic process with a single-step instrument. Finally, it makes the DWI processing much easier for the officer by eliminating the problems of excuses, special procedures for female offenders, absence of facilities, or handling of specimens.

H_2 *competition.* The innovation has only one application in the CPD: to test breath samples of drivers arrested for DWI. Establishment of priorities and resource allocation are thus not important issues.

H_3 *service-related payoffs.* The benefits from the innovation have been derived first and foremost by the arresting officers. They can process a DWI case within fifteen minutes and have all the information they need to complete their reports. Time for processing the case and court time per case have been reduced. Overall, however, court time appears to have increased for the officers because of the larger number of arrests.

At the same time, the larger number of arrests and convictions has also benefited the CPD, the prosecutor's office, and the city population. The CPD can point to the number of arrests as evidence of more effective job performance. The prosecutor is able to spend less time per case because the results of the Breathalyzer test are more easily understood by a jury and are accepted by the court as proof of impairment. The conviction rate with the urinalysis procedure was only about 5 percent less than with the Breathalyzer (90 percent), but the number of cases processed was only about six hundred, compared to the three thousand currently being handled. The city also benefits from the extra revenue brought in by the cases and from a declining rate of deaths from vehicular accidents.

There has been at least one formal evaluation of the innovation during its operation. It was carried out in 1974 as a part of the ASAP evaluation done by the Institute of Governmental Research at the University of Cincinnati. Although most of the report dealt with arrest strategy and ASAP performance, it did identify specific payoffs of the Breathalyzer. In addition, successive roadside surveys in 1973, 1974, and 1975 found that there had been a reduction of 42 percent in the number of drivers on the road with a BAC of .10 percent or higher as a result of the ASAP enforcement.

However, the innovation has not been without problems. The Breathalyzer has made the arrest procedure simpler; consequently, more arrests are being made. The increased arrests, however, mean that the officers must spend more time in court and less time on the street. During the ASAP operation, the twelve officers would often spend all day in court and all night patrolling, with little time left to rest from the workload. Court time is also expensive for the division, because each officer must be given a minimum of three hours compensatory time for every occasion in which he goes to court. The increased workload therefore indirectly incurs greater costs. The excessive court time also has a drawback for the officers. Many of them do not like to spend time in court. Others find that after they have been in court a few times, they are perceived by the attorneys as "experts" and are singled out for extra questioning. With the long hours and difficult experiences in court, many of the men have shied away from DWI arrests and from volunteering to become Breathalyzer operators.

External Environment.

H_4 *crisis conditions.* Prior to the innovation, Cincinnati was facing a twofold problem with respect to drunken driving. The state had estimated that there were over twenty-five thousand problem drinkers on the road in the metropolitan area, many of them well over the impairment level of .10 percent BAC. Most of the thirty thousand automobile accidents the city experienced every year involved the use of alcohol. But to combat DWI, the CPD had to rely on the commitment of the officers and the lengthy procedures of the urinalysis, and only five hundred to six hundred arrests were being made each year. Most of the respondents agreed that the CPD would have implemented the Breathalyzer eventually, but it would not have been on nearly the same scale or with the same commitment. The impetus for the innovation's use really came from outside the agency. It came from the federal government through the ASAP program and through the state highway operation. Both parties recognized the service need in Cincinnati and were able to put the resources into meeting those needs.

H_5, H_6 *client-community support.* The innovation is entirely limited to the internal operations of the local government and police agency; there are no "clients" per se in the community to support the innovation. City park police use the Breathalyzer as needed and, in theory, other cities in Hamilton County (outside of Cincinnati) can also make use of the instruments. It is unlikely, however, that there would be any kind of organized support for the innovation if the CPD discontinued it.

The only enthusiastic supporters outside the local government have been the Institute of Governmental Research, the state board of health, the state department of transportation, and the NHSA, all of which have been extensively involved in the several enforcement programs. There is general support from the community, but it is directed at the overall enforcement program and not merely the innovation. It appears that the community would express little opposition to the removal of the Breathalyzer as long as the accident rate did not increase.

The amount of publicity for the innovation has been steadily declining since it was first introduced. The federal government gave extensive publicity to the ASAP project in 1972 and to the fact that Cincinnati was a test site. The state has also publicized the fact that there are special teams of officers patrolling the highways for cases of DWI. Local coverage, which appears primarily around holiday time, focuses attention on both the enforcement program and the Breathalyzer itself. The heavy publicity initially given to the program was intentionally reduced as the backlog of arrests grew. The division has attempted to maintain a public awareness of the program to serve as a deterrent to DWI. Because the deterrent factor comes from the possibility of arrest and not from the Breathalyzer itself, little emphasis is placed on the instrument. The traffic section still feels that over half the potential DWIs know about the innovation and about the enforcement program.

Internal Characteristics.

H_7 *administrators.* The innovation has received continued support from the top administration in the CPD. One sign of support on the part of the chief has been the continuation of the innovation after federal funding stopped; the chief approved the funding of officer overtime and the expenditures for instrument supplies. In addition, the chief reallocated $5,000 in discretionary funds to acquire five more instruments, approved the continued training program, and authorized release time for the training of officers.

There is also strong support and awareness for the innovation from other parts of the Cinicinnati government. Six of the nine city council members are familiar with the Breathalyzer, and four showed strong backing for the ASAP program. At one point, the mayor (elected from the council) was very supportive of the enforcement program and the innovation; the current mayor, however, has little awareness of the instrument. Eleven of the thirteen judges in the municipal court readily accept the use of the Breathalyzer and feel it has been very helpful in processing DWI cases. Even defense attorneys have come to accept the results of the breath test, while the assistant prosecutor has gone so far as to become a trained senior operator.

H_8 *innovator.* Although the commander of the traffic bureau has responsibility for the coordination and supervision of the innovation, the role of innovator is actually shared by several officers in the bureau. The commander provided the initial thrust for the use of the instrument and its procedures but then quickly involved the officers in the implementation and problem solving. For example, the revisions made in the intoxication report resulted from the suggestions of traffic officers that information frequently requested in court be recorded directly on the form. Similarly, the changes in the procedure manual were developed by the officers based on their experiences. These changes were then officially instituted by the program management section.

Technical expertise is also shared by the bureau officers. All have been trained to repair and maintain the instruments; however, to minimize inconsistent repairs to the instrument, one of the officers has been designated as the primary technician. As such, he is responsible for making the weekly or monthly repairs and for much of the preventive maintenance. The technician also provides instruction on the use of the Breathalyzer at the academy and frequently handles the scheduling of classes, ordering of materials, etc. Often these various responsibilities are rotated among the other officers so that everyone remains familiar with each aspect of the operation. Thus, it appears that the innovation has been supported by multiple innovators under the coordination of the commander and that it has not developed a dependency on any single officer.

H_9 *practitioners.* The innovation is not relevant to the officers' career advancement, and there is no monetary incentive system for becoming involved in the enforcement operation. All operators maintain their regular CPD rank; they must take the civil service examination for any promotions and are not given special consideration as a result of being Breathalyzer operators. Operating the instrument does not interfere with the other duties or experiences of the officer and, therefore, is not a handicap in the promotion process. Because the CPD views the skill of operating a Breathalyzer the same as any other technical skill of the officers, such as marksmanship, there is no extra pay associated with the title of operator.

Among those officers who had processed DWI cases using urinalysis, there was ready acceptance of the new instrument. However, other officers, particularly the older ones, showed some resistance to the extra time involved in the training and the additional demands of court appearances. As the men learned about the heavy workload entailed, the list of volunteers diminished. For the most part, the only reaction to the innovation itself has been either positive or neutral.

H_{10} *adversary group.* There are no groups within the local agency that oppose the innovation or that would support a substitute.

Dallas Fire Department, Dallas, Texas

Persons interviewed

Chief, Ambulance Division

Chief, Dallas Fire Department

Chief of Operations Division

Chief, Planning and Research Division

Lieutenant, Ambulance Division

Two Paramedics, Unit 11

Cardiologist; chairman, Training Committee, EMS Program; assistant professor, Medical School, University of Texas; member, State EMS Committee

Surgeon; member of the Training Committee; associate professor, Medical School, University of Texas

Registered Nurse; member, Training Committee, EMS Program; director of EMS Research

Member of State Department of Public Health; director of Training, EMS Program

Member of State Department of Public Health; EMS Skills instructor

Budget officer, Office of Management Services, City of Dallas

Background

Dallas is a "low-rise" city composed of about 340 square miles and a population of about 912,000. In contrast to many of the rapidly expanding cities in the Southwest, Dallas has experienced a relatively stable population and geographic size over the last decade, although there has been some annexation of the many small, independent enclaves within the city boundaries. The economic and tax base of the city has also been stable for several years, allowing for moderate growth in construction and services.

Although the city is headed by a mayor elected from an eleven-member city council, the day-to-day administration is handled by a strong city manager and staff. In fiscal year 1977, Dallas operated on a budget of $307,420,000 (including revenue-sharing funds) of which $30,676,000 (10 percent) was allocated to the fire department. Current city manpower is approximately 13,000 employees, of which 1,400 (11 percent) work in the fire department. All of these employees are covered by a city-wide civil service system; all hiring and promotions are done solely by examination plus an efficiency evaluation by the supervisor. For the most part, the system is very competitive.

The Dallas Fire Department has fared better than most city agencies. The overall budget for fire protection has been increasing at a gradual rate over the last several years, and some new fire stations have been built. In mid-1976, the department underwent a major turnover in its top administration. The chief, who had been in office for six years and who was a part of an administration that had been in control for over thirty years, retired and was replaced by a division chief from the planning and research division of the department. At the same time, several other top positions opened and were also filled from within the ranks, including the chief of operations and the chief of planning and research. Whereas the previous administration was very "closed" in its attitudes toward personnel matters and operations, the new administration has actively tried to confront many of the department's longstanding problems. This has changed the internal atmosphere from one opposing new ideas to one encouraging experimentation and open discussion.

The Innovation

Throughout the 1960s, Dallas contracted biennially with one of the several local funeral homes to provide emergency ambulance service. The contract was written on an annual basis. The primary contractor then subcontracted with other funeral homes around the city to operate the ambulances. Calls for emergency assistance would be received by the police; the police would then call the primary contractor to dispatch the ambulance. Equipment on the ambulances was minimal, and the attendants' main function was simply to transport people. The contractor would charge the patient $32.50 per trip, and the city agreed to pay the contractor 80 percent of that if the contractor could not collect from the individual. In essence, the city was subsidizing the contractor to provide the service.

Three groups gradually became dissatisfied with the service: the public was upset about the slow response time (over ten minutes on the average), the doctors were dissatisfied with the level of prehospital care, and the local politicians and media were distressed by the numerous citizen complaints. During this time, the fire department maintained a neutral stand, although some officials did expect to eventually get involved in the provision of ambulance service.

In 1969, an ambulance committee was formed, consisting of representatives from the city council, the mayor's office, Southwestern Medical School, Dallas Hospital Council (representing the thirty-four hospitals in the area), the Dallas County Hospital District, and others. Much of the impetus for organizing the committee came from the Dallas County League of Municipalities. The size of the committee prevented it from working effectively, and so in early 1970 the league asked a consulting firm to study the problem. The consultant's recommendation was a county-wide system of emergency medical services (EMS). If that was not possible for political reasons, then Dallas was to: (a) regulate private ambulances directly, (b) set up its own EMS program, or (c) transfer the ambulance service to the fire department.

The political environment precluded the county-wide system. At first, the city tried to get the surrounding cities in the county to cooperate in an EMS program. This failed because these cities already had a program of their own or they were not experiencing service problems. Although the cities did agree to a one-dollar charge on license plate fees to support a county-wide system, opposition from truckers and funeral homes killed the proposed bill in the 1971 legislature.

The defeat of the bill forced the city to look elsewhere for a solution. The city manager and council finally decided to put the EMS program in the fire department because: (1) it had the physical plant to take care of the equipment, (2) it had a full-time core staff, and (3) the record of fire departments' EMS service elsewhere (for example, Baltimore, Miami) was good. The assistant city manager and several council members made site visits to other cities to view their EMS operations.

To prepare for the transition to an EMS system, the chief assigned a member of the department's research and planning staff (who later became the head of the EMS program) to develop the budget and procedures for the service. Based on additional site visits but very little available EMS literature or other outside help, a proposal was drafted. Private ambulance companies had been responding to about sixty-eight calls per day according to police records, and so the demand for EMS was projected higher, at eighty-five per day. With a response time of six to eight minutes as the overriding constraint on system design, a computer simulation was used to estimate the number and location of EMS vehicles. The computer simulation model was a cooperative effort of the fire department, the city office of management services, and the data processing division. The results indicated a need for sixteen mobile intensive care units (MICUs) with an additional six units in reserve.

The recommendation of the department to the council was for a first-year budget of $423,187 for EMS. That amount was increased to $600,805 during negotiations to include: twenty-two vehicles, $96,696 for salaries, increases for clothing and travel, and additional funds for tools and chemicals. The vote approving the budget was five to four. However, when the department went back to the council for approval of the type of vehicle to be purchased (prior to the bids going out) the program was again in doubt. The council was divided five in favor of fire department operation, five in favor of private operation, and one—the legal counsel of the funeral home which was a subcontractor—abstaining. After several weeks, the vote finally shifted to nine:one:one and passed in January, 1972. The medical community had lobbied behind the scenes in favor of the new service.

The EMS system began in October, 1972 with 150 EMTs. Two were assigned to each MICU for each shift, with the remainder assigned to various engines. The system was headed by a division chief for EMS, and it was part of the ambulance division (one of nine fire department divisions). The EMTs had been trained in five classes, with each class completing a 176-hour course, and the EMTs were qualified to perform advanced first aid and to prepare an emergency patient for transport.

From the beginning, however, the division chief had planned to upgrade the system to include the use of paramedics. Rather than doing everything at once and risking failure, the first phase concentrated on the implementation of the ambulance service. In January 1974, the second phase of the program was initiated with the training of 120 paramedics from the existing EMTs. Life support equipment (Amb-paks), telemetry equipment, and drug kits were purchased to upgrade the ambulances to fully equipped MICUs. There are currently 160 EMTs and 138 paramedics. Most are assigned to the seventeen active and six reserve MICUs with some EMTs assigned to engines. All the officers, like regular fire officers, are located in stations throughout the city and work in twenty-four-hour shifts with forty-eight hours off between shifts. Each MICU has a squad of two firemen, one of whom is a paramedic and the other a trained EMT.

Each MICU contains a great deal of sophisticated medical and communication equipment. A portable Amb-pak contains an electrocardiograph, an oscilliscope, and a defibrillator. A portable five-channel radio can be attached to the Amb-pak to transmit ECG information to a radio receiver in the hospital base station. A drug kit contains a variety of medications for use in reviving heart attack patients, as well as other medications used for tending to accident victims. When the unit arrives at the scene, the two men carry the necessary equipment to the patient and begin to give care. Because the exact nature of the call is not always known, the men must carry most of their equipment with them each time; the equipment packages can weight as much as sixty to seventy pounds, which makes them difficult to carry.

At the scene, the paramedic decides whether the patient needs to be transported to a hospital for further treatment. If it is not an emergency, the patient is told that he must find his own transportation to the hospital. If it is an emergency and the patient refuses to be transported, he is asked to sign a statement to the effect. There is a forty-dollar charge to anyone transported, but on-site care is provided without charge. From the time the MICU arrives at the scene until the time it arrives at the hospital, the paramedic is in constant voice contact with the physician at the hospital base station. All voice contact and telemetry is recorded by the fire department dispatcher and by the base station for reference.

Status of Routinization

Budget and Equipment. The budget for the EMS operation has increased each year since its implementation, from $600,805 for fiscal year 1971-72 to $1.6 million in 1974-75 to $2.1 million for 1976-77. The passage from external to local (that is, soft to hard) funding occurred in 1971, at the same time that the program changed from its start-up phase to its operational phase. The initial funds in fiscal year 1971-72 had been part of the city's revenue-sharing money for that year; the funding for the following year, however, was totally from the city's general fund. The program has continued to operate on local funds since then, although revenue-sharing funds were used again in 1974 to pay for the new telemetry equipment for the paramedics.

It should be noted that the EMS program generates some revenue for the city, but the revenue does not directly benefit the program. The city charges forty dollars to transport a patient to the hospital, regardless of the distance involved (generating approximately $400,000 in revenue annually). The city also contracts with neighboring cities who wish to participate in the telemetry link to one of the hospitals. There are currently three communities that are under such a contract. Citizen donations have amounted to only a few hundred dollars, but a large donation of $34,000 was made by a private citizen to purchase a new MICU for the program; the unit is in the process of being acquired.

The substantial yearly funding by the city has allowed the program to own all its equipment, with the exception of the few dedicated telephone lines. Most of the equipment was purchased in 1972, with the telemetry and additional drugs added in 1974. In fiscal year 1975, the 23rd MICU was added, to bring the active force up to 17 units (with six in reserve); in 1976, money was appropriated by the city council to purchase a twenty-fourth unit, but, through an administrative mix-up, the unit is now being purchased with the funds from the private donation. The council is currently being asked to fund an additional unit.

The EMS program has not had to face any cutbacks in its annual funding level and has enjoyed an overall increase in expenditures even though the department's resources have become constrained. There are two reasons why the EMS program would not likely suffer severe budgetary cutbacks and why in some ways it would be given preferential treatment. First, the program is functioning at the absolute minimum staffing level. The chief and other administrators have agreed that the program could not function with fewer than two men and the present complement of equipment. Moreover, any reduction in the number of MICU units would be immediately noticeable to the community and would become a source of complaints.

A second reason for the preferential treatment of the EMS program is the double duty performed by its staff. In 1973, a new pension plan for the department reduced overall manpower by over 100 men; at the same time, another 46 men were taken off the rigs to staff the EMS program. Thus, because the paramedics are fire officers first and paramedics second, the department was able to economize in filling its paramedic positions. A group of 106 recruits was then hired to fill the vacancies left by the 146 firemen, and the engines/trucks were restaffed with slightly fewer men. The paramedics now serve as a supplement to the fire companies when the need arises. Because of the dual role performed by the paramedics, any budget cutbacks would probably result in the release of some of the 106 new recruits rather than any of the EMS personnel.

Personnel and Training. There are approximately 318 firemen in the department who are trained either as EMTs or paramedics. All of the 170 paramedics and 34 of the EMTs are functionally assigned to the ambulance division and perform their job on a regular, full-time basis. The rest of the EMTs are within the operations division and are assigned as regular members of the engine or truck companies. Although all of the fire officers are covered by a civil service system, there is no special classification for the EMTs or paramedics. Instead, the officers receive their distinction by having state certification and are put on "special assignment" within the department. The department pays the paramedic/firemen on special assignment an additional $25 per month but provides no other type of special distinction. Other personnel who are involved full time with the innovation include: a division secretary, three lieutenants (paramedics), one Captain (EMT), and four EMTs who rotate as radio operators at the hospital base station. There are also six dispatchers who send out the

MICUs and a cadre of training personnel who are indirectly involved with the innovation.

Currently, the department has about twenty volunteers a month who wish to transfer into the ambulance division—just enough to balance the number of officers leaving the division. The volunteer has to be in the department for at least one year before being selected. There is no entry examination, only a subjective evaluation by the chief of operations and the chief of the ambulance division. Once selected, the men are sent through an intensive training course conducted outside the department. At the end of the class, they are given an exam by the state department of public health to be certified as either EMTs or paramedics. The certification is good for two years, and at the end of that time the fire officer must take a five-day refresher course for EMTs or a ten-day refresher course for paramedics, and another exam. All exams for the EMT and paramedic rating were created prior to the first training programs for the Dallas firemen and are also used for personnel trained from elsewhere throughout the state.

The initial training program for EMTs was the product of an advisory subcommittee to the city council ambulance committee appointed by the mayor in 1972. The subcommittee advised the chief of the ambulance division for the training program. The content of the program was based on the U.S. Department of Transportation's recommendations, although some modifications were made to include suggestions from other EMS programs. The committee also served as liaison to the various hospitals participating in the training program. By the end of 1972, the subcommittee's role was delegated to an associate professor at the medical school. Thus, when the paramedic program was started, its training program was designed almost exclusively by the associate professor, the chief of the ambulance division, and an ad hoc training committee. Members of the committee include a surgeon, a cardiologist, a registered nurse assigned to the EMS program full time, a coordinator from the department of public health, a skills instructor, and the chief of the ambulance division.

The training program for both EMTs and paramedics is conducted on a periodic basis by the University of Texas Southwestern Medical School. Until 1976, the school only trained Dallas fire officers and could handle only about five classes of thirty officers each year. The training was provided free of charge to the fire department, although there was never any formal contractual arrangement between the department and the medical school. There appear to be three major reasons for the medical school's contribution of training. First, the president of the Health Science Center (previously the dean of the medical school) strongly supports the EMS program and feels that the school should be doing the training as part of its public service. Second, the doctors in the medical school also support the program and are willing to donate their time. Finally, the medical school receives a large amount of fire department equipment and additional staff support in the emergency room from the arrangement.

As the training program leveled off for the Dallas Fire Department in 1976, the training committee decided to begin training other fire officers from other jurisdictions in the metropolitan area. Currently, the committee will accept fire officers from other cities if the city has first shown a genuine commitment to the EMS program, i.e., committed funds to purchase the necessary equipment. The cities then pay directly to the medical school a $300 tuition for each EMT trainee or $1,200 for each paramedic trainee. In all, there have been twelve training cycles since the EMS program began.

The medical school staff has provided considerable technical assistance to the program as have the two advisory committees that were initially established. However, once the program was started, there was little outside technical assistance from consultants. Two sources of assistance that were particularly helpful in the early stages were the management and communications services provided by the city. Initially, the city provided its own management services to help the department plan the EMS operation. These services are used infrequently now, having been replaced by the department's own management experience and in-house computer system. Similarly, the initial planning, installation, and debugging of the telemetry equipment was handled by the communications services of the city, but the department developed its own capacity to solve equipment problems and modify the equipment when necessary.

The EMS program has been marked by a relatively low level of turnover among personnel. Out of the over 330 personnel trained, only a handful have left the department. Others have requested transfers out of the ambulance division because of being "burned out by the pace," but they have remained available for duty on the regular engines and trucks. There has been no turnover among supervisory lieutenants; the captain who supervised these lieutenants and served as an assistant to the division chief was replaced by a batallion chief in 1976. Most important, however, is the absence of any turnover at the division chief level; the same person who designed and initiated the program is still in command. Several respondents stated that if the division chief were to leave suddenly, the program would be in serious trouble because much of the EMS information and procedures have not been formally written. Because of the relative isolation of the program, the recent turnover of other top level administrators (including the department chief) has had little effect on the EMS program.

Organizational Governance. Because the innovation was a new function added to existing department operations, there was little revision needed in specific forms already in use. The innovation has, however, generated a large number of new forms to be filled out by EMTs and paramedics. Some of the forms have already gone through one or two revisions as procedures have been updated and refined. In addition, as with the establishment of the new, separate ambulance division (which is a formal unit on the department's organization chart), new procedures and regulations to be followed by the EMTs and paramedics were issued as "orders" from the division chief's office; thus, some formalized and official procedures do exist for the innovation.

The innovation is mandated by a single city council ordinance which took effect in November, 1972 at the expiration of the city's contract for private ambulance services. The ordinance has been mainly drafted by the chief of the ambulance division, with the assistance of the city's legal affairs office. There are also several state statutes that affect the operation of the innovation but which do not serve as mandates. For example, the state law requires that all EMTs and paramedics must be certified by the state health department. The health department in turn has a set of regulations governing the requirements for certification. Other state regulations govern the safety features of the equipment involved but, again, only indirectly affect the innovation.

The innovation has not been a part of any collective bargaining with the unions. State law prohibits any binding arbitration, and so the unions are relatively weak and inactive. The International Firefighters Association (IFFA) to which the fire officers belong has, however, been involved with the innovation and has lobbied the city council for certain changes. In particular, the IFFA sought better pay for the paramedics on the basis of their increased workload, but the move was unsuccessful. It has only been with the recent change in department administration that the paramedics have had any kind of organization, and the new chief has tried to deal with many of the long-standing grievances of the men such as pay and recognition.

Another addition to the department as a result of the innovation has been a set of purchasing specifications and maintenance procedures. When the EMS program was initiated, all of the equipment (MICUs and telemetry) had to be purchased. The chief of the ambulance division wrote the specifications for the equipment, and he has written the revised specifications for the fourteen chassis that have since worn out and been replaced. The purchase of medical and communication equipment has followed the traditional department procedures, using the specifications generally provided by the manufacturer. The most extensive modification required by the innovation, other than making space in the fire stations to park the MICU, has been to find closet space at each station to keep the medical supplies.

To handle the increased demand on vehicle maintenance, the department hired two more mechanics and one body/fender specialist to work full-time on MICUs. Arrangements were made between the ambulance division and the maintenance shop to hire the additional staff and to budget the replacement costs for the equipment annually. The EMS program had only to bear the initial cost of the equipment, the other years being built into the depreciation budget. Maintenance on the radio equipment and the Amb-paks is handled in a similar manner by the division of equipment services: EMS buys the initial equipment, but it is maintained and replaced by the maintenance section. Thus, the necessary maintenance and replacement procedures have been built into the regular operations of the fire department.

There have been a few design changes on some of the equipment to account for needed improvements. For example, the brakes on the MICUs were modified to hold up under heavy stop-and-go travel. Fifty-foot patch cords were added to the radios in order to transmit via telephone when radio transmission was not possible. In addition, to give better care, the paramedics made modifications in the types or use of medical supplies. However, there have been no major modifications, and no new models of equipment have been purchased.

Reasons for Routinization Status

Service Applications and Outcomes.

H_1 *core application.* Although the EMS program replaced no functions within the fire department, it did replace the emergency ambulance service that had been provided to the public by private suppliers. The innovation met the two requirements imposed by public and professional concerns: it provided emergency medical care to the public with a shorter response time, and it provided appropriate and satisfactory treatment in doing so. It did not totally replace the several private companies, however; such companies can continue to transport non-emergency cases as long as they comply with the new standards of operation.

H_2 *competition.* There is only a single application for the innovation, even though the innovation is capable of accomplishing several tasks simultaneously. Therefore, there is no competition for either the manpower or resources of the EMS program from the other divisions in the department. If a shortage of manpower occurs at the location of a fire, the chief in charge at the fire scene can reassign the paramedics to a firefighting role. (This situation has not yet occurred). If tradeoffs are to be made within the EMS program, they are usually made by the chief of the ambulance division.

H_3 *service-related payoffs.* The primary beneficiary of the innovation has clearly been the general public. They are now receiving faster, better-quality emergency medical care. The incidence of fatal heart attacks and the complications from trauma have both decreased since the start of the program. Specific measures for the benefits of the program, however, are difficult to judge because of the nature of the service. The department claims only partial credit for the total decrease in fatal heart attacks and will only discuss benefits in terms of improved response time (from ten minutes down to six). Department statistics only show that the number of responses and the number of people served increase each year, and that the types of service calls have also expanded.

The secondary beneficiaries of the innovation are the hospitals and the fire department itself. The hospitals benefit from the improved care the patient receives at the scene of the accident and are able to better prepare for the patient's arrival at the emergency room. The EMS program, in essence, increases the success rate of the hospital by starting the care sooner. The fire department has benefited from the increased public exposure; the image of the department has changed from one of "firemen sitting around all day playing checkers" to one of "firemen providing rescue and emergency care twenty-four hours a day." The change in the public image has meant a higher status among city services and perhaps an easier time during budget proceedings.

The innovation has not been without its problems, however. The fact that there is a special class of firemen called "paramedic" that performs a different function from the regular firefighter but is housed in the same station, has caused some conflict among the men in the department. On the the one hand, the paramedics feel they are not appreciated, are underpaid, and are given excessive workloads. On the other hand, the regular fire officers feel the paramedics have a comparatively easy job in the MICUs. Hard feelings are exacerbated by the abuse that paramedics sometimes face in answering calls in certain parts of the city; occasionally, individuals will obstruct the fire officers in the performance of their duties. These internal problems have not affected the operation of the innovation but may have caused a decline in the number of men volunteering for special assignment.

External Environment.

H_4 *crisis conditions.* The use of the innovation began as the result of a chronic need for quick and competent emergency medical care. This need was recognized by both the city council and the local news media and reflected a widespread public dissatisfaction with the private ambulance service. The medical profession was also acutely aware of the problem and expressed its concern about the condition of the arriving emergency patients.

H_5, H_6 *client-community support.* The clients of the innovation, that is, the general public in Dallas, are not formally organized to support the innovation. Their support is expressed instead through the local media and through the city council. Several community groups have expressed an interest in the EMS operation and requested speakers to inform them of the program. At times, the public will make small monetary donations as well.

Outside of the local government, the strongest supporters of the innovator are the medical school, the local EMS committee, and other municipalities that contract with Dallas for service. The medical school provides support through the contribution of training programs and through the informal lobbying of the city council. The local EMS committee similarly works toward generating public support and making its opinions known to the city council.

Finally, the other communities that contract with Dallas either for direct service or for the use of the telemetry equipment show support for the innovation through their service demand and through the status they confer on the city for operating such a program.

Although the EMS committee and the medical school are the most enthusiastic supporters of the innovation, the strength of the program comes from broad public awareness. When the program was introduced and again when the paramedics were added, there was substantial press coverage of the innovation. The public affairs division organized a public relations campaign to make the community highly aware of the service and to inform residents about how to call for assistance. Since then, other articles have appeared periodically in the press, and there has been limited television coverage. The program was given an additional boost at campaign time when several of the candidates for city council included an EMS plank in their platform. The division chief occasionally writes articles for national publications describing the operation of the Dallas program.

The only opposition to the innovation occurred at the outset of the program. Private ambulance companies opposed the move because of the business they would lose and because of the new set of regulations. Several city council members were also opposed to the idea on the grounds that private enterprise should be allowed to provide service where possible without government interference. The council members changed their opinions after examining the private service more thoroughly, and the private companies have not expressed any criticisms of the innovation for several years.

Internal Characteristics.

H_7 *administrators.* The change in top level administrators in 1976 represented an increase in the department's support for the EMS program. The previous chief and the operations division head had not been exceptionally strong supporters (the program had been mandated by the city council), but they did implement the program and make the appropriate budget approvals and assignments of personnel. The planning and operation of the innovation were delegated to the chief of the ambulance division, who was allowed to pursue the program as long as it did not interfere with other regular department operations.

With the change in administration, the department has taken a somewhat new direction. The new administrators are much stronger in their support of the EMS program, even though their knowledge of the program's operation is still limited and they are willing to continue delegating responsibility for the program to the division chief. Many of the administrative roadblocks have been removed from the innovation's operation, and many of the longstanding problems are being confronted. The chief has always supported and continues to support the EMS operation through annual budget appropriations.

H_8 *innovator.* The chief of the ambulance division has clearly been the single innovator for the EMS program. He was originally assigned to the innovation from the planning and research section and was given the job of planning and implementing the council's mandate. He worked mostly by himself within the department but drew on outside resources from the city offices, the medical school, and other EMS programs. He is responsible for specifications for the MICU units, the final equipment arrangements with Motorola Corporation, the telemetry, and the Amb-paks. He has been instrumental in the design of the training curriculum and the drafting of the initial council ordinance. He is trained as a paramedic, knows the equipment inside out, fights for the funding annually, and has a never-ending supply of ideas for improving the EMS operation. As mentioned before, there is some concern that the division chief has been so instrumental that if he were to leave the division, the program might suffer.

H_9 *practitioners.* There was no resistance on the part of the fire officers to the innovation in the early stages of the program; many were happy to volunteer, and many still are quite enthusiastic about their work. However, attitudes have changed somewhat over the last two years, with the result that fewer men are volunteering for the division, and those who are already inside show some disappointment. Almost all of the fire officers are committed to the EMS program and would resist any move to drop the program, but they are dissatisfied with some of the working conditions and the limited recognition for their effort. The new administration is actively trying to resolve these problems and to encourage the next round of volunteers for the innovation (the planning for the innovation was based on a three-year tour for the paramedics because of the heavy workload).

Service as an EMT or paramedic does not contribute toward career advancement within the department. At times, it has been seen as a disadvantage because it reduces a fire officer's firefighting experience and takes away from the time available to study for promotional exams. Thus, because there is no promotional credit for EMS duties and because the experience necessary for passing promotional exams comes from firefighting and not emergency work, serving in EMS positions may actually have a negative effect in terms of career advancement. Similarly, the additional twenty-five dollars a month in special assignment pay is not seen as a strong incentive because it does not compensate for the additional workload. To the paramedic or EMT, the real incentive is internal—the satisfaction of helping people in emergency situations. The administration is currently trying to establish a career path that includes the ambulance division and to boost the special assignment pay.

H_{10} *adversary group.* Some officers within the fire department were initially unenthusiastic about the innovation because of the belief that emergency medical care was not a proper function of the department. Such feelings, however, ceased shortly after the program was mandated by the council. Private interests represented by the city council also initially opposed the change on grounds that private enterprise should be allowed to provide the service, but such opposition has also subsided. Currently, there are no groups in the department or the city government that strongly oppose the EMS program.

Miami Police Department, Miami, Florida

Persons interviewed

Assistant to the City Manager

Assistant to the Chief

Commander, Information Services Section

Supervisor, Computer Operations

Manager, Systems Development Group

Assistant Commander, Records Section

Public Information Officer

Officer, Patrol Section

Sergeant, Operations Analysis and Research

Background

As of the fall of 1976, the Miami Police Department employed approximately 799 sworn and 382 non-sworn personnel to serve a central city of about 350,000 people. Since 1969, the department has been undertaking a massive program to modernize its facilities and to expand its capabilities. This program has been supported by a $20 million bond issue approved by city voters in 1970, and it is expected to be concluded in 1978. The full-scale planning activities, however, did not start until April 1972, when the department contracted with Stanford Research Institute (SRI). For four years, SRI worked closely with department administrators, providing intensive technical assistance and preparing a master plan of several hundred pages.

In October 1976, the department moved into its newly constructed $11 million headquarters building and began to operate with about $3 million of new computer and communication hardware. Tentative plans exist for spending an additional $3 million on the computer and communications systems. The department's new computer system will support two innovative programs: computer-aided dispatch (CAD) and computer-assisted report entry (CARE). CAD uses the computer to record information from incoming complaint calls and to route them to the appropriate dispatcher for immediate assignment. The system replaces an old, three-step, conveyor belt and status board dispatch system. CARE uses the computer to record the data from officers' reports (for example, reported crime, suspect's characteristics, and stolen property) and to print out a wide range of statistical analyses. Mobile digital terminals, to be added in 1977, will allow the officers to query the record files directly.

The Innovation

One of the most important resources for a police department is information about crimes and the department's own performance. The increasing sophistication of criminal techniques requires that data be kept on names, vehicles, methods of operation, etc. Administrative and planning activities further necessitate the analysis of data on officer performance, case status, and monthly crime statistics. Most departments have responded to this demand by implementing automated or computer-assisted data systems.

Like most departments, the Miami Police Department traditionally tabulated by hand the statistics needed for the FBI's Uniform Crime Report (UCR). In the late 1960s, the department acquired its own IBM Tab reader/sorter to automate statistical reporting. Even before the bond issue planning in 1969, it was realized that the Tab machine was inadequate for the amount of analysis being requested, and therefore money for the department's first computer was approved in the 1969-70 budget, with the computer (NCR Century 100) being installed in early 1971.

The NCR Century was a small business computer limited in both its capacity and speed; all jobs had to be processed singly and only in batch mode. There was no on-line capability, and the operation required an intermediary programmer/operator to translate user language into computer language. Thus, the application and turnaround time of the computer depended on the number of personnel available to run it, as well as the capacity of the machine itself.

The approximately 350 programs written for the computer[1] were roughly equally divided for payroll, program development, and statistical purposes. The payroll section of the department was given a printout of personnel attendance and functions, which was forwarded to the city payroll office. The strategic planning section received all of its printouts on weekly and monthly crime statistics, status of arrests and warrants, reponse times, methods of operation, etc. The UCR data were sent to Tallahassee on magnetic tape, and a printed copy was returned for verification. The first section of the UCR data (Part I) was also printed out by area, sector of the city, and day of the week. Each shift sergeant was given a copy of the printout from his sector, showing criminal activity for the previous calendar week. Finally, the chief himself reviewed most of the printouts in order to closely monitor all of the department's activities.

The department leased the NCR computer until very recently, when the first new computer system purchased from the bond revenues (two PDP 11/45's) assumed all of the NCR functions plus many new ones. The Miami computer system has thus included two generations of equipment, with the most recent generation using several computers to accommodate both the array of older functions as well as the CAD and CARE applications.

Status of Routinization

Budget and Equipment. The funding support for the NCR computer and support staff was made a part of the department's budget in 1969-70. There were no federal or state funds involved in the data processing operation, although outside grants were utilized for special programs (such as investigations of organized crime) that relied on statistical analyses. Funds from the 1970 bond issue, which contained about $6 million for computer hardware and software, were not used until late 1974, when the department contracted for the two PDP 11/45's from the Digital Equipment Corporation. At about the same time, six new staff were hired to program the new computer and to facilitate the conversion of programs from the NCR to the PDP system. These six positions are funded from the bond revenues for development work. It is anticipated that the bond revenues will end by 1978, at which time the hardware (including two PDP 11/70's now being installed) and software will be transferred back to general funding. Thus, funding for the system will have been entirely from local funds (that is, hard money) but from different local budget categories.

The NCR system was maintained over six budget cycles, with apparently little change in its annual level of funding. There has been no project-by-project accounting, since all data processing was charged to a single account. Because the computer was leased and maintenance was included as part of the agreement, operating expenses were limited to about $2,200 per month. With the acquisition of the new computers, staff costs have been the single greatest expense for data processing, with the annual expenditure approaching $400,000 for the past two years. In 1977, the department has had to face an across-the-board 4.5 percent budget cut. The cutback caused the abolishment of two vacant civilian positions in data processing: a programmer and a keypunch operator.

Personnel and Training. All the personnel directly involved with the computer are under the auspices of the city's civil service system, a fact that had created some problems in introducing new data processing specialties. At the time the NCR computer was acquired, the positions and job descriptions for the four to

six coders and four to six keypunch operators had already been long established. When the PDP 11/45 computers were purchased, three new civil service
classifications had to be created because the existing "programmer" classification was far too limited. After several months delay, the department was finally
allowed to hire two senior systems analysts, two systems programmers, and two
application programmers.[2] A seventh staff member was also hired at that time
to serve as systems development manager. Unlike the other new positions that
were funded from bond revenues, the manager was paid from the general fund.

For the support staff, the basic skills of reading, keypunching, and programming are now prerequisites built into the qualifying exam for each respec-
tive position. New personnel are selected from two to three people on a civil
service list of those passing the qualifying examination. Similarly, the newer
staff classifications—analysts and programmers—are also covered by a civil
service qualifying examination and certain educational qualifications.

Organizational Governance. The use of the computer has been marked by three
major changes in governance organization and rules. First, a reorganization
of the administrative division has established the data processing system as a
separate administrative entity. Second, the department has modified the incident reporting forms to reduce the duplication of data and paperwork. In the
1960s, a single report form was successfully substituted for several shorter
ones. A more recent change has resulted in a single form for filing all reports.
The new form is formatted for easy entry directly into the CARE system, and
a manual has been written specifically to help officers complete this form.
Third, the department has entered into a formal agreement with the state of
Florida to submit its monthly UCR data on magnetic tape rather than written
forms. Thus, the computer system is reinforced by the requirement for collecting UCR data and by the agreement to submit the data via tape.

Reasons for Routinization Status

Service Applications and Outcomes.

H_1 *core application.* Even a limited capacity computer such as the NCR
supported a variety of applications. In Miami, these applications replaced manual
systems and thus were part of the core information-gathering and analysis
functions of the department. For instance, data were needed for the UCR
report and for tracking department performance (status of arrests, response
time, and deployment). Even though the printout was often seven to nine
days old when first available, it nevertheless enabled both the chief and the unit
sergeant to monitor criminal activity in a particular sector. Equally important
was the collection of facts and characteristics on suspects, crimes, property,

etc. Officers and investigators could not rely solely on the specialized printouts because of the limitations of the data and computer, but the system was called upon four or five times each month to provide information. Finally, a portion of the computer's time was devoted to the simple function of payroll. Because the payroll was actually handled by the city finance department, the police department's responsibility was only for maintaining the complex attendance records.

H_2 *competition.* With the expanded computer system, these applications will be enhanced by two other core functions, dispatching and case entry. Thus, the computer system has continued to grow and to provide important services to the department. Initially, the payroll function was considered secondary to the other statistical functions, but conflicts did arise regarding the actual time to be allocated to each. With the exception of the monthly UCR report, investigations and other projects usually followed a flexible schedule. Since there were no formal priorities established for the computer time, jobs would be processed on a first-come, first-served basis and according to the preferences of the head of data processing. Payroll, however, soon "created its own priority" because everyone wanted to be paid on time. When competition arose for computer time, the conflict had to be settled by the manager of systems development, or it proceeded up the hierarchy for resolution. With the new PDP computers, such conflicts will no longer exist because there is ample capacity for all of the older functions as well as the new ones.

H_3 *service-related payoffs.* To date, the actual payoffs from the computer system have been minimal, if measured in terms of changes in productivity; but it must be remembered that expanded computer operations only began in October, 1976. Very few of the officers know anything about the computer, its uses, or the staff running it, and no critical cases are known to have been solved simply because of computer assistance. Those people involved in planning police deployment have experienced some benefit from the data in balancing sector manpower, but again the payoff is not clearly identifiable. (These kinds of payoffs may become more evident with the new system.) The single, most useful feature of the NCR system, however, has perhaps been that it has symbolized the department's modernization program.

External Environment.

H_4 *crisis conditions.* The operation of the computer system did not follow any specific crisis conditions. The adoption of automated data processing was more the result of a slowly emerging problem—the rising incidence of crimes that had to be tabulated and reported.

H_5, H_6 *client-community support.* By far the strongest supporter of the computer system outside the department is the general public. The wide margin by which the 1970 bond issue passed affirmed the public demand for better police services. The new computer and communications hardware were clearly proposed as part of the bond issue, and a picture of the NCR computer was included in the referendum literature, even though the NCR had not actually been installed. The emphasis on new equipment, such as computers, appears to have captured voter attention, primarily because the shock of the 1967-69 demonstrations, riots, and other disorders was still vividly remembered.

The continuing problem of crime in the streets reinforces the use of the computer in two other ways. First, the greater frequency and sophistication of criminal activity requires increased monitoring. Organized crime, for example, is perceived as a long-term phenomenon, and both the public and public officials place great faith in the computer as being instrumental in actions against organized crime. Second, the exchange of information among law enforcement agencies is handled by computer, either directly or indirectly. The state's acceptance of UCR reports on magnetic tape is one example. The department's query of national criminal justice data banks via remote terminals is another.

Internal Characteristics.

H_7, H_8 *administrators and innovator.* The greatest internal support for the system comes from the department's top administrators. The police chief who was responsible for the entire program and for bringing the department "into the 20th century" was a highly controversial figure recruited from outside the department in 1969. Although he understood very little about computers and their technical potential in police work, the chief was convinced that they were an essential part of the future of the department. He took the responsibility for organizing and coordinating the task forces and steering committees that handled the bond issue and supervised the entire planning program.

The chief's efforts survived his departure in October, 1974 and the appointment of a new chief from within the department. The new chief had been the assistant chief for operations and had been actively involved in the planning of the new computer system. It is felt that he has become an even stronger proponent of the system than his predecessor, a view that is partially confirmed by the fact that he personally reviews most of the printouts. Other top administrators who were involved in the computer planning are equally committed, either because they believe in its benefit for police work or because they feel that the dollar expenditure thus far is so great that there is no choice but to continue the program.

One particularly strong supporter within the municipal administration is the assistant to the city manager. He was closely associated with the previous chief, was instrumental in the computer's early design and planning, and has been responsible for guiding the data system through its budget and implementation cycles. Yet, he is not involved in the daily operation of the computer or in the technical aspects of the new system. There has been no turnover in his position since the computer system was initiated, and so his own role has been a major factor in the incorporation of the system.

H_9 *practitioners.* As mentioned earlier, practitioner support for the computer system is mainly limited to those few persons who actually use its output. Most officers have only seen the Part I UCR printout for their own sector. However, even this brief exposure has built up some support among the officers, whose primary interest is "what it can do for me on the street." The officers appreciate feedback on how they are performing, especially relative to other sectors. They also want data on the types and location of criminal activity so they can be more aware of what to observe while on patrol. More importantly, they want other kinds of data available to them on the street and have been disappointed when the data have not been accessible in the past. With the new applications effective in 1977 (CARE and CAD), and the remote/mobile terminals, all officers will be linked directly to the computer system and will be able to make their own requests. This kind of direct participation will, no doubt, foster strong practitioner support for the system.

H_{10} *adversary group.* There has been no opposition to the innovation by individuals within or outside of the department.

Oakland Unified School District, Oakland, California

Persons interviewed

Acting director of Data Processing

Mathematics teacher

Staff person in Testing and Evaluation

Background

The Oakland Unified School District was the site of a field visit on computer assisted instruction (CAI). Approximately 53,000 students are enrolled in Oakland's six senior high schools, sixteen junior high schools and sixty-four elementary schools. Another 14,000 students attend special classes for adult or handicapped students, bringing the overall district enrollment to approximately 64,000 students. The district has a large minority population: two-thirds of the students are black and 15 percent are Spanish-surnamed, Asian, Native American, or Filipino. The enrollment level has increased slightly over the past five years.

District expenditures for 1975-76 totalled $136,472,969. Although local and state money provided the largest proportions of these revenues, the expenditures included a federal contribution of over $16 million. The district's large minority population qualifies it to receive most of these federal funds, with 60 percent of the schools eligible for outside assistance. However, even with the slight increases in enrollment and the availability of federal aid, Oakland's school district operates under severe budgetary stress. Respondents attributed this to the recent increases in employee salaries and fringe benefits. In addition, they reported that it is becoming more and more difficult for the district to raise local revenues, and therefore the budgetary strains are likely to continue.

The Innovation

The data processing department has a district-owned Honeywell 6025 computer, which is used for instructional applications but which is primarily dedicated to such administrative functions as budgeting, payroll, and class scheduling. The department operates on an annual budget of about $700,000. About $300,000 of the budget is applied to salaries, with the remainder for equipment and supplies. Oakland schools, however, used computers for instructional purposes before the arrival of the Honeywell 6025. In the early 1960s, six of the district's high schools purchased programmable calculators, which they used in conjunction with the teaching of programming in various advanced mathematics classes. This type of computer programming continues to be part of the curriculum in some high schools. In addition, several of the district's schools experimented with the form of CAI that enables students to receive individually paced instruction in a variety of school subjects. This type of CAI was typically associated with experimental programs supported by outside funds and is currently not in use in the district.

Status of Routinization

Budget and Equipment. A general-purpose fund provides all the money currently used in connection with CAI. All charges for central processing unit (CPU) time are absorbed by the data processing group, which does not charge separate departments for the service it renders. The seventy-five-dollar-per-month payment for each of the thirteen teletype terminals rented from the telephone company and distributed among the six high schools is paid for through a special budget category that has been part of the standard school allocations since the days when they had the calculators. The terminals do not appear as separate line items but are part of a general equipment category that includes typewriters and other standard office machines. Such equipment is considered essential to the daily operation of the schools, and this funding arrangement, therefore, makes it highly unlikely that the terminals will be singled out and eliminated from the budget.

Although the Oakland schools have used a computer for administrative applications for over fifteen years, the third-generation Honeywell 6025 purchased in 1971 was the district's first computer that could be used for instructional as well as administrative purposes. There were, however, some instructional uses of the computer under way prior to the purchase of the Honeywell 6025, mainly the use of the programmable calculators by the six high schools in the early 1960s. In addition, three elementary schools in 1969 used money from a state grant for the improvement of mathematics education to lease a total of fifteen teletype terminals and associated drill-and-practice oriented software from IBM. The terminals were linked via telephone lines to an IBM central computer in San Francisco, and IBM provided in-service training and equipment maintenance in connection with the project. However, the project was only in operation for six months and was plagued by equipment breakdowns. Many of the teachers involved said they would be unwilling to support future proposals for introducing CAI in the schools.

With regard to the in-house capacity for CAI, the data processing staff in part selected the Honeywell 6025 to replace their second generation IBM 1401 because it could accommodate a variety of instructional applications. Honeywell offered a software package in mathematics, reading, and other subjects, and the data processing staff initially leased some of these programs.

Despite early hopes that the purchase of the new computer would encourage the introduction of more classroom use of CAI, the presence of the Honeywell 6025 resulted in only minimal expansion in the use of the computer for instructional purposes.

When the Honeywell 6025 was purchased, the six high schools that taught programming gave up their programmable calculators and became part of the central system. Funds previously used for the maintenance of the calculators were used to lease thirteen teletype terminals from the telephone company, which assumed responsibility for maintenance of the terminals. These terminals have continued to be leased by the schools, and the same model terminals that were at the school sites in 1971 are still there today.

Otherwise, the Honeywell 6025 has only been used for CAI in a few sporadic cases. One junior high school used federal funds to lease a telephone company terminal and used the Honeywell software for a three to four week mini-course in mathematics. The course was popular, and the school continued to maintain a terminal for several years. However, when the teacher who had offered the course left the district, computer use was discontinued. Three elementary schools also used compensatory education funds to lease terminals. Each used mathematics or reading software for two to three years, but in all cases the program was eventually abandoned. In one of these cases, the teacher who had backed the program left the district; in the other two, the school was closed down.

Personnel and Training. The only personnel who are currently involved in CAI are a few teachers from the six schools where there are now terminals for teaching computer programming. Such involvement with the computer is completely voluntary, and respondents noted that in several cases the terminals would not continue to be used if the teacher who currently uses the computer were to leave. Most of these teachers have learned computer programming in college courses, although a few teachers acquired their programming skills in in-service courses that were once offered by the data processing department.

Organizational Governance. There is not now, nor has there ever been, any official central coordination of staff positions dedicated to CAI. The current acting director of data processing has informally supported such positions, however. When the new computer was purchased, he attempted to set up a users' group that met on a few occasions to share ideas and experiences. He also offered classes in programming, arranged for teachers to receive in-service credit for these classes, and had funds allocated for the data processing budget to cover the cost of the classes. About 40 teachers took advantage of the offerings that continued for a two-year period. Lack of interest on the part of central instructional personnel and administration officials proved discouraging, however, and data processing has discontinued most of these efforts.

There appear to be no laws or regulations that directly bear on the use of CAI. It was mentioned, however, that the procedures governing the distribution of special project funds have created certain problems with respect to the purchase of computer terminals for the schools. The special project money, which is the main source of school funds that can be applied to CAI, can only be allocated on a yearly basis, with no assurance that the individual school will receive special funding the next year. This creates a situation where schools are unable to commit themselves to a lease-purchase agreement, and equipment must be bought outright or not used at all.

Reasons for Routinization Status

Service Applications and Outcomes.

H_1 *core application.* As was noted previously, the primary applications of the computer are administrative in nature. There is little question that the payroll, budgeting, scheduling, report cards, and other administrative functions are firmly implanted as part of the core operations of the district.

In contrast, the main instructional application of the computer is related to the teaching of programming in a few mathematics courses. Individual teachers decide whether they want their students to be exposed to the computer, and only a few teachers have moved in this direction. At most schools, whether or not the computer is used in the classroom depends on the disposition of a single teacher; if that teacher were to leave, the instructional application would disappear. This situation, coupled with the fact that efforts to use CAI in a drill-and-practice form have proved short-lived, clearly indicates that the instructional uses of computers have not been integrated as part of the core of the academic program.

H_2 *competition.* There has been no competition among the administrative and CAI functions in Oakland. Although administrative applications are of prime importance, the data processing staff has been committed to encouraging the development of CAI. Part of the rationale for purchasing the Honeywell 6025 was its adaptability in both administrative and instructional areas. The computer is currently not being used to capacity, and the data processing staff would still be willing to support instructional applications if district administrators expressed any interest in having them take on that responsibility.

H_3 *service-related payoffs.* Respondents did not cite any service-related payoffs that derived from CAI. Moreover, they described an unfortunate development related to an administrative application, one which they felt had a detrimental effect on the overall image of the data processing group and which led to district-wide discontent with all data processing services.

Shortly after the purchase of the new computer, the department agreed to serve as a trial site for a computerized payroll package that had been developed by the state of California. In exchange for the trial, the state agreed to provide the district with technical assistance and with free software. However, the district's efforts to implement the program proved disastrous. There were serious flaws in the software, and the state failed to provide adequate assistance in working through the problems. Paychecks were often late or made out for the incorrect amount.

As a result of this "trial," data processing developed a reputation for incompetence that led to the rapid resignation of two directors. District personnel were constantly critical of the data processing staff, and the operation became the scapegoat for many problems for which it was not at fault. Although the payroll system operates smoothly today, the respondents reported that some district personnel still have serious qualms about the data processing operation, and these feelings may alter perceptions of the usefulness of CAI.

External Environment.

H_4 *crisis conditions.* The computer operation did not emerge because of a crisis but was originally purchased for various administrative operations within the district. Similarly, the purchase of the programmable calculators, which were the forerunners of the current operations, was not associated with a crisis situation in the district. Rather, it appears that these were acquired at a time when budgets were not as tight as they are now and when school personnel felt that such expenditures were a worthy use of available funds.

H_5, H_6 *client-community support.* Because so few students use the computer, there is little opportunity for wide-scale client support. The three terminals at the school we visited were in constant use, and the school boasts an active thirty-five-member computer club, but we were told that students at other schools do not necessarily have the opportunity to use the computer on such a regular basis.

For the most part, the community is unaware of the computer and therefore would not be active supporters of CAI. There has been at least one exception to this situation. In a junior high school, several parents became so interested in their children's CAI work that they arranged to visit during evening hours to work with the programs. About ten parents came to classes on a regular basis. However, the support by parents was not great enough to sustain the use of the computer after the teacher who had used CAI in that school left the district.

Internal Characteristics.

H_7 *administrators.* There appears to be no support for CAI by school administrators, and the respondents reported that the administrators have resisted all efforts to obtain their backing. In part, this may be due to the fact that Oakland did not have central curriculum specialists when the new computer was purchased. Thus Oakland, unlike other school districts that now have well-established CAI programs sanctioned or actively supported by the instructional personnel, has never had the benefit of having a mathematics coordinator who was enthusiastic about the computer and who was willing to work closely with data processing to develop a constituency favoring CAI.

H_8 *innovator.* If any individual were to be singled out as an innovator with respect to the district-wide instructional applications, it would be the current acting director of data processing. He assumed the greatest responsibility in developing data processing's abilities to handle CAI and has attempted to provide support services, such as teacher in-service training, which would help establish CAI in the district.

However, his official responsibilities are to oversee the entire computer operation, which is viewed as a support service for the administrative rather than the instructional functions of the district. This places him in an unlikely position to be an effective innovator for an instructional innovation. He could possibly be more effective if there were strong administrative or practitioner backing for the innovation, but this is not the case in Oakland.

H_9 *practitioners.* There also appears to be very little support for CAI among teachers, although there are clearly a few who feel the computer makes a contribution to their students' education and who sustain the limited current CAI applications. These teachers are often willing to have a noisy teletype terminal in the back of their classrooms, and they typically put in extra hours so all students who wish to use the terminals have an opportunity to do so. These teachers have no incentives for being involved with the computer other than the personal satisfaction they derive from exposing students to the computer, which they view as an important and effective instructional tool. Teachers with this level of commitment to the computer operation are rare, however, and it has often been the case that when a teacher who has worked actively with the students on the computer leaves a school, there is no other teacher available who is willing to assume the computer activities.

H_{10} *adversary group.* Respondents noted that many teachers feel insecure about having the computer "take over" their jobs, and they therefore resist efforts to introduce CAI in the classroom. There was some speculation that this resistance stemmed from a general lack of awareness about what the computer can and cannot do and that such doubts could be alleviated by the appropriate in-service activities. However, there appears to be little chance that such activities will be offered in Oakland, and teacher resistance to the computer is therefore likely to continue.

Portland School District, Portland, Oregon

Persons interviewed

Supervisor, Television Services

Television Services staff, production responsibilities

Television Services staff, curriculum responsibilities

Television Services engineer

Two former ITV operation supervisors

Director of educational media

Portland teacher; former ITV teacher

Background

Portland is the nation's twenty-sixth largest school district with thirty-four primary, six intermediate, fifty-three elementary, fourteen secondary, and thirty special and alternative schools. There are approximately 62,000 students enrolled in the Portland schools, and the annual budget for the district is slightly over $100 million. Local property taxes account for 68.8 percent of these funds, and funds from the state of Oregon account for another 24.8 percent of the general fund. In addition, the district receives several million dollars in federal, state, and private funds for special programs outside the general fund budget.

In 1970, the school district decentralized into three administrative areas, a change that was to have a profound impact on the closed-circuit television (CCTV) operation. As a result of the decentralization, each of the three areas was made responsible for the development and administration of its own instructional program, within established district-wide guidelines. Each area has had its own superintendent and has been advised by a separate citizen's committee responsible for counseling the area administration on such matters as educational programs, building needs, school operation, and other area problems. The central administration is headed by the superintendent of schools, and it provides coordination of the district's needs and services, public information, and leadership in the evaluation and overall direction of the educational programs.

Like other urban school districts, Portland has been confronted with declining enrollments during the 1970s. Since 1970, enrollment has dropped by nearly 13,000 students, thus creating the potential for substantial decreases in district funding. Funding problems have been averted because of increases in the local school tax rate, coupled with increases in property values. In addition, the amount of state and federal money available to the district has nearly doubled since 1970. Thus, instead of budgetary famine, there has been a steady increase in the funds available.

Portland has also met another challenge common to urban districts—the need to achieve racial balance—with less public disruption than other cities. The district has used a twofold strategy to implement school desegregation. First, Portland established a policy supporting voluntary "administrative transfers," which enabled students from schools with racial imbalances to volunteer to transfer to cooperating suburban schools or to other schools in the Portland School District in order to achieve a more desirable racial mix. In addition, the district has adopted a "magnet" schools approach with such special emphasis as "performing arts and technical education" in an effort to attract more white students to schools that previously had a predominantly black student body.

The Innovation

The closed-circuit television operation (CCTV) in the Portland School District has gone through several distinct stages since it was first conceived in 1967. Although these transitions have been largely influenced by external events, the sweeping changes evidenced in the philosophical and day-to-day direction of the operation itself have also reflected the outlook of the three supervisors who have successively directed the CCTV operation.

The initial impetus for the program (1967-69) was tied to the availability of funds for a model school operation. The district was awarded a three-year grant of state and federal funds to be used for improving the education of disadvantaged students. The district was to use part of the funds to establish a cable television operation that would produce instructional programs and distribute them to students in nine elementary schools, and a project staff consisting of a supervisor, four teachers, and six technical personnel was assigned to the project. The major portion of the first year of the grant was spent in planning and producing programs, and in April, 1969 the first programs were transmitted.

The basic approach was to produce programs that would be compatible with the regular class material and to enrich the classroom experience by introducing what were then popular approaches to instruction, such as discovery learning and indirect questioning. District-level curriculum specialists chose social studies, science, and art as the three subjects for instructional television (ITV) activities. Each week, two fifteen-minute programs for grades three, four, and five were produced in each of these subjects, with each program being transmitted over the cable at two or three different times. The programs were designed to correspond with the topics that students would normally be studying in their classes, and teachers in the model schools were required to have their students view these programs as part of their regular instructional program. To facilitate use of the system, half-day in-service training sessions were offered for teachers once or twice a year.[3]

The administrative decentralization that began in 1970 had a profound effect on this CCTV operation. As part of the decentralization, the CCTV supervisor was assigned to a deputy superintendent position in one of the three new administrative areas while retaining his responsibilities as director of the CCTV operation. Because of the intensity of the demands of the new job, he could devote little time to CCTV, and this essentially left the operation without a leader. In addition, the decentralization distributed the nine model schools among different area administrations, each of which had autonomy with respect to instructional decisions. This made it impossible to continue the program of mandatory viewing that had previously characterized the CCTV efforts.

After the CCTV operation had stagnated for about a year and a half, the central administration decided to appoint a new director and to place the operation under the aegis of a central service, the Educational Media Department. The new coordinator was responsible for converting the operation into a program that would serve the entire district, and was given considerable freedom in shaping the CCTV operation. The major portion of the funding still came from state funds for disadvantaged students, but a small amount of money was added from the educational media budget (the general fund) to justify television use by students who were not considered disadvantaged.

The emphasis of the CCTV operation shifted considerably during this second stage. Although there was still some effort made to produce programs relevant to traditional classroom subjects, all efforts at central coordination were abandoned. There were no mandatory viewing requirements, and decisions regarding the kinds of programs that should be produced were most frequently made on the basis of teachers' requests. Rather than producing a series of programs on a limited number of subjects, the CCTV operation produced a few programs on each of a wider range of subjects. Moreover, the focus of the in-service training shifted to emphasize the production aspects of television, and teachers were invited to sessions where they would receive instruction in creating their own programs for classroom use. The CCTV operation continued in this manner for a little over two years (1972-74), when the supervisor resigned. A new supervisor was immediately hired to replace the outgoing one, and the CCTV operation entered into its third phase (1974 to present).

The CCTV operation in the Portland schools today bears little resemblance to its earlier counterparts. The new supervisor has rejected the "down the line" transmission in which a single program is sent to many classrooms at the same time, and instead has embraced a grass roots approach in which teachers are encouraged to adapt television to their individual classrooms. Thus, when the five-year lease with the telephone company for cable services expired shortly after the new supervisor's arrival, he decided not to renew that contract and instead applied the $11,500 annual expenditure toward the purchase of video equipment (videotape recorders, monitors, and portable cameras) to be located in schools throughout the district.

This marked the beginning of a service-oriented operation that, unlike its predecessors that had produced and distributed programs to supplement classroom instruction, encourages the use of over-the-air television programs and teaches students and teachers to produce their own TV programs. The name of the operation has been changed from "instructional television" to "television services," and the group now engages in four major categories of activities: (1) recording over-the-air television programs and making them available for classroom playback, (2) providing in-service training to teachers in television production and in using TV as an instructional tool, (3) coordinating an equipment pool that distributes video production kits and other equipment to teachers in the district, and (4) teaching career-oriented television production courses to students in Jefferson High School, one of the district's magnet schools.

Status of Routinization

Budget and Equipment. During the first phase of the CCTV operation, the major support came from federal funds. During the second phase, the overall expenditures for the CCTV operation were reduced somewhat, and the funding became part of a standing state disadvantaged fund that the state routinely distributes to school districts on the basis of the number of disadvantaged students enrolled in the schools. During the third and current phase of the CCTV operation in Portland, the amount of state disadvantaged money available to the program has remained about the same, but the amount of district funds allocated to the television operation has increased to such a great extent that the majority of support now derives from district money. About one-third of the current television budget comes from the Jefferson High School budget. At this magnet high school, the television services operation has assumed responsibility for a career-oriented program of professional courses in television production. As part of the agreement regarding the Jefferson operation, the television services staff designed two television studios and moved their offices to the high school grounds. The studios and other equipment needed for the Jefferson program are used by television services as part of their district-wide operation.

This budgetary arrangement appears to have helped establish television services as an ongoing operation in the Portland schools. Having money available from three different sources gives the CCTV coordinator considerable flexibility in allocating equipment and personnel to different funds, and the television services supervisor has been careful to allocate some staff and some equipment expenditures to each of the funds. Thus, cutbacks in any one of them are not likely to debilitate the overall operation. Moreover, the diversity in budgetary sources has enabled the television services operation to serve such special groups as disadvantaged and magnet school students as well as the general school district population. Because of the sensitive nature of cutting back the services available to these groups, any moves in that direction are likely to be very carefully considered before they are approved by the board of education and top district officials.

Television services has also recently begun to receive small outside grants to produce television programs for use throughout the state. Work is now under way for programs on local government and on handicapped children. If these programs are well received, they will likely bring favorable publicity to Portland's television operation and will further contribute to the operation being viewed as an asset to the district.

When considering the purchase and replacement of equipment in the context of a CCTV operation, it is important to remember that the audio-visual field is one where there have been continual and rapid advances in the capabilities of the available equipment. The range of equipment now available to a district that is planning to set up a CCTV operation presents a far greater opportunity for flexibility in the design and use of the corresponding instructional program than did the equipment that was available in 1968 when the CCTV operation began. One of the most striking advances has been in the area of videotape technology. Videotape equipment provides an opportunity for relatively simple production and playback of programs, processes that can easily be mastered by students and teachers. With the videotape technology, cassette tapes of television programs can be made available to teachers who use a tape recorder-like machine connected to a video monitor to view the tapes at any time they find convenient. In addition, it is possible for a teacher to stop a tape midstream to discuss various points or to rewind the tape to have the class view selected portions of the program a second or third time.

These advances in videotape essentially made possible the shift toward the individual classroom approach that currently characterizes the Portland CCTV operation. Because the television services operation carries out a considerable variety of television-oriented activities adapted to the desires of the individual classroom teacher, it is necessary to examine two general categories of equipment: (1) the equipment available to the television services staff for program production and instruction in career-oriented production classes, and (2) the equipment available for use at the local level.

The central production capabilities of Portland's television services are substantially richer than those of the typical CCTV school district operation. Portland has both black and white and color production capabilities and boasts the largest educational TV studios in the Northwest. The television services operation also has a video van with relatively sophisticated remote production capabilities. There was a near complete replacement and updating of equipment in 1975, when television services officially assumed responsibility for instruction in television production at the magnet schools. Because the magnet school program is designed to offer career-relevant experience to students, there is a justification for (and the funds appear to be available for) a continual expansion and updating of this equipment to keep pace with the state of the art.

The situation is less promising at the local level, where the availability of equipment for classroom use has not kept pace with the demands. When the operation originally began, each classroom in the nine model schools received a television set. After decentralization took place, these were redistributed so that each school in the district had at least two sets. However, because of the district's commitment to a videotape approach, additional equipment has been needed for these sets to be used with videotape programs. Money derived primarily from the educational disadvantaged fund and the educational media fund has been used to purchase eighteen Porta-Paks containing portable equipment that lends itself to on-site production of television programs. These have been purchased on an ongoing basis, with three to six portable cameras added every year. The older portable cameras are still in acceptable operating conditions and have not been replaced.

The television services equipment is distributed through an equipment pool. The television services group receives requests for equipment and schedules its use, and generally delivers and picks up the equipment. The radio shop, another group that falls within the Educational Media Department, once had responsibility for the equipment pool and still occasionally delivers the equipment to the school site. There have only been three weeks in the last three years when all the equipment had not been checked out for classroom use. In addition to equipment deliveries and pickup, the radio shop is responsible for equipment repair. This has created some problems for television services because the radio staff is not always proficient in the upkeep of new model television equipment.

Despite the apparent interest in television services equipment, few local schools have purchased any television equipment with their own funds. The respondents expressed some frustration over this situation and claimed that it had, to some extent, limited the television services activities.

Personnel and Training. The size of the staff has fluctuated over the years, depending on the level of funding available for the operation. However, there has been some continuity in the production personnel, several of whom were hired during the first two years of the operation. During the model schools period, the staff included several teachers—certified personnel who wrote the scripts for the programs and appeared in the productions. All of these teachers left the staff after the district was decentralized, and most returned to regular classroom teaching. They were not replaced, and since that time there have been few certified personnel (teachers) on the staff. Certified personnel are occasionally used as consultants, however, and there are funds set aside for this purpose.

One of the first activities of the current supervisor was the establishment of approved classifications for members of the technical staff. Before he arrived, the classifications had been informal in-house designations, and salary levels did not reflect the true activities of many of the staff. In order to obtain the official job classifications, it was necessary to write job descriptions and provide evidence of salary levels offered elsewhere for comparable positions.

At the local level, each school has a designated radio-televison coordinator. The coordinator is a teacher who receives about two hundred dollars extra per year for assuming various responsibilities associated with the position. Decisions regarding who should be designated as the radio-television coordinator and what his or her responsibilities should be rest with the individual school principals, and it is frequently the case that the person appointed has little interest in television services. The television services supervisor now meets with the radio-television coordinators four times a year, but the coordinators do not appear to play a very active role in publicizing or assisting in the television services activities.

Organizational Governance. In 1975, the Portland Board of Education passed a resolution requiring that a program of instruction in television production be part of the Jefferson High School's curriculum. The passage of this resolution assures the television services group of at least a limited level of funding each year, and, as a result, the operation is likely to continue actively operating in the district.

One other event that was briefly mentioned earlier also relates to organizational governance. It occurred when the CCTV operation was placed under the aegis of the Educational Media Department. This move linked the interests of the television operation with those of a firmly established service department in the district. In addition, this integration of the television operation into the regular school bureaucracy helped to dispel the notion that the television operation was to be a short-lived special program in this district.

Reasons for Routinization Status

Service Applications and Outcomes.

H_1 *core application.* Television production is a core program at Jefferson High School, and the television service's assumption of responsibility for the development and day-to-day operation of this magnet school program has been important in assuring the continued existence of the television services group. The expenditure for new equipment for Jefferson's studios is itself such a sizable investment that it would be difficult to justify a substantial program cutback. Moreover, the Jefferson program is in line with the district administration's commitment to career education and school desegregation, two other factors that would make cutbacks unlikely.

In contrast, the other school functions of the television services department are generally unrelated to core aspects of the local schools' instructional programs. The early efforts to make the CCTV program an ongoing part of the core elementary school curriculum by requiring teachers to have their students regularly view programs in science, social studies, and art proved unsuccessful in that they were discontinued after the first director resigned. The operations today stress the use of popular television as a supplementary aid to instruction, and all decisions regarding the use of television in the classroom are left to the discretion of the individual teacher. Thus, television may be used in some classrooms in connection with the teaching of basic subjects, but there is no available information that would suggest whether this is or is not the case.

H_2 *competition.* There appears to be no competition among the major applications of the television services operation. Instead, the existence of each application appears to enhance the continued use of the others. For example, the arrangements for offering instruction in television production at Jefferson provide excellent facilities for producing programs for district-wide use. Likewise, the district benefits by having available students trained as working professionals to assist them in television-related classroom activities. This arrangement also benefits the Jefferson students, who gain career-related experience and expertise that they would find difficult to acquire if the classroom opportunities were not available to them. Moreover, the fact that the television services operation is a district-wide function justifies the presence of a larger professional staff at Jefferson. Jefferson students thereby have the opportunity to be exposed to and instructed by a wider range of television professionals than would be available if the magnet school activities did not coincide with those of the rest of the district.

H_3 *service-related payoffs.* There have been no formal evaluations of the outcomes or effectiveness of the television services operation. Respondents did seem to feel, however, that the program was moving in a productive direction, indicated by informal feedback they had received from practitioners. In particular, respondents noted that teachers had reported that the popular television approach was especially effective in teaching English grammar and vocabulary to students who previously had been difficult to motivate. The continued demand for television equipment has also been interpreted as an indication that television makes a contribution to classroom instruction. In addition, the scope and sophistication of the Jefferson television operation was singled out as having a certain amount of prestige value for the district.

External Environment.

H_4 *crisis conditions.* The evolution of the CCTV system did not follow any specific crisis. The main impetus at the outset was the desire to improve educational opportunities for disadvantaged students and the availability of external funds to support the CCTV operation.

H_5, H_6 *client-community support.* We did not have the opportunity to speak with any students who were either enrolled in the production courses or who had been exposed to the services supported by the television operation in their classes. Because district-wide classroom use of television is scattered and typically sporadic, it is unlikely that students would form a strong support group. There might, however, be some support by students for continuing television activities in the few schools that produce their own news broadcasts on a regular basis. Pupils who are studying television production at Jefferson are the only clients who would currently be likely to have a strong objection to television services cutbacks, and who might actively lobby for continued program operation.

Although a few community groups have used the production facilities at Jefferson for their own activities, the community at large is for the most part unaware of the television activities conducted in the district. However, those who are concerned with the education of the disadvantaged could be called upon for support of the television services activities associated with the disadvantaged if either the funding were cut or if the funding were targeted at another group of students.

Internal Characteristics

H_7 *administrators.* The instructional television operation has only received modest support from agency administrators. This is shown by the fact that the administrators allowed the CCTV operation to stagnate for a year and a half after administrative decentralization before appointing a new CCTV supervisor. Respondents expressed the view that the operation might well have been phased out at that time had not an experienced television teacher, who was a friend of the superintendent and who had recently returned from Samoa where television is the predominant educational medium, convinced the superintendent that she could turn it into a worthwhile operation.

The current supervisor is of the opinion that there was also thought given to phasing out the program when he was interviewed for his position. However, the decisions of administrators to hire new supervisors in both cases would seem to indicate that they are not hostile to the program and are willing to allocate some district resources to it.

Despite the general lack of enthusiasm by top district administrators, respondents indicated that there are at least two members of the board of education who favor continued operation of television services. In addition, the director of educational media appears to firmly support the operation and noted that it strongly coincides with the district's commitment to career education.

H_8 *innovator.* Throughout the history of CCTV in Portland, the most active innovator has always been the instructional television supervisor, the individual in charge of the instructional television operation. There has been little programmatic direction or supervision of the television operation from more senior individuals in the school bureaucracy, and the supervisor, therefore, has had near total autonomy in determining the allocation of the budget, in hiring the staff, and in directing the overall television operation. As a result, the television operation has largely reflected the background and disposition of the individual supervisors, and one comes away with the sense that the turnover in the supervisor's slot has resulted in little continuity in the CCTV operation over the years.

Unlike his predecessors, the current television services supervisor appears to be developing his programs to assure that there will be a continuing demand for the type of television activities he favors. He came to the Portland School District with a strong background in television production, after having spent several years as an instructor in television techniques at a local college. This background contributed to his enthusiasm for linking the existing district-level service with the Jefferson program. One of his first activities was to present the administration with a detailed proposal for linking the CCTV with Jefferson's programs. His expertise in studio design brought him administrative support for the merger, and his administrative prowess enabled him to formulate an ongoing role for his group in the new program. The association with the Jefferson program probably has been the single most important factor contributing to the secure positioning of the television services within the district.

With the Jefferson arrangement in operation, the supervisor is now directing a concerted effort at generating interest in television services' in-service training. The assumption underlying this approach is that teachers who are exposed to and appropriately instructed in the use of popular television and in production techniques will create a demand for increased television-related services that will justify an expansion of the television services' activities.

H_9 *practitioners.* At present, there is no clearly established base of practitioner support for the television operation, although there are several indications that teachers who use the service find it to be of value in their classrooms. The demands for television equipment are great and typically exceed the amount of equipment now owned by television services. In addition, interest in the television in-service workshops for teachers has led television services to offer several workshops each month, and sometimes as many as one per week.

The limited availability of equipment for school activities appears to be a prime factor that inhibits the growth of practitioner support for the television services operation. Because the operation is a district-wide service, it is necessary to distribute equipment among all schools in the district. This creates a situation where there is little equipment available at any one school, and thus there are, at most, only a few teachers at each school who can use the equipment on a regular basis. This creates a situation where individual practitioner support is likely to be scattered throughout the district and, as a result, it will be quite diffuse. Moreover, competition for equipment among practitioners at the school sites is a potential source of frustration that could detract from practitioner support for the operation.

H_{10} *adversary group.* There seems to be little opposition to the instructional use of television or to the teaching of television production in the Portland School District. There are some indications that relationships with the radio shop are strained, but the problems appear to have more to do with establishing procedures acceptable to both the radio shop and television services, and do not reflect organized opposition to television services activities.

San Diego City Schools, San Diego, California

Persons interviewed

> Director, Data Systems Department
>
> Senior systems analyst and ITSS project director
>
> District resource teacher for computer science
>
> Member, District Finance Department
>
> Member, Guidance Services
>
> Curriculum specialist, Mathematics Department
>
> Director, Planning and Research Department
>
> Assistant director, Planning and Research Department
>
> Time Share coordinator, La Jolla High School
>
> Time Share coordinator, Farnum Elementary School
>
> Time Share coordinator, Collier Junior High School
>
> Time Share coordinator, Henry High School
>
> Time Share coordinator and principal, Taft Junior High School
>
> La Jolla High School student

Background

The San Diego School District (fifteen senior high, nineteen junior high, and 123 elementary schools) has been faced with a slightly declining student population over the last several years in spite of a stable city population and an expanding economic tax base. The decline in students has forced a direct reduction in the district's operating budget because schools receive most of their funding directly from the state on a per pupil basis. The same statute providing for the state funding also limits yearly increases due to inflation to 6 percent, further reducing the district's ability to handle anything but basic instructional programs. Currently, there are some 120,000 students in the school system.

A school bond issue in 1975 has helped to inject new resources into facilities and instructional equipment for most secondary schools. Thirty new schools have been built in the last two years to comply with new state earthquake standards, but few old schools have as yet been closed.

Individual schools in San Diego assume additional importance due to the extensive decentralization of the operating budget for the district. In 1973-74, under the guidance of a new superintendent, each school was designated a separate cost center whose budget was determined by the average student enrollment and whose allocations were determined by the principal rather than the central administration. Each school receives not only its per pupil share of state funds but also its per pupil share of special funding such as Title I and funds for the gifted. It is up to the school principal to decide if he wishes to involve the teaching staff in the budgeting of these funds, and most do actively seek input from the teachers. During the decentralization process, citizen advisory councils were also created to work with the principal of each school on matters of finances, curriculum, and personnel.

The central administration still continues to provide a core of services to schools, however. Audio-visual, accounting, program specialists, and counseling are all offered and funded through the central offices, as are evaluation and data processing. The data systems department (DSD) provides technical assistance for computer assisted instruction (CAI), the focus of the present case study. The department has been in existence since 1951 and has been continually upgrading its capability and programs to meet district demands. Currently, the DSD owns and operates an IBM 370 system. Most of the computer programs pertain to student records, accounting, demographic analysis, budgeting, and other administrative tasks. However, there is no instructional use of the IBM 370 system because of its very limited ability to handle time sharing and because of the high demand for administrative applications.

The Innovation

Although the district was not interested in using its central computer system for CAI, there were several informal attempts to use other systems. For example, a local computer company sponsored a Boy Scout training program in computer science and programming. In addition, several of the mathematics teachers in the district taught pilot programs in a few special areas of instruction in the early 1970s. Each summer, fifteen students were enrolled in a class taught by one of the mathematics teachers. The instructor was paid from discretionary funds, while the classroom facilities and the computer time were provided free of charge by a local college. The program had strong support among mathematics teachers and showed some promising results, but the administration was not interested in funding the program during the regular school year.

A survey among the district's mathematics teachers showed there was a growing interest in acquiring a computer to be used in the classroom on a regular basis. When the district underwent decentralization, discretionary funds became available at each school. A few of the more interested teachers began to interest school principals in pooling resources to support their own instructional computer system, albeit on a very small scale.

By the end of the 1972-73 school year, a core of mathematics specialists had sold their idea to the director of the DSD, who was then willing to risk committing funds on behalf of the participating schools, which would reimburse the DSD later in the year, to acquire a CAI system (which is called "instructional time share system" in San Diego). An assessment was made of whether to attempt to upgrade the existing IBM equipment to handle time sharing or whether to acquire a totally separate system. A committee of mathematics instructors and data processing personnel agreed that, based on costs and the difference in use, it would be better in the long run to purchase a separate minicomputer.

The committee members approached the principals of all the junior and senior high schools in May and June of 1973. The members explained their idea and asked for tentative commitments from the principals. In June, 1973, with only eleven users signed up, bid specifications were sent out. In August, the school board approved the purchase of the computer, primarily because the project was to be financed by the schools themselves and did not require additional district funds. With board approval, the DSD acquired a Hewlett-Packard 2000 minicomputer in September, 1973; it was installed in February, 1974 and was to be paid through a four-year, lease-purchase agreement. The participating schools were linked to the computer via business telephone lines. The computer itself was installed in the same toom with the IBM system, although it was totally separate; teletype terminals were installed in each of eight schools, usually in the mathematics classrooms. As a part of the package for each school, the terminal came with access to a 1,300 program library and storage for 1,000 records.

The HP 2000 was thus physically maintained within the DSD, and the DSD was financially responsible for any shortfalls in funding. The administrative responsibility for instructional time sharing, however, rested with the mathematics teachers in each school. From 1972 until 1975, one of the curriculum specialists spent about 25 percent of his time working with principals and teachers on the time sharing system. He had assumed the responsibility of promoting the idea with other schools, training the teachers, coordinating the use of the terminals, and arranging for the funding of the account from individual school budgets. In 1975, DSD assigned a full-time systems analyst to coordinate the system. The other curriculum specialists also remained actively involved.

As teachers' interest grew and the number of schools participating increased, the funding of the system became more stable. The increased demand for the system also necessitated the purchase of two more minicomputers and numerous terminals. In August 1975, the second HP 2000 was added by the DSD, and a third was added a year later, both on four-year, lease-purchase arrangements. Currently, the CAI system (with all three computers treated as one system) is operating at almost 90 percent capacity, with eighty-five out of a possible ninety-six ports used. There are sixty-one terminals distributed among eight elementary schools, sixteen junior high schools and fifteen high schools. In addition, some schools have purchased supplementary time sharing equipment, including twelve HP card readers, two printers for tabular material, and one plotter for graphic material.

There are several other district and non-district users linked to the CAI system as well. In 1975, the planning and research department purchased a port for computing enrollment projections, and evaluation services purchased one for computing test trends. More recently, the transportation department used the computer to determine bus routes in the face of shifting residential location patterns. Outside the district, several other education agencies have purchased their own ports: Point Loma College, San Diego Community College, and the Adult Education Program of the County Department of Education. These non-district users must provide their own terminals, but they are charged the same rates as the district users.

A school's use of the time sharing system is determined by the number and background of interested teachers, and the resulting applications differ greatly at each of the participating schools. The schools have access to a wide variety of computer programs, ranging from elementary to college levels and covering many of the disciplines. Teachers and students also write their own programs. The most structured use of the CAI system is the drill-and-practice application found in the mathematics or language centers, while the most frequent use appears to be enrichment programs available through media centers. In both instances, the programs provide supplementary rather than primary instruction.

Some of the schools also use CAI for other than classroom purposes. For example, one of the popular new programs is a guidance information system used in twenty-five of the secondary schools to help students select colleges. The program lists colleges and universities by such characteristics as location, SAT levels, occupations, and extracurricular activities. The advantage of the system is that it forces the student to make decisions about colleges and it allows him to easily explore other interest areas. Another application of the CAI system is to record books checked out of the library.

Status of Routinization

Budget and Equipment. The DSD functions very much as a service bureau for other units in the district. The work performed for the central administration (accounting and recordkeeping for example), is funded through a fixed item in the annual budget, while work for the instructional units must be handled on a contractual basis. If a school or department, for example, wanted the DSD to initiate a project, the school would prepare a proposal and the DSD would estimate the cost. If the school accepted the estimate, it would write a contract with the DSD and pay for the work from its own budget. The DSD would then assemble the necessary resources for the project and assign the necessary staff. The CAI system receives no central funding for non-personnel costs through the DSD.

Initially, each user was charged $2,000 per year for the use of the computer and the terminal (each user had the same equipment and therefore was charged the same amount), and the funds were placed in the same account as the IBM 370 system. However, the commingling of funds caused great accounting difficulty in relation to special-purpose funds received from the federal government. To solve the difficulty, the DSD requested the budget office in 1976 to establish a special account to handle only CAI revenues and payments. The separate account has line items for supplies, contractual services, equipment, and special programs.

The fact that CAI was started in February, 1974 with only eleven of thirty-two participating schools meant that the system would potentially incur a loss for its first year which the DSD would have had to cover. However, the purchase of several more ports by new users in 1975 adequately covered the first-year costs, and new subscribers have been added each year. Currently, the CAI account needs to sell the remaining ports on the third HP 2000 to cover the costs for the 1978-79 school year and to complete the last of the four-year purchase agreements. The DSD anticipates that the costs for the CAI system in 1977-78 will be approximately $90,000.

Each school or user is no longer charged the same flat fee, thereby making the accounting system somewhat more complex. In 1975, when a full-time coordinator was assigned to CAI and schools started using different types of terminal equipment, it was decided to charge each user according to the real costs incurred. The management committee for CAI (one elementary, one junior high, and one senior high principal, a director in the secondary division, the CAI coordinator, the data systems director, and the mathematics curriculum specialist) now divides the total costs, including an estimate for repairs and maintenance, for the year by the number of users and adjusts for the particular equipment used. Users are not charged, however, for the salary of the CAI coordinator, who is a full-time staff member of the DSD.

The decentralized budgeting system allows principals to pay for CAI from any of the funds allocated to the school. There are, however, two restrictions affecting the principal's decision. First, state accounting procedures require that lease-purchase agreements be treated as capital expenditures; therefore, the funds have to come from captial outlay accounts. Second, the use of special funds, such as for the gifted, restricts the use of the equipment to only those eligible children; therefore, funds are frequently taken from more than just one special account to support the use of CAI. Non-school users also make their own decision as to the source of funding for CAI. For example, the guidance department spent $6,000 to purchase its software package, but it does not pay for computer services because it does not have a port line exclusively for its own use. The planning and research department simply budgets its payment for its port line as a budget item under contractual services.

Thus, although CAI receives a substantial amount of funding and has a separate project account, the innovation is not really a formal part of the district or school budget. Similarly, because it does not appear as a part of the annual budget, the CAI system is not considered in discussions of budget increases or cuts. Other kinds of budget cuts can, of course, indirectly affect the CAI system—for example, when special project funding is reduced.

Budget decisions directly affecting CAI are made at the individual school level by the principal or the principal and faculty. In the three budget cycles that have been completed since the implementation of CAI, only four schools have reduced their use of CAI. However, most of the respondents agreed that it would be difficult to eliminate the CAI project altogether because of its support through discretionary funding.

Fortunately, most of the users will be facing declining costs for CAI in the future as the lease-purchasing agreements for the computer equipment expire. Some of the terminals, like the three HP 2000s, were also acquired under a lease-purchase agreement. The growth in the number of users has allowed some of this equipment to be paid off earlier than anticipated. Currently, one of the minicomputers and all of the terminals are owned by the schools, after four years on the system. The only charges to the schools are for maintenance. It is interesting to note that if a school drops out of the system at any point, it automatically forfeits its accrued payoff for the central costs. It may keep any terminals or other peripheral equipment which have been purchased, but it is disconnected from the HP 2000.

Personnel and Training. The CAI system has no full-time staff of its own, that is, one paid out of project funds. Instead, the two staff members assigned to CAI are employees of other departments diverted from other duties to operate the innovation. The CAI coordinator, in place since 1975, is a regular senior systems analyst for the DSD. Although there is no job description for the coordinator's role, there is general agreement within the DSD administration that the position should be formalized in the near future.

The other staff member to work on the innovation is a district-wide resource teacher for computer science, hired in 1975 as a part of the curriculum staff but paid through the federal Comprehensive Employment and Training Act (CETA). While the coordinator spends most of his time dealing with the technical aspects of the innovation, the resource teacher is primarily responsible for teacher training and program development. She will respond to principal or teacher requests for help, advise on the use of books and software programs, solve minor technical problems, and work directly with students who want more instruction in programming. The district has recently recognized the need for a full-time person in this capacity and intends to make the position permanent when the CETA funds expire.

There are several other district personnel who work on CAI on a part-time basis. A few of the curriculum specialists in mathematics and languages are active in showing teachers how CAI can be used in their classes and in coordinating supplementary materials. At each participating school, there is also a time share coordinator who helps train teachers and who handles the scheduling of the terminals. The school coordinators are not paid extra for their additional responsibilities, but they do gain slightly more access to the terminals. All of the school coordinators will meet three to four times a year with the main CAI coordinator to exchange ideas.

If several teachers in one school are interested in CAI, the resource teacher will give a training class. In fact, CAI has an extensive in-service training component. One course is a "get acquainted" series that covers the CAI concept, available programs, operation of the terminal, and practice. A second course covers the BASIC programming language to enable the teacher to write his or her own programs (about half of the teachers on the system do their own programming). Teachers receive one full unit of district credit for attending each course; the course is held after school for eight weeks and is usually open to any interested teacher. However, it is difficult to estimate the number of teachers in the district who have either received some training or who currently use the CAI system.

The district has occasionally sought outside technical assistance for CAI, both in hardware maintenance and in programming. San Diego contains a large number of private computer firms, and many of the parents in the community are affiliated with or knowledgeable about computer systems. A group of experts from the community was used by the district to help establish a summer computer program. Since 1973, however, the technical expertise for CAI has all been provided by the DSD, and outside assistance is no longer used.

While much of the necessary technical expertise has been internalized in the CAI project through the assignment of the two full-time staff, the problem solving capacity of the project has been maintained through a very low turnover among all of the personnel involved. There has been no turnover among the DSD staff people involved in the innovation, and the curriculum specialist involved in the early administration of the project is still active. The majority of school coordinators have remained in that role since the system was initiated, even though they may now be assigned to different schools. Thus, the only significant personnel change was the shift of administrative responsibility to the CAI coordinator in 1975.

There has been no apparent change in the procedures for teacher certification or evaluation as a result of the innovation. An ability to use CAI and to operate computer terminals has not been integrated with any teacher job description or promotional considerations. It has, however, been used as an informal criterion in transferring teachers. For example, many of the teachers assigned to the three new schools that opened in 1976 had CAI training.

Organizational Governance. Because the CAI only exists as a special project and a separate cost account, there has been no need for a reorganization of administrative units to accommodate the innovation. There has not been sufficient need to create a separate computer sciences department or to have a distinct CAI section with the DSD.

Similarly, there have only been minor changes in the forms and paperwork of the district due to CAI. Among the changes, the CAI coordinator has created a new billing form to send to the schools. In addition, the various curriculum departments are just beginning to adopt textbooks that are geared to CAI programs or that have computer programs integrated with the text material. The mathematics department, for example, is revising its textbooks (a process which takes place every five years) and selecting a few books that incorporate BASIC programming.

The innovation has been strictly a grass roots effort since 1972, and it has succeeded in spite of the absence of explicit administrative or legislative mandates. CAI has been supported, however, through a district bond issue initiated in 1975. The bond issue officially amended the list of standard equipment for schools to include four computer terminals per high school and two terminals per junior high school. The bond issue provided the capital funds for each school to make computer-related purchases. Thus, although CAI itself is not formally established by district policy, the equipment to operate the system has in part been financed by a public mandate.

Centrally, the procedures for purchasing the terminals and other hardware for CAI are the same as those for purchasing any piece of computer equipment. These procedures were previously established by the DSD and have not been modified for the innovation. Individual schools do have the option of purchasing terminals, printers, etc. directly from private suppliers without consulting the DSD or the CAI coordinator, but it is generally discouraged. The coordinator wants to avoid the problems of inferior equipment and weak maintenance contracts and so has established the policy that if a school does have a direct contact with a supplier, the school cannot use the CAI account to cover the cost of the equipment.

The innovation has not been a part of any collective bargaining sessions or the subject of any other union-related discussions.

Maintenance and Repair. Once a terminal has been installed, the school is responsible for requesting the supplies to maintain the terminal. The maintenance needs of the terminals are actually minimal. Minor operational malfunctions are often corrected by the teacher using the terminal, because most of the teachers have completed a one-and-one-half-hour maintenance and repair course. Serious equipment malfunctions are repaired by a maintenance firm or, in the case of couplers, by the district's audio-visual repair shop.

Prior to 1975, all of the maintenance and repair work was included in a service contract between the school district and the terminal suppliers. All of the servicing for the minicomputers was performed by the DSD personnel. In 1975, the DSD entered into a single, full-maintenance contract with all of the schools. As a service bureau, the DSD now provides all repair and servicing of equipment on a formal, paid basis through a third party.

The CAI system has continued to expand the number of users and the amount of equipment. Although the additional minicomputers do not represent a newer generation of equipment, there is a new generation of terminals. In 1975, the CAI coordinator convinced the schools that they could purchase a quieter and faster terminal at a lower cost than they had been paying for their teletype terminals, and a newer generation of terminals was phased in over an eight-month period. Today, it is up to each school to decide whether it wants to upgrade its equipment further and to select new terminals.

The number of software programs available through CAI has been gradually reduced. Under lease-purchase, the minicomputers came with 1,300 prepackaged programs, ranging in level from elementary through college graduate courses. The coordinator noted that many of the upper-level programs were never accessed and were simply a burden to the system. He and the resource teacher have since reviewed most of the programs in the library and removed many of them. In 1976, the number of programs was reduced to 950; and in 1977, it was further reduced to 750; any program thus removed can be replaced upon request.

The only other modification made by the DSD staff has been the upgrading of the HP system to allow an interface with the district's IBM system.

Reasons for Routinization Status

Service Applications and Outcomes.

H_1 *core application.* CAI has provided teachers with a useful instructional tool in mathematics, science, language, and social studies. Using a terminal located in the school, the teacher can assign individualized programs to help students to correct their deficiencies. The drill-and-practice technique is used to help students master routine procedures, while enrichment programs enable the student to explore areas on his own that the teacher would not otherwise have time to cover. The innovation is clearly a supplement to the existing instructional programs and has not replaced any of the existing functions.

H_2 *competition.* Each participating school has at least one port and one terminal on-site. The terminal can be used for a variety of purposes ranging from instructional to administrative applications. As interest in the CAI program grows at each school, conflicts can arise among (a) teachers wanting to make assignments for students, (b) teachers wanting to do their own programming, (c) administrative uses such as recordkeeping, and (d) students wanting to do their own special projects. The conflict is usually a scheduling problem which will be resolved by the time share coordinator for the school. Ultimately, it is the principal's decision as to how the terminal will be used and who will receive priority in scheduling. In those cases where some conflict has occurred, the school has acquired a second terminal and port before the problem has become too severe.

H_3 *service-related payoffs.* There has been no formal evaluation of CAI during its operation, but those affiliated with the innovation do perceive that there are definite benefits from having it. The primary benefits go to the teacher in three ways. First, the teacher is able to provide the student with additional instruction in a problem area via CAI, thereby allowing more time to work with other students having special problems. Second, the teacher can use his CAI training as a bargaining tool with the principal for classes he wants to teach by offering to handle CAI in return for being able to teach a favorite class. Third, the teacher is able to gain advanced credit (and therefore more pay) for undergoing the two training courses offered for CAI.

The administration appears to benefit from the cost savings involved in the innovation. The cost for one student to work through an instructional program at the terminal for an hour is $1.18, whereas the cost for a teacher's aide to provide the same individualized instruction for an hour is $3.09. As school budgets are cut back, the innovation becomes a more attractive way to provide routine instruction and practice.

The CAI system has not been without its problems, however. One problem encountered early in the project was the tendency for certain teachers to monopolize the use of the terminals. It was only when the coordinator explained to the teachers that their department within that school would have to bear the full costs of funding the terminals that the teachers became more willing to share with others. The related problem of a few students monopolizing the terminals has been partially resolved by better supervision of the terminals.

New principals have sometimes posed a problem because they are often unfamiliar with CAI. They may not wish to continue the school's commitment to CAI; and they may make the decision to discontinue in September, although all CAI arrangements have already been settled for the school year. In such cases, the CAI personnel or the head of the DSD is usually able to show the principal the value of retaining the innovation.

Perhaps the most serious problems occur during in-service training, when teachers are first exposed to the new technology. Some of the teachers lack the typing skills necessary to operate the terminal. Others are reluctant to admit they do not know anything about CAI, even though their students are already using the terminals. Finally, some teachers are simply afraid of the machine; they are accustomed to having complete control over a situation, and they are not really certain what will happen when they press the "send" button.

External Environment

H_4 crisis conditions.   The adoption of the innovation was neither the result of a crisis condition faced by the district nor attributable to a chronic deficiency in instructional functions. Rather, it was the result of several teachers' perception that computers could be a useful tool in the classroom in that some types of instruction and practice could be handled by pre-packaged programs and students could be taught about computers and computer programming. As teachers saw the success that CAI was having in the mathematics curriculum, they started applying it to similar problem areas in their own subjects.

H_5, H_6 client-community support.   There are only a few individuals outside the district who are aware of the CAI project. Some of the other institutions that use CAI would be able to advocate the system's continuation, and there are several other private schools that might be interested in purchasing CAI time from the system. In general, there has been very little publicity about the innovation, and, because CAI does not require the use of community resources nor affect anyone in the community, there are no community groups to support or oppose it.

The parents of students who use CAI support the project, however. Many of these parents have a computer background and can readily understand the objectives and operation of the innovation. Other parents have simply seen their children take a new interest in school and spend many hours using the terminals. The parents are not formally organized to support CAI except through PTAs, but the fact that several of the PTAs have made donations to the project would indicate a strong support for it from at least some parents.

Internal Characteristics

H_7 *administrators.* During the early 1970s when the interested mathematics specialist was trying to marshall support for CAI, there was very little support from the top administration. The superintendent felt that the time for funding unusual projects had passed, and the school board was reluctant to provide any funding. The few summer pilot programs were funded from private contributions and from discretionary funds in the mathematics department budget. When the DSD director and math specialist presented the idea to the board that the innovation be self-financed through the participating schools, however, the board gave its approval.

Although the board concurred that the project was worthwhile, there was still no strong support behind it. As the project expanded, the board became more familiar with its objectives and teacher support; at least one board meeting was held in a room with the CAI terminals and included a program by students to explain the system. In 1975, the board agreed to modify the standard list of equipment for schools to include computer terminals, and it included funds for purchasing terminals in the bond issue.

The key support for the innovation has come primarily from the director of the DSD and the math specialist. Once he had been approached by the teachers, the director helped to get other schools interested, made available the initial funding for the CAI equipment, and supported the schools during the summer funding gaps. Later, he assigned one of the DSD systems analysts to the CAI project full time, requested the special accounting category for the innovation, and supported the hiring of a full-time resource teacher.

The support of the principals has also been important to the success of the innovation. Because they provide the actual funding for the system, they are the administrators who must make the greatest commitments. They not only provided funding but also spoke to the central administration on behalf of the project. Thus, it is mainly their decision whether or not the innovation will continue.

H_8 *innovator.* The role of innovator has been shared by several individuals during the system's evolution. A curriculum specialist in the mathematics department was the first to be responsible for developing school support for the innovation and for establishing the procedures for acquiring equipment and for billing. He also allocated a portion of the department's discretionary funds to pay for time sharing and for the instructional materials needed to train teachers.

During the time the specialist was coordinating the project, the DSD director was active in allocating his staff for technical support and creating the accounting procedure for funding.

The role of coordinator was shifted to the current incumbent in 1975. His assignment from within the DSD combined the tasks of technical support with administrative responsibility for the system. Perhaps the coordinator's greatest contribution to the innovation is his enthusiasm and ability to provide schools with new ideas on uses for CAI.

H_9 *practitioners.* The adoption, implementation, and growth of the innovation has been essentially a grass roots movement on the part of teachers. A core group of interested teachers, primarily from the mathematics departments, supported the CAI concept and convinced other teachers of its potential value. Although a few teachers did object to the innovation in faculty meetings (usually because they favored other budget priorities), there was little opposition. Many teachers no doubt resist the project because of lack of training or a fear of the computer, and they simply avoid using the innovation. The growing demand for terminals and training, however, indicates growing support among practitioners. The respondents agreed that the teachers would most likely voice strong resistance if the CAI system were to be removed.

Support for the innovation has developed among department heads as well. As more and more departments invest in materials geared to CAI, they have a greater stake in its continuation. Further, the departments have realized the advantages of using CAI to increase the capacity of teachers to deal with student problems. Departments have also been investing their own discretionary funds in the innovation and in the training of their teachers.

For most teachers, the innovation is not associated with career advancement or monetary reward. There are some teachers who do benefit from involvement in CAI because of the district credit (one unit for each eight-week course) given for in-service training. The credit counts on the district pay scale for teachers and toward consideration for transfers. Thus, the innovation and related training can, in conjunction with other educational activities, be an incentive to a teacher.

H_{10} *adversary group.* There are no organized groups within the district who oppose the CAI system. Because the approval for participation in the CAI system is an annual decision by the principal and faculty, there are always a few teachers who may advocate reallocating the funds for other purposes. In only three schools has the decision been made to drop a part or all of CAI and to use the money in other ways. Thus, the potential exists for supporting an alternative innovation or project, but there is no strong opposition to the CAI system.

Hillsborough County School District, Tampa, Florida

Persons Interviewed

Supervisor of Mathematics (secondary education)

Director of Data Processing

Programmer in data processing

Assistant Superintendent for Instruction

Head of Mathematics Department, Brandon High School

Mathematics teacher, Brandon High School

Mathematics teachers in other high schools, who gathered for a workshop session

Background

The Hillsborough County School District (somewhere between the twentieth and twenty-fifth largest in the country) was the site for a field visit on computer-assisted instruction. The school district covers the area around Tampa, Florida; it has about 120,000 students, an annual operating budget of about $136 million, and about 13,000 employees. Pertinent to the site visit is also the fact that there are 11 senior high schools which have been the main participants in the CAI system.

The Innovation

The school district grew steadily until 1973, after which enrollment leveled off somewhat. The development of the CAI system is tied closely to the development of the school's computer system, which began in 1961 (an IBM 402) with an emphasis on such school-related applications as grade reporting, student scheduling, and testing. Such applications are considered by data processing officials to be neither business applications (for example, payroll, finance, property accounting), which were added in 1963, nor instructional applications (such as drill and practice and advanced computer mathematics), which began in 1972. At the time that the IBM 402 was initiated, the head of the data processing unit was first appointed. (This position is still held by the same person.) The data processing unit had begun as part of the administrative operations of the school district, but for the last eight years it has been under the direction of the assistant superintendent for business and research. The current utilization rates for the computer system are divided roughly one-third each for school-related applications, business applications, and instructional applications.

The main instructional application is related to the teaching of computer programming (BASIC), and regular and advanced computer mathematics courses. There is only minimal use of the system for routine classroom applications—that is, for drill and practice, for portions of regular mathematics classes, or for portions of classes other than mathematics. The computer science interest has been quite high, however, and, because of the time-sharing limitations in the current system, several high schools have been considering the purchase of mini-computers. The minicomputers allow a school to have on-site capabilities and support the use of at least one additional terminal, which can be a CRT terminal with or without a printout capability. One high school, Brandon, purchased an Altair model and began using it during the current year. The total cost of Brandon's minicomputer was about $8,000, with the funds coming from the capital budget in relation to the addition of a new wing for the school building; maintenance for the minicomputer is provided by the regular school maintenance shop, so that the high school itself has required few funds to support the computer following the initial outlay. Other schools that are considering the purchase of minicomputers hope to be able to use capital budget funds in a similar manner.

Status of Routinization

Budget and Equipment. The central data processing operation currently has about thirty-seven full-time staff and a budget of about $1 million annually. The budget support has been almost totally derived from local funds, with the few exceptions being a small grant from LEAA (which was for a juvenile home project and which supported the purchase of some software) and one from the Office of Education, Title III (which was for a student grading project). Of the $1 million, about $350,000 is for hardware, $525,000 for personnel, $135,000 for paper, $25,000 for software, and $35,000 for other expenses. The core computer was purchased in 1972, with the earlier generations having been leased. District officials have been pleased with the purchasing agreement because it has reduced costs in the long run and because the current computer still has considerable resale value. In fact, because of continued demands for more computer time, the officials are considering new ways of increasing the core capacity, and a purchasing arrangement would be the most desirable for whatever new equipment is involved. Although there have been no formal studies of the cost savings attributable to the computer operation, the system has recently assumed the responsibility for a substantial test-scoring job that had previously been subcontracted to an outside computer firm at a cost of about $150,000.

The costs for renting the CAI terminals and telephone lines average about $100 per month per terminal. These costs, in contrast to the costs for maintaining all central equipment, are part of the budget of the instructional (curriculum) department, and the use of the CAI terminals has been coordinated by the mathematics supervisor. There appears to be continued demand for additional terminal time among the high schools. The main constraint has been a shortage of ports and the limitation in central processing capability, rather than the unavailability of funds.

In summary, budgetary support for the CAI system has mainly been from local funds, with little transition required from federal or other outside grants to such local support. The system has also moved from a leasing to a purchasing arrangement for the core computer, and the staffing requirements all appear to be an integral part of the school budget. There is every indication that, from a budgetary standpoint, the computer system would be treated as any other item in the budget, whether there were increased or decreased funds available.

The core computer is now in its fourth generation. Following the IBM 402 were an IBM 1401 (installed in 1963), an IBM 360 (1969), and an IBM 370/135 (1972). The current system is compatible with the Hillsborough County computer (which serves county-level agencies), and each serves as a backup system for the other. Some batch processing of instructional applications was done on the IBM 360, but the major CAI applications began in 1972 with the IBM 370/135, when nine teletype terminals were placed in the high schools. There are presently ten such terminals, divided among the eleven high schools, and these terminals share four of the ports to the core computer. (The other four ports are used by CRT terminals in relation to non-instructional applications.)

Personnel and Training. Because the major instructional application has been in the mathematics area, the CAI system is coordinated by both the data processing unit and the supervisor for mathematics instruction. As previously noted, the CAI-related costs are shared between the data processing unit and the instructional department. Both the head of the data processing unit and the mathematics supervisor are the first incumbents to have held their positions since the initiation of CAI. Some CAI planning had been done by the mathematics supervisor's predecessors, however. In addition, initial enthusiasm in CAI had been shown by both the science supervisor and mathematics supervisor, but the advanced computer courses were accepted by students as part of their mathematics rather than science (that is, engineering) electives. As a result, there appears to be little interest in CAI on the part of the science supervisor or most of the supervisors of other subjects.

As for the data processing personnel, their job classifications and entrance exams have been covered since 1970 under the Hillsborough civil service system rather than the school system, which has meant that: (1) the classifications and salaries have been competitive with those in other industries, and (2) there has been little of the undesirable competition between instructional and non-instructional jobs.

All high school mathematics teachers have had at least one opportunity to participate in in-service training courses for using CAI. Such courses were offered regularly by the instructional department (with assistance from a vendor) until most of the mathematics teachers had been exposed to the training, but the courses are now only offered sporadically. There is no formal requirement for new teachers to have CAI training, but the local university from which most of the teachers are recruited has incorporated a CAI course into its curriculum.

Organizational Governance. There appear to have been no specific laws or regulations that have affected the computer operation. The state has recently passed an accountability law that will increase pressure to provide compensatory training to students who cannot pass a criterion level in mathematics or reading. However, how this law will be implemented (the first round of testing will be next year) and what its effect will be on the computer system is unclear. As for textbook adoption (for example, for CAI-oriented algebra books), this issue is not relevant because CAI is not regularly used for the general mathematics classes; the computer mathematics classes, of course, do have special texts.

Reasons for Routinization Status

Service Applications and Outcomes.

H_1 *core application.* The computer system, as previously noted, is used for school-related applications, business applications, and instructional (CAI) applications. There is little doubt that the computer operation now performs many essential functions in the first two areas. In instructional applications, however, the main application has been for computer science and advanced mathematics students (courses in BASIC as well as computer mathematics) rather than for the core curriculum. This means that students are exposed to CAI either as part of an elective course or as an additional activity in which advanced students can conduct special problem-solving exercises, such as the development of a program to produce different versions of the same type of test to help a teacher minimize cheating in a regular mathematics class. Because these applications are limited to a minority of the students, most of the students and teachers can continue their functions without involvement with CAI. In contrast, CAI could be deemed a more integral part of the curriculum if it involved the drill and practice applications associated with regular mathematics or science classes, or if it involved the problem-solving applications associated with regular courses in algebra, geometry, trigonometry, and so on. Thus, unlike the school-related and business applications, the CAI applications do not appear to have displaced core functions.

H_2 *competition.*   To a certain extent, the fact that the computer tends to perform essential functions in the school-related and business areas but more peripheral functions in the instructional area is evidenced by the competition and priorities among applications. First, half of the ports for terminals are dedicated to administrative applications, and only the other half (four ports) are dedicated to the CAI terminals. This allocation has continually caused scheduling problems among the schools, which must share the ports, and the CAI lines appear to be in continual use. (Two or three schools are explicitly assigned to each port line; if a line is exceedingly busy, a school that wants some teletype time will telephone the sharing school(s) to indicate its needs. Thus, the sharing arrangements are maintained without having to go through the central facility.)

In general, the data processing unit has attempted to maintain a one-third split among the three broad areas of applications, but the CAI applications naturally require much less in CPU time. Secondly, the current considerations for expanding the computer system are primarily based on anticipated increases in school-related and business, but not CAI, applications. Instead, the major CAI expansion is likely to occur through individual schools acquiring their own minicomputers, so that the CAI applications are likely to be less centralized in the future.

H_3 *service-related payoffs.*   The biggest service-related payoffs have been in the test-scoring applications, which have saved both money and teacher time. The saving of time previously devoted to grading tests is appreciated by the older teachers who have had to perform such functions before the installation of the computer system. The cost savings have only been informally documented. It is known, however, that a California company previously had a contract to distribute, collect, and score certain elementary school tests. By performing this application by itself, the data processing unit saved the district $150,000. Moreover, high school test-scoring will be conducted by the data processing unit this year, which will produce further savings. As yet, the CAI applications appear to have had no documented effect in terms of cost savings or specific service payoffs, such as examples of students who have performed exceedingly well in school or after graduation as a result of CAI. An implicit service payoff has been the general acknowledgment that computers are part of contemporary life, so that any exposure to computer techniques will help a student in his or her subsequent career.

External Environment.

H_4 *crisis conditions.* The computer operation did not emerge because of a crisis. In 1961, when the first computer was acquired by the district, it was a result of the efforts of a group of five high school principals who were interested in computer applications in the area of student administrative records. Most school districts that used computers at that time had systems oriented toward business applications. The Hillsborough system, however, started out with school-related data processing because of the influence of the initiators.

An additional early factor was that the supervisor of mathematical instruction for the district had attended a computer workshop in the summer of 1970. At that time, he was chairman of the mathematics department in one of the high schools. He became very interested in computers, and, in 1970-71, he and another teacher team-taught FORTRAN, using a Wang-370 programmable calculator. He also made an arrangement with the head of data processing to process student jobs in batch mode. Even though there were problems, the supervisor was highly enthusiastic about computers. He was promoted to his present position of supervisor in the fall of 1971, just in time to be able to help develop the request for proposals (RFPs) that the district was issuing for bids on a new computer system (which eventually became the IBM 370/135). During his first year as supervisor, he also bought a portable Wang-3330 computer, which he used to train teachers and to generate enthusiasm for the computer as an instructional tool.

The specifications for the new system mandated that the vendor provide software to support cathode ray tubes (CRTs), teletypes, and CAI applications. This was the first time instructional applications were included in the computer system on an interactive basis.

H_5, H_6 *client-community support.* Two students were interviewed who were especially enthusiastic supporters of the computer. They appeared to have spent much time with the terminals during after-school hours, and they were mainly challenged by having to create computer programs for solving a variety of problems. However, these students were probably not average members of the student body. Most students do not come into contact with CAI. Those that do are enrolled in computer mathematics courses. Except for the very enthusiastic support of a few students, the students in general may not be very supportive of CAI. In fact, a contrasting report was made by a mathematics teacher (the only one in the school who knows any programming) at one school which has been one of the most infrequent computer users. Her computer science course is part of the honors program, but her description of her students was at variance with the notion of honor students. She said they were apathetic and that they only took the course to fill up their schedules.

According to the head of data processing and the supervisor for mathematical instruction, the community is generally unaware of the computer system, and therefore there is no active support. There has been an occasional newspaper article on CAI, but such publicity has been minimal.

Internal Characteristics.

H_7 *administrators.* The computer system falls under the overall direction of the assistant superintendent in charge of business and finance. The assistant superintendent in charge of instruction also has contact with the computer system, mainly for its CAI applications. It is difficult to determine the degree to which either of these persons supports the computer. However, as for other instructional innovations, the district is involved in CCTV in a minor way. At least one high school in the district is fully equipped for CCTV, and the district has had a mobile TV unit for the last several years. One innovation that appears to generate more interest among administrators, possibly because it is in the process of being installed, is a word-processing unit in the elementary education department.

H_8 *innovator.* For the computer system, the role of innovator is shared between the head of data processing and the mathematics supervisor. The data processing director has guided the district through three new generations of computers and has coordinated both the preparation of applications programs and their priorities of usage. The department grew under her direction to its present staff of thirty-seven people. The group provides the technical expertise required by teachers or administrators. The innovator for the instructional applications alone, however, is more clearly the supervisor of mathematical instruction.

If the director of data processing were replaced, the system would probably continue in its present state. However, if the supervisor of mathematical instruction were replaced, the instructional applications could possibly diminish unless his replacement happened to be another computer enthusiast.

H_9 *practitioners.* The only teachers who use the system at present are mathematics instructors. However, the number of these instructors who are involved may be limited. For instance, in the most active user-school, only two mathematics teachers appear to use the computer. Other departments, such as science, business, language, and social studies, appear not to be involved in CAI at all. One potential barrier is that the drill and practice and other CAI applications that might be appropriate for the average student require some administrative procedures in which many teachers have not been trained. For instance, a teacher would not only have to be taught the mechanics of switching onto and off the computer and using special computer programs, but he would also have to know all the administrative procedures involved in registering and monitoring each student. Also, the teletype terminal is inappropriate for drill-and-practice applications because it is too slow and cumbersome, and only one student would be able to work on a program at a time because of the limited number of terminals.

Thus, except for the enthusiastic backing of several mathematics teachers, CAI does not appear to have active supporters among the staff. The same is probably true among the instructional supervisors, where the mathematics supervisor is the major supporter, but where there may be little interest among the supervisors of other subject areas.

H_{10} *adversary group.* There appears to be little opposition to the use of CAI. The supervisor of mathematical instruction of the district does encounter resistance on the part of the supervisors in other instructional areas when he tries to persuade them to use the computer. From his perspective, they do not appear interested. There is also some resistance among department heads and teachers in the schools, primarily from those who view CAI as an undesirable substitute for the more traditional methods of learning mathematics. There appears, however, to be no active opposition to CAI.

Notes

1. No packaged programs were leased or purchased from NCR when the computer was first introduced.

2. The new positions had been presented to the civil service board by the chief of police. The board, however, acted only after an extended period of time marked by numerous discussions between civil service personnel, the city manager, and the police chief.

3. Not all respondents agreed on the level and nature of in-service training during the early years. We have presented the view agreed upon by the majority of the respondents.

Appendix D
Responses to Ninety
Telephone Interviews

Number	Variable and Coding Categories	Number	Percent
001	Case Number		
002	Type of innovation		
	Police computer	13	14.4
	MICU	16	17.8
	CAI	16	17.8
	CCTV	14	15.6
	Jet-Axe	15	16.7
	Breath testing	16	17.8
	Total	90	100.0
003	City Code (see table 1–2 of text)		
004	Type of respondent		
	Chief of service	1	1.1
	Administration staff head	16	17.8
	Line staff head	19	21.1
	Administration staff	30	33.3
	Line staff	24	26.7
	Total	90	100.0
005	Innovation use		
	Currently in use	78	86.7
	No longer in use	12	13.3
	Total	90	100.0
006	Innovation use (same as 005)		
	Total	90	100.0
007	Administration of innovation		
	By department alone	84	93.3
	By department with another agency	5	5.6
	No response	1	1.1
	Total	90	100.0
008	Number of preceding models of the innovation		
	0	26	28.9
	1	21	23.3
	2	14	15.6
	3	10	11.1
	4	2	2.2
	Not applicable	17	18.9
	Total	90	100.0

Number	Variable and Coding Categories	Number	Percent
009	Year innovation first used		
	1965 and before	18	19.9
	1966-1970	27	30.1
	1971-1975	33	36.6
	1976 to present	4	4.4
	No response	8	8.9
	Total	90	100.0
010	Size of innovation		
010A	Size of innovation (number of on-line terminals, police computer)		
	0-20	5	38.5
	21-40	5	38.5
	41 or more	3	23.1
	Total	13	100.0
010B	Size of innovation (number of MICU vehicles)		
	2	3	18.8
	3	4	25.0
	4	1	6.3
	5	3	18.8
	6 or more	5	31.1
	Total	16	100.0
010C	Size of innovation (number of on-line terminals, CAI		
	0-20	4	25.2
	21-40	5	31.5
	41 or more	4	25.2
	No response	3	18.1
	Total	16	100.0
010D	Size of innovation (number of television receivers, CCTV)		
	0-50	5	35.8
	51-999	4	28.5
	1,000 or more	4	28.5
	No response	1	7.1
	Total	14	100.0
010E	Size of innovation (number of Jet-Axes ever detonated)		
	None	6	40.0
	0-10	5	33.3
	11 or more	4	26.8
	Total	15	100.0

Number	Variable and Coding Categories	Number	Percent
010F	Size of innovation (number of officers trained as breath-testing operators)		
	0-30	6	37.5
	31-60	6	37.5
	61 or more	4	25.0
	Total	16	100.0
011	Equipment ownership status		
	Purchased	65	72.2
	Leased	1	1.1
	Lease-purchase plan	7	7.8
	Not applicable	16	17.8
	No response	1	1.1
	Total	90	100.0
012	Year of equipment purchase		
	1965 and before	4	4.4
	1966-1970	18	19.9
	1971-1975	35	38.9
	1976 to present	6	6.7
	Not applicable	16	17.8
	No response	11	12.2
	Total	90	100.0
013	Number of years of lease		
	(applicable to less than 25 percent of cases)		
014	Initial technical assistance		
	From manufacturer	30	33.3
	From another agency	1	1.1
	From a university	2	2.2
	From consultants and/or manufacturer	23	25.6
	Combination of above	10	11.1
	None	22	24.4
	No response	2	2.2
	Total	90	100.0
015	Continuing technical assistance		
	From manufacturer	11	12.2
	From another agency	1	1.1
	From a university	3	3.3
	From consultants and/or manufacturer	23	25.6
	Combination of above	4	4.4
	None	48	53.3
	Total	90	100.0
016	Provisions for repair and maintenance		
	Contract with manufacturer	33	36.7
	Contract with other outside group	6	6.7
	Performed in-house	26	28.9

Number	Variable and Coding Categories	Number	Percent
	Provided by other agencies	9	10.0
	Not applicable	15	16.7
	No response	1	1.1
	Total	90	100.0
017	Number of coordinators (full-time equivalent)		
	Less than 1	7	7.8
	1	45	50.0
	2	3	3.3
	3	3	3.3
	Not applicable	31	34.4
	No response	1	1.1
	Total	90	100.0
018	Is coordinator's position permanent?		
	Yes	50	55.6
	No	1	1.1
	Not applicable	31	34.4
	No response	8	8.9
	Total	90	100.0
019	Is coordinator's position primarily classified in personnel system?		
	Yes	32	35.6
	No	19	21.2
	Not applicable	31	34.4
	No response	8	8.9
	Total	90	100.0
020	Number of mid-level staff positions (full-time equivalent)		
	Less than 1	22	24.4
	1-10	17	18.9
	11 or more	3	3.3
	Not applicable	31	34.5
	No response	17	18.9
	Total	90	100.0
021	Are mid-level staff positions permanent?		
	Yes	17	18.9
	No	2	2.2
	Mixed	1	1.1
	Not applicable	31	34.4
	No response	39	43.3
	Total	90	100.0
022	Are mid-level positions formally classified in personnel system?		
	Yes	15	16.7

Number	Variable and Coding Categories	Number	Percent
	No	5	5.6
	Not applicable	31	34.4
	No response	39	43.3
	Total	90	100.0
023	Number of support staff positions (full-time equivalent)		
	Less than 1	8	8.9
	1-10	21	23.3
	11-20	6	6.6
	21 or more	6	6.6
	Not applicable	31	34.5
	No response	18	20.0
	Total	90	100.0
024	Are staff support positions permanent?		
	Yes	32	35.6
	No	0	0
	Mixed	2	2.2
	Not applicable	31	34.4
	No response	25	27.8
	Total	90	100.0
025	Are support staff positions formally classified in personnel system?		
	Yes	19	21.1
	No	10	11.1
	Mixed	4	4.4
	Not applicable	31	34.4
	No response	26	28.9
	Total	90	100.0
026	Is the use of the innovation part of an employee examination?		
	Yes, civil service	10	11.1
	Yes, other than civil service	45	50.0
	No	14	15.6
	Not applicable	15	16.7
	No response	6	6.7
	Total	90	100.0
027	Number of coordinators throughout innovation's history		
	0	1	1.1
	1	42	46.7
	2	18	20.0
	3	8	8.9
	4	7	7.8
	5 or more	6	6.6
	No response	8	8.9
	Total	90	100.0

Number	Variable and Coding Categories	Number	Percent
028	Preceding coordinator's new position		
	Practitioner	3	3.3
	Head of agency	1	1.1
	Senior supervisor	8	8.9
	Administrator	2	2.2
	Junior supervisor	8	8.9
	Technician	1	1.1
	Outside of agency	5	5.6
	No response	53	58.9
	Total	90	100.0
029	Innovator's position at time of adoption of innovation		
	Head of agency	14	15.6
	Staff person in agency	29	32.2
	Staff person in other agency	9	10.0
	Outside city government	4	4.4
	Group of innovators	1	1.1
	Combination of above	10	11.1
	Other	12	13.3
	No response	11	12.2
	Total	90	100.0
030	Is innovator still with department?		
	Yes	43	47.8
	No	16	17.8
	No response	31	34.4
	Total	90	100.0
031	Innovator's current position		
	Practitioner	5	5.6
	Head of Agency	11	12.2
	Senior Supervisor	17	18.9
	Administrator in Agency	6	6.7
	Junior supervisor	2	2.2
	Retired	3	3.3
	No response	46	51.1
	Total	90	100.0
032	Prior need for innovation		
	Increasing service demands	17	18.9
	Specific need	14	15.6
	Other reasons	49	54.4
	Not applicable	6	6.7
	No response	4	4.4
	Total	90	100.0
033	Primary source of software		
	In-house	18	20.0
	Other agency	1	1.1
	External group	8	8.9

Number	Variable and Coding Categories	Number	Percent
	Prepackaged programs	13	14.4
	Users of innovation	2	2.2
	Other	1	1.1
	Not applicable	47	52.2
	Total	90	100.0
034	Source of current operating funds for innovation		
	Regular agency budget	63	70.0
	Other funds, excluding federal	3	3.3
	Federal funds	4	4.4
	Combination of above	1	1.1
	Other	3	3.3
	No response	16	17.8
	Total	90	100.0
036	Formal organizational status (no meaningful responses)		
037	Source of first external funds		
	LEAA or revenue-sharing	10	11.1
	State government	12	13.3
	Department of Transportation or Public Broadcasting Service	19	21.1
	Department of Health, Education, and Welfare	22	24.4
	National Science Foundation	3	3.3
	Private organization	1	1.1
	Unidentified	3	3.3
	No response	31	34.5
	Total	90	100.0
038	Year in innovation's history that external funds were first used		
	Same year that innovation was adopted	32	35.8
	A year or more after innovation had been adopted	30	33.1
	No response	28	31.1
	Total	90	100.0
039	Amount of first external funds		
	$0-5,999	12	13.3
	$6,000-10,000	10	11.0
	More than $10,000	14	15.6
	No response	54	60.0
	Total	90	100.0
040	Source of second external funds		
	(applicable to less than 25 percent of cases)		

Number	Variable and Coding Categories	Number	Percent
041	1976 budget for innovation		
	$0-50,999	16	17.6
	$51,000-100,999	6	6.6
	$101,000-500,000	13	14.3
	More than $500,000	3	3.3
	No response	52	58.2
	Total	90	100.0
042	1975 budget for innovation		
	$0-50,999	18	19.9
	$51,000-100,999	5	5.5
	$101,000-500,000	9	9.9
	More than $500,000	2	2.2
	No response	56	62.4
	Total	90	100.0
043	1974 budget for innovation		
	$0-50,999	20	22.0
	$51,000-100,999	4	4.4
	$101,000-500,000	8	8.8
	More than $500,000	1	1.1
	No response	57	63.8
	Total	90	100.0
044	Have there been organizational changes related to the innovation?		
	Formal changes	23	25.6
	Less formal changes	14	15.6
	No changes	19	21.1
	Other	17	18.9
	Not applicable	15	16.7
	No response	2	2.2
	Total	90	100.0
045	Is there dedicated space for the innovation?		
	Yes	48	53.3
	No	26	28.9
	Mixed	11	12.2
	No response	5	5.6
	Total	90	100.0
046	Is the use of the innovation mandated by law?		
	Yes	5	5.6
	No	54	60.0
	Not applicable	31	34.4
	Total	90	100.0

Number	Variable and Coding Categories	Number	Percent
047	Is the use of the innovation regulated by law?		
	Yes	38	42.2
	No	48	53.3
	No response	4	4.4
	Total	90	100.0
048	Was there any initial practitioner training?		
	Yes, informal	8	8.9
	Yes, given by manufacturer	2	2.2
	Yes, classes held by agency	23	25.6
	Yes, in agency's academy	23	25.6
	Yes, other	9	10.0
	Combination of above	5	5.6
	None	19	21.1
	No response	1	1.1
	Total	90	100.0
049	Has there been any update training for practitioners?		
	Yes, informal	6	6.7
	Yes, given by manufacturer	4	4.4
	Yes, classes held by agency	36	40.0
	Yes, in agency's academy	7	7.8
	Yes, other	12	13.3
	Combination of above	7	7.8
	No	9	10.0
	No response	9	10.0
	Total	90	100.0
050	Has there been any service payoff from the innovation?		
	Yes, reported or discussed in budget	17	18.9
	Yes, reported in evaluation studies	10	11.1
	Yes, both of above	25	27.8
	Yes, other	14	15.6
	No	1	1.1
	No response	23	25.6
	Total	90	100.0
051	Type of service payoff		
	Better information	9	10.0
	Reduced manpower demands	2	2.2
	Expansion of service practices	20	22.2
	Quicker response	13	14.4
	Better output of agency practices	21	23.3
	Coordination of manpower	1	1.1
	Public recognition	2	2.2
	No response	22	24.4
	Total	90	100.0

Number	Variable and Coding Categories	Number	Percent
052	Has there been any resistance from inside the agency in using the innovation?		
	Yes	48	53.3
	No	42	46.7
	Total	90	100.0
053	If there has been resistance, of what type?		
	Regarding specific applications	3	3.3
	Only at time of adoption	15	16.7
	Over entire use of the innovation	20	22.2
	Other	8	8.9
	Combination of above	2	2.2
	No response	42	46.7
	Total	90	100.0
054	Has there been any publicity regarding the innovation?		
	Yes, local mention	46	51.1
	Yes, national media	1	1.1
	Yes, both of above	23	25.6
	No	19	21.1
	No response	1	1.1
	Total	90	100.0
055	If there has been publicity, has it been favorable?		
	Yes	63	70.0
	Mixed	6	6.7
	Not applicable	19	21.1
	No response	2	2.2
	Total	90	100.0
056	Support from the Mayor for the innovation		
	Yes	39	43.3
	No	47	52.2
	No response	4	4.4
	Total	90	100.0
057	Opposition from the Mayor for the innovation		
	Yes	3	3.3
	No	83	92.2
	No response	4	4.4
	Total	90	100.0
058	Support from other municipal officials for the innovation		
	Yes	44	48.9
	No	44	48.9

Number	Variable and Coding Categories	Number	Percent
	No response	2	2.2
	Total	90	100.0
059	Opposition from other municipal officials		
	Yes	6	6.7
	No	82	91.1
	No response	2	2.2
	Total	90	100.0
060	Support from local legislators for the innovation		
	Yes	35	38.9
	No	50	55.6
	No response	5	5.6
	Total	90	100.0
061	Opposition from local legislators		
	Yes	6	6.7
	No	80	88.9
	No response	4	4.4
	Total	90	100.0
062	Support from citizen groups		
	Yes	31	34.4
	No	57	63.3
	No response	2	2.2
	Total	90	100.0
063	Opposition from citizen groups		
	Yes	2	2.2
	No	86	95.6
	No response	2	2.2
	Total	90	100.0
064	Support from interest groups		
	Yes	34	37.8
	No	11	12.2
	No response	45	50.0
	Total	90	100.0
065	Opposition from interest groups		
	Yes	4	4.4
	No	41	45.6
	No response	45	50.0
	Total	90	100.0
066	Support from any other group		
	Yes	15	16.7
	No	6	6.7
	No response	69	76.7
	Total	90	100.0

Number	Variable and Coding Categories	Number	Percent
067	Opposition from any other group		
	Yes	7	7.8
	No	11	12.2
	No response	72	80.0
	Total	90	100.0
068	Difficulties foreseen in operating innovation during coming year		
	Staff training	5	5.6
	Reorganization in department	4	4.4
	Interdepartmental problems	3	3.3
	Overuse or excessive demands	6	6.7
	Legislative or regulatory problems	2	2.2
	Change in basic nature of innovation	2	2.2
	Survival of innovation in doubt	4	4.4
	Other	2	2.2
	No difficulties	62	68.9
	Total	90	100.0
069-071	Questions related to computer innovations only		
	(applicable to less than 30 percent of cases)		
072	Total number of groups of external supporters		
	0	20	22.2
	1	17	18.9
	2	18	20.0
	3	10	11.1
	4	11	12.2
	5	14	15.6
	Total	90	100.0
073	Total number of groups of external opposers		
	0	71	78.9
	1	13	14.4
	2	4	4.4
	3	2	2.2
	Total	90	100.0
074	Extent of practitioner use of innovation		
	None	50	55.6
	Low	11	12.2
	Moderate	13	14.4
	High	16	17.8
	Total	90	100.0
075	Number of core applications		
	0	8	8.9
	1	14	15.6

Number	Variable and Coding Categories	Number	Percent
	2	15	16.7
	3	12	13.3
	4	15	16.7
	5	26	28.9
	Total	90	100.0
076	Number of core applications among top priorities		
	0	41	45.6
	1	15	16.7
	2	10	11.1
	3	21	23.3
	4	3	3.3
	Total	90	100.0
077	Number of business applications performed by computer		
	0	12	13.3
	1 to 5	8	8.9
	6 or more	9	9.9
	Not applicable	61	67.8
	Total	90	100.0
078	Number of service applications performed by computer		
	1 to 5	23	25.6
	6 or more	6	6.6
	Not applicable	61	67.8
	Total	90	100.0

Note: These responses were coded from the six original instruments found in appendix B. Wherever possible, identical questions were used in each instrument and coded here; in other cases, the final codes are based on similar questions from each instrument.

Appendix E
Review of Four
Traditional Approaches
for Studying
Bureaucratic
Innovation

This appendix summarizes much of the literature on bureaucratic innovation. Its main purpose is to show that the study of innovations is still dominated by four different approaches:[1] research, development and diffusion; social interaction; innovative organizations; and organizational change. Although these approaches have become modified, and although specific studies may combine two or more of them, current empirical research on local services, as illustrated by the studies cited in chapter 1 (see table E-1), still tends to follow one of these approaches. In general, the review shows that, of the four approaches, only organizational change provides even rudimentary assistance for analyzing innovation life histories.

Research, Development and Diffusion

The R,D&D approach views the innovative process from a multi-institutional viewpoint, covering the macrosystem that produces, markets, and implements new technology. The three R,D&D steps are the conduct of basic research—

Table E-1
Recent Empirical Research Illustrating Four Approaches to the Study of Innovation

Approach	Studies Reviewed
R, D&D	Radnor (1975)
	Baer et al. (1976)
Social Interaction	Feller, Menzel, and Kozak (1976)
Innovative Organizations	Bingham (1976)
	Nelson and Sieber (1976)
	Danziger and Dutton (1976)
Organizational Change	Bale (1976)
	Berman and McLaughlin (1977)

the research component; the development of specific innovations that can be applied to service problems—the development component; and the communication of such innovations to potential users—the diffusion component. The approach also includes the final installation and implementation of an innovation (adoption). For local services, the approach has been best articulated in education, following the work of David Clark and Egon Guba (Clark and Guba, 1965, and Guba, 1968). According to one observer, the major federal initiatives in education were in fact undertaken on the basis of this approach (House, 1974). Table E-2 provides a schematic chart of the various steps and the components for each of them.

Another version of the R,D&D approach may be found in the work on technology delivery systems (Wenk, 1970; Committee on Public Engineering Policy, 1973; and Ezra, 1975). A technology delivery system (TDS) is seen as that system which is composed of the various institutions that produce innovations and influence the innovative process. Thus, the TDS framework makes explicit some of the actors that are usually implicitly assumed within the R,D&D approach, including lending institutions, private manufacturers, regulatory commissions and, wherever relevant, the role of the federal government.

This R,D&D approach has been the basic framework within which many studies of local service innovations have been conducted. Studies of the development of new police equipment, for instance, have attempted to identify the institutional problems that occur in producing and implementing change in law enforcement agencies (see Radnor, 1975). A major problem revealed by such studies is the difficulty that private manufacturers encounter in dealing with the fragmented market represented by local services. Because of the fragmented market, consumer needs are more difficult to assess and potential products are more difficult to market. A second example comes from a recent study on the curriculum changes in the educational system that followed the post-Sputnik surge of interest in science education (Quick, 1978). The study identified the key role of two institutions in the education TDS that had previously been overlooked: (1) the publishing companies that produce new textbooks, and (2) state adoption boards that decide which textbooks will be used in the various schools.

The macroview of the innovative process has been very useful in calling attention to all the institutions that must interrelate and whose activities must in some way be coordinated, whether through market or administrative mechanisms. In most studies of innovation, all the relevant institutional relationships have generally not been elaborated, so the approach serves as a reminder that such relationships need to be explicitly identified. Furthermore, the incentives by which the various institutions operate do not necessarily coincide and may help to explain difficulties in the innovative process. The R,D&D approach suffers, however, from a perspective that is biased toward the environment external to the innovating organization. As such, the approach typically gives

Table E-2
The Research, Development and Diffusion Approach

	Development			Diffusion			Adoption	
	Research	Invention	Design	Dissemination	Demonstration	Trial	Installation	Institutionalization
Objective	To advance knowledge	To formulate a new solution to an operating problem or to a class of operating problems, i.e., *to innovate*	To order and to systematize the components of the invented solution; to construct an innovation package for institutional use, i.e., *to engineer*	To create widespread awareness of the invention among practitioners, i.e., *to inform*	To afford an opportunity to examine and assess operating qualities of the invention, i.e., *to build conviction*	To build familiarity with the invention and provide a basis for assessing the quality, value, fit, and utility of the invention in a particular institution, i.e., *to test*	To fit the characteristics of the invention to the characteristics of the adopting institution, i.e., *to operationalize*	To assimilate the invention as an integral and accepted component of the system, i.e., *to establish*
Criteria	Validity (internal and external)	Face validity (appropriateness) Estimated viability Impact (relative contribution)	Institutional feasibility Generalizability Performance	Intelligibility Fidelity Pervasiveness Impact (extent to which it affects key targets)	Credibility Convenience Evidential assessment	Adaptability Feasibility Action	Effectiveness Efficiency	Continuity Valuation Support
Relation to Change	Provides basis for invention	Produces the invention	Engineers and packages the invention	Informs about the invention	Builds conviction about the invention	Tries out the invention in the context of a particular situation	Operationalizes the invention for use in a specific institution	Establishes the invention as a part of an ongoing program; converts it to a "noninnovation"

greater attention to the production and diffusion of new R&D products in the marketplace than to conditions within the innovating organization; it considers the progression from research to development to diffusion to be a linear process; and it assumes that innovations with the exact same form have general applicability to several if not many different local sites. These and other implicit assumptions have been consistently pointed out by those concerned with the dynamics of change as an innovation is actually implemented in an organization. Such critics suggest, for instance, that a more relevant approach for local service organizations would begin with a better understanding of the service practitioner's routine activities and constraints (see House, 1974; Pincus, 1974; Berman and McLaughlin, 1974; and Warner, 1974).

As a macroview, the R,D&D approach thus tends to skim lightly over the critical events within a given institution. This means that there is only very superficial concern for a process such as routinization. Although the R,D&D approach may provide a general context for understanding the place of routinization in the overall innovative process, it contributes few insights into the specific decisions, procedures, and organizational behaviors that occur as a specific innovation becomes routinized at a specific site. From the point of view of understanding routinization, the relevant conceptual issues must be spelled out in greater detail at the organizational level.

Social Interaction

This approach applies to situations where individuals adopt specific innovations. The individuals may learn about these innovations from other adopters, creating a communications network through which information about the innovation and the experiences of other individuals passes. Thus, social interactions become a key element to the adoption process, which is a step included in but not emphasized by the R,D&D approach.

Much research has followed this approach, mainly in the form of studies of the diffusion of innovations (Rogers and Shoemaker, 1971). The set of adopters may be physicians concerned with a new drug, farmers considering new agricultural techniques, consumers concerned with birth control devices, or any number of groups of individuals for whom a particular innovation may be relevant. The research has typically found that the adoption pattern follows an S-shaped curve over time,[2] and various studies have also attempted to identify the conditions that may predict the rate of adoption. For instance, many studies have compared the characteristics of individuals who are early adopters with those who are late, while other studies have examined the characteristics of the communications network or of the innovation that may lead to rapid or slow rates of adoption. Figure E-1 provides a schematization of the adoption process, together with some of the relevant conditions that have been identified.

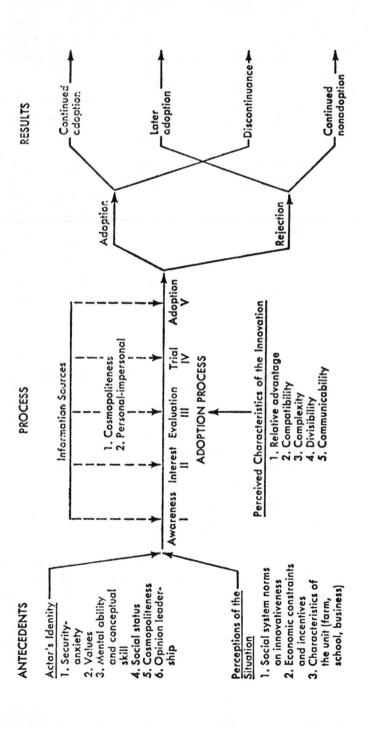

Source: Everett M. Rogers, *Diffusion of Innovations*, (New York:: The Free Press) 1962, p. 306. Reprinted with permission.

Figure E-1. The Adoption Process (Social Interaction Approach)

Because the social interaction approach has mainly dealt with the behavior of individuals, it has not been viewed useful in describing or explaining the innovative process for organizations. In some cases, where the organization is, for instance, a state legislature, and the innovation is a new piece of legislation (see Walker, 1969), the social interaction approach may be applied without too much difficulty. This is because the act of adoption may be seen as a unitary act, embodied in a specific vote, and because the implementation steps that follow adoption may not play an important role. However, major problems arise when the approach is applied to the implementation of new programs or other innovations by service agencies (Warner, 1974). In such cases, the decision to adopt may not be a unitary decision, and there may be no single individual that may be regarded as the adopter. Studies conducted along these lines have therefore had to arbitrarily identify an adopter, usually naming the head of the agency as the adopting individual (see Mytinger, 1968). More important, the critical implementation factors in the organizational innovation process cannot be studied as a simple act of adoption.

As a result of these difficulties, there has been some attempt to redefine the social interaction approach so that it can be applied to organizations rather than to individuals as adopting units. Rogers and Eveland (1975), for instance, suggest that one possibility is to add an implementation stage to the original approach, making the decision to adopt merely an intervening step and hence not the main focus of study, and defining permanent changes in organizational practice as the new set of outcomes to be explained. This does not entirely solve the problem, for the major work of conceptualizing the implementation process remains incomplete. Moreover, to the extent that it is completed, the effort represents such a significant shift away from the concern with adoption that the social interaction approach may no longer be recognizable.

In a similar manner, the social interaction approach is not helpful for studying the later events that characterize the routinization process. Any understanding of routinization must cover the organizational events that take place after an innovation has already been implemented for some period of time; yet, the approach does not extend over such a period of time.

Innovative Organizations

This approach is more static than the first two because it has attempted to identify the critical characteristics of innovative organizations, without developing an explicit explanation of organizational changes over time. Clues about the innovative process are thus inferred from the characteristics that have been found to be shared by innovative organizations but no direct attempt is made to test hypotheses about the process itself.[3] Tannon and Rogers (1975), for instance, reviewed eight major studies of innovations in health care systems, with all studies attempting to arrive at a definitive set of characteristics of innovative organizations.

Another example of the innovative organization approach is represented by the research of Burns and Stalker (1961) on the distinction between mechanistic and organic organizations. Mechanistic organizations are defined as highly differentiated, formalized, hierarchical, and inward directed, and are not seen as innovative organizations. Organic organizations are mainly defined in terms of the opposing attributes, and are therefore more innovative. In a similar manner, there have been several reviews of the literature in which the characteristics of innovative versus noninnovative organizations have been compared (see Becker and Whisler, 1967; Rowe and Boise, 1973 and 1974; Rothman, 1974; and Public Affairs Counseling, 1976). No dominant set of characteristics has emerged from these reviews. Moreover, even if a consistent set of organizational attributes were found, little would be learned about the innovative process (that is, how an organization innovates) other than by inferring change processes from clusters of static characteristics (Rogers and Agarwala-Rogers, 1976).

This approach encounters another difficulty when actual data from organizational cases are analyzed. The data are usually aggregated in some manner, so that innovative organizations are defined by some aggregate index, such as one based on the number of innovations that have occurred in the organizations, and the entire analysis is conducted at an aggregate level—which may be inappropriate because the results are averaged over a heterogeneous group of organizations and innovations (Downs and Mohr, 1976). In other words, different research studies will use different groups of innovations in defining innovativeness; therefore, the identification of key organizational characteristics does not apply to a specific innovation, but to a mixed group of innovations. As Downs and Mohr (1976) point out, it is not surprising that because the mixed group varies from study to study, there has been little consistency in the findings of these studies as to the key organizational characteristics.

The innovative organizations approach may, nevertheless, provide a possible starting point for studying implementation and routinization. For instance, Yin (1977) hypothesized two innovative processes within local service agencies. One process was associated with production efficiency and resulted in service improvements; the other was associated with the fulfillment of bureaucratic self-interests such as agency growth and prestige and resulted in incorporation. The findings of the study suggested that, although certain conditions such as practitioner training promote both service improvement and incorporation, other characteristics of the situation, such as support for the innovation by the chief executive of the jurisdiction and initiative from a coalition of individuals within the innovating agency, were important to incorporation but not service improvement; other characteristics were important to service improvement but not incorporation. The overall conclusion was that local agencies often incorporate innovations such as computer systems that serve bureaucratic self-interests, even though no service improvements are clearly evident. Conversely, innovations that lead to service improvements may not be incorporated unless they also serve some bureaucratic self-interest.

Despite the apparent utility of research that has followed the innovative organizations approach, the approach can only provide indirect clues about the underlying processes. The clues must then be pursued by some systematic hypothesis testing about the important causal changes over time, and care must be taken in the design of any study to avoid aggregating an overly heterogeneous set of experiences. Because this hypothesis-testing stage has rarely taken place, it is difficult to assess the ultimate utility of the innovative organizations approach. Judged by its present use, however, it falls short of providing an adequate conceptual framework for studying the routinization process.

Organizational Change

This fourth approach provides what is probably the most useful context for analyzing the routinization process. In essence, the approach focuses on events within an organization as it undergoes change, and the innovation process is seen as but one variant of organizational change. The process has not really been defined in great detail, but there are usually four stages that have been identified:

1. *Prior stage* of the organization before change, in which dissatisfaction or a sense of opportunity may arise and there is a recognition of the need for change
2. *Initiation*, or the process of planning for specific changes and identifying the resources to be used and procedures to be followed
3. *Implementation*, or the actual occurrence of change when the plan becomes a reality, and during which unanticipated responses may occur
4. *Routinization*, or the establishment of the new changes as a stable and normal part of organizational procedures and behavior

This same basic conceptual framework has been applied in numerous studies of both public and private organizations. Table E-3 is an adaptation of a table originally developed by Hage and Aiken (1970) and indicates the different labels that have been applied, even though the conceptualizations are similar. For instance, the systems dynamics and equilibrium theory espoused by Kurt Lewin provides the labels "unfreezing," "change," and "refreezing" in reference to the final three stages (Lewin, 1958; Barnes, 1971; and Alderfer, 1976), whereas the organizational theory developed by Berman and McLaughlin (1974) uses the terms "initiation," "implementation," and "incorporation."

This kind of change process occurs continually in all but the most static

Table E-3
Variations in Organizational Change Approach

Hage and Aiken (1970)	Mann and Neff (1961)	Barnes (1971)	Berman and McLaughlin (1974)
Evaluation	State of organization before change	–	–
	Recognition of need for change		
Initiation	Planning change	Unfreeze	Initiation
Implementation	Taking steps to make change	Change	Implementation (mutual adaptation is necessary)
Routinization	Stabilizing change	Refreeze	Incorporation

organizations, and the general purpose of previous research has been to identify desirable innovative behavior, to reduce the barriers to change, and to promote more change-oriented organizations. In fact, the general thrust of such managerial initiatives as *planned change* or *organizational development* is based on the premise that a chronic capacity for change is a desirable state of affairs for most organizations (see Bennis, Benne, and Chin, 1969). The classic studies have attempted to suggest the conditions most conducive to change, such as the existence of performance gaps (March and Simon, 1958, pp. 176, 182-184; and Downs, 1967, p. 169), slack resources (Cyert and March, 1963; and Thompson, 1969, pp. 44-45), or even bureaucratic conditions in which self-interests, the extending of career goals, and changes in organizational goals, can all lead to a constant state of change (Blau, 1955). Other studies have described the role of change agents in instigating change through training programs and other methods of attitude change among the employees of an organization (Bennis, 1965). In fact, one way of depicting organizational change is to describe it in terms of the stages of conflict between the individual proponents and opponents to a particular proposal (Watson, 1969).

One of the significant developments in the organizational change approach has been the increasing number of studies on implementation. This marks a shift from earlier research, which tended to focus on the conditions for initiating change, but not on the later stages of change (Bennis, 1965). Studies of the implementation process in private organizations, for instance, have received considerable impetus from those interested in operations research. This research, though primarily concerned with innovations such as the use of quantitative models, now explicitly treats implementation as a behavioral process

(Schultz and Slevin, 1975). Similarly, studies of organizational changes in public organizations, typically following initiatives taken by the federal government, have now begun to examine the implementation process and to compensate for the earlier gap in the literature noted by Pressman and Wildavsky (1973).

Only fragmentary work, however, has been done on the final stages of organizational change, or routinization. Hage and Aiken (1970) suggest that:

> Perhaps the best sign of the routinization of [a] new program occurs when the men who were originally involved in implementing the program are replaced. If the program remains essentially the same. . . we can then say that it has been stabilized. Another sign of routinization is the development of job training programs for the new replacements.

In other words, if a new practice survives despite personnel turnover, this may be one sign that the practice has become routinized. Another suggestion is that routinization will more easily follow if the changed practice is central to an agency's priorities (Berman et al., 1975). However, aside from a few suggestions such as these, there has been no comprehensive study of the routinization process. Thus, even though the organizational change approach provides a potential framework for analyzing the routinization process, the relevant issues have not yet been developed in detail.

Table E-4
Four Approaches to the Study of Bureaucratic Innovation

Approach	Main Focus	Innovative Stage that Tends to be Subject of Study		
		Adoption	Implementation	Routinization
Research, Development and Diffusion	Institutional relationships in the production of a new technology	x		
Social Interaction	Communication networks among individual adopters or organizations	x		
Innovative Organizations	Characteristics of innovative organizations and their environment	x	x	
Organizational Change (also problem-solving approach)	Change processes and individual behavior within an organization		x	x

Summary

This appendix has reviewed four traditional approaches for studying innovation in local services. Each of the four tends to focus on one or another aspect of the innovative process, and no single approach is all-encompassing. Table E-4 summarizes the complementary contributions that can be expected from each approach. A full understanding of all aspects of organizational innovation would thus require some element of each approach. For the purpose of studying the routinization process, however, our argument is that the organizational change approach is more relevant than the other three, and hence must play the central role in any discussion of routinization. This means greater emphasis on specific change processes and behaviors within a service organization, and less emphasis—at the outset, at least—on inter-organizational patterns of communication and community characteristics across jurisdictions.

Notes

1. Ronald Havelock (1969) has done an excellent job of reviewing the work for three of these approaches (all but the innovative organizations approach). He uses the label "problem-solving" in referring to the organizational change approach. This author has previously described these same approaches, but mainly in the context of problems of adoption and implementation, and not routinization. See Yin (1976) and Yin, Heald, and Vogel (1977).

2. More precisely, the logistic follows the general form:

$$P = \frac{K}{1 + e^{-(a+bt)}}$$

where P is the percentage of adopters who have adopted the innovation; e is the base where the natural log $\ln = 1$; K is the asymptotic value of P; a is the constant of integration locating the curve on the time scale; b is the rate of growth coefficient; and t is time.

3. An excellent critique of this approach appears in Eveland, Rogers, and Klepper (1976).

References

Aberbach, Joel D., et al. "Exploring Elite Political Attitudes." *Political Methodology* (1975): 1-27.

Alderfer, Clayton P. "Change Processes in Organizations," in *Handbook of Industrial and Organizational Psychology*, edited by Marvin D. Dunnette. Chicago: Rand McNally, 1976, pp. 1591-1638.

Allison, Graham. *Essence of Decision: Explaining the Cuban Missile Crisis.* Boston: Little, Brown and Company, 1971.

Allison, Graham, and Peter Szanton. *Remaking Foreign Policy: The Organizational Connection.* New York: Basic Books, 1976.

American Association of School Librarians, ALA, and Association for Educational Communications and Technology. *Media Programs: District and School.* Chicago and Washington, D.C., 1975.

Atkinson, R.C., and H.A. Wilson. "Computer Assisted Instruction." *Science* (October 1968): 73-77.

Baer, Walter S. *Cable Television: A Handbook for Decisionmaking.* New York: Crane, Russak and Company, 1974.

Baer, Walter S., et al. *Analysis of Federally Funded Demonstration Projects: Final Report.* Santa Monica, Calif.: The Rand Corporation, R-1926-DOC, April 1976.

Bale, Richard L. "Organizational Change and Innovation in American Elementary Schools: The Case of 'The Electric Company.'" Ph.D. dissertation. Department of Sociology, Florida State University, Tallahassee, May 1976.

Barbach, Eugene. *The Implementation Game: What Happens After A Bill Becomes a Law.* Cambridge, Mass.: The MIT Press, 1977.

Barnes, Louis B. "Organizational Change and Field Experiment Methods," in *Organizational Design and Research,* edited by James D. Thompson and Victor H. Vroom. Pittsburgh, Pa.: University of Pittsburgh Press, 1971, pp. 57-111.

Battelle-Columbus Laboratories. *Interactions of Science and Technology in the Innovative Process: Some Case Studies.* Columbus, Ohio, March 1973.

Beard, Marian. "Computer Assisted Instruction: The Best of ERIC, 1973-May 1976." Stanford, Calif.: ERIC Clearinghouse on Information Resources, Stanford University, August 1976.

Becker, Theodore M., and Peter R. Meyer. "Empathy and Bravado: Interviewing Relevant Bureaucrats." *Public Opinion Quarterly* 38 (Winter 1974): 605-613.

Becker, Selwyn, and Thomas L. Whisler. "The Innovative Organization: A Selective View of Current Theory and Research." *Journal of Business* 40 (October 1967): 462-469.

Bennis, Warren G. "Theory and Method in Applying Behavioral Science to Planned Organizational Change." *Journal of Applied Behavioral Science* 1 (1965): 337-359.

Bennis, Warren G., Kenneth D. Benne, and Robert Chin, eds. *The Planning of Change*, 2d ed. New York: Holt, Rinehart and Winston, 1969.

Berman, Paul, and Milbrey McLaughlin. *Federal Programs Supporting Educational Change*, Vol. 1 Santa Monica, Calif.: The Rand Corporation, R-1589/1-HEW, September 1974.

Berman, Paul, and Milbrey McLaughlin. *Federal Programs Supporting Educational Change*, Vol. 7. Santa Monica, Calif.: The Rand Corporation, R-1589/7-HEW, April 1977.

Berman, Paul, and Milbrey McLaughlin. *Federal Programs Supporting Educational Change*, Vol. 8. Santa Monica, Calif.: The Rand Corporation, R-1589/8-HEW, 1978.

Berman, Paul, et al. *Federal Programs Supporting Educational Change*, Vol. 5. Santa Monica, Calif.: The Rand Corporation, R-1589/5-HEW, April 1975.

Bingham, Richard D. *The Adoption of Innovation by Local Government*. Lexington, Mass.: Lexington Books, D.C. Heath, 1976.

Bitzer, Donald, and D. Skaperdas. "The Economics of a Large-scale Computer-based Education System: Plato IV," *Computer-Assisted Instruction, Testing, and Guidance*, edited by Wayne H. Holtzman. New York: Harper and Row, 1970, pp. 17-29.

Blau, Peter M. *The Dynamics of Bureaucracy: A Study of Interpersonal Relations in Two Government Agencies*. Chicago: University of Chicago Press, 1955.

Booth, Ethel. "CATV/School Colloboration." *Educational and Industrial Television* (May 1972), pp. 14-16.

Borko, Stephen B. "Local Government Experience with Cable Television." *Urban Data Service* 5 (July 1973): 1-15.

Boyd, Harper W., and Ralph Westfall. *Marketing Research*, 3d ed. Homewood, Ill.: Richard D. Irwin, 1972, pp. 143-159.

Bretz, Rudy. *Handbook for Producing Educational and Public-Access Programs for Cable Television*. Englewood Cliffs, N.J.: Educational Technology Publications, 1976.

Bukoski, William J., and Arthur L. Korotkin. "Computing Activities in Secondary Education." *Educational Technology* 16 (January 1976): 9-29.

Bukoski, William J., and Arthur L. Korotkin. *Computing Activities in Secondary Education*. Washington, D.C., American Institutes for Research, September 1975.

Burns, Tom, and G.M. Stalker. *The Management of Innovation*. London: Tavistock Publications, 1961.

Carpenter-Huffman, Polly, Richard C. Kletter, and Robert K. Yin. *Cable Television: Developing Community Services*. New York: Crane, Russak and Company, 1974.

Chaiken, Jan M., and Robert J. Gladstone. *Some Trends in the Delivery of Ambulance Services*. Santa Monica, Calif.; The Rand Corporation, R-1551-RWJF, July 1974.

Charters, W.W., Jr., and Roland J. Pellegrin. "Barriers to the Innovation Process." *Educational Administration Quarterly* 9 (1973): 3-14.

Clark, David, and Egon Guba. "An Examination of Potential Change Roles in Education," paper presented at Seminar on Innovation in Planning School Curricula, Airlie House, Warrenton, Va., October 1965.

Clark, Richard E. "The Best of ERIC: Recent Trends in Computer Assisted Instruction." Stanford, Calif.: ERIC Clearinghouse on Educational Media and Technology, Stanford University, April 1973.

Collins, M. Clagett. "State Laws for Ambulance Attendants and Advanced Emergency Medical Technicians." *Journal of the American College of Emergency Physicians* 3 (May-June 1974): 161-167.

Colombotos, John. "Personal vs. Telephone Interviews: Effects on Responses." *Public Health Reports* 84 (September 1969): 773-782.

Colton, Kent. "Computers and the Police: Police Departments and the New Information Technology." *Urban Data Service* 6 (November 1974): I-19.

_____ . "The Dedicated Police Computer—Does it Really Make a Difference?" *The Bureaucrat* 1 (Winter 1972b): 357-365.

_____ . "Use of Computers by Police: Patterns of Success and Failure." *Urban Data Service* 4 (April 1972a): 1-21.

Committee on Public Engineering Policy, National Academy of Engineering. *Priorities for Research Applicable to National Needs*. Washington, D.C., 1973.

Comptroller General of the United States. *Progress, But Problems in Developing Emergency Medical Services Systems*. Washington, D.C., July 13, 1976.

Corwin, Ronald G. "Innovation in Organizations: The Case of Schools." *Sociology of Education* 48 (Winter 1975): 1-37.

Costello, Timothy W. "Change in Municipal Government: A View from the the Inside." *Journal of Applied Behavioral Science* (March-April 1971): 131-145.

Cyert, Richard M., and James G. March. *A Behavioral Theory of the Firm*. Englewood Cliffs, N.J.: Prentice-Hall, 1963.

Danziger, James N., and William H. Dutton. "Technological Innovation in Local Government: The Case of Computers in U.S. Cities and Counties." Irvine, Calif.: Urban Information Systems Research Group, University of California, July 1976.

Darby, Charles A., et al. "A Survey of Computing Activities in Secondary Schools." Washington, D.C., American Institute for Research, 1970.

deLeon, Peter. *The Sun Also Sets: The Evaluation of Public Policy*. Santa Monica, Calif.: The Rand Corporation, P-5826, March 1977.

Dexter, Lewis Anthony. *Elite and Specialized Interviewing*. Evanston, Ill.: Northwestern University Press, 1970.

Dillman, Don A., et al. "Reducing Refusal Rates for Telephone Interviews." *Public Opinion Quarterly* 40 (Spring 1976): 66-78.

Downs, Anthony. *Inside Bureaucracy*, Boston: Little, Brown and Company, 1967.

Downs, George. *Bureaucracy, Innovation, and Public Policy.* Lexington, Mass.: Lexington Books, D.C. Heath, 1976.

Downs, George, and Lawrence B. Mohr. "Conceptual Issues in the Study of Innovation." *Administrative Science Quarterly* 21 (December 1976): 700-714.

Dozier, Phillip C., and John Moulden. "Breath Testing the Drinking Driver." *Target* 6 (May 1977): 2-3.

Ellis, Allan B. and David V. Tiedeman. "Can a Machine Counsel?" in *Computer-Assisted Instruction, Testing, and Guidance*, edited by Wayne H. Holtzman. New York: Harper and Row, 1970, pp. 345-373.

Eveland, J.D., Everett M. Rogers, and Constance A. Klepper. "The Innovation Process in Public Organizations." Ann Arbor, Mich.: Department of Journalism, University of Michigan, August 1976.

Ezra, Arthur A. "Technology Utilization: Incentives and Solar Energy." *Science* 187 (February 1975): 707-713.

Federal Register 41 (September 23, 1976): 4137.

Feinberg, Barry M. "Nationwide Survey of School Superintendents on Future Utilization of the Instructional Television Fixed Service." Washington, D.C.: Bureau of Social Science Research, Inc., November 15, 1976.

Feller, Irwin, Donald C. Menzel, and Lee Ann Kozak. *Diffusion of Innovations in Municipal Governments*. University Park, Pa.: Institute for Research on Human Resources, Pennsylvania State University , June 1976.

Festinger, Leon, and Daniel Katz, eds. *Research Methods in the Behavioral Sciences*. New York: Holt, Rinehart and Winston, 1966.

Flores, A.L. "Results of the First Semi-Annual Qualification Testing of Devices To Measure Breath Alcohol." Cambridge, Mass.: Transportation Systems Center, DOT-TSC-NHTSA-74-6, January 1975.

Frohman, Alan, et al. *Factors Affecting Innovation in the Fire Services.* Cambridge, Mass.: Pugh-Roberts Associates, March 1972.

Fyke, James L. "Records and Communications." in *Municipal Police Administration,* edited by George D. Eastman and Esther M. Eastman. Washington, D.C.: International City Management Association, 1971, pp. 247-275.

Gebolys, Suzette. *Evaluation Report: Planning for the Utilization of the Texas Telecomputer Grid in Elementary and Secondary Schools.* Dallas, Tex.: Independent School District, 1974.

Gibson, Geoffrey. "Emergency Medical Services." *Proceedings of the Academy of Political Science* 32 (1977): 121-135.

Grace, William J., and John A. Chadbourn. "The Mobile Coronary Care Unit." *Diseases of the Chest* 55 (June 1969): 452-455.

Guba, Egon G. "Development, Diffusion and Evaluation," in *Knowledge Production and Utilization in Educational Administration*, edited by Terry L. Eidell and Joanne M. Kitchel. Eugene, Oreg.: Center for the Advanced Study of Educational Administration, University of Oregon, 1968.

Gunter, Margaret J. *A Comparative Study of Community Planning for Emergency Medical Services: The Impact of Social and Political Factors on Program Implementation*. Pittsburgh, Pa.: Department of Industrial Engineering Systems Management, Engineering and Operations Research, University of Pittsburgh, August 1975.

Hage, Jerald, and Michael Aiken. *Social Change in Complex Organizations.* New York: Random House, 1970.

Hargrove, Erwin C. *The Missing Link: The Study of the Implementation of Social Policy*. Washington, D.C.: The Urban Institute, 1975.

Hartley, Boyd A. "Emergency Medical Services." *Municipal Yearbook* (1971): 83-90.

Havelock, Ronald G. *Planning for Innovation through Dissemination and Utilization of Knowledge*. Ann Arbor, Mich.: Institute for Social Research, the University of Michigan, July 1969.

Hearle, Edward F., and Raymond J. Mason. *A Data Processing System for State and Local Governments.* Englewood Cliffs, N.J.: Prentice-Hall, 1963.

Hirschman, Jim C., et al. "Mobile Physician Command: A New Dimension in Civilian Telemetry-Rescue Systems." *Journal of the American Medical Association* 230 (October 14, 1974): 255-258.

Hochstim, Joseph R. "A Critical Comparison of Three Strategies of Collecting Data from Households." *American Statistical Association Journal* 62 (September 1967): 976-989.

Hoffman, Lily. "Alcohol and Traffic Safety: Screening Out the Drunken Driver," in *Technological Shortcuts to Social Change*, edited by Amitai Etzioni and Richard Remp. New York: Russell Sage Foundation, 1973, pp. 79-102.

Holtzman, Wayne H., ed. *Computer-Assisted Instruction, Testing, and Guidance*. New York: Harper and Row, 1970.

House, Ernest R. "The Micropolitics of Innovation: Nine Propositions." *Phi Delta Kappan* (January 1976): 337-340.

_____. *The Politics of Educational Innovation*. Berkeley, Calif.: McCutchan Publishing Co., 1974.

Hunter, B., et al. *Learning Alternatives in U.S. Education* Englewood Cliffs, N.J.: Educational Technology, 1975.

Hyman, Herbert, et al. *Interviewing in Social Research*. Chicago: University of Chicago Press, 1954.

IIT Research Institute. "Technology in Retrospect and Critical Events in Science." Chicago: December 1968.

Jones, Ralph K., et al. *Final Report on a Background Study of Technology*

Utilization in the Field of Public Works. Bloomington, Ind.: Indiana University; Chicago: Research Foundation, American Public Works Association, March 1974.

Kaufman, Herbert. *Are Government Organizations Immortal?* Washington, D.C.: The Brookings Institution, 1976.

_____. *The Limits of Organizational Change.* University, Ala.: University of Alabama Press, 1971.

_____. "The Natural History of Human Organizations." *Administration and Society* 7 (August 1975): 131-149.

Kimberly, John R. "Issues in the Design of Longitudinal Organizational Research." *Sociological Methods and Research* (February 1976a): 321-347.

_____. "Organizational Size and the Structionalist Perspective." *Administrative Science Quarterly* 21 (December 1976b): 571-597.

Knight, Fred S. "Mini-Computers: An Alternative for Local Government." *Municipal Management Innovations Series.* Washington, D.C.: International City Management Association, October 1975.

Kraemer, Kenneth L., et al. "Information Technology and Urban Management in the U.S." Irvine, Calif.: Public Policy Research Organization, University of California, March 1976.

Lambright, W. Henry. *Governing Science and Technology.* New York: Oxford University Press, 1976.

Lambright, W. Henry, and Paul J. Flynn. "Bureaucratic Politics and Technological Change in Local Government." *Journal of Urban Analysis* 4 (1977): 93-118.

Leavitt, Harold J. "Applied Organizational Change in Industry," in *Handbook of Organizations*, edited by James G. March. Chicago: Rand McNally, 1965, pp. 1144-1170.

Lewin, Kurt. "Group Decision and Social Change," in *Reading in Social Psychology*, 3d ed., edited by E.E. Maccoby, T.M. Newcomb, and E.L. Hartley. New York: Holt, Rinehart and Winston, 1958, pp. 197-211.

Lewis, A. James, et al. "Pre-Hospital Cardiac Care in a Paramedical Mobile Intensive Care Unit." *California Medicine* 117 (October 1972): 1-8.

Liebert, Roland J. *"The Electric Company" In-School Utilization Study. Vol. 2: The 1972-73 School and Teacher Surveys and Trends Since Fall 1971.* Tallahassee, Fla.: Center for the Study of Education, Florida State University, in conjunction with statistics Research Division, Research Triangle Institute, October 1973.

Locander, William, et al. "An Investigation of Interview Method, Threat, and Response Disportion." *Proceedings*, American Statistical Association, 1974, pp. 21-27.

Mann, Floyd C., and F.W. Neff. *Managing Major Change in Organizations.* Ann Arbor, Mich.: Foundation for Research on Human Behavior, 1961.

March, James G., and Herbert A. Simon. *Organizations.* New York: John Wiley and Sons, 1958.

Margolin, Joseph B., and Marion R. Misch. *Computers in the Classroom.* New York: Spartan Books, 1970.

Mason, M.F., and K.M. Dubowski. "Breath-Alcohol Analysis: Uses, Methods, and Some Forensic Problems—Review and Opinion." *Journal of Forensic Sciences* 21 (January 1976): 9-41. Portions reprinted with permission.

_____. "Alcohol, Traffic, and Chemical Testing in the United States: A Resume and Some Remaining Problems." *Journal of Clinical Chemistry and Clinical Biochemistry* 20 (1974): 126-140. Portions reprinted with permission.

McLaughlin, Milbrey. "Implementation as Mutual Adoption," in *Social Program Implementation*, edited by Walter Williams and Richard Elmore. New York: Academic Press, 1975, pp. 167-180.

McLaughlin, Milbrey, and Paul Berman. *Macro and Micro Implementation.* Santa Monica, Calif.: The Rand Corporation, P-5431, May 1975.

Mohr, Lawrence B. "Determinants of Innovation in Organizations." *American Political Science Review* 3 (March 1969): 111-126.

Moulden, John V., and Robert B. Voas. "Breath Measurement Instrumentation in the U.S." Washington, D.C.: National Highway Traffic Safety Administration, U.S. Department of Transportation, DOT-HS-801 621, June 1975.

Murphy, Stephen M. "Countrywide Program in California." *Hospitals* 47 (May 16, 1973): 119-124.

Myers, Sumner, and Donald G. Marquis. *Successful Industrial Innovations.* Report to the National Science Foundation, NSF 69-17, Washington, D.C., May 1969.

Mytinger, Robert E. "Innovation in Local Health Services: A Study of the Adoption of New Programs by Local Health Departments with Particular Reference to Newer Medical Care Activities." Arlington, Va.: U.S. Department of Health, Education, and Welfare, Public Health Service, 1968.

National Emergency Medical Services Information Clearinghouse. "National Paramedic Service Listing." Unpublished manuscript. Philadelphia: University of Pennsylvania, no date.

National Highway Traffic Safety Administration. "Emergency Medical Services: A Subject Bibliography from Highway Safety Literature." Washington, D.C.: SB-07, September 1976.

Nelson, Margaret K. *The Adoption of Innovation in Urban Schools.* New York: Bureau of Applied Social Research, Columbia University, March 1975.

Nelson, Margaret, and Sam Sieber. "Innovations in Urban Secondary Schools." *School Review* 84 (February 1976): 213-231.

Oregon Board of Education. "Oregon Total Information System," Salem, Ore.: May 1971.

Page, James O. *Emergency Medical Services for Fire Departments.* Boston: National Fire Protection Association, 1975.

_____. *National Study of Paramedic Law and Policy.* Buffalo, N.Y.: Lakes Area Emergency Medical Services, 1976.

Pantridge, J.F., and J.S. Geddes. "A Mobile Intensive-Care Unit in the

Management of Myocardial Infarction." *Lancet* 2 (August 1967): 271-273.

Pennings, Johannes. "Measures of Organizational Structure." *American Journal of Sociology* 79 (November 1973): 686-704.

Perry, James L., and Kenneth L. Kraemer. *Executive Influence in the Adoption of Computer Applications in Local Government*. Irvine, Calif.: Public Policy Research Organization, University of California, WP-76-21, 1976.

Pincus, John. "Incentives for Innovation in the Public Schools." *Review of Educational Research* 44 (Winter 1974): 113-144.

Plaas, Hyrum, et al. *The Evaluation of Policy-Related Research in Emergency Medical Services*. Knoxville, Tenn.: The Bureau of Public Administration, The University of Tennessee, August 30, 1974.

Policy Sciences 7 (June 1976) whole issue.

Pressman, Jeffrey L., and Aaron Wildavsky. *Implementation*. Berkeley, Calif.: University of California Press, 1973.

Public Affairs Counseling. *Factors Involved in the Transfer of Innovations*. Washington, D.C.: Report to U.S. Department of Housing and Urban Development, January 1976.

Pyo, Yoon H., and Richard W. Watts. "A Mobile Coronary Care Unit: An Evaluation for Its Need." *Annals of Internal Medicine* 73 (July 1970): 61-66.

Quick, Suzanne K. Ph.D. dissertation. Stanford, Calif.: School of Education, Stanford University, January 1978.

Radnor, Michael. "Studies and Action Programs on the Law Enforcement Equipment R&D System." Evanston, Ill.: Graduate School of Management, Northwestern University, January 1975.

Rein, Martin, and Francine Rabinowitz. "Implementation: A Theoretical Perspective." Working Paper No. 43. Cambridge, Mass.: Joint Center for Urban Studies, March 1977.

Renner, William F. "Emergency Medical Service: The Concept and Coronary Care." *Journal of the American Medical Association* 230 (October 1974): 251-254.

Roessner, J. David. "Federal Policy and the Transfer of Technology to State and Local Government." Unpublished paper. Washington, D.C.: National Science Foundation, August 1976.

Rogers, Everett M. *Diffusion of Innovations*. New York: The Free Press, 1962, p. 306.

Rogers, Everett M., and Rekha Agarwala-Rogers. *Communications in Organizations*. New York: The Free Press, 1976.

Rogers, Everett M., and F. Floyd Shoemaker. *Communication of Innovations*, 2d ed. New York: The Free Press, 1971.

Rogers, Everett M., with John Dudley Eveland. "Diffusion of Innovations Perspectives on National R&D Assessment: Communication and Innovation in Organizations," in *Technological Innovation: A Critical Review of Current Knowledge, Vol. 2, Aspects of Technological Innovation*, edited by Patrick Kelly et al. Atlanta, Ga.: Advanced Technology and Science Studies Group, Georgia Institute of Technology, February 1975, pp. 301-368.

Rogers, Theresa F. "Interviews by Telephone and in Person: Quality of Responses and Field Performance." *Public Opinion Quarterly* 40 (Spring 1976): 51-65.

Rothman, Jack. *Planning and Organizing for Social Change: Action Principles from Social Science Research*. New York: Columbia University Press, 1974.

Rowe, Lloyd A., and William B. Boise, eds. *Organizational and Managerial Innovation: A Reader*. Pacific Palisades, Calif.: Goodyear Publishing Company, 1973.

Rowe, Lloyd A., and William B. Boise. "Organizational Innovation: Current Research and Evolving Concepts." *Public Administration Review* 34 (May-June 1974): 284-293.

Salisbury, A.R. "Computers and Education: Toward Agreement on Terminology." *Educational Technology* 11 (September 1971): 35-40.

Schon, Donald A. *Technology and Change: The Impact of Invention and Innovation on American Social and Economic Development*. New York: Delta Books, 1967.

Schultz, Randall L., and Dennis P. Slevin. "Implementation and Management Innovation," in *Implementing Operations Research/Management Science*, edited by Randall L. Schultz and Dennis P. Slevin. New York: American Elsevier, 1975, pp. 3-20.

Selltiz, Claire, et al. *Research Methods in Social Relations*. New York: Holt, Rinehart and Winston, 1976.

Sheehy, Gail. *Passages: Predictable Crises of Adult Life*. New York: E.P. Dutton, 1976.

Smith, Barry D., and Mildred P. Cooper. "Instructional TV Program: An Evaluation." Washington, D.C.: District of Columbia Schools, 1974.

Smith, Leslie R. "Fire Rescue Personnel Serve as Paramedics." *Hospitals* 45 (August 16, 1971): 62-64.

"Standard for Devices to Measure Breath Alcohol." *Federal Register* 38 (November 5, 1973).

Street, Paul W., ed. "Computerized Instruction in Mathematics." Lexington, Ky.: College of Education, University of Kentucky, June 1972.

Sullivan, Ronald. "New York City Plans to Overhaul Outmoded System of Ambulances." *The New York Times* (May 30, 1977): 1.

Suppes, Patrick, and Mona Morningstar. "Four Programs in Computer-Assisted Instruction," in *Computer-Assisted Instruction, Testing, and Guidance*, edited by Wayne H. Holtzman. New York: Harper and Row, 1970, pp. 233-265.

Tannon, Christian P., and Everett M. Rogers. "Diffusion Research Methodology: Focus on Health Care Organizations," in *The Diffusion of Medical Technology,* edited by Gerald Gordon and G. Lawrence French. Cambridge, Mass.: Ballinger, 1975, pp. 51-77.

Tansik, David A., and Michael Radnor. "An Organization Theory Perspective on the Development of New Organizational Functions." *Public Administration Review* 31 (November-December 1971): 644-652.

Thompson, Victor A. *Bureaucracy and Innovation.* University, Ala.: University of Alabama Press, 1969.

Walker, Jack L. "The Diffusion of Innovations among the American States." *American Political Science Review* 63 (September 1969): 880-899.

Warner, Kenneth E. "The Need for Some Innovative Concepts of Innovation." *Policy Sciences* 5 (December 1974): 433-451.

Watson, Goodwin. "Resistance to Change," in *The Planning of Change.* 2d ed. edited by Warren Bennis et al. New York: Rinehart and Winston, 1969, pp. 488-498.

Watson, Paul G. *Using the Computer in Education.* Englewood Cliffs, N.J.: Educational Technology Publications, 1972.

WCET-TV. "Report of Television Multi-Channel System in Lincoln Heights Elementary School." Cincinnati, Ohio: October 1973.

Weidman, Donald R. "Writing A Better RFP: Ten Hints for Obtaining More Successful Evaluation Studies." *Public Administration Review* 37 (November/December 1977): 714-717.

Weiss, Robert. *Marital Separation.* New York: Basic Books, 1975.

Wenk, Edward, Jr. "The Social Management of Technology, in *Science for Society,* edited by John E. Mock. Atlanta, Ga.: Proceedings of the National Science Conference, October 1970.

Whisenand, Paul M., and Tug G. Tamaru. *Automated Police Information Systems.* New York: John Wiley and Sons, Inc., 1970.

Wigren, Harold E., et al. *A Survey of Instructional Closed-Circuit Television 1967.* Washington, D.C.: National Education Association, 1967.

Williams, Walter. "Implementation Problems in Federally Funded Programs," in *Social Program Implementation,* edited by Walter Williams and Richard Elmore. New York: Academic Press, 1976, pp. 15-40.

Wilson, O.W., and R.C. McLaren. *Police Administration.* New York: McGraw-Hill, 1972.

Wiseman, Frederick. "Methodological Bias in Public Opinion Surveys." *Public Opinion Quarterly* 36 (Spring 1972): 105-108.

Wolfson, Stanley. Personal communication. Washington, D.C.: International City Management Association, 1976.

Yin, Robert K. "Production Efficiency vs. Bureaucratic Self-Interest: Two Innovative Processes?" *Policy Sciences* 8 (December 1977): 381-399.

_____. *R&D Utilization by Local Services: Problems and Proposals for Further Research*. Santa Monica, Calif.: The Rand Corporation, R-2020-DOJ, December 1976.

_____. *The Workshop and the World: Toward an Assessment of the Children's Television Workshop*. Santa Monica, Calif.: The Rand Corporation, R-1400-RF, October 1973.

Yin, Robert K., and Margaret Gwaltney. "Local Public Services as Consumers of Energy Resources." Unpublished paper. Santa Monica, Calif.: The Rand Corporation, July 1977.

Yin, Robert K., Karen A. Heald, and Mary Vogel. *Tinkering with the System: Technological Innovations in State and Local Services*. Lexington, Mass.: Lexington Books, D.C. Heath, 1977.

Zaltman, Gerald, et al. *Innovations and Organizations*. New York: John Wiley and Sons, 1973.

Zamoff, Richard, et al. "Improving Technology Transfer." Working note. Washington, D.C.: The Urban Institute, December 1974.

Zinn, K. *An Evaluative Review of Uses of Computers in Instruction*. Ann Arbor, Mich.: University of Michigan, 1970.

Selected Rand Books

Averch, Harvey A., Stephen J. Carroll, Theodore S. Donaldson, Herbert J. Kiesling, and John Pincus. *How Effective is Schooling? A Critical Review of Research.* Englewood, Cliffs, N.J.: Educational Technology Publications, 1974.

Bagdikian, Ben H. *The Information Machines: Their Impact on Men and the Media.* New York: Harper & Row, 1971.

Bretz, Rudy. *A Taxonomy of Communication Media.* Englewood Cliffs, N.J.: Educational Technology Publications, 1971.

Brewer, Garry D., and James S. Kakalik. *Handicapped Children: Strategies for Improving Services.* New York: McGraw-Hill Book Company, 1979.

Carpenter-Huffman, Polly, Richard C. Kletter, and Robert K. Yin. *Cable Television: Developing Community Services.* New York: Crane, Russak & Company, 1975.

Cohen, Bernard, and Jan M. Chaiken. *Police Background Characteristics and Performance.* Lexington, Mass.: Lexington Books, D.C. Heath and Company, 1973.

Comstock, George, Steven Chaffee, Natan Katzman, Maxwell McCombs, and Donald Roberts. *Television and Human Behavior.* New York: Columbia University Press, 1978.

Dalkey, Norman C. *Studies in the Quality of Life: Delphi and Decision-Making.* Lexington Mass.: Lexington Books, D.C. Heath and Company, 1972.

DeSalvo, Joseph S., ed. *Perspectives on Regional Transportation Planning.* Lexington, Mass.: Lexington Books, D.C. Heath and Company, 1973.

Downs, Anthony. *Inside Bureaucracy.* Boston: Little, Brown and Company, 1967.

Fisher, Gene H. *Cost Considerations in Systems Analysis.* New York: American Elsevier Publishing Company, 1971.

Greenwood, Peter W., Jan M. Chaiken, and Joan Petersilia. *The Criminal Investigation Process.* Lexington, Mass.: Lexington Books, D.C. Heath and Company, 1977.

Greenwood, Peter W., Sorrel Wildhorn, Eugene C. Poggio, Michael J. Strumwasser, and Peter de Leon. *Prosecution of Adult Felony Defendants: A Policy Perspective.* Lexington, Mass.: Lexington Books, D.C. Heath and Company, 1976.

Jackson, Larry R., and William A. Johnson. *Protest by the Poor: The Welfare Rights Movement in New York City.* Lexington, Mass.: Lexington Books, D.C. Heath and Company, 1974.

Kakalik, James S., and Sorrel Wildhorn. *The Private Police: Security and Danger.* New York: Crane, Russak & Company, 1977.

Levien, Roger E. *The Emerging Technology: Instructional Uses of the Computer in Higher Education.* New York: McGraw-Hill Book Company, 1972.

McKean, Roland N. *Efficiency in Government through Systems Analysis: With Emphasis on Water Resource Development.* New York: John Wiley & Sons, 1958.

Meyer, J.R., J.F. Kain, and M. Wohl. *The Urban Transportation Problem.* Cambridge, Mass.: Harvard University Press, 1965.

Novick, David, ed. *Program Budgeting: Program Analysis and the Federal Budget.* Cambridge, Mass.: Harvard University Press, 1965.

Pascal, Anthony H., ed. *Racial Discrimination in Economic Life.* Lexington, Mass.: Lexington Books, D.C. Heath and Company, 1972.

Pascal, Anthony H., ed. *Thinking About Cities: New Perspectives on Urban Problems.* Belmont, Calif.: Dickenson Publishing Company, 1970.

Pincus, John, ed. *School Finance in Transition: The Courts and Educational Reform.* Cambridge, Mass.: Ballinger Publishing Company, 1974.

Quade, Edward S. *Analysis for Public Decisions.* New York: American Elsevier Publishing Company, 1975.

Quade, E.S., and W.I. Boucher, eds. *Systems Analysis and Policy Planning: Applications in Defense.* New York: American Elsevier Publishing Company, 1968.

Sackman, Harold. *Delphi Critique: Expert Opinion, Forecasting, and Group Process.* Lexington, Mass.: Lexington Books, D.C. Heath and Company, 1975.

Sharpe, William F. *The Economics of Computers.* New York: Columbia University Press, 1969.

Wildhorn, Sorrel, Marvin Lavin, and Anthony Pascal. *Indicators of Justice: Measuring the Performance of Prosecution, Defense and Court Agencies Involved in Felony Proceedings.* Lexington, Mass.: Lexington Books, D.C. Heath and Company, 1977.

Williams, J.D. *The Compleat Strategyst: Being a Primer on the Theory of Games of Strategy.* New York: McGraw-Hill Book Company, 1954.

Wirt, John G., Arnold J. Lieberman, and Roger E. Levien. *R&D Management: Methods Used by Federal Agencies.* Lexington, Mass.: Lexington Books, D.C. Heath and Company, 1975.

Yin, Robert K., and Douglas Yates. *Street-Level Governments: Assessing Decentralization and Urban Services.* Lexington, Mass.: Lexington Books, D.C. Heath and Company, 1975.

Yin, Robert K., Karen A. Heald, and Mary Vogel. *Tinkering with the System: Technological Innovations in State and Local Services.* Lexington, Mass.: Lexington Books, D.C. Heath and Company, 1977.

Index

About the Authors

Robert K. Yin is a visiting associate professor at the Department of Urban Studies and Planning, Massachusetts Institute of Technology. He divides his time between Cambridge and Washington, D.C., where he maintains an independent consulting practice.

Previously, Dr. Yin worked for nine years at The Rand Corporation. He has authored several books, including *Street-Level Governments* and *Tinkering with the System* (Lexington Books, 1975 and 1977, respectively); and published numerous articles in such journals as the *Journal of Experimental Psychology*, *Administrative Science Quarterly*, *Policy Sciences*, and *Sociological Methods and Research*.

Peter M. Bateman is currently a doctoral student in urban studies and planning at the Massachusetts Institute of Technology, where he is researching the social psychology of policymaking groups. His research interests also extend into the areas of institutional analysis and economic development. In the former area, Mr. Bateman has studied the decisionmaking networks of city agencies and universities, and has assisted in the fieldwork conducted for this book. In the latter area, Mr. Bateman has coauthored *Fishing Cooperatives and Economic Development* (Cambridge, Mass.: Center for Community Economic Development, 1979); and is completing a study of community-development corporations. His work as a consultant to numerous research projects is complemented by teaching at Northeastern University's College of Business Administration.

Ellen L. Marks was formerly a research assistant and is now a consultant with The Rand Corporation. She received the B.A. in political science from Emory University in 1974, the M.A. in political science from George Washington University in 1979, and is currently a Ph.D. candidate at the Department of Political Science, University of Minnesota.

Suzanne Quick received the Ph.D. from Stanford University in 1978. From 1976 to 1978, she was a resident consultant at The Rand Corporation's Washington, D.C. office. She is presently employed by the American Psychiatric Association, Washington, D.C.